Thirteenth Brief Edition

Principles of Speech Communication

Thirteenth Brief Edition

Principles of Speech Communication

Bruce E. Gronbeck
The University of Iowa

Kathleen German
Miami University • Oxford, Ohio

Douglas Ehninger
Alan H. Monroe

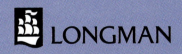
LONGMAN

An imprint of Addison Wesley Longman, Inc.

New York • Reading, Massachusetts • Menlo Park, California • Harlow, England
Don Mills, Ontario • Sydney • Mexico City • Madrid • Amsterdam

Senior Acquisitions Editor: Deirdre Cavanaugh
Development Editor: Cathy Richard
Editor-in-Chief: Priscilla McGeehon
Development Manager: Lisa Pinto
Supplements Editor: Tom Kulesa
Project Coordination and Text Design: York Production Services
Cover Design: Kay Petronio
Cover Illustrator: Tina Vey
Photo Researcher: Mira Schachne
Full Service Production Manager: Valerie Zaborski
Manufacturing Manager: Hilda Koparanian
Electronic Page Makeup: York Production Services
Printer and Binder: R.R. Donnelley & Sons, Co.
Cover Printer: Coral Graphic Services, Inc.

Library of Congress Cataloging-in-Publication Data

Principles of speech communication/Bruce E. Gronbeck . . . [et al.].—13th brief ed.
    p.   cm.
  Includes bibliographical references and index.
  ISBN: 0-321-01004-3
  1. Public speaking.   I. Gronbeck, Bruce E.
  PN4121.E36 1997
  808.5′ 1—dc21
                                                 97-7433
                                               CIP

ISBN: 0-321-01004-3

12345678910—DOC—00999897

Brief Contents

Detailed Contents   vii
Preface   xv

Part 1   Public Speaking and Critical Listening   1

1 Responsible Speechmaking in an Age of Diversity   3
2 Getting Started: Where Responsibility Begins   16
3 Critical Listening for Responsible Speakers   33
4 Public Speaking and Cultural Life   44

Part 2   Planning and Preparing Your Speech Responsibly 63

5 Understanding Your Audience   65
6 Finding Supporting Materials   83
7 Using Supporting Materials   96
8 Organizing and Outlining Your Speech   114
9 Beginning and Ending Your Speech   129

Part 3   Responsible Presentation   147

10 Wording Your Speech   149
11 Delivering Your Speech   169
12 Using Visual Aids   186

Part 4   Types of Public Speaking   203

13 Speeches to Inform   205
14 Speeches to Persuade   231
15 Argumentation and Critical Thinking   259

Credits   283
Index   285

v

Detailed Contents

Preface   **xv**

Part I   Public Speaking and Critical Listening   **I**

1 Responsible Speechmaking in an Age of Diversity   **3**

The Functions of Speechmaking in Society   **3**

Individual Diversity 3 • Community Building 4

**The Advantages of Speech Training to
the Responsible Speaker**   **5**

Basic Elements in the Speechmaking Process   **6**

Responsibilities for Successful Speechmaking   **8**

Ethics 9 • Respecting Human Diversity 11

Your First Speech   **12**

Assessing Your Progress   **14**

Chapter Summary 14 • Key Terms 14 • Assessment
Activities 14 • References 15

Speaking of . . . Apprehension   *First-Time Fears*   **10**

Speaking of . . . Ethics   *Ethics and Public Speaking*   **13**

2 Getting Started: Where Responsibility Begins   **16**

Selecting and Narrowing Your Subject   **16**

Determining Your Purposes and Central Idea   **18**

General Purposes 19 • Specific Purposes 20 • Central Ideas 20

Responsible Analysis of Audience and Occasion   **22**

Gathering Your Speech Material   **22**

Making an Outline   **23**

Practicing Aloud   **24**

Developing Confident Delivery   **25**

Sample Speech on Diversity: Bill Veeck by David Mellor   **28**

Assessing Your Progress 31

Chapter Summary 31 • Key Terms 31 • Assessment
Activities 31 • References 32

Speaking of . . . Skills *Brainstorming to Generate Topics* 18

Speaking of . . . Apprehension *State and Trait Apprehension* 25

Speaking of . . . Skills *Practicing Your Speech* 26

3 **Critical Listening for Responsible Speakers** 33

Hearing and Listening 33

Barriers to Good Listening 34

Practical Listening Techniques 35

Know Your Purposes 35 • Listening
for Comprehension 36 • Critical Listening 38

Developing Skills for Responsible Listening 41

Assessing Your Progress 42

Chapter Summary 42 • Key Terms 43 • Assessment
Activities 43 • References 43

Speaking of . . . Skills *Good Note Taking and Active Listening* 37

Speaking of . . . Ethics *Deliberately Misguiding Listeners* 40

4 **Public Speaking and Cultural Life** 44

Understanding Cultural Processes 47

The Dynamics of Culture 47 • The Challenge of Cultural
Diversity 50

**Communicating Unity Through Diversity:
Possible Strategies** 50

Recognizing Diversity 50 • Negotiating Diverse
Values 52 • Accepting Multiple Paths to Goals 53 • Working
Through the Lifestyle Choices of Others 55 • Maintaining
Self Identity When Facing Difference 56

Assessing Your Progress 59

Chapter Summary 59 • Key Terms 60 • Assessment
Activities 60 • References 60

Speaking of . . . Apprehension *Xenophobia* 45

Speaking of . . . Skills *What Others Are Saying: Oral Culture* 56

Speaking of . . . Ethics *Considering Cultural Practices* 57

Part 2   Planning and Preparing Your Speech Responsibly   63

5 Understanding Your Audience   65

Analyzing Your Audience Demographically   66

Age 66 • Gender 66 • Education 67 • Group
Membership 67 • Cultural and Ethnic Background 68 • Using
Demographic Information Responsibly 68

Analyzing Your Audience Psychologically   69

Beliefs 70 • Attitudes 71 • Values 72

Discovering Demographic and Psychological Factors   74

Surveying Your Listeners 74 • Observing Your
Listeners 75 • Using Your Psychological Profile 75

Responsible Use of Audience Analysis in Speech Preparation   76

Developing Your Purposes 76 • Developing Your
Goals 77 • Developing Your Appeals 78

A Sample Audience Analysis   79

Assessing Your Progress   81

Chapter Summary 81 • Key Terms 81 • Assessment
Activities 82 • References 82

Speaking of . . . Ethics   *Using Audience Analysis Ethically*   69

Speaking of . . . Skills   *Handling Hostile Audiences*   78

6 Finding Supporting Materials   83

Determining the Kinds of Supporting Materials You'll Need   83

Sources of Supporting Materials   85

Computerized Database Searches 85 • Print Materials 88 •
Radio and Television Broadcasts 90 • Interviews 90

Recording Information   90

Using Source Material Responsibly   91

Assessing Your Progress   94

Chapter Summary 94 • Key Terms 94 • Assessment
Activities 94 • References 95

Speaking of . . . Skills   *How Much Is Enough?*   84

Speaking of . . . Skills   *Conducting an Interview*   91

Speaking of . . . Ethics   *What Is the Ethical Response?*   93

7 Using Supporting Materials   96

Functions of Supporting Materials   96

Forms of Supporting Materials   97

Explanations 98 • Comparisons and Contrasts 99 •
Examples 100 • Statistics 102 • Testimony 106

Critical Thinking and the Use of Supporting Materials 106

Sample Outline for an Informative Speech: How We Breathe 108

**Sample Outline for a Problem-Solution Speech:
The Heartbreak of Childhood Obesity**   109

Assessing Your Progress   111

Chapter Summary 111 • Key Terms 112 • Assessment
Activities 112 • References 112

Speaking of . . . Skills   *Choosing Supporting Materials*   100

Speaking of . . . Ethics   *The Numbers Game*   104

8 Organizing and Outlining Your Speech   114

Developing Your Speech Plan   114

Developing Your Central Idea 115 • Choosing Your
Organizational Plan 115

Types of Organization   116

Chronological Patterns 116 • Spatial Patterns 116 • Causal
Patterns 117 • Topical Patterns 118

Audience-Centered Patterns of Organization   118

Familiarity-Acceptance Order 119 • Inquiry Order 119 •
Question-Answer Order 119 • Problem-Solution
Order 120 • Elimination Order 120

Outlining Your Speech   121

Types of Outlines 121 • Guidelines for Preparing Outlines 125

Assessing Your Progress   127

Chapter Summary 127 • Key Terms 127 • Assessment
Activities 128 • References 128

Speaking of . . . Skills   *Memory and Organization*   123

9 Beginning and Ending Your Speech 129

Capturing and Holding Attention 129

Activity 130 • Reality 130 • Proximity 131 • Familiarity 131 •
Novelty 131 • Suspense 131 • Conflict 132 • Humor 132 •
The Vital 132

Beginning Your Speech 133

Referring to the Subject or Occasion 134 • Using a Personal
Reference or Greeting 134 • Asking a Question 136 • Making a
Startling Statement 136 • Using a Quotation 137 • Telling a
Humorous Story 137 • Using an Illustration 138 • Completing
Your Introduction 138

Ending Your Speech 139

Issuing a Challenge 140 • Summarizing the Major Points
or Ideas 140 • Using a Quotation 140 • Using
an Illustration 141 • Supplying an Additional Inducement
to Belief or Action 141 • Stating a Personal Intention 142

Sample Outline for an Introduction and Conclusion 143

Assessing Your Progress 144

Chapter Summary 144 • Key Terms 145 • Assessment
Activities 145 • References 145

Speaking of . . . Ethics   *Revealing Responsible Intentions* 133
Speaking of . . . Skills   *How Long Should It Be?* 139

Part 3   Responsible Presentation 147

10 Wording Your Speech 149

Selecting Your Style 149

Accuracy 151 • Simplicity 152 • Restatement 152 • Coherence 153

Creating an Atmosphere 155

Intensity 155 • Appropriateness 156

Using Language Strategically 158

Definitions 158 • Imagery 160 • Metaphor 164

Sample Speech: "On Accepting the Nobel Prize for Literature"
by William Faulkner 164

Assessing Your Progress 166

Chapter Summary 166 • Key Terms 167 • Assessment
Activities 167 • References 167

Speaking of . . . Skills   *Oral Versus Written Style*   **151**

Speaking of . . . Ethics   *Doublespeak*   **157**

11   Delivering Your Speech   169

Selecting the Method of Presentation   170

The Impromptu Speech 170 • The Memorized Speech 170 •
The Manuscript Speech 170 • The Extemporaneous Speech 171

Using Your Voice to Communicate   171

The Effective Speaking Voice 172 • Practicing Vocal Control 175

Using Your Body to Communicate   175

Dimensions of Nonverbal Communication 176 • Adapting Nonverbal
Behavior to Your Presentations 181

Assessing Your Progress   183

Chapter Summary 183 • Key Terms 184 • Assessment
Activities 184 • References 185

Speaking of . . . Skills   *Vocal Exercises*   **176**

Speaking of . . . Apprehension   *Breathe Through Your Fears* **181**

12   Using Visual Aids   186

The Functions of Visual Aids   186

Comprehension and Memory 187 • Persuasion 187

Types of Visual Support   187

Actual Objects 187 • Photographs and Slides 188 • Videotapes
and Films 188 • Chalkboard Drawings 190 • Overhead
Projections 190 • Graphs 190 • Charts
and Tables 193 • Models 194

Strategies for Selecting and Using Visual Aids   194

Consider the Audience and Occasion 195 • Consider the
Communicative Potential of Various Visual Aids 196 •
Integrate Verbal and Visual Messages Effectively 196 • Evaluate
Computer-Generated Visual Materials 198

Assessing Your Progress   200

Chapter Summary 200 • Key Terms 200 • Assessment
Activities 200 • References 201

Speaking of . . . Skills   *Using Visual Aids in Business*   **195**

Speaking of . . . Ethics   *Can Pictures Lie?*   **197**

Part 4 Types of Public Speaking 203

13 Speeches to Inform 205

Facts, Knowledge, and the Information Age 205

Types of Informative Speeches 206
Speeches of Definition 207 • Instructions and Demonstrations 207 • Oral Reports 207 • Lectures 207

Essential Qualities of Informative Speeches 208
Clarity 208 • Associating New Ideas with Familiar Ones 210 • Clustering Ideas 211 • Relevant Visualizations 212 • Motivating Your Audience 212

Structuring Informative Speeches 212
Speeches of Definition 213 • Instructions and Demonstrations 214 • Oral Reports 216 • Lectures 218

Assessing Your Progress 228
Chapter Summary 228 • Key Terms 228 • Assessment Activities 229 • References 229

Sample Outline for an Oral Report: Report from the Message Therapy Committee 217
Sample Outline for a Speech of Definition: What is Diabetes? 220
Sample Outline for a Demonstration Speech: How to Build a Picket Fence 222
Sample Speech: "The Geisha" by Joyce Chapman 226
Speaking of . . . Skills *Choosing a Topic* 209
Speaking of . . . Apprehension *Information Overload* 211
Speaking of . . . Ethics *Suppressing Information* 213

14 Speeches to Persuade 231

Changing Audiences' Minds and Actions 233
Analyzing the Needs and Desires of Listeners 233 • Turning Needs and Desires into Motivational Appeals 235 • Using Motivational Appeals 235 • Using Motivational Appeals 242

Organizing Persuasive Speeches: The Motivated Sequence 243
Structuring Actuative Speeches 243 • Structuring Persuasive Speeches 249

Assessing Your Progress 255
Chapter Summary 255 • Key Terms 256 • Assessment Activities 256 • References 256

Speaking of . . . Skills: *Persuading the Diverse Audience*   **234**

Speaking of . . . Ethics: *Using Fear Appeals*   **241**

Sample Outline for an Actuative Speech: Numbers That Can Save Your Life   **247**

Sample Outline for a Persuasive Speech: The Positive Negative Political Ad   **249**

Sample Speech: "For a Declaration of War Against Japan" by Franklin Delano Roosevelt   **254**

Assessing Your Progress   **255**

Chapter Summary 255 • Key Terms 256 • Assessment Activities 256 • References 256

15 **Argumentation and Critical Thinking**   **259**

Rational Thinking and Talking: Argumentation   **260**

Types of Claims 261 • Types of Evidence 263 • Forms of Reasoning 265

Evaluating Arguments   **267**

Reasoning from Examples 268 • Reasoning from Generalization 268 • Reasoning from Sign 269 • Reasoning from Parallel Case 269 • Reasoning from Cause 269

Detecting Fallacies in Reasoning   **270**

Tips for Developing Argumentative Speeches   **272**

A Look at Debates   **273**

Assessing Your Progress   **279**

Chapter Summary 279 • Key Terms 280 • Assessment Activities 280 • References 281

Sample Arguments from the Second Presidential Debate, 1996   **275**

Speaking of . . . Apprehension *The Personal Risk of Argumentation*   **265**

Speaking of . . . Skills *Evaluating Arguments*   **268**

Speaking of . . . Ethics *Name Calling*   **273**

Credits   **283**

Index   **285**

Preface

A Tradition of Excellence

Principles of Speech Communication has guided students for over a half century by setting the standard for education in the basic speech course. It originated when the armed forces of the United States asked Professor Alan Monroe of Purdue University to write a brief textbook for officer candidates schools around the country during World War II. Monroe adapted his successful public speaking textbook, *Principles and Types of Speech;* he shortened it, added military examples, and brought out the "Military Edition" in 1943. It was such a hit that after the war he brought out the "Brief Edition" in 1945, modeled on the Military Edition. Your textbook is the Thirteenth Edition of the book that went to war.

Principles of Speech Communication, Thirteenth Brief Edition, builds on those fundamental principles that have helped thousands of students gain the expertise and confidence to speak in public. This edition will guide students successfully into the twenty-first century because it incorporates the following characteristics:

1. **This textbook gets you on your feet quickly and easily.** While you will need a communication vocabulary to prepare and critique speeches, you also must put concepts into practice early. In this edition, Chapter 2, "Getting Started," will get you on your feet and speaking to your classmates. Later chapters will develop ideas more fully so that you can increase your expertise as a speaker and listener.

2. **The textbook focuses on communication in your college life, but also draws examples from the worlds of work, politics, and social activism.** We recognize that your college environment probably requires your immediate attention, but we're also sensitive to the fact that you're preparing for a lifetime of public participation, so we've incorporated applications and examples from both.

3. **This textbook challenges you technically, intellectually, and morally.** Throughout your life, you will be expected to know how to accomplish goals (technical skills), how to analyze situations and propose courses of action (intellectual skills), and how to lead your social and professional life in trustworthy ways (moral development). You can prepare now to become a more effective communicator later. Our textbook challenges you not only to develop your skills and thought processes through public speaking, but to understand the responsibilities a speaker faces as well.

New Features

This textbook always has taught the basics, and it always will. Nevertheless, *Principles of Speech Communication,* Thirteenth Brief Edition, like its predecessors, is still evolving to meet your needs. It offers the latest thinking of scholars in rhetorical and communication theory, and blazes new trails in speech communication pedagogy. In this way, you are encountering the best thinking in the field of communication studies. Some of the newest features of this textbook include:

1. *An appreciation for cultural diversity,* which has led to the inclusion of a new Chapter 4, "Public Speaking and Cultural Life," which specifically focuses on the role of culture in communication. Serious attention to the role of cultural practices throughout the textbook reflects the fact that we live and interact in an increasingly diverse society and successful public speakers can adjust their styles accordingly.

2. *An increased awareness of ethics in speech communication,* which manifests itself in a discussion of speech ethics in the first chapter and, more importantly, in a series of boxed features, "Speaking of . . . Ethics." These boxes reflect contemporary concern with the moral consequences of communicating and help you to explore your own thinking about ethical choices. Topics include "Considering Cultural Practices" in Chapter 2 and "Suppressing Information" in Chapter 13.

3. *Practical applications to speechmaking in society* through a special boxed feature called "Speaking of . . . Apprehension" and "Speaking of . . . Skills." These boxes focus on speakers' questions, especially those regarding their fears about public speaking. These boxes foreshadow situations in which you might find yourself, and they ask you to look at the big picture—the role of public speaking at work in our society.

4. *Expanded coverage of electronic and World Wide Web databases* in recognition of the special information skills that you need in the age of the CD-ROM and the information superhighway. The computer has changed the way we store and retrieve information, and it will affect the research you conduct to become an informed speaker. Chapters 6 and 12 will guide you in using these new technologies to find supporting materials and evaluate use of computer-generated visual materials.

Better than Ever

In addition to the new features in the Thirteenth Brief Edition of *Principles of Speech Communication,* we have kept the text lively by rewriting, revising, and restructuring the following features:

1. **Appreciating diversity.** Throughout this textbook, we recognize the heterogeneity of contemporary speakers and their audiences. Both the explanation of concepts and their applications should reveal an appreciation for the complexity of the communication process.

2. **Streamlined chapters.** This edition has been shortened and streamlined so that more classroom time can be spent on basic speechmaking skills and activities. We think that you'll find the chapters in the Thirteenth Brief edition comprehensive, easy to read, and practical.

3. **Critical-thinking emphasis.** With critical thinking as an important part of speech instruction and overall education, we've expanded our coverage of it throughout the chapters, featuring it in Chapter 3, "Critical Listening for Responsible Speakers," and in Chapter 15, "Argumentation and Critical Thinking."

4. **Full-color printing.** This book was the first college-level public speaking textbook to be printed entirely in full color. Color improves the readability of the book and research shows that it helps students learn concepts more easily. Our contemporary design is used to invite you into the book and, ideally, hold your attention.

5. **Sample outlines and speeches.** As always, a key feature is the application of speechmaking principles in sample outlines and speeches. In this edition, you'll find new outlines and speeches that allow you to see how others face the challenges of public speaking. Annotations are added to many of the outlines and speeches so that you can examine the rhetorical strategies being used in them.

6. **Refining the central concepts developed by Monroe and Ehninger.** For years, Alan Monroe (1903–1975) and Douglas Ehninger (1913–1979) worked with students and teachers to develop strategies for teaching public speaking to students of varied backgrounds and talents. As a student at the dawn of the twenty-first century, you are heir to the pedagogy they built:

   ✓ Monroe's motivated sequence, the greatest formula for putting together a speech this century has seen. Others have copied it, but none have topped it.

   ✓ A critical examination of the forms of supporting materials.

   ✓ Exploration of types of language use, including imagery.

   ✓ Exploration of various kinds of introductions, organizational patterns, and conclusions.

   ✓ A discussion of the factors of attention that help you capture and keep your listeners's interest.

   ✓ A focus on argumentation that teaches you how to build an argumentative speech and analyze the arguments of others.

This pedagogy is seamlessly woven throughout the text. We call it out here in the preface so you know how the earlier authors and thus this book formed the foundation of basic public speaking instruction.

The Plan of the Book

Principles of Speech Communication, Thirteenth Brief Edition, is organized into four parts, reflecting the four major emphases of most contemporary courses in public speaking.

1. Part I: "Public Speaking and Critical Listening" provides you with *an orientation to the communication process.* Most teachers help you to relate the particular skills involved in public speaking to a variety of real-world contexts. Teachers want you to develop skills to enhance your success at work and in society, to understand the conceptual underpinnings of public communication, and to adapt your ideas to the folks who make all the difference—the people in your audience. Part I of this book introduces important ways to think about speechmaking even as, with the help of Chapter 2, you give your first classroom speeches.

2. Part II: "Planning and Preparing Your Speech" offers a *step-by-step approach to speech preparation.* You learn to conquer the complex task of public speaking by breaking it down into its component parts: setting your purposes, articulating cen-

tral ideas, finding and assessing supporting materials, organizing and outlining these materials, and building introductions and conclusions.

3. Building a speech is the first half of the speech making process. The other half is actually giving it—*putting your presentation into words, gestures, bodily actions, vocal patterns, and visual aids.* That's what Part III, "Presenting Your Speech," is all about. You're communicating by way of four channels—language, sounds, movements, and visuals—every time you speak. Part III will help you learn how to send and control the messages flowing through each channel.

4. There are many different kinds of speeches, each with its own demands and conventional rules. In Part IV, "Types of Public Speaking," we introduce you to *three broad types of speeches*—speeches to inform, speeches to persuade, and argumentative speeches. As a result, you will refine your speechmaking skills, and learn how to adapt them to particular speaking occasions.

Resources for Instructors

The latest in ancillary support for instruction is available to make your classroom even more challenging. The resources program for *Principles of Speech Communication,* Thirteenth Brief Edition, includes the following instructional supplements:

1. **Instructor's Resource Guide.** This is an extensive guide to teaching the course written by Kathleen German of Ohio University. For each chapter, it includes an outline of key concepts, questions to check student comprehension and to encourage critical thinking, detailed descriptions of classroom activities, impromptu speaking exercises, and a bibliography for further reading.

2. **Teaching Public Speaking.** Also written by Kathleen German, this introduction to teaching the basic course in public speaking offers suggestions for everything from lecturing to designing assignments and examinations to incorporating cultural diversity in the classroom. Essential for graduate teaching assistants and first-time instructors, it may also provide new ideas for the experienced instructor. An extensive general bibliography and list of references for media resources is also included.

3. **Test Bank.** A comprehensive test bank including over 3,000 test items: true/false, multiple choice, short answer, and essay questions written by Terry Perkins of Eastern Illinois University.

4. **Public Speaking TestGen EQ.** Our print test bank is available digitally through Longman's TestGen-EQ with QuizMaster-EQ. This fully networkable testing software is available in Windows and Macintosh versions. TestGen-EQ's friendly graphical interface enables instructors to easily view, edit, and add questions, transfer questions to tests, and print tests in a variety of fonts and forms. Search and sort features let the instructor quickly locate questions and arrange them in a preferred order. QuizMaster-EQ enables instructors to create and save tests and quizzes using TestGen-EQ so students can take them on a computer network. Instructors can

set preferences for how and when tests are administered. QuizMaster-EQ automatically grades the exams and allows the instructor to view or print a variety of reports for individual students, classes, or courses.

5. **Great Ideas for Teaching Speech (GIFTS).** Descriptions and guidelines for assignments successfully used by experienced public speaking instructors in their classrooms

6. **Supplemental Chapters: Speaking on Special Occasions and Public Group Communication Booklet.** For instructors who include coverage of public group communication or speaking on special occasions in their public speaking course, Longman is pleased to offer a manual covering these two areas. The 30-page manual that includes coverage of speeches of introduction, speeches to entertain, group discussion techniques, and team presentations is available free of charge when packaged with student copies of *Principles of Speech Communication 13/e.*

7. **ESL Guide for Public Speaking.** A supplemental guide written by Debra Gonsher Vinik of Bronx Community College includes strategies and resources for instructors teaching in a bilingual or multi-lingual classroom.

8. **Transparencies.** 75 four-color transparencies of diagrams and outlines from the text are available upon adoption to qualified college adopters.

9. **Longman's Public Speaking Video Library.** Three professionally produced videos are available to qualified college adopters and are accompanied by an **Instructor's Video Guide,** written by Kathleen German of Miami University. The Instructor's Guide offers suggestions for classroom exercises, discussion, and applications.

   ✓ **Speaker Apprehension Video.** This video addresses student speech apprehension and provides students with methods for overcoming anxiety in speaking.

   ✓ **Audience Analysis Video.** This video offers strategies and suggestions for students on how best to plan speech delivery based on the demographics of an audience and the context in which a speech is presented.

   ✓ **Student Speech Video.** This video features three complete students speeches and special analysis sections on key speech components such as introductions and conclusions. Outlines of each presentation are available in the accompanying Instructor's Video Guide.

10. **Supplements Crate.** For a limited time, qualified college adopters of *Principles of Speech Communication 13/e* will enjoy our convenient Supplements Crate that aids instructors in organizing our comprehensive ancillary package. In one convenient and durable location, you can store key print supplements, software, and video material. Additional space is available for you to store personal class material such as lecture notes and grade books.

   For previews of this convenient crate and additional information on all of our instructor and student ancillaries, please contact your local Longman representative, call Customer Service at 1-800-322-1377, or visit us on the internet at http://longman.awl.com.

Resources for Students

The Speech Writers Workshop Speech Outlining Software

This interactive software will assist students with speech preparation and enable them to write better speeches. It contains a topic dictionary and powerful documentation tool that includes coverage of how to cite new bibliographic types like on-line sources and e-mail correspondence. Available for Windows and Macintosh machines.

Assessment Guide for Public Speaking

Written by Bruce E. Gronbeck and Ray McKerrow, this manual provides chapter-by-chapter objectives and activities that help you focus on assessing your progress through the book and the course. Based on SCA guidelines for "Assessing College Student Competency in Speech Communication," this is an invaluable resource for classrooms, departments, and institutions who are focused on assessment.

Supplemental Chapters: Speaking on Special Occasions and Public Group Communication

A 30-page manual written by Bruce E. Gronbeck and Kathleen German provides coverage of special occasion speaking and group discussions and presentations. Specific topics covered include speeches of introduction, speeches of courtesy (acceptances and toasts), speeches to entertain, the responsibility of group discussion leaders, the responsibility of group discussion participants, and presentations in teams.

Faculty can order these student supplements packaged with the textbook or in bulk for classroom use through a campus bookstore. For ordering and price information, please contact the local Longman representative, call us at 1-800-322-1377, or visit us on the web at http://longman.awl.com

Acknowledgments

We owe a great debt to instructors who took the time to review the previous edition and offer feedback and suggestions for the preparation of this edition: Ozzie Banicki, Prairie View A&M University; Nancy Kiefer, John Carroll University; Stephen F. Nielsen, University of Nevada, Las Vegas; Gwenn Schultze, Portland Community College; Arlie V. Daniel, East Central University; Cheri Frey-Hartel, Cardinal Stritch College; Dorotha O. Norton, University of Tennessee at Martin; Richard A. Rogers, Northern Arizona University; and Dr. Mary Y. Mandeville, Oklahoma State University. We also thank the following reviewers for their special attention to our coverage of culture: Al González, Bowling Green State University, and Scott D. Gratson, Ball State University.

A special thank you is also due to the thousands of students and instructors who have used this textbook. Their support and suggestions over the years have helped to make *Principles of Speech Communication* comprehensive and enduring. In this way, this textbook belongs to all those who have shared it.

Part I

Public
Speaking
and
Critical
Listening

1 Responsible Speechmaking in an Age of Diversity

The Functions of Speechmaking in Society

You've been speaking most of your life. From the time you started gurgling in your crib, you have used speech to interact with others. Since speaking with others has been a part of your life for such a long time, you're probably asking yourself, "What am I doing in a public speaking class?"

You're in this class because public speaking is something that you must be able to do well if you hope to contribute to society. Since the first schools of public speaking opened in ancient Greece in the sixth century B.C., training in the art of public discourse has held a special place in education. It will prepare you to add your voice to the chorus of public conversation.

Individual Diversity

As a responsible member of society you have an opportunity to help build your community. As an individual, you also have a responsibility to contribute your unique viewpoints to the public conversation. When you articulate your perspective, you help others broaden their understanding of society.

Throughout history, people with ideas have presented them in the public forum for consideration by others. For example, following the lead of Frederick Douglass, a former slave who urged the abolition of slavery, African Americans demanded the right to speak for themselves. They asserted their selfhood in public. In the language of his times, Douglass said, "Men may combine to prevent cruelty to animals, for they are dumb [mute] and cannot speak for themselves; but we are men and must speak for ourselves, or we shall not be spoken for at all."[1] Similarly, the women attending the Seneca Falls, New York, convention for women's rights in 1848 argued that they should be allowed to talk publicly. Originally, they had been assigned only to watch the proceedings from the gallery, but they were determined to define their own rights by exercising the freedom to speak afforded in the First Amendment to the Constitution.

As you see, you have inherited this tradition of public speaking. Today, speaking in public is still a measure of your personhood, a recognition of your uniqueness in society. If you are silent, you become invisible, a nonperson. The Jews of Hitler's Germany were talked about as "silent animals" in *Mein Kampf;* American slaves were thought of as personal property; Native Americans were viewed as children, to be seen and not heard; and whole groups in Africa, Central America, and eastern Europe have been silently "cleansed" from their homelands. When people are silenced, they lose their ability to speak for themselves. As a result, they risk being ignored, controlled by others, or eliminated.

There is an important connection between being heard publicly and being accepted as a human being. It is this very need for recognition that often calls for public speaking as we try to create understanding and respect for diversity. Public speaking is a primary vehicle for representing individual identity. However, because we are all constrained by social groups, our individual voices must be understood in terms of the community.

Community Building

Like individuals, communities are also defined by public talk. The words *community* and *communication* both come from common Latin root words—*cum,* meaning "with," and *munis,* denoting "public work." Communicating is doing public work—defining, exercising, maintaining, or saving *communities*—groups of individuals with shared characteristics and goals. These groups are created and maintained symbolically, largely through public talk. Boy Scouts take their oaths together; churchgoers pray aloud and together offer public declarations of shared beliefs; the Pledge of Allegiance echoes through American schoolhouses every weekday; during lunch breaks, work groups share their corporate culture; Olympic athletes pledge to uphold the common ideals of international competition.

Your sense of community is created in large part through public address. Social communities take shape from the sharing of common interests through public discussion. Most of the groups you value influence your life through public talk. We become bonded together in a community as we discover common interests through public discourse. We learn that we are related by blood, locale, nationality, race, occupation, gender, or other shared experiences and attributes. Senator Ben Nighthorse Campbell of Colorado expresses this idea when he speaks of the "Indian way." He explains, "To Indians . . . success isn't what you have, it's what you've given away. The most revered member of the tribe may be the poorest, because giving away increases your stature. We should place greater value on what we contribute to society rather than on what we accumulate."[2]

Public speech serves both to maintain and to change our communities. You'll even end up creating a small community in your speech classroom. You'll see firsthand the power of public speech to build a community from a collection of strangers as you develop a classroom atmosphere and a set of relationships for learning together.

To Senator Ben Nighthorse Campbell of Colorado, the "Indian Way" places greater value on contributions to society than ownership of material possessions.

The Advantages of Speech Training to the Responsible Speaker

Let's turn back to the question of why you are taking this course. You probably realize that public speaking skills are not developed overnight. You're taking this course because you need to become more skilled in the kind of communication that goes on publicly. It is important for you to be able to express your ideas to others effectively, especially in situations in which you address many people at once. For now, you'll talk in your classes, meetings of organizations to which you belong, and in other familiar settings. Later, you will encounter even more occasions for public talk: meetings of parent groups, church organizations, your kid's scout troop, professional presentations, weddings, neighborhood get-togethers, city government hearings.

As a society, Americans traditionally have thought that self-expression is important enough to merit special legal protection in the First Amendment to the Constitution. And, following the Western heritage of training in public speaking, we have placed special emphasis on it in our educational systems. Specifically, you will realize these benefits from your class:

1. *A speech classroom is a laboratory, an ideal place for experimentation.* You can try out new skills in the safety of the classroom. Use your classroom as a lab to develop your repertoire of speaking skills.

2. *You can practice effectively getting your message across to others.* As you plan, prepare, and deliver speeches, you will learn the techniques that will help you be a
   more effective communicator. You will discover what works and what doesn't
   work.

3. *Practicing public speaking in a classroom brings you face-to-face with listeners.* Becoming audience-centered is a key to becoming a more powerful speaker. Your
   speech classroom is a great place to learn how to do that. As you get to know your
   classmates, you can focus on them as listeners, learning to work with them to accomplish your speech goals.

4. *You can learn from the feedback of others.* Your classmates can provide you with
   valuable feedback on the effectiveness of your speaking skills. As you become more
   adept as a speaker, they can help you assess your progress.

5. *Studying oral communication helps you to become a more shrewd consumer of messages.* In your lifetime, you'll be exposed to thousands of messages demanding your
   attention. To protect yourself, you'll need to become a critical listener and thinker.
   You can practice those skills in this class as you listen to your classmates' speeches
   and evaluate their ideas.

6. *Adapting to listeners helps you cope in an increasingly diverse society.* Predictions suggest that in the next fifty years, the United States will undergo a profound ethnic
   shift. Your understanding of the complexity of the communication process can
   help you appreciate differences among people and cope with the increasing diversity of lifestyles and ideas in our society.

Speechmaking in the classroom prepares you to participate more fully in your community. You can acquire the necessary basic skills to voice your opinions effectively in an
age of diversity and change. Your speechmaking skills will enhance your ability to affect
people's minds in your neighborhood, in the coffee room at work, in government meetings, and in the associations and clubs to which you belong. Speechmaking will prepare
you to live productively in our changing society.

Basic Elements in the Speechmaking Process

Public speaking is an **interactive process.** That is, it is a transaction or exchange among
people in public, rather than interpersonal, settings. Four basic elements of speaking
work together to create the speech process—a speaker, a message, listeners, and the context. Let's consider each of these four basic elements.

The **speaker** is the primary communicator in the public speaking situation. As the
source of the message, the speaker brings an individual perspective and experiences to
the communication transaction.

The **message** is comprised of both the factual content of the speech and the attitudes
and values that represent the speaker's view of the topic. The message is transmitted by
selecting and arranging words and ideas in a particular pattern.

The **listener** is a partner in the speech transaction. While you may think of public
speaking as communication flowing in only one direction from speaker to listener, this is

Studying communication helps you become a more shrewd consumer of messages.

not an entirely accurate picture. Listeners bring prior knowledge, attitudes, and interests to the speech situation. They also provide verbal and nonverbal **feedback** such as frowns, laughter, yawns, or questions during and after the presentation.

Speakers and listeners engage each other in a communication **context.** Some parts of the communication context are obvious, such as the physical setting in which the speech takes place. Other elements, however, are more subtle. The context of the speech also includes the social expectations and cultural rules that come into play when speakers and listeners interact.

To understand the interactive nature of the speech communication process, consider actor Christopher Reeve's appeal to a congressional subcommittee. Reeve offered his unique perspective as a paraplegic when he spoke on behalf of increased research funding

Listeners react to the speaker with verbal feedback such as questions or comments and nonverbal feedback such as frowns, puzzled looks, or laughter.

for spinal cord injuries. Members of the subcommittee probably recognized Reeve as "Superman" or from news bulletins about his riding accident. During the speech, they listened with looks of concern, encouragement, and interest. Afterward, they asked questions. The context was defined by the formal room and format of the hearing.

You can easily identify the basic elements of speechmaking in this transaction. Each element is an integral part of the process. If any single part of the process is changed, the entire transaction is altered.

Responsibilities for Successful Speechmaking

Because public speaking is an interactive process, you have certain responsibilities to your listeners. You should consider your ethical responsibilities and respect for human diversity as you contribute to the community dialogue.

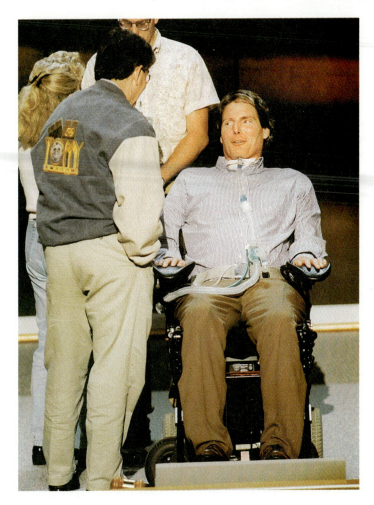

As a speaker, you contribute your unique perspective to the communication interaction. Christopher Reeve often speaks on behalf of the handicapped.

Ethics

Each time you speak publicly, you are contributing to the process of community building and affecting the lives of others. The act of speaking involves making ethical choices. Ethical choices pivot on the questions of justice and injustice, goodness and badness, rightness and wrongness. As a speaker, you might ask yourself questions like these: Is it ethical to make explicitly racial references when describing an individual or a group? Should you tell both sides of the story when giving people information about a new wonder drug? Should you suppress certain kinds of information when trying to change people's minds? Is it fair to use language that you know will trigger emotional reactions in your listeners? These and hundreds of other ethical questions will surface as you prepare and deliver your speeches. While no one can presume to tell you precisely what ethical codes you ought to adhere to when giving a speech, acknowledging the role of ethics in public speaking and working through ethical dilemmas will make you a more thoughtful speaker.

Your reputation for reliability and truthfulness is a powerful means of influencing others because it expresses your concern for your audience. Integrity is important, especially in an age of diversity, when fragmented groups may not understand each other's intentions. Listeners who have no personal experience with a particular subject seek information and advice from speakers they trust. Ancient writers recognized the importance of the speaker's reputation as seen by the audience and labeled it **ethos.** *Ethos* is the credibility attributed to you by your listeners based on their perceptions of your honesty and intentions in the speech.[3]

Demonstrating expertise is an essential ethical quality. So, even though you know a lot about a topic through personal experience, take time to do some extra reading, talk with other experts, and find out what aspects of the topic will engage your listeners. You must know both what you're talking about and to whom you're talking.

Speaking of . . . *apprehension*

First-Time Fears

When you get up to speak for the first time, if you haven't already, the biggest thing on your mind will most likely be stage fright. Some fears can be overwhelming, interrupting good ideas and stopping otherwise great talks dead in their tracks.

Stage fright or fear isn't an actual fear aroused by the perception of a real danger. Instead, it is anxiety that comes from an imagined threat that exists mostly in your mind. Your listeners aren't likely to storm the podium. They're probably a lot more sympathic than you realize.

Performance anxiety is normal. You'd be surprised at the people who experience and have experienced it for years. James Stewart, Sir Laurence Olivier, Luciano Pavarotti, Madonna, Randy Travis, Carly Simon, Pablo Casals, Barbra Streisand—all have experienced feelings of anxiety. It's an integral part of performing—the risk that comes from commanding the attention of others.

The key is to use your anxiety to energize your performance. Expect that you'll be anxious, but don't let it get the best of you. The rush of adrenaline that comes just before you get up to speak should be used to fuel your speech. Below are some tips to help you cope with stage fright.

1. Prepare ahead of time. Uncertainty about what you're going to say just adds to the anxiety. You don't need that.
2. Breath slowly and deeply. You can't expect to support your voice and movement without oxygen.
3. Think about your ideas. Concentrate on what you're sharing with your listeners, not on how you're feeling.
4. Don't let your imagination run wild. A listener who yawns probably didn't get enough sleep last night. Make it your goal to keep him awake during your speech.
5. Brace yourself for the natural physical symptoms of adrenaline. Expect damp palms, a dry throat, or your own peculiar symptoms.

Above all, give yourself a break. Don't expect perfection the first time you speak—or even the second. Speaking well sometimes takes years of practice. Give yourself a chance and take every opportunity to develop and polish your skills.

Fluency, poise, vocal control, and coordinated movements of your body also contribute to your ethos because they mark you as a skilled speaker. These oral skills are achieved through practice. Such practice is a matter of rehearsing both inside and outside your classroom, aiming at becoming an animated, self-confident, and conversational speaker. You'll have many opportunities in your classroom to sharpen your skills.

Respecting Human Diversity

For many centuries since the rise of Western oratory in ancient Greece, public speaking was a privilege reserved for white, economically secure, socially prominent males. Upper-class, white, propertied men ran the legislatures, the courts, government, and religion. Women, nonwhites, and lower socioeconomic classes were silenced.

The movement to include others followed John Locke's seventeenth-century treatises on government and continued through the social and political revolutions of the ensuing centuries. This emancipation has empowered and given public voices to some previously silenced segments of our society. While progress toward public empowerment continues, we've come far enough toward the goals of justice and equality to demand that public speakers keep human diversity in mind while preparing to speak.

This is not a question of being liberal or conservative, it is just plain social fact. Nonwhites, the economically disadvantaged, women, the elderly as well as the young, those protected by the Americans with Disabilities Act, gays, lesbians—all of these segments of American society will be represented in your audiences. As a speaker, you must recognize that human diversity will affect your public messages.

Most successful speakers are "other-directed," concerned with meeting their listeners' needs and solving their problems. The best speakers recognize and respect listeners and their needs; they are rhetorically sensitive. **Rhetorical sensitivity** refers to speakers' attitudes toward listeners during the speech preparation and delivery process.[4] Rhetorical sensitivity is the degree to which speakers:

   a. Recognize that all people are different and complex and, therefore, should be considered individually. To treat listeners as a uniform mass instead of as people with individual heritages and needs is to dehumanize them. A speaker can't really talk to each member of the audience individually, but he or she can convey respect for their opinions.

   b. Adapt their messages and themselves to particular audiences. Sensitive speakers work at clearly conveying their ideas to each group of listeners. They draw supporting materials out of their listener's experiences and employ language that is suitable to the groups being addressed. Political candidates, for example, talk about local issues and problems.

   c. Consciously seek and react to audience feedback. In responding with clarification to puzzled looks or laughter and clapping, speakers recognize the interactive nature of communication. They acknowledge that their listeners are an important part of the speech transaction process.

   d. Understand that words sometimes cannot bridge the differences between people. To force them to do so is to ignore the humanity and individuality of people. There are limitations of talk. Speech sometimes cannot express the inexpressible. You must recognize that you can't always speak for everyone. In the face of utter personal tragedy, for example, perhaps the best we can do is to hug the victims, hold their hands, and say "I'm sorry"; more words may be insensitive.

Being rhetorically sensitive does not mean saying only what you think others want to hear. Rather, it is a matter of respecting human diversity, conducting careful audience analysis, and making responsible decisions. What are your reasons for speaking? To what degree will those reasons be understood and accepted by others? Can you maintain your own integrity while adapting your purposes to your audience's preferences? Do your listeners respect you and your ideas? These questions demand your sensitivity for your audience as individuals.

Your First Speech

Now, it's time to get you started—up on your feet and ready to speak. Your first speech will probably not be elaborate, but it should follow a few simple guidelines. Structuring the speech in three main parts works well—the introduction, the body, and the conclusion.

Begin by stating your main idea clearly in your introduction. This will help listeners follow your ideas through to the end of your speech. Likewise, the last few sentences should recapture the main idea of the speech to wrap it up and give it a sense of finality.

Most speakers draw on their own knowledge as they develop their ideas. Notice how a beginning student, Delores Lopez, did this in her first speech assignment "Who Am I?" Delores explains why she is in a public speaking class:

> One word that describes my life is "change." Ever since I can remember, things around me have constantly changed. I'm forty-two years old and as I look back, I see lots of change.
>
> When I was a kid, a high school education was enough. My parents didn't go to college; no one in my family did. Although education was respected in my family, there wasn't enough money for us to go on to school. My dad was partially disabled in an industrial accident and we depended on my mom's job to support us.
>
> While I was in high school, I had a weekend job and after graduating, I found a full-time job to help support my younger brothers and sisters. At the time, I never considered going to college. It wouldn't have mattered if I had wanted to go. I didn't have the time or money.
>
> But things have changed. After I had my oldest son, my mom took care of him and I went back to work. Now he's seventeen and I want him to go to school—to have an opportunity I didn't have. I want his life to be different than mine has been.
>
> My life has changed too. The corporation where I work has been downsizing and looking for leadership within the ranks. My supervisor has encouraged me to go back to school. She thought I was smart enough to make it, and I know I can study hard. The company is even paying part of my tuition. In this economic climate I realize that to be without higher education is to be more disadvantaged than ever. Maybe those of you who don't have kids, don't realize the financial pressures of raising kids.

Speaking of ... *ethics*

Ethics and Public Speaking

Occasionally, we'll include a boxed area devoted to "ethical moments"—ethical decisions public speakers must make in preparing and delivering their talks. We hope that you'll take a moment to think about the problems presented and their solutions in your life. You might discuss some of these problems with others to get alternative perspectives.

Here are some typical ethical questions that you might face in the speeches you'll give this term:

1. You read a fascinating article about fund-raising ideas for organizations. Should you borrow these ideas and present them as your own at your next club meeting? Do you need to acknowledge everything you learn from others? Must you always cite sources?

2. You recognize that a major portion of a speaker's informative speech came from an article that you read last week. The speaker does not cite the source. During the critique session, should you blow the whistle on the speaker or should you talk with the person later? Should you tell your teacher or let it go?

3. An article says exactly what you intended to say about the use of tanning beds. Then you find a more recent article claiming that new research contradicts the first article. Should you ignore the new evidence?

4. An authority whom you wish to cite uses the words *perhaps, probably, likely,* and *often.* Should you strike these words from the quotation to make it sound more positive? After all, you're not tinkering with the ideas, only the strength of assertion.

5. A student in your class disagrees strongly with your analysis of cheating on college campuses. You know that he was caught cheating in another class a year ago. If you bring this student's past up in response to his challenge, it may deflect focus from his point of view. Should you do it?

Ethical decisions such as these will confront you regularly, both in your speech classroom and throughout rest of your life. Take a few moments now to consider such situations and to articulate your position. Identify your moral standards before you face ethical dilemmas on the platform.

There is one skill that is in demand in my company. They're looking for leadership qualities in their employees—especially the ability to present oneself and communicate well with others. That's why I decided to take this class in public speaking.

As you can see, there has been a lot of change in my life. Some of those changes have come from outside—my job, my family. But, I'm changing inside too. I am more confident about what I want in my life and I'm finding ways to meet my goals.

I'm looking forward to working with all of you; I think we can learn from each other.

Notice how Delores's speech was divided into three main sections. In the introduction she mentioned the theme of change. She elaborated on that idea by tracing changes in her own life, building on what she knew best, her own experiences. Examples from her family supported and elaborated the theme. Delores answers the question "Who Am I?" by explaining how she has come to be in her public speaking class. The final sentences of the speech summarize the main theme of change.

Of course, there's more to consider as you develop your skills in public speaking. Chapter 2 will give you additional advice to get you started.

Assessing Your Progress

Chapter Summary

1. Although you have been communicating with others all of your life, public speaking offers special opportunities for expressing individual diversity and building communities.

2. Your speech classroom gives you a unique opportunity to practice your skills on a live audience, get others' feedback, become a better consumer of oral messages, and cope in an increasingly diverse society.

3. Speaking is a transaction involving a speaker, listeners, and a message within a context.

4. As a speaker, you should be able to demonstrate ethics and respect human diversity.

5. Rhetorical sensitivity refers to the speaker's attitudes toward listeners during the preparation and delivery of a speech.

6. Your first speech should have an introduction, body, and conclusion that develop a main idea.

Key Terms

context (p. 7)

ethics (p. 9)

ethos/credibility (p. 10)

feedback (p. 7)

human diversity (p. 11)

interactive process (p. 6)

listener (p. 6)

message (p. 6)

rhetorical sensitivity (p. 11)

speaker (p. 6)

Assessment Activities

1. Interview a representative of a local group that schedules public lectures, the director of the campus speakers' bureau, or someone in a position to discuss the speech skills that are characteristic of professional speakers. Bring a list of those skills to class and be prepared to share your notes with others. Identify the basic competencies of effective speakers.

2. Meet with a classmate to discuss your first speech assignment. How did you obtain and select the information for your speech? What role did your perception of the audience play in the development of your speech?

3. Prepare an inventory of your personal speaking abilities. (Your instructor may make this an assignment in a journal that you will maintain throughout the term.) What is your ethical standard for speaking? How does your speaking reflect a respect for human diversity? Estimate your integrity as a speaker.

References

1. Frederick Douglass, "Speech at the National Convention of Colored Men [1883]" reprinted in *The American Reader: Words That Moved a Nation,* edited by Diane Ravitch (New York: HarperCollins, 1990), 172.

2. Quoted by Wallace Terry, "Success Isn't What You Have—It's What You've Given Away," *Parade,* June 2, 1996, p. 17.

3. William L. Benoit, "A Cognitive Response Analysis of Source Credibility." *Progress in Communication Sciences, 10* (1991): 1–19.

4. See Roderick P. Hart and Don M. Burks, "Rhetorical Sensitivity and Social Interaction," *Speech Communication Monographs, 47* (1980): 1–22.

2 Getting Started: Where Responsibility Begins

You learned about your role as a public speaker in our society in Chapter 1. While there's a lot to discover about the intricacies of speech preparation and speechmaking, you can learn enough about the basics to begin responsible speechmaking right away. As you prepare to speak, you'll probably ask questions like:

- ✔ How do I choose a topic?
- ✔ How do I make ethical choices for the content of my speech?
- ✔ What will my listeners want to hear?
- ✔ Where do I find the material for my speech?
- ✔ What kind of notes should I make?
- ✔ What's the best way to practice delivering my speech?

These may seem like a lot of decisions, but strategic planning is the key to platform success. You can save time and effort by planning carefully instead of wandering aimlessly through the library or waiting endlessly at your desk for inspiration.

There's no magical formula for speaking responsibly. However, if you follow the seven steps offered in this chapter—either as they are presented here or in another order that works for you—you'll be ready for your audience. By the end of this chapter, you'll have mastered the basic steps for delivering your first speeches.

Selecting and Narrowing Your Subject

The most difficult task for many speakers is to choose a subject. Sometimes the subject is chosen for you, but often you will choose your own topic for classroom speeches. You might begin the process of choosing a topic by asking yourself questions: What do you know something about? What are you interested in talking about? What topics do you think will interest your listeners? Does the occasion or situation suggest a topic for dis-cussion? It's important to answer these questions carefully. Your answers will help you select and narrow your subject. A well-chosen speech topic is the first step to a successful speech. Let's examine in more detail the processes of choosing and narrowing a topic.

It's a good idea to begin selecting a topic by listing those subjects that you have knowl-edge of, choosing the ones you're willing to talk about in front of others, and thinking about ways you can relate them to your listeners. If the purpose of your first classroom speech is to inform your classmates about a subject, you might come up with the follow-ing list of things you know something about:

High school football (you played football)

Sharks (you did a science project on this subject)

Halloween (it's your favorite holiday and you love to make costumes)

Nintendo (you like the games)

Soap operas (you watch them)

Smoking (you quit two years ago)

Careers in accounting (you're considering them now)

Photography (you like taking amateur photos)

Skin cancer (you're worried about the side effects of tanning)

Next, you need to consider the people who make up your audience. Which topics would interest them most? When you ask yourself this question, you realize that several topics such as making Halloween costumes, careers in accounting, and photography are mainly of interest to you. Members of your audience have made career choices and they already have hobbies. You should probably cross these topics off your list.

You should also think about your listeners' expectations. What do they already know, and what do they expect to learn? They may already know more than you do about Nin-tendo and soap operas. You'll certainly need to eliminate these topics from your list. Now you have a narrower list of potential topics—those that will interest your audience and meet your listeners' expectations.

After some additional thought, you decide to inform your classmates about sharks be-cause you've done a lot of research on this subject and know you can arouse their inter-est. This general subject can be broken into more specific topics, including:

The types of sharks

The life cycle of the shark

Endangered species of sharks

Shark habitats and habits

Famous shark stories

Sharks as a source of human food

Movies about sharks

Shark cartilage as a potential cure for cancer

Shark attacks and how to prevent them

The historical evolution of the shark

Brainstorming to Generate Topics

Having trouble coming up with possible speech topics? Try this brainstorming exercise:

1. Get a large blank sheet of paper and a pencil.
2. On the left-hand side of the paper, write the letters of the alphabet in a column.
3. Then, as quickly as you can, write down single words beginning with each of the letters. Write down any word that comes to your mind. Repeat until you have the entire sheet filled. You might begin like this: A—apples, alphabet, alarm, alimony; B—bazaar, balsa, baboon, bassoon, balloon; C—comics, cologne, colors, confetti.
4. Next, consider each of the words as a key to potential topics. For example, *apples* might suggest apple pie recipes, Johnny Appleseed and other early American legends, pesticide controversies, fruit in our diets, farm and orchard subsidies, or government price controls of farm produce. This is just the beginning. From one key word, you can derive many possible speech topics.
5. Obviously, not all of these topics would be great speech topics, but this exercise gives you a creative and quick way to generate lots of ideas.

Given this list of subtopics, begin to ask yourself additional questions to narrow the topic even further. How much time do I have to deliver this speech? What do my classmates already know about my topic? Can I group some of these ideas together? After you answer these questions, you may end up with an informative speech focusing on three topics that cluster around the characteristics of sharks:

The types of sharks

The life cycle of the shark

Shark habitats and habits

As you can see from this example, you begin with a list of potential topics. Then, you select those that reflect your knowledge, the expectations of your listeners, and the requirements of the occasion. Finally, you consider the possible subtopics and choose several that fit the time limits and go together naturally. This kind of systematic topic selection is the first step in successful speaking. The next step is to identify your speaking purpose and central idea.

Determining Your Purposes and Central Idea

Once you know what you want to talk about, you still need to ask yourself more questions. Why do you wish to discuss this subject? Why might an audience want to listen to you? And, is what you're discussing appropriate to the occasion? To answer these questions you must analyze the reasons for your topic choice. First, think about the *general purpose,* the primary reason you will speak in public. Next, consider your *specific purposes,* the concrete goals you wish to achieve in a particular speech. Finally, focus your thoughts on a *central idea,* the statement guiding the thoughts you wish to communicate.

General Purposes

If you examine most speeches, you'll come up with three **general purposes** for speeches: to inform, to entertain, and to persuade. This chart summarizes the general purposes for speaking:

General Purpose	Audience Response Sought
To inform	Clear understanding
To entertain	Enjoyment and comprehension
To persuade	Acceptance of ideas or behaviors

Throughout this book, we will emphasize speeches to inform and speeches to persuade. The reason is that these types of speeches dominate the speaking occasions you'll face in life.

Speaking to Inform When you speak *to inform,* your general purpose is to help listeners understand an idea, concept, or process or to help widen their range of knowledge. This is the aim of scientists who gather at the International AIDS Conference to report their research results to colleagues, of presidential press secretaries who make public announcements, of a job supervisor who explains the operation of a new piece of equipment, and of your professors in college classes.

To create understanding, you must change the level or quality of information possessed by your listeners. They should leave your speech knowing more than they did before they heard it. For example, you might inform your classmates about herbal medicine, photographic composition, laser surgery, personal computers, tornadoes, Individual Retirement Accounts, anorexia nervosa, the battle of Bunker Hill, or any number of topics. If you talk about laser surgery, for instance, assume that they may already have some knowledge. To increase their understanding, you will need to focus on innovative surgical techniques using lasers, such as radial keratotomy. You might even speculate about how lasers will change standard surgical operations in the future. By providing explanations, examples, statistics, and illustrations, you expand your listeners' knowledge.

Not only must an informative speech provide facts, but it must be structured so that listeners can easily understand and remember those facts. For example, an informative speech on how to assemble a sound system must include the necessary instructions in the correct sequence of steps. Your goal as an informative speaker is to impart both knowledge and overall understanding. Understanding how to assemble a sound system depends not only on learning what to do but also on knowing when to do it and why.

Speaking to Persuade If you seek to influence listeners' beliefs and actions, then your purpose is *to persuade.* Celebrities sell us on the benefits of cars and shampoos; lawyers convince jurors to recommend the death penalty; activists exhort tenants to stand up to their landlords; politicians debate taxes.

As a persuasive speaker, you usually seek to influence the beliefs and attitudes of your listeners. You might want to convince them that John F. Kennedy was shot by several assassins, that education is the cornerstone of freedom, or that life exists after death. In these cases, you are attempting to alter beliefs or attitudes. Sometimes, however, you will want to persuade your listeners to act. You may want them to contribute money to the Humane Society, sign a petition against a landfill project, vote for a new tax levy, or boycott a local grocery store. In this type of persuasive speech, called a speech *to actuate,* you ask your listeners for specific actions. You might ask your classmates to quit watching television, cut back on caffeine consumption, sign prenuptial agreements, start stock portfolios, or register to vote.

To inform, to entertain, and to persuade are the general purposes of speaking. By thinking about general purposes, you begin your orientation process and assessment of the task ahead. The next step is to focus on the specific purposes of your speech.

Specific Purposes

Specific purposes are the actual goals you want to achieve in a speech. They can be extremely wide-ranging. For example, if your topic is aircraft and your general purpose is to inform, then your specific purpose might be to inform your audience about the role of aircraft in military combat *or* to inform your listeners about safety regulations governing air travel *or* to provide them with a history of aircraft design. The specific purpose combines the general purpose with the topic of the speech.

While some specific purposes are public, some are private—known only by you. For example, as a responsible speaker you probably hope you'll make a good impression on an audience, although you're not likely to say that aloud. Some purposes are short-term; others are long-term. If you're speaking to members of a local organization on the importance of recycling, your short-term purpose might be to convince them to save their aluminum cans, while your long-term purpose could be to gather support for a citywide recycling program.

Theoretically, you have multiple private and public as well as short-term and long-term specific purposes whenever you speak. Practically, however, you need to identify a dominant one that can guide your speech preparation. A single specific purpose, one that you can articulate for an audience, focuses you on precisely what you want your audience to understand, believe, or do.

Suppose that you wanted to take on the challenge of getting more of your classmates to use electronic databases. Consider various ways of wording your specific purpose:

- ✓ "The purpose of my speech is to tell students about the variety of electronic databases" (understanding).
- ✓ "The purpose of my speech is to relate how electronic retrieval systems can put the resources of other libraries at your fingertips" (information).
- ✓ "The purpose of my speech is to reduce students' levels of anxiety about using computers for electronic searches" (feelings).
- ✓ "The purpose of my speech is to change the belief that computers are good only for playing games" (beliefs).
- ✓ "The purpose of my speech is to get half of the class to agree to search electronic databases for their next speech" (action).

All these purposes involve electronic databases, yet each has a different specific focus, making it a different speech. Locking onto a specific purpose allows you to zero in on your primary target.

Central Ideas

Once you've settled on a specific purpose for your speech, you're ready to translate that goal into concrete sentences. You first need to cast into words the controlling thought of your speech. This **central idea** (sometimes called a *thesis statement*) is a statement that captures the essence of the information or concept you wish to communicate to an audience, usually in a single sentence. For example, your central idea for a speech on diamonds might be: "The value of a diamond is largely determined by four factors—color, cut, clarity, and carat." In a persuasive speech, the central idea phrases the belief, attitude, or action you want an audience to adopt. Your central idea for a persuasive speech on dieting might be: "Avoid fad diets because they create dangerous imbalances in essential nutrients and break down muscle tissue."

The precise phrasing of central ideas is very important because wording conveys the essence of your subject matter, setting up audience expectations. Examine Table 2.1 for examples of ways to word speech purposes. Then consider this example—assume that you've decided to give an informative speech on fixing a leaky faucet. You might phrase your central idea in one of three ways:

1. "With only minimal mechanical skills, anyone can fix a leaky faucet."
2. "With a few simple supplies, you can fix a leaky faucet for less than $10."
3. "Fixing a leaky faucet yourself will give you a sense of accomplishment as well as free you from depending on plumbers for making home repairs."

Note that the phrasing of the central idea controls the emphasis of the speech. The first version stresses the individual audience member's ability to complete the task. Presumably, the speech would offer a step-by-step description of the repair process. The second version suggests a quite different speech, focused on securing the inexpensive supplies. In contrast, the third version concentrates on benefits to the listener.

The process of selecting your subject, determining your general and specific purposes, and phrasing your central idea is the process of narrowing. When you put it all together, here is the result for an informative speech:

Subject: Plumbing repair

General Purpose: To inform

Specific Purpose: To explain how you can fix a leaky faucet.

Central Idea: Most leaky faucets require a new washer that you can install in less than an hour for about $2.00.

TABLE 2.1 Speaking Purposes

This table provides a guide to the relationships between the general purpose, specific purpose, and central idea of your speech.

General Purpose	Specific Purpose	Central Idea
To help your listeners understand an idea, concept, or process (to inform)	To teach your listeners about the Federal Reserve Board	"The most important influence on interest rates in this country is the Federal Reserve Board."
To influence your listeners' actions (to actuate)	To get your listeners to walk to classes this week (short-term goal)	"You should start a fitness program today to improve the quality of your life."
	To get your listeners to develop a fitness program (long-term goal)	
To influence your listeners' thoughts (to persuade)	To increase your listeners' appreciation of the role of pure scientific research	"While science doesn't always yield a better mousetrap, it is still an important human activity."

Work on your general and specific purposes before constructing your speech. Your speaking purposes clarify your relationship to your audience. They also guide your search for speech materials.

Responsible Analysis of Audience and Occasion

Communication is a two-way street. That means you need to consider your listeners when you are preparing to speak. It's tempting to focus only on yourself—your goals, your fears, and your own interests. However, if you want to speak so that others will know what you know, believe what you believe, feel what you feel, and do what you believe is in their best interests, then you've got to construct the speech from your listeners' viewpoint.

Responsible speakers regularly ask questions such as: "How would I feel about this topic if I were in their place?" "How can I adapt this material to their interests and habits, especially if their experiences or understandings are different from mine?" Putting yourself in your listeners' shoes is what researchers call **audience orientation,** an ability to understand the listener's point of view. Being audience-oriented will push you to construct speeches from the receiving end of the communication process, investigating aspects of the audience's psychological and sociological background that are relevant to your speech.

Chapter 5 takes up the topic of audience orientation in detail. For now, you should find out how much your listeners already know about your subject so that you can adjust to their level. You should also discover their attitudes toward your subject. If they are apathetic, you must create interest; if they are hostile or favorable, you must adapt what you say. In a public speaking class, this type of investigation is easy enough to conduct—you can ask. Start asking questions early—after all, your whole purpose in speaking is to connect with your listeners!

It is also important to consider the occasion on which you're speaking. The occasion is what brings people together, and, consequently, it often determines listeners' expectations. Do they expect to hear a comic monologue? Does the situation demand a serious approach such as a lecture? In addition to answering these questions, you should consider the nature and purpose of the occasion. Is this a voluntary or captive audience? How many people will attend? Will the speech be delivered indoors or outdoors? Will the audience be sitting or standing? Will there be competing noise? Will you need to make special arrangements for equipment such as a public address system or an overhead projector?

Throughout the process of developing your speech, consider your listeners and the occasion. Your listeners' expectations and the reasons they have gathered to hear you will influence your choice of topic and the focus of your speech. As you examine the remaining steps in the process of speech development, remember that your ultimate goal is to communicate with your listeners.

Gathering Your Speech Material

Once you've considered the subject and purpose of your speech and analyzed the audience and occasion, you'll be ready to gather the materials for your speech. Ordinarily, you'll start by assembling what you already know about the subject and deciding what ideas you want to include. Nearly always, however, you'll find that what you already know is not enough. You'll want to supplement what you know with additional information—facts, illustrations, stories, and examples. You can gather some of this material from newspapers, magazines, books, government documents, or radio and television programs. You can acquire other information through interviews and conversations with people who know something about the subject that you do not know. And, more and more information is becoming available through electronic databases.

As you search for materials, if you plan to deal with a current question of public interest, you should consult such sources as the "The Week in Review" section of the Sunday *New York Times, U.S. News and World Report, The Wall Street Journal, Harper's,* and *The Observer.* Many magazines of general interest are indexed in the *Readers' Guide to Periodical Literature* or can be accessed via electronic database searches; numerous encyclopedias, yearbooks, government reports, almanacs, and other reference materials can be found in your college library. This important topic—locating supporting materials—will be covered in detail in Chapter 6.

Making an Outline

Early in your preparation, make a rough sketch of the points you wish to include in your speech. A complete outline can be drawn up once you've gathered all of the necessary material. When this material is at hand, set down in final order the principal points you expect to present, together with the subordinate ideas that will be necessary to explain or prove these points. Flesh out your ideas with supporting materials such as examples, statistics, and quotations.

In Chapter 8, you'll find a number of specific organizational patterns for arranging the ideas in a speech. There, too, you'll find the form that a complete outline should take. For

FIGURE 2.1   The Essential Steps in Planning, Preparing, and Presenting a Speech

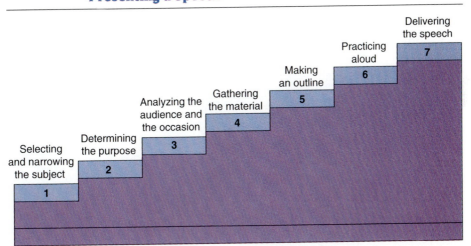

Systematic planning and preparation will save you time and frustration as you develop your speeches. These are the seven basic steps involved in effective speech preparation. Do you usually prepare your speeches in this order? Which steps are the easiest and which are the most difficult for you?

the present, remember two simple but important rules: (1) arrange your ideas in a clear sequence and (2) make sure that each point is directly related to your specific purpose. If you follow these rules, your speech should be coherent.

Practicing Aloud

Once you have completed your outline, you're ready to practice your speech (see Figure 2.1.). Even though you may feel silly talking to yourself, practice aloud to refine the ideas and phrasing of your speech and to work on delivery skills.

Many people practice alone, sometimes in front of a mirror, before delivering their first speech to an audience.

Give practice a chance. It can mean the difference between an adequate effort and an outstanding speech. Repeatedly read through the outline until you've made all the changes that seem useful and until you can express each idea clearly and smoothly. Then write out a note card with brief cues for each of your main ideas. Next, try to talk through the speech by looking at your note cards. As you practice aloud, you may inadvertently leave out some points; that's okay. Practice until all of the ideas come out in their proper order and the words flow easily. Talk in a full voice to get used to the sound—don't mumble. Finally, if possible, get a friend to listen to your speech, give you direct feedback, and help you practice making eye contact with a real person.

Developing Confident Delivery

Now you're ready to present your speech. Even if you've prepared fully, you still might be asking, "How can I deal with my nervousness? If I'm anxious, how can I convey a sense of self-confidence to my listeners?" If you have thought about some strategies for coping with anxiety, you'll be ready to deal with it. Although there's no foolproof program for developing self-confidence, there are some practical ways to communicate confidently:

1. *Realize that tension and nervousness are normal.* They can even benefit you. Remember that tension can provide you with energy. As adrenaline pours into your bloodstream, you experience a physical charge that increases bodily movement and psychological alertness. A baseball pitcher who's not pumped up before a big game may find that his fastball has no zip. Similarly, a speaker who's not pumped up may come across as dull and lifeless. Practice speaking often so that you learn how you react to stress and develop strategies for coping with it.[1]

Speaking of . . . apprehension

State and Trait Apprehension

Research distinguishes between two kinds of speech anxiety: state apprehension and trait apprehension. **State apprehension** refers to the anxiety you feel in particular settings or situations. For example, perhaps you can talk easily with friends but are uncomfortable when being interviewed for a job. This sort of apprehension is also known as *stage fright*, because it's the fear of performing that leads to your worries about failure or embarrassment.

Stage fright has physiological manifestations that vary from one person to another. You can probably list your own symptoms—clammy hands, weak knees, dry mouth, and a trembling or even cracking voice. Its psychological manifestations include mental blocks (forgetting what you're going to say), vocal hesitation and nonfluency, and an internal voice that keeps telling you that you're messing up. The knowledge that you're being evaluated by others brings on these anxious moments.

While some aspects of nervousness are characteristic of the situation, others are a part of your own personality. This kind of apprehension, called **trait apprehension,** refers to your level of anxiety as you face any communication situation. A high level of anxiety leads some people to withdraw from situations that require interpersonal or public communication with others.

Speaking of . . . skills

Practicing Your Speech

If you're ever learned to play the piano or drive a car with a standard transmission, you know that you can't do it all at once. You must practice to improve. The same principle can be applied to improving your public speaking skills. Practice repeated over time will result in more improvement than a single practice session. In addition, remember these guidelines:

1. Keep practice sessions brief. It's better to practice your speech for a few minutes at a time over the course of several days than to go through it repeatedly for two hours the day before it's due.
2. Practice in different settings. Deliver your speech as you walk to classes, in front of your friends, or in an empty classroom. This kind of varied practice encourages flexibility.
3. After you start your speech, finish it without stopping to correct errors or to restart it. You aren't going to deliver your speech exactly the same way every time you give it. Expect some changes in your speech delivery and phrasing.

2. *Focus on your ideas.* Think about what you want to communicate to your listeners. When you speak, you want their minds to be focused on your ideas, not on the way you're presenting them. Speech anxiety arises in part because of self-centeredness; sometimes you're more concerned with your personal appearance and performance than with your topic. One means of creating confidence is to select topics that will take your mind off yourself. By doing this, you make the situation topic-centered rather than self-centered. Have you ever wondered why you can talk at length with friends about your favorite hobby, sports, or political interests without feeling anxious but you find yourself in a nervous state when standing in front of your history class to report on something you've read? Talking about a subject that interests you may be part of the answer.

3. *Look at your listeners.* Americans tend to mistrust anyone who doesn't look them in the eye. They also may get the impression that you don't care about them or that you aren't interested in their reactions to your message if you look at your notes and not at them. Eye contact with members of your audience promotes visual bonding. This will signal your eagerness to communicate with them. In addition, you can watch your listeners' faces for feedback and make minor adjustments as you speak. If you notice looks of puzzlement, for example, you'll certainly want to adjust by further explaining your ideas.

4. *Communicate with your body as well as with your voice.* Realize that you are being seen as well as heard. Bodily movements and changes in facial expression can help clarify and reinforce your ideas. You might smile as you refer to hu-

morous events or step toward your listeners as you take them into your confidence. Keep hands free at your sides so that you can gesture easily. Let body movements be natural and appropriate to your message. As you say, "On the other hand," you might raise one hand to reinforce your statement. As you speak, your body uses up the excess adrenaline it generates. The very act of talking aloud reduces fear.

5. *Speak in public as often as you can.* Public speaking experience will not eliminate your fears, but it will make them more controllable. Speaking frequently in front of your classmates will help reduce your anxiety. Repeated experiences with different audiences and situations also will increase your self-assurance and poise, which, in turn, will lessen your apprehension. Force yourself to speak up in class discussions, join in discussions with friends and others, and contribute as a member of organizations. Find time to talk with people of all ages. Attend public meetings and contribute to the discussion. Maybe you'll decide to run for office!

There are no shortcuts to developing speaking confidence. For most of us, gaining self-confidence results from experience and from understanding the process of communication. The uneasy feeling in the pit of your stomach may always be there, but it need not paralyze you. As you gain experience with each of the essential steps—from selecting a subject to practicing the speech—your self-confidence as a speaker will grow.

You should practice your speaking skills whenever the opportunity arises.

Sample Speech

The following speech was given by David Mellor of Southern Connecticut State University at a speech contest. It's a comparatively simple, thought-provoking talk about diversity of educational goals. David opens with some reflections on the current job market and successful preparation for it. Then, he turns his attention to diversity. Using the unique life of Bill Veeck, David elaborates on his theme. Notice how the specific examples David uses make this speech interesting. The speech is easy to follow, thoughtful, and well adapted to student listeners.

Bill Veeck[2] David Mellor

The speaker uses supporting material to show the problems in the current job market for college graduates. The answer he proposes is to take chances by choosing creative careers. Bill Veeck is an example.

By parents, peers and professors, we, as college students are pressured to succeed. This pressure is now at an all-time high. According to an April 19th article in the *New York Times,* "the job search for this year's graduates is the worst ever." Regardless of this hindrance, we see that in order to be successful, one must not only be intelligent but innovative and unique. In short, one must be creative. According to *The Journal of Higher Education,* we college students are anything but that. Over 33 percent of 1990 college graduates received business-oriented degrees. Of the remaining students, over half were divided between communications, political science, and computer studies. The problem is obvious: we need diversity. The solution is simple. We should not look to these overcrowded areas, but direct our attention towards individuals; people who chase chances rather than rest in routines. Baseball's business executive Bill Veeck was such a person. Of course, being a corporate baseball boss is not the only avenue to success. But the example shown to us by Veeck is an enlightening one. An amputee with . . . impaired vision and hearing, Bill Veeck far exceeded all expectations of him. It has been said ". . . when life gives you lemons, make lemonade." Bill Veeck did just this with his product: the game of America, the game of baseball; with his employees; our heroes, our idols, the players; and finally, with his patrons, all of us. We'll first see how Bill Veeck's creative product innovation made baseball the creative successful game that it is today. Next, we'll see how Bill Veeck's employee relations are not only the epitome of employee relations for baseball coaches, but for business executives everywhere. We'll finally see how Bill Veeck's patron appreciation has made him a man worthy of our admiration and praise. Unique, innovative individuals are hard to come by, as is success. Bill Veeck embodies a lesson we can all learn from./1

From his autobiography *Veeck as in Wreck,* Bill Veeck stated ". . . baseball's greatest asset is the long sense of continuity that comes with a deep personal affiliation." Indeed Bill Veeck had long been affiliated with baseball. He merely followed in his father's footsteps when he purchased his first team. However, Bill Veeck was by no means a follower. His creative innovations upon baseball had never been seen before and may never be duplicated again. A typical day at the ballpark we'll hear, ". . . a deep drive to the center field fence, it's going, it's going, it's gone for a homerun. The scoreboard is exploding with light and a pitching cart will be out of the bull pen soon with a relief help." We hear that and it is commonplace, but we hear that courtesy of Bill Veeck. The exploding scoreboard was one of the many in-Veeck-ions that ignited both the crowd and the game of baseball. The pitching cart: a means by which the pitcher can make his grand tour of the stadium before taking to the mound—not quite. Bill Veeck created the pitching cart as a means by which to avoid lulls in the game and keep the action continuous by getting the pitcher from the bullpen to mound quicker. From the highly acclaimed business book, *Swimming with the Sharks without Being Eaten,* we see that Bill Veeck was correct in saying ". . . promotion is a state of mind long before it becomes a state of action." It was these creative innovations that brought us to Comiskey and ballparks all over the nation. This is because Bill Veeck owned several teams as a major league executive: the St. Louis Browns, the Chicago White Sox, and the Chicago Cubs just to name a few. Now some may see hints of inconsistency in wandering from team to team. Such is not present with Bill Veeck. What is present is his means by which to adopt an ailing franchise and help it achieve success. How was this done? By dealing all employees the same policy, honesty./2

In 1977, pitcher Steve Stone started out with Veeck's Chicago White Sox. After winning 18 games his rookie season, his demand throughout the league skyrocketed. Bill Veeck could not keep up with Stone's comparable offers. Though Stone wished to stay in Chicago, Bill Veeck referred him elsewhere. Now, Bill Veeck could have easily taken advantage of Stone's success and allegiance but did not. Steve Stone went on to win 25 games and the Cy Young Award in 1980, but went on to praise Bill Veeck as being the person who opened the door to his stellar career. Events such as this earned Veeck respect and admiration throughout the league. In his book, *A Hustler's Handbook,* coauthor Ed Linn cites, ". . . if wealth could be measured by admiration Bill Veeck is indeed the richest man in the world." We see that Bill Veeck did have a rich reputation. But his treatment of Stone was not exceptional. Bill Veeck treated all players, major and minor leaguers, to that same honest policy and so strived to refine the echelons of his own business before intruding upon others. Such is seen with his treatment of the minor league teams. According to a 1989 *Sporting News* article, ". . . most today are mere drop-offs for hero has-beens." This was not the view of Bill Veeck, who looked to minor league teams as a means by which to recruit young talent, refine young ball players, and so set up a steady chain of progression from the minors to the majors. With Bill Veeck, few if any players were considered to be in the "minor league." The story of Eddie Gadell proves this fact. In 1951, Veeck sent the 3-foot 11-inch Gadell to the plate for the St. Louis

The speaker develops his first point. Bill Veeck introduced innovations to baseball, including the exploding scoreboard and the pitching cart.

*The second point is
expanded. Veeck earned
respect from his
employees by treating
them honestly and equally.
Examples of specific
instances and testimony
provide support for this
point.*

Browns. Equal opportunity was provided at all levels of business under Bill Veeck. In turn, business was attracted to Bill Veeck./3

Again from his autobiography *Veeck as in Wreck*, Bill Veeck stated ". . . baseball consists of three dimensions, the customer brings a fourth." We all know that customers are the business to any business, but no one acknowledged this commonsense theory more than Bill Veeck. Most sports corporations today, be it Nike with the Air Jordan Shoe or Starter with the Pro-Line Jacket, offer a glitzy product but for a glitzy price. Bill Veeck took his product, the game of baseball, and not only made it affordable and accessible but enjoyable to all. An old archive rule in baseball states the pitcher must release the ball 20 seconds after it has been returned to him with the bases empty. Now some may protest this foolish rule, but Bill Veeck took full advantage of it. He went as far as to install a 20-second pitchometer that would bleep, scream, and siren every time the opposing pitcher exceeded 20 seconds. Baseball often falls victim to the weather. But rain did not foil the fun for the fan or Bill Veeck. Any day rain was expected fans would be given a team-emblemmed poncho upon entering the ballpark. Should the rain continue, the tarp that was rolled out onto the infield was also a chess/checkerboard on which the ground crew would be the pawns. Two lucky fans would then be recruited up into the press box and announce their moves over the public address system to the ground crew. Should chess or checkers not be the choice, the exploding scoreboard was also a movie screen that would show past highlights. We see that Bill Veeck confronted life's handicaps as he would hurdles, clearing them all. Be it with the exploding scoreboard, the checkerboard, or the complimentary ponchos, Bill Veeck has adopted all of life's abandoned apples and made a pie to please all. Eventually fans do have to leave the ballpark, but not without the continued gratuity and respect of Bill Veeck. Annually, he donated hundreds of thousands of dollars to clean up the communities beyond the stadiums. So be it in the ballpark or our own backyards, Bill Veeck is indeed worthy of our admiration and praise./4

*The final point extends
the central ideas of the
speech, Veeck never
forgot that the customer
was the heart of the game
of baseball. Examples of
the pitchometer, team
ponchos, checkerboard
tarps, and other baseball
fan involvement support
this point.*

Veeck upheld many high traits. He was genuine, a true fan and follower of the game. He was grateful to have long been affiliated with baseball, and he was generous with his product, the game of baseball, to all of us, all of his patrons. Chances are many of us may have never made it to Comiskey. But Jerry Reinsdorf, owner of the Chicago White Sox, in the *New York Times* stated, ". . . memories won't leave, just the building is coming down." How true this is since the memory of the man who brought ivy greens to Wrigley Field and a midget to the plate in Eddie Gadell is everlasting. His employee relations, customer courtesy and creative innovations have made him a man of unequal imitation. Unfortunately college students today live in a world of imitation. It is time we seek alternatives. In this case, we need not address our congressman but rather the idea of our own originality and ingenuity. We need look no further than Bill Veeck./5

*The speaker summarizes
the three main points of
the speech, then returns
to the idea of creativity
that introduced this
speech.*

Assessing Your Progress

Chapter Summary

Getting started is a matter of thinking about choices you have to make as a responsible speaker. Here are some things to consider when planning and preparing your speech:

1. Select and narrow your subject, making it appropriate to you and your listeners.

2. Determine your general and specific purposes, then word the central idea to guide your development of the key ideas.

3. Analyze your audience and the occasion to discover aspects of both that may affect what you say and how you say it.

4. Gather your material, beginning with what you already know and supplementing it with additional research.

5. Arrange and outline your points to package your ideas clearly and coherently.

6. Practice your speech aloud, working from outlines and then note cards, first alone and then with an audience.

7. Recognize that self-confidence can be developed by understanding the communication process and through public speaking experience.

Key Terms

audience orientation (p. 22)

central idea (p. 20)

general purposes (p. 19)

specific purposes (p. 20)

state apprehension (p. 25)

trait apprehension (p. 25)

Assessment Activities

1. Prepare and present a speech. Go to the library and read several popular magazines and newspapers from the week that you were born. Sort out the events of that week and write a clear central idea for a brief informative speech. Organize your ideas, and use some illustrations or perhaps some expert testimony from the sources you examined. Follow the rest of the steps suggested in this chapter for developing a speech; then deliver it to your classmates. After the speech, ask for feedback. Was the central idea clear? Did your listeners follow the structure of the speech easily? Did your delivery convey confidence?

2. Rewrite each of the following statements, making it into a clear and concise central idea for a speech to inform:

   a. "Today I would like to try to get you to see the way in which the body can communicate a whole lot of information."

   b. "The topic for my speech has to do with the high taxes people have to pay."

   c. "A college education might be a really important thing for some people, so my talk is on college education."

   Be ready to present your central ideas in a class discussion.

3. For each of the following statements, write a central idea for a persuasive speech that incorporates the three ideas. Compare your phrasing of the central ideas with those of your classmates.

a. Many prison facilities are inadequate.

b. Low rates of pay result in frequent job turnover in prisons.

c. Prison employees need on-the-job training.

a. Few doctors practice general medicine; most doctors specialize in one or two areas.

b. The present system of delivering medical service is excellent.

c. Rural areas have a shortage of doctors.

4. To learn brainstorming, you must practice it. Form groups, appoint a recorder to jot down all ideas, then practice brainstorming with the questions listed below. Don't evaluate or editorialize until the brainstorming session has stopped. The goal is to list as many ideas as possible. To evaluate the success of the brainstorming session, compare the number of ideas generated.

a. How can an egg be packaged so that it will not break when dropped from the top of a 20-foot ladder?

b. What can we do with all the disposable diapers clogging our landfills?

c. What adjustments would our society have to make if there were three sexes instead of two?

d. Pretend that aliens have been spotted hovering over our cities in spacecraft. How can we communicate with them?

e. You are a scientist who has just discovered a potent narcotic. It has tremendous pain-relieving properties, but it is also highly addictive. What should you do with the drug?

References

1. Michael Neer, "Reducing Situational Anxiety and Avoidance Behavior Associated with Classroom Apprehension." *Southern Communication Journal, 56* (1990): 49–61; John Gorhis and Mike Allen, "Meta-Analysis of the Relationship Between Communication Apprehension and Cognitive Performance," *Communication Education, 41* (1992): 68–76; James McCroskey, "Oral Communication Apprehension: A Summary of Current Theory and Research," *Human Communication Research, 4* (1977): 78–96.

2. David Mellor, "Bill Veeck," *Winning Orations, 1991* (the Interstate Oratorical Association). Reprinted by permission of Larry Schnoor, Executive Secretary, Interstate Oratorical Association, Mankato State University, Mankato, Minn.

3 Critical Listening for Responsible Speakers

In your daily life, you spend more time listening than you do reading, writing, or speaking. Listening accounts for over 40 percent of your communicative time.[1] While you may assume that you're a good listener from all that practice, you really don't know until you discover you've missed something important. The fact is, you've probably never had any training in listening, especially for situations such as class lectures where you're expected to acquire technical or abstract materials aurally.

Through conversations, classroom lectures, group meetings, electronic media, and other forms of aural communication, you amass an amazing amount of information. You also learn to anticipate the actions of others and to gauge their feelings and moods through listening. Listening is a fundamental activity in the communication process. Both speaker and listener are active partners in communication events. As a speaker, you reach out to your audience; and in turn, as a listener, you respond.

After more fully introducing the idea of listening, this chapter will focus on practical listening techniques you can use in almost any listening situation. We'll finish by suggesting how you can put new listening skills to work in your classes.

Hearing and Listening

Hearing is the first step in the listening process. To listen to a message, you first must hear it. **Hearing** is the physiological process of receiving sound waves. Sound waves travel through the air and set up vibrations on the eardrum; these vibrations, in turn, are transmitted to the brain. Hearing is affected by the laws of physics and the neurophysiology of the body. Any number of factors can interfere with hearing—distracting noises in the environment, sounds too loud or too soft for the aural mechanisms, or impediments such as illness or hearing loss. The speaker can change speaking volume, seating arrange-

33

The speaker receives verbal and nonverbal feedback both during and after the communication transaction. Immediate feedback occurs during the speech. Delayed feedback happens after the communication transaction.

ments, or conditions in the room before talking in order to facilitate hearing. Listeners can provide feedback to the speaker if their hearing is blocked.

Listening, on the other hand, is the cognitive process whereby people attach meanings to aural signals. After sound waves are translated into nerve impulses by the middle ear and the auditory nerve, they're sent to the brain for interpretation. The process of interpretation—registering impulses, assigning them to meaningful contexts, and evaluating them—constitutes listening.

Barriers to Good Listening

Listening is easy to define but hard to practice. You've probably developed some barriers to good listening. You'll have to recognize and remove those barriers if you're going to become a better listener. Most of us experience these five barriers to good listening:

1. *Passive listening.* Many of us are just plain lazy listeners, hoping the speaker will be exceptionally clear. As a result, we forget more of the speech than we remember. Listeners are partners in the communication transaction, and this requires active listening, including identifying your purpose for listening, taking notes, and evaluating the ideas in the message.

2. *Drifting thoughts.* You can comprehend many more words per minute than someone can utter; you probably can process about 400 words per minute, while most speakers produce only about 125 to 175 words per minute. As a result, you may fill

the time lag with other thoughts. Your **internal perceptual field** is the world of your own thoughts. While someone is speaking, you may be remembering a television show you saw last night or planning the menu for supper or thinking about a topic for your next term paper.

3. *Physical distractions.* Sometimes your attention may be diverted by elements in your **external perceptual field.** These are things in your physical environment such as a loud truck, the sun's glare off your teacher's bald head, or a banging radiator. Our attention can be sidetracked by physical interference, so that we hear and process only part of a spoken message.

4. *Trigger words.* We often bring our feelings, values, and attitudes into the speech setting. Memories of past events or strong feelings can be triggered by a mere word or a reference to a place. Many people spend time mentally debating with speakers and remain stuck on one idea while the speaker moves ahead to others. For example, some listeners become hostile when they hear a speaker refer to a secretary as "my girl." They may spend several minutes fuming and miss the next part of the speaker's message.

5. *Self-fulfilling prophecies.* Preset ideas can get in the way of good listening. You may have heard that Professor Rogers is a dull lecturer, so you enter the class expecting to be bored. Or, previous encounters with a speaker can color your expectations.

Like most people, you probably have beliefs and attitudes about topics and people. But, if you let your feelings, musings, and guesses get in the way of careful listening, you're likely to miss the important parts of speeches. It is important to overcome these barriers to become an active listener and a better participant in the communication transaction. Here are some suggestions for developing your listening skills.

Practical Listening Techniques

While hearing is a more or less natural physiological process for most people, listening is another matter. You've got to work hard to listen well. The good news, though, is that you can train yourself to listen better. You can begin to practice better listening habits in three ways: (1) determine your purposes for listening; (2) develop techniques that help you comprehend speeches; and (3) design questions that help you evaluate or assess speeches on criteria that matter to you.

Know Your Purposes

This may sound foolish, but the first thing good listeners must do is figure out why they're listening. That's not really a silly thing to do, because, if you think about it, you engage in many different kinds of listening. On any given day, you may listen intently to your instructors in order to learn new concepts, you may listen to your favorite music to relax, and you may listen attentively to be sure that a car salesperson isn't skipping over essential features of the dealer's guarantee.

Researchers have identified five kinds of listening that reflect purposes you may have when communicating with others:[2] appreciative, discriminative, therapeutic, comprehension, and critical.

Appreciative listening focuses on something other than the primary message. Some listeners enjoy seeing a famous speaker. Others relish the art of good public speaking. On these occasions, you listen primarily to entertain yourself.

Discriminative listening requires listeners to draw conclusions from the way a message is presented rather than from what is said. In discriminative listening, people seek to understand the meaning behind the message. You're interested in what the speaker really thinks, believes, or feels. You're engaging in discriminative listening when you draw conclusions about how angry your parents are with you, based not on what they say but on how they say it. An important dimension of listening is based on inferences drawn from—rather than found in—messages.

Therapeutic listening is intended to provide emotional support for the speaker. Although it is more typical of interpersonal than public communication, therapeutic listening does occur in public speaking situations, for example, when a sports figure apologizes for unprofessional behavior, a religious convert describes a soul-saving experience, or a classmate thanks friends for their help in solving a personal problem.

Listening for comprehension occurs when you want to gain additional information or insights from the speaker. You are probably most familiar with this form of listening. When you listen to a radio newscast, to a classroom lecture on the principal strategies in the 1996 presidential campaign, or to a school official explaining new registration procedures, you're listening to understand—to comprehend information, ideas, and processes.

Critical listening requires you to both interpret and evaluate the message. This is the most sophisticated and difficult kind of listening. It demands that you go beyond understanding the message to interpreting it, judging its strengths and weaknesses, and assigning it some value. You'll practice this sort of listening in class. A careful consumer also uses critical listening to evaluate television commercials, political campaign speeches, advice from talk show guests, or arguments offered by salespeople. When you are listening critically, you decide whether to accept or reject ideas and whether to act on the message.

You may have many different purposes for listening, and that's why the first question you ought to ask yourself is: "What's my purpose in listening?" Do you expect to gain information and insight to make a decision? Or are you listening to enjoy yourself, to understand the feelings of another human being, to assess someone's state of mind, or to test ideas? Knowing why you're listening will help you listen more efficiently and effectively. In the rest of this chapter, we'll focus on listening for comprehension and critical listening because those are the kinds of listening you use primarily in a public speaking situation.

Listening for Comprehension

Listening for comprehension is the kind of listening you usually do in class lectures. Fully comprehending what's being said requires that you understand the three essential aspects of speech content: *ideas, structure,* and *supporting materials.* You've got to understand clearly what ideas you're being asked to accept, how they're related to each other, and what sorts of facts and opinions underlie them. Asking three questions will help you to comprehend a message:

1. *What are the main ideas of the speech?* Determine the central idea of the speech and look for the statements that help the speaker to develop it. These main ideas should

Speaking of ... skills

Good Note Taking and Active Listening

One of the easiest ways to practice your listening skills while in college is to work on note taking. As you become a better note taker, you'll also become a better listener. Here are some tips for improving your note-taking skills.

1. *Get organized.* Develop a note-taking system like a loose-leaf notebook so you can add, rearrange, or remove notes. Use separate notebooks for different subjects to avoid confusion.
2. *Review your notes regularly.* This will prepare you to ask questions while the lecture or readings are still fresh in your mind and will help to keep you oriented to the class. Research shows that students who review their notes achieve significantly more.
3. *Leave a 2- to 3-inch blank margin.* Later, you can add facts, clarification, reactions, and other alterations after comparing your notes with other students' or after doing related reading. Such critical commentary is an important stage in merging the material in the notes with your own thoughts.
4. *Write more.* Making a conscious effort to record more ideas and more words related to a speech or lecture will help you to remember the important ideas, structure, and supporting evidence. Research shows that most students don't take enough notes. The problem is compounded with long messages; students take even fewer notes as the speech or lecture continues.
5. *Develop a note-taking scheme.* Consider using abbreviations such as the ampersand (&) for *and*, *btwn* and *w/o* for *between* and *without* or specialized notations like *mgt* and *acctg* for *management* and *accounting*. Color-code your notes or use highlighter pens to remind yourself of the most important parts of the material.

     By taking these steps, you can become an active listener who's engaging in a two-way communication channel. And the more you practice, the more you'll get out of every communication situation.

See: Kenneth A. Kiewra, "Note-taking and Review: The Research and Its Implications," *Instructional Science,* 16 (1987): 233–249.

serve as the foundation on which the speaker builds the speech. The next time you listen to a soap commercial, listen for the main ideas: are you encouraged to buy it because of its cleaning ability, smell, sex appeal, or gentleness to your skin? Before you decide to buy a new brand of soap, you ought to know something about its characteristics. Transfer that same listening behavior to a speech. Always know what ideas you're being sold.

2. *How are the main ideas arranged?* Once you've identified the main ideas, you should figure out and assess the relationships between them. In other words, identify the structure of ideas and then probe the speaker's use of that form. If a speaker is explaining affirmative action laws, does the explanation seem reasonable? Is the speaker limited only to one perspective? Who is defined as the victim? Does the speaker express sympathy for one point of view over another? What information is excluded from the explanation?

3. *What kinds of materials support the main ideas?* Consider the timeliness, quality, and content of the supporting materials. Are facts and opinions derived from

sources too old to be relevant to today's problems? Is the speaker quoting the best experts? Ask yourself whether the materials clarify, amplify, and strengthen the main ideas of the speech. For example, if someone tells you that the 1996 bombing at the Olympic Games in Atlanta is reminiscent of the murders in Munich at the 1972 games, ask yourself several questions: Were both examples the same kind of terrorist actions? Is the twenty-four year gap between the two events important to consider? Examine the relationship asserted between the events.

To comprehend the content, in other words, make sure you've got it straight so that you know what ideas, relationships, and evidence you're being asked to accept. To be an active listener, you should constantly *review, relate,* and *anticipate (RRA):*

Take a few seconds to *review* what the speaker has said. Mentally summarize key ideas each time the speaker initiates a new topic for consideration.

Relate the message to what you already know. Consider how you could use the information in the future.

Anticipate what the speaker might say next. Use this anticipation to focus on the content of the message.

By reviewing, relating, and anticipating, you can keep your attention centered on the message. Using the **RRA Technique** keeps you on your toes. It keeps *you* in charge of the ideas you receive.

Critical Listening

Once you've figured out why you're listening, how the ideas are arranged, and what supporting materials are being presented, you're in a position to form some opinions. You, after all, are the reason the speech is being given, so you're the one who must make the judgments: good/bad, beautiful/ugly, just/unjust, fair/unfair, true/false. Making such assessments is the only way to keep yourself protected from inflated claims, dated information, and unethical speakers. Completely assessing a speech could include asking yourself about the situation, the speaker, and the message. The following questions will help you listen critically:

Listening well has been a human (and canine) concern for a long, long time.

1. *How is the situation affecting this speech and my reception of it?* Is this the featured speaker or a warm-up act? Is the speaker expected to deal with particular themes or subjects? Am I in sympathy with this speech occasion? Speeches in churches, basketball arenas, and Rotary Clubs are very different from each other, and you must adjust your judgment-making criteria accordingly.

2. *How is the physical environment affecting the speaker and my listening?* Is the room too hot or too cold? Too big or too small? What other distractions affect us? The physical environment can have an important impact on your listening. You might have to compensate: lean forward, move up, or concentrate more closely.

3. *What do I know about the speaker?* The reputation of this person *will* influence you, whether you want it to or not, so think about it. Are you being unduly deferential or hypercritical of the speaker just because of his or her reputation? Do you think the speaker will be fair and honest because he or she represents your interests or is similar to you? Don't let your assumptions about the speaker get in the way of critical listening.

4. *How believable do I find the speaker?* Are there things about the person's actions, demeanor, and words that make you accepting or suspicious? Does the speaker use adequate and compelling supporting material to reinforce the message? Try to figure out why you're reacting positively or negatively and then ask yourself whether it's reasonable for you to believe this person.

5. *Is the speaker adequately prepared?* Imprecise remarks, repetitions, backtracking, vague or missing numbers, and the lack of solid testimony are all signs of a poorly prepared speaker. For example, a speaker talking about how audiences influence TV programming decisions should discuss, among other things, the networks' use of focus groups. If the speaker doesn't discuss this, you'll know that he or she hasn't gotten very far into the topic. Similarly, if the speaker can't clearly explain the different rating systems, you should question the reliability of other information in the speech.

6. *What's the speaker's attitude toward the audience?* How is the audience being treated: cordially or condescendingly, as individuals or as a general group, as inferiors or as equals? Answering these questions will help you not only to assess your experience but also to form some questions for the speaker after the speech.

7. *How solid are the ideas being presented?* We've been stressing this point throughout the chapter because it's crucial for you to assess the ideas in terms of your own knowledge and experience. Just one warning: you could be mistaken yourself, so don't automatically dismiss new ideas. That's how you stagnate intellectually. But listen more carefully when ideas seem strange, making sure that you understand them and that they're well supported.

8. *Are the ideas well structured?* Are important concepts missing? For example, anyone who talks about the branches of the federal government but then ignores the Supreme Court has a defective set of ideas. Are logical links visible? The comparisons must be fair; the cause-and-effect links clear and logical; and the proposals for correcting social wrongs both feasible and practical. Structural relationships between ideas are what give them their solidity and coherence as a package.

Speaking of ... *ethics*

Deliberately Misguiding Listeners

Some advertisers, politicians, sales representatives, and even friends have learned how to misguide their listeners without actually lying. They hope, of course, that you'll draw the conclusions they want you to on the basis of distracting or misdirective statements. You can recognize these situations by thinking and listening critically. Here are some things to listen for:

1. *Percentages rather than absolute numbers.* If you're told that women's salaries went up 50 percent more than men's last year. Should you cheer? Maybe not. Even if women got a 3 percent raise when men got 2 percent, there's such a differential in their salaries that the actual dollar amount of women's and men's raises was probably about the same.

2. *Characteristics of the sample.* Beware when the manufacturer tells you that "Four out of five of the dentists surveyed preferred the ingredients in Smiles-Aglow toothpaste." How big was the sample? Were the dentists surveyed working in Smiles-Aglow labs or were they in private dental practice? You need to know more about them to know whether this claim is solid.

3. *Generic substitution.* Were the dentists asked if they preferred the Smiles-Aglow toothpaste or only "the ingredients"? Since most toothpastes use the same ingredients, the claim may be meaningless.

4. *Hasty generalization.* The neighbor who tells you that "Most folks on this block are against the widening of our street" may have talked to everyone, although that's not likely. He probably means "most folks I know on this block"—and then you'd better find out how many that it is. Press him for details before you accept or reject his judgment.

5. *Convenient bases.* Politicians talking about economic change carefully pick a base year for their analyses that makes their cases appear strong. For example, Republicans are fond of going back go 1981 to show how much inflation was reduced during the Reagan-Bush years, while Democrats prefer to go back to 1988 to show how much growth was slowed and the debt increased under Bush. Each party picks an economic yardstick to make its opponents look bad.

Are speakers lying when they use these distracting or misguiding techniques? Are they acting unethically? Where does ethical responsibility lie—with the speaker or with the audience?

Source: Andrew Wolvin and Carolyn Coakley, *Listening* (Dubuque, IA: Wm. C. Brown, 1982), pp. 3–11 and chaps. 4–8.

9. *Is sufficient evidence offered?* The world is filled with slipshod reasoning and flawed evidence. Bad reasoning and a refusal to test the available evidence, after all, are what led the American high command to believe that Pearl Harbor was an impregnable port in 1941. Listen for evidence; write down the key parts so you can mull it over, asking yourself if it's good enough to use as a basis for changing your mind or taking on some new job. Be demanding; adopt a "show me" attitude. Insist on adequate evidence and logical reasons when a speaker asks you to make crucial decisions.

You may not ask all of these questions every time you hear a speech because your listening purposes vary considerably from occasion to occasion. However, you will need most of these questions when doing critical listening before you make important decisions such as who to vote for, whether to take the job offer, or if you should make a major purchase. To practice critical listening you can begin now in your classes.

Developing Skills for Responsible Listening

As noted in Chapter 1, your speech classroom is set up to teach skills that you can use for the rest of your life. Listening is one of the skills you'll need to survive in the worlds of work, politics, and social life. You'll have to listen to understand your employer's explanation of a new computer system, to make reasonable decisions between two political candidates who offer different views of health care reform, and to follow a neighbor's instructions as she tells you how to rewire a light fixture. The ability to listen can help you make money, be a good citizen, and keep you from frying your fingers on a 110-volt circuit!

Your classes are excellent settings for practicing new listening skills and refining old ones. Use the Speech Evaluation Form in Table 3.1 as a checklist when listening to speeches. It will challenge your listening skills. During this term, we also suggest that you improve your listening in the following ways:

1. *Practice critiquing the speeches of other students.* Practice note-taking techniques; ask questions of the speaker; take part in postspeech discussions. You can learn as much from listening well as from speaking yourself.

2. *Listen critically to discussions, lectures, and student-teacher interactions in your other classes.* You're surrounded with public communication worth analyzing when you're in school. You can easily spot effective and ineffective speech techniques in those classes.

3. *Listen critically to speakers outside of class.* Attend public lectures, city council meetings, religious rallies, or political caucuses. Watch replays of presidential or congressional speeches on C-SPAN. You'll be amazed by the range of talent, techniques, and styles exhibited in your community every week.

4. *Examine the supporting materials, arguments, and language used in newspapers and magazines.* Refine your critical listening skills by practicing critical reading. Together, they represent the skills of critical thinking you need to survive in this world. **Critical thinking** is the process of consciously examining the content and logic of messages to determine their bases in the world of ideas and to assess their rationality. Critical thinking is the backbone of evaluation. It's what happens when you actively listen and read others' messages.

Overall, then, listening makes public speaking a reciprocal activity. Listeners seek to meet their diverse needs, ranging from personal enjoyment to crucial decision making, through specialized listening skills designed for each listening purpose. When both speakers and listeners work at making the speech transaction succeed, public speaking reaches its full potential as a partnership in communication.

TABLE 3.1   Speech Evaluation Form

Use this form to evaluate your own speeches.

The Speaker

- ☐ Poised?
- ☐ Positive self-image?
- ☐ Apparently sincere?
- ☐ Apparently concerned about the topic?
- ☐ Apparently concerned about the audience?
- ☐ Apparently well prepared?

The Message

- ☐ Suitable topic?
- ☐ Clear general purpose?
- ☐ Sharply focused specific purpose?
- ☐ Well-phrased central idea or proposition?
- ☐ Adequately supported (enough, varied, trustworthy sources)?
- ☐ Supporting materials tailored to the audience?
- ☐ Introduced adequately?
- ☐ Concluded effectively?
- ☐ Major subdivisions clear, balanced?
- ☐ Use of notes and lectern unobtrusive?

The Channel

- ☐ Voice varied for emphasis?
- ☐ Voice conversational?
- ☐ Delivery speed controlled?
- ☐ Body alert and nondistracting?
- ☐ Gestures used effectively?
- ☐ Face expressive?
- ☐ Language clear (unambiguous, concrete)?
- ☐ Language forcible (vivid, intense)?

The Audience

- ☐ All listeners addressed?
- ☐ Their presence recognized and complimented?
- ☐ Their attitudes toward subject and speaker taken into account?

The Speech as a Whole

Audience's expectations met?

_____
_____
_____
_____

Short-range effects of the speech?

_____
_____
_____
_____

Long-range effects?

_____
_____
_____
_____

Possible improvements?

_____
_____
_____
_____

Assessing Your Progress

Chapter Summary

1. Both the speaker and listener are critical participants in the communication transaction.

2. Hearing and listening are two different processes. *Hearing* is physiological. *Listening* is a psychological process by which people seek to comprehend and evaluate aural-visual signals.

3. One way to improve your listening skills is to know why you're listening. There are five types of listening: appreciative listening, discriminative listening, therapeutic listening, listening for comprehension, and critical listening.

4. A second way to improve your listening skills is to sort out the essential aspects of speech content: ideas, structure, and supporting materials. The RRA Technique can help you listen more efficiently.

5. To improve your speech evaluation skills, practice assessing the situation, the speaker, and the message.

6. Practicing and refining your listening skills in your classes will help you to acquire important tools for academic, financial, political, and social success.

Key Terms

appreciative listening (p. 36)

critical listening (p. 36)

critical thinking (p. 41)

discriminative listening (p. 36)

external perceptual field (p. 35)

hearing (p. 33)

internal perceptual field (p. 35)

listening (p. 34)

listening for comprehension (p. 36)

RRA Technique (p. 38)

therapeutic listening (p. 36)

Assessment Activities

1. Conduct a class discussion on a controversial topic: for example, doctor-assisted suicide, multiculturalism and political correctness, the rights of smokers, or welfare reform. Establish the rule that before anyone can speak, he or she first must summarize to the satisfaction of the previous speaker what that person said. To assess their effectiveness, determine if they were fair, accurate, and complete. What conclusions can you draw about people's ability to listen and provide feedback? How do good listening and feedback reduce the amount and intensity of disagreement?

2. Keep a listening log. For two or three days, record your oral communication interactions, noting (a) to whom you were speaking, (b) what your listening purposes were, and (c) how effectively you listened given your purposes. After completing the log, do a self-assessment: What are your strengths and weaknesses as a listener? What changes would make you a better listener?

3. Make a line drawing of an irregular geometric figure. Describe it verbally to an audience. Then ask each listener to draw the figure. How good are you at helping listeners "see" what you've described? What could you say to improve the accuracy of their drawings? What listening skills could they improve?

References

1. Steven Rhodes, "What the Communication Journals Tell Us About Teaching Listening," *Central States Speech Journal, 36* (1985): 24–32.

2. Andrew Wolvin and Carolyn Coakley, *Listening* (Dubuque, Ia.: William C. Brown Co., 1982), chaps. 4–8.

4 Public Speaking and Cultural Life

At its simplest, a **culture** is a social group's system of meanings. We can usefully think of "culture" as the sorts of meanings a people attaches to persons, places, ideas, rituals, things, routines, and communication behavior. You've been taught since you were an infant who's important or not (persons), how to act on the playground and in public buildings (places), what's true and false about the world (ideas), how to greet friends and strangers (rituals), what's valued or not (things), what's safe to talk about at parties with friends or strangers (routines), and the most effective and ineffective ways to get favors from your parents (communication behavior). Your culture thus is comprised of pieces of social knowledge that represent how you've been taught to comprehend and act effectively within the world.

What's true of you and your life, of course, is true for everyone else as well. We've all been taught about persons, places, rituals, ideas, and the rest. The problem is that the meanings for those entities that you've been given may not be the same as the meanings someone else has learned. Your experiences are different from those of others. This happens not only on an individual basis but also on a group basis. Men and women in some important ways have been given different social educations; so have whites and Hispanics, rich people and poor people, sighted and visually challenged people. All of our differences in psychological, social, political, economic, and behavioral—which is to say, cultural—education can cause speakers some serious problems.

"I can't go out there and speak!" Melissa was distraught. She was a delegate from the Panhellenic Council about to speak to a gathering of the campus African American, Hispanic, and international students' associations on working together on a weekend of fun and games for all students. "Here I am, a white sorority member born in Iowa, a state that's ninety-seven and a half percent white. And there they are, from the ghettoes of Chicago and LA, from foreign countries totally different from mine. They'll

*resent me. What do we have in common?" "That's the question you must answer,"
replied her best friend Sherri. "What do you have in common? You're all students
here, you all need a weekend off from studies to celebrate spring, you all enjoy group
competition, you'll all dance the night away—you have a lot in common!" "Well, I
guess we do, but . . . ." "But nothing!" said Sherri. "Quit emphasizing your differences
as barriers to a successful spring celebration. Think of what you share and of ways
your differences will become a strength at party time! That's what to talk about."*

Training in public speaking is in part a matter of learning about the cultural expectations of one's audience. Speakers must learn what those expectations are in order to be
seen as socially competent. Speakers who want considerable impact on audiences must
learn to be exceptionally good at phrasing ideas and engaging the feelings of others
within the communication traditions of a group or society.

Learning about the cultural expectations of one's audience, however, is easier said
than done; the doing—meeting those expectations—can be a most difficult task. There is
always perhaps (especially in the United States, where almost all children have been
taught to maximize their own potentials, to be their own persons) a tension between the
self and society—between the individual and the collectivity. On the one hand, you are
you, a unique individual with your own life experiences, your own thoughts about the
world; but on the other, you always are marked by social categories. You're an individual,

Speaking of . . .   apprehension

Xenophobia

As the story of Melissa indicates, people can become terrified when talking to listeners whom they perceive to
be significantly different from themselves. Men can stammer when facing female listeners, African Americans can
fear that no white will accept what they have to say, and most people are convinced that they'll be misunder-
stood by or even offend foreigners—*xenophobia*, a word whose meaning should be expanded to include fear of all
kinds of "different" people. How can you overcome or at least control such fears and misgivings?

1. Engage in conversation members of the groups you fear so as to explore the bases of your fears. Get to
   know some African Americans or Mexican Americans well enough to discuss your concerns. The more men
   and women talk informally about their relations, the less likely their differences will affect public speaking.
2. Talk with members of groups you fear after you've spoken to see what their reactions were. Don't take a
   simple "You were fine!" or "You're great!" from them. Ask specific questions about specific things you said
   and did in order to force particular judgments about your speaking skills and strategies.
3. Accentuate the positive. When talking to a diversified audience, concentrate on your shared values and
   outlooks, not your differences. That was Sherri's advice to Melissa. It's good advice.
4. Focus on actions, not beliefs, attitudes, values, and ideologies. Getting people to act together—to work together for a cause—often can be advocated without exploring too many of their cultural differences. Even
   people who outrightly dislike each other will work together if there's a gain for all of them.

but simultaneously you're female, Russian, a twentysomething person, an atheist, a junior in college. . . . Yes, you're an individual, but part of your self identity—and certainly a major part of everyone else's perception of you—is socially and culturally determined.

This is the sort of world you must learn how to speak in:

✓ Can you respect individual difference and cultural diversity even while attempting to get a group of people to think alike and work together?

✓ Can you learn to speak publicly with success even while recognizing the importance of the motto you carry around on the dimes and nickels in your pockets: *e pluribus unum,* "out of many, one"?

✓ What sort of person does the successful public speaker embody?

✓ How can you recognize the diversity of your classmates's lived experiences, even their ideological schisms, while you nonetheless attempt to enact a public image that is credible?

These are not easy questions to answer, and you probably won't think about them every time you raise your hand in class to disagree with your instructor. But, especially as you address the variegated sorts of audiences that Melissa faced when talking about a spring celebration, you'll want to follow her friend Sherri's advice, looking for the common ground that turns a group of listeners into a people unified in thought and action.

In this chapter, we'll discuss relationships between public speaking and cultural life by first examining the components of "culture" more specifically and then reviewing some strategies that you can use to unify and direct your listeners' thoughts and actions even

The ability to communicate across gender, racial, and class lines is an essential skill for all members of diverse communities.

when they come from diverse cultural backgrounds. Having an understanding of cultural diversity and how it has impacts on speechmaking will give you a framework for thinking responsibly about all aspects of preparing and delivering public talks.

Understanding Cultural Processes

We've defined *culture* generally. Before you can think about public speaking strategies that you'll need to know how to use in the face particularly of cultural diversity, however, you'll want to think more about how it affects your everyday life.

The Dynamics of Culture

If *culture* is a concept broad enough to include all of a society's meanings for ideas, things, and activities, then we need a systematic vocabulary for breaking it down into units for analysis and study. That vocabulary is a bit abstract, but will be easier to understand if you focus on three dimensions of social life: culture as lived, thought, and performed.

Culture as Lived: Demographic Categories of Social Organization   One way to examine cultural life is via the social categories by which we're defined by others. You have learned to define yourself by gender (male, female, transsexual), ethnic background (Norwegian American, Mexican American), age (young, old), sexual orientation (straight, gay), nationality (Slovene, Chinese), educational background (high school dropout, college grad), disability (hearing impaired, visually challenged), socioeconomic status (underclass welfare recipient, upper-bracket taxpayer). Insofar as you think about yourself or others with whom you come in contact via such demographic categories, those social markers become amazingly important in your relationships with people; in the story of Melissa, she thought about herself in terms of race, gender, and reference or organizational group. Such markers can become determinative of **culture as lived.**[1]

Gender identification starts at a young age, as little boys and little girls generally learn even to play differently from one another; those differences become more and more important as they mature, governing personal identity (straight or gay), social relations (the dating game), extracurricular activities (different high school sports for females and males), and even work (women paid an average of 41 percent less for comparable work than men). Ethnic background can produce similar sets of differences, especially because whites tend to have much easier access to social-economic-educational institutions than people of color, other things being equal. But, of course, they're not equal, so that one's economic status can neutralize or exacerbate racial differences. As well, age can enter in, for racial differences tend to harden with age.

And so it goes: culture as lived, especially as you move out of your immediate family and neighborhood, becomes increasingly focused on cultural differences. Those differences have always been around, though the Black, Hispanic, gay/lesbian, and women's empowerment movements of the 1960s and 1970s, the growing emphasis on **cultural diversity** in the 1980s, and the passage of the Americans with Disabilities Act in 1991 have sensitized most of us to their roles. **Multiculturalism**—the recognition that a country such as the United States possesses, not a unitary culture with several **sub-cultures,** but rather a series of **co-cultures** that interpenetrate yet are separate from each other—is a fact of life.[2] And its effect on public speaking, as we'll see, is considerable.

Culture as Thought: Ideology and Hegemony   Not only have you been socialized to act in particular ways through lived experiences, but you've also been conditioned to think in particular patterns as well. You've been conditioned to think, perhaps, that freedom is worth dying for, that beet roots taste better than jicama roots, that your personal safety is affected by the skin color of people around you, that with hard work anyone can succeed in life, that "blood is thicker than water." That is, others have taught you to think that certain values (e.g., freedom) are positive, and others (e.g., forced obligation to others) are negative; that personal tastes (such as for foods) are grounded in real differences between things rather than in mere preference; that people can be usefully stereotyped by such accidental characteristics as skin color; that rules for succeeding in your own society (e.g., about hard work) hold true everywhere; and that folk wisdom (often captured in aphorisms such as the one mentioned) contains eternal verities.[3]

A system of thought that embodies social values and perceptual orientations to the world is called an **ideology.** The key to ideology's power in your life is that it is naturalized,[4] that is, thought of merely as "what everyone knows" or "how things are done around here." Ideologically grounded values and perceptions of the world are rooted in cognitions that always have been part of your environment, unquestioned and regularly reinforced by people important to your life—parents, siblings, friends, authority figures in your community and schools. A person in your locale who doesn't believe in freedom will be thought deviant; someone who prefers jicama to all-American vegetables will be regarded as a little strange; and someone who leaves his or her family (blood ties) to join a Hari Krishna community might even be chased down by de-programmers.

But, ideologies are powerful not only because familial, religious, social, and political institutions reinforce them; they're also powerful in your life because of your own volition. Not only do you seldom question fundamental tenets of living with like-minded others, but you even reinforce them in your own talk to others. You're liable to try to rein in a child running off to school without eating breakfast by saying "That's not the way we do things around here, kid." When a bigger and older bully beat you up on the playground, you likely thought simply that that's the way the world is—that the bigger and older folks rule the roost. If you were raised in a small mill town where all of the working families gathered on Labor Day for a communal picnic and dance, you probably assumed that working class families were pretty much alike. In all of these instances you internalized a series of cultural rules and beliefs and made them a part of your perceptual and valuative equipment.

Hegemony is a word for relationships between more powerful and less powerful people that are maintained in part or whole by complicity on the part of the less powerful people. Hegemonic relationships are often signaled by such phrases as "That's the way we do things," or "That's the way it goes," or "That's a fact of life." Relationships between classes (rich and poor), between racial groups (white and non-white), even between the sexes (male and female) often are maintained as much by complicitous acceptance of one's status as by direct force. The idea of hegemony in part accounts for why it's so difficult to change social relations quickly; even when women or Hispanics or gays have been "liberated" from some dimensions of their oppression by others, not all of them join in the singing of a chorus of "Free at last! Free at last! Thank God Almighty, we're free at last!" There still are women who sneer at feminist thought, Mexican Americans who don't look forward to the revolution, and gays, lesbians, and bisexuals who haven't come out of the closet. Naturalized attitudes and social relations resist alteration. **Culture as thought** has a lock on many of our minds, thanks to the forces of ideology and hegemony.[5]

Culture as Performed: Embodiment and Enactment   The rules and thoughts governing life can be put into words, as when you recite the Pledge of Allegiance, promise to tell the truth, the whole truth, and nothing but the truth in court, or inform a friend that you're not going to write a term paper tonight by saying "Haste makes waste." More usually, however, cultural rules and the social roles we come to accept or at least live out are not only heard but also seen. **Embodiment** is the process whereby ideas, attitudes, values, and social character are given corporeal existence in communication acts.[6]

You come to understand what a "governor" is by watching your governor on TV. A television show such as *Mad About You* exaggerates husband-wife gender talk; the acting out in comedic ways of gender roles serves to critique the relationships existing between too many husbands and too many wives. In *ER* we see how the personal and the professional aspects of people's lives actually are inseparable. You come to understand what education is by watching people teach. The idea of police brutality came to be understood by Americans who watched the use of night sticks and cattle prods on civil rights demonstrators in the early 1960s and the capture of Rodney King in Los Angeles in the 1990s. You learn many—probably most—of the cultural rules you know because particular people embody them in their activities.

In turn, then, you work to enact them. **Enactment** is a communication process whereby a person behaves in a manner consonant with a society's cultural rules. Insurance agents go to school to learn how to sell policies; they learn to talk like insurance agents are expected to in the United States. Individual athletic achievements are recounted by stars, often, with such phrases as "I couldn't have done this without my teammates, who . . ."; such modest behavior is consonant with rules for sports ettiquette. In this course, you practice giving speeches with introductions, bodies, and conclusions on the assumption that such an arrangement pattern for public talks is expected. Rules for speaking are grounded in audience expectations, which you try to enact so as to be judged a competent speaker.[7]

Culture as performed, therefore, takes us to heart of the matter of this book: how it is that members of a society communicate with each other. The forms of public talk (introductions, bodies, conclusions), the substance of public talk (accepted ways of thinking), the relationships between speaker and audience (grounded in lived experiences), and even the outcomes of public speeches (who'll listen to whom) are affected by your skills in "performing" those speeches in culturally sensible and accepted ways. In different societies, you'll likely have to learn different forms of talk.[8] Performance ought not be thought of here as a theatrical term, a term for acting out a script in such as way as to become someone else. In communication studies, the idea of performance is tied to life roles and cultural rules,[9] not artistic license. Theatrical performance is judged by aesthetic standards; speech performance is judged by pragmatic standards, by whether people accept you and what you have to say. You learn those standards by seeing others embodying them, and then you enact them yourself in hopes of affecting the beliefs, attitudes, values, and behaviors of others.

The Challenge of Cultural Diversity

Earlier we raised this question: Can you respect individual difference and cultural diversity even while attempting to get a group of people to think alike and work together? Yes, we think you can. We think that you can embody in your speaking some generally accepted cultural standards for interpersonal relationships. What those standards are and ways in which you can embody them are the next topics we address.

Communicating Unity Through Diversity: Possible Strategies

The number of ways you can make a group of individuals feel unified, of course, is huge. Rather than catalog every rhetorical technique you might use, we will concentrate on five strategies in this chapter. These have been chosen for analysis because each seemingly honors diversity while recognizing the importance of group or collective action.

Recognizing Diversity

Most fundamentally, speakers recognizing that members of their audience have had different cultural experiences should acknowledge those differences and yet call for unified thought and action. Even in their differences, members of a group must learn to think alike on particular matters and to find ways of acting together. Perhaps the most famous speaker of our time who uses this strategy often is Jesse Jackson. His 1988 speech to the Democratic National Convention illustrates his skill. First, he recognized the diversity of American political audiences:

> *America's not a blanket woven from one thread, one color, one cloth. When I was a child growing up in Greenville, S.C., and grandmother could not afford a blanket, she didn't complain and we did not freeze. Instead, she took pieces of old cloth—patches, wool, silk, gabardine . . . —barely good enough to wipe off your shoes with.*

Having recognized the fundamental fact of diversity ("pieces of old cloth" in Jackson's metaphor), he then calls for unified action:

> *But they didn't stay that way very long. With sturdy hands and a strong cord, she sewed them together into a quilt, a thing of beauty and power and culture.*
>
> *Now, Democrats, we must build such a quilt. Farmers, you seek fair prices and you are right, but you cannot stand alone. Your patch is not big enough. Workers, you fight for fair wages. You are right. But your patch, labor, is not big enough. Women, you seek comparable worth and pay equity. You are right. But your patch is not big enough. Women, mothers, who seek Head Start and day care and pre-natal care on the front side of life, rather than jail care and welfare on the back side of life, you're right, but your patch is not big enough.*
>
> *Students, you seek scholarships. You are right. But your patch is not big enough. Blacks and Hispanics, when we fight for civil rights, we are right, but our patch is not big enough. Gays and lesbians, when you fight against discrimination and [for] a cure for AIDS, you are right, but your patch is not big enough. Conservatives and*

Jesse Jackson's speech rhythms come in part from his experiences in African American churches, also in part from his personal goals—to give hope and inspiration to the downtrodden.

progressives, when you fight for what you believe, right-wing, left-wing, hawk, dove—you are right, from your point of view, but your point of view is not enough.

But don't despair. Be as wise as my grandmama. Pool the patches and the pieces together, bound by a common thread. When we form a great quilt of unity and common ground we'll have the power to bring about health care and housing and jobs and education and hope to our nation.

We the people can win.[10]

Jackson's is a prime example of this strategy because he never lets the audience forget their multiculturalism but yet also hammers at the consequences of respecting diversity at all costs—"your patch is not big enough" becomes the refrain. As well, by finishing with a list of common goals, he gives his listeners reasons for working with different kinds of people to achieve programs they all want.

Inventorying the diversity of cultures in one's experience is a technique you can quickly learn to use. For example, in a speech on why students in your school's Study Abroad program should consider going to school in Malta, you might say: "Malta has earned its reputation as 'The Crossroads of the Mediterrean,' and that fact can be highly significant for you. You'll be educated in English, but will hear a dozen languages spoken on the streets. You'll experience the mixing of Christian and Islamic cultures. You'll vacation in both the Adriatic-European and the Mediterranean-African spheres, eating scampi in Slovenia and cous cous in Morocco. Your palate—and your mind—will be opened to a dozen cultures on Malta."

Even if the topic you're addressing doesn't seem inherently multicultural, you'll want to be sensitive to diversity all of the time. In mentioning dating in a speech on teenagers' urban lifestyles, you'll want to make sure you don't suggest that you're talking only about heterosexual relationships. When talking about the crisis in medical practice in this country, be careful you don't unnecessarily gender the professions, calling doctors "he" and nurses "she."

Negotiating Diverse Values

Often, before you can move an audience to action, you must make it realize that different segments see the world in different ways—use some of the same words but mean quite different things by those words because of varied value orientations. Consider, for example, how much the phrase "family values" has been knocked around in the 1990s. Everyone supports family values, but varied ideologies lie behind liberal and conservative uses of that label (Table 4.1).[11]

These, of course, are simplified positions, but when many people talk about values in public, they in fact deal in such simplicities. That "family values" can mean such different things to people should not be surprising, for the American culture is strongly divided on this issue, and what counts as family units can affect a full range of public actions. The divisions are so deep that, as a speaker, you cannot ignore them. Rather, you're better ad-

TABLE 4.1 The Diversity of "Family Values"	
Conservative Ideology:	America is in moral decline and must return to older family values. We've become a permissive society characterized by divorce, illegitimacy, juvenile crime, and spoiled children. We must bolster the traditional two-parent, heterosexual family as the best environment for children, and eliminate governmental (including school) interference with the family's operations.
Liberal Ideology:	America has to give parents more aid in the raising of children. Everyone, not just parents, has a stake in making sure that children are cared for, supported, and raised to be good citizens. Because financial resources are so varied in this country and because so many families are troubled, government at local, state, and even national levels must help parents with child care, health care, paid parental leave when children are infants, and other forms of financial assistance. It is better to help all forms of family—single- and dual-parent, traditional and nontraditional couples—with their children than to have to deal with juveniles in prisons later.
Middle-of-the-Road Ideology:	The raising of children should be primarily a matter of parental responsibility but with governmental safety nets in place. Parents must be made more responsible for the growth and actions of their children, yet should have help available in the form of family planning agencies, subsidized adoption and abortion services, and sex education in the schools. If parents fail or abuse their children, the state should rescue children from such situations, but, if not, then parents should be made to take responsibility for care, feeding, and nurture.

vised to recognize those differences, defining a phrase like "family values" in multiple ways so as to make sure every one of your listeners understands that the value of family is disputed in this country, and then seeking ways to negotiate among those definitions. Only after recognizing such diversity of opinion can you then ask your audience, "All right, then, on what do we agree? How far can we go together in helping parents raise their children?" It was precisely that kind of thinking that got liberals, conservatives, and middle-of-the-roaders together in 1993 to form a coalition in Congress. That coalition passed the Family Leave Act in the name of both fostering traditional families (by requiring businesses to pay a parent while staying at home with an infant) and yet recognizing a child's needs (by guaranteeing him or her parental support in the earliest stages of social life). The middle-of-the-roaders saw the Act as a perfect example of family-business-government cooperation. Speakers sought out and found some common goals in the political debates surrounding the hot-button issue of family values.

The tricky part of negotiating across valuative differences is to make sure that negotiation doesn't turn into erasure. If you're using as a theme for a speech Rodney King's plea, "Can't we all just get along?" make sure you don't interpret that as meaning that blacks must learn to think and act like whites. Getting along doesn't mean becoming all the same, but rather looking for actions or activities that respect differences and yet achieve aims common to multiple groups in society.

Accepting Multiple Paths to Goals

A more difficult challenge, often, is to convince people that there are many ways for them to reach a shared goal. Yet, it often is a highly useful tactic for bringing together a diverse audience. Thus, some colleges and universities allow their students to meet a physical education requirement in varied ways: a demonstration of skills (playing a set of tennis well with an advanced beginner), life experiences (having a record of having played tennis in a city league for three years), and in-class instruction (taking a class). Likewise, you can urge smokers to try quitting with the help of hypnosis and psychotherapy, the "patch" or nicotine gum, group programs, or cold-turkey regimens.

More difficult problems in demonstration and persuasion, however, face people who are working in situations in which goals traditionally have been pursued only in one way. So, many's the child who's heard a parent say, "There's only one way to do this: the *right* way!" (that is, *my* way!). So, how can speakers create a sense of tolerance and acceptance of multiple paths leading to common goals?

Metaphors and allegories (see Chapter 10) are useful ways for letting people see the utility of allowing multiple paths to lead to common goals. In his speech to the Atlanta Exposition in 1894, black social activist Booker T. Washington used the metaphor of the hand, whereby individual ethnic groups (the fingers) were depicted as attached to and part of the same social system (the hand). And, in urging the U.S. Forest Service to hire a more culturally diverse workforce, Native American woman Henri Mann Morton used the metaphors of a former chieftain to argue that multiple paths can lead to the same goal:

> Finally, I would like to leave you with the words of one of our Cheyenne philosophers, High Chief, who said:

> In this land there are many horses—red, white, black, and yellow. Yet, it is all one horse.

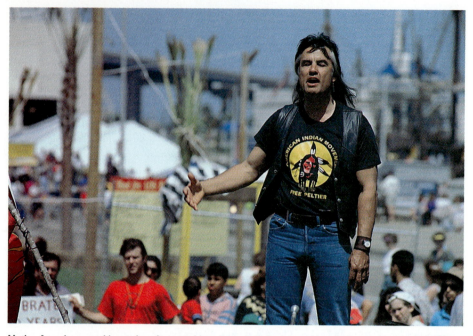

Native American speaking styles often combine characteristics learned in tribal experiences with those needed for talking to broader cultural audiences.

> *There are also birds of every color, red, white, black, and yellow. Yet, it is all one bird. So it is with all living things.*
> *In this land where once there were only Indians, there are different races, red, white, black, and yellow. Yet, it is all one people.*
> *It is good and right.*
>
> *High Chief was a wise man. He knew that cultural uniquenesses have a strength of their own. At the same time he recognized our common humanity.*
> *You, too, know this, as indicated by your powerful theme of "Strength Through Cultural Diversity."[12]*

The metaphor of colors—even Jesse Jackson's political group was called the Rainbow Coalition in the 1980s—is useful because its suggests how differences can be focused into a whole, just as the color spectrum is blended together to make "light." Thus, the metaphor works to make multiple paths to shared goals seem commonsensical. Similarly, historical examples can be equally useful: e.g., pointing to the success of multinational forces in times of war (the Allies of World War II), multinational cooperation in times of peace (UNICEF programs in the United Nations), interpersonal and group efforts in times of disaster (people-to-people support programs in Southeast Asia), and the overcoming of differences in times of celebration (the building of the multiracial South African Olympic team for the first time in 1996). Teaching people to accept multiple paths to shared goals is a technique you must learn to use almost daily in your talk if you're going to successfully get past things that divide listeners into distrustful groups.

So, think about using such speaking techniques as these:

In a speech on getting people to vote: "So, register to vote. Those of you who aren't American citizens still can participate by working in voter-registration booths or by providing rides to voters who need them on election day. This country can use everyone's help in making it a truly participatory democracy."

In a speech on allowing prayer in public schools: "I realize this is a difficult issue for many, especially non-Christians and atheists. The question, though, is not whether everyone should pray a prayer together—they should not. The question is not whether everyone even has to pray during a time set aside for prayer—of course not. Rather, the question is, can children with various religious convictions be allowed a time for self-reflection during the school day? Some will pray, some will think about their life at home. Some will pray, others will play. Some will pray to God, some to Allah, and maybe even one or two to Rah the Sun-God of ancient Egypt. It is the concept, not the content and the form, that is important."

Working Through the Lifestyle Choices of Others

An old saying recommends that "When in Rome, do as the Romans do." Often, you do. You might eat with chopsticks and a flat-bottomed spoon when in a Chinese restaurant, remove your shoes when entering the home of a Finn, kiss a Romanian on both cheeks when greeting him or her, or take a *siesta* after lunch when visiting the Patagonian region of Spain. Urging people to accommodate the lifestyles of (especially) other cultures is something you'll need to do on occasion, particularly if that's the only way to come together, and if coming together is important to you.[13]

A classic Western story of accommodation, of surrender to another's lifestyle, comes from the Old Testament, from the book of Ruth. There, Ruth (a Moabite) had been married to Mahlon (an Israelite from Judah). Mahlon and his brother died, so their mother Naomi decided to return from Moab to Judah. Ruth pleaded with Naomi to take her to Judah. Naomi kept thinking of reasons for Ruth not to move to what for her would be a foreign country. Ruth finally gave a short speech:

> *Entreat me not to leave you or to return from following you; for where you go I will go, and where you lodge I will lodge; your people shall be my people, and your God, my God; where you die I will die, and there will I be buried. May the Lord do so to me and more also if even death parts me from you.*[14]

And the Book of Ruth records that "And when Naomi saw that she was determined to go with her, she said no more" (Ruth 1:18). Furthermore, her actions led her future husband, Boaz, to notice her accommodation: "All that you have done for your mother-in-law since the death of your husband has been fully told me, and how you left your father and mother and your native land and came to a people that you did not know before. The Lord recompense you for what you have done, and a full reward be given you by the Lord, the God of Israel, under whose wings you have come to take refuge!" (Ruth 2:11–12).

Here, we see an extraordinary effort at persuasion built around a full surrender to the lifestyle of others. In offering to engage in a series of acts reflective of another's lifestyle—living (lodging) with Naomi, dwelling among her people, worshipping her deity, and being buried with her—Ruth was able to enter into a complete and apparently mutually satisfying relationship with Naomi and all of Israel. Indeed, as a result of these promises

Speaking of . . . skills

What Others Are Saying: Oral Culture

Oral specialists in many ancient societies composed and recited poems that served as encyclopedias long before written languages were invented. Those societies with oral specialists were able to preserve more information than those without them. A few of those societies that developed elaborate oral technologies evolved into civilizations.

An interesting area of contemporary studies is the orality-literacy distinction—the notion that information and ideas organized and stored orally are quite different from those organized and stored in writing, that is, literately. Oral cultures existing before literate cultures had to preserve history, laws, and literature in devices built into oral codes. While you of course live in a society that has available not only oral but also literate and electronic communication technologies, you don't need a lot of oral encyclopedias, though you have some oral mnemonics you learned before you could write: "Thirty days hath September, April, June, and November . . . ." "'Do,' a deer, a female deer; 're,' a drop of golden sun; 'mi,' a name I call myself . . . ." "'I' before 'e,' except after 'c,' or when sounded as 'ay' as in 'neighbor' or 'weigh.'" You still can help your audiences store information in its orally conditioned memories through wording and rhythm choices.

Source: Carl Couch, *Information Technologies and Social Orders* (New York: Aldine de Gruyter, 1996), 29.

Ruth became the great-grandmother of the most famous of Israel's kings, David. Obviously, such a strategy of accommodation can have great personal consequences, for one's own lifestyle may well be sacrificed. And that sense of personal sacrifice, perhaps, is why it's such a powerful approach to the transcendence of difference: if you're willing to give up part of your own identity, it seems, you are demanding to be taken with the utmost of seriousness.

So, in urging your classmates to put pressure on Congress to pass a more aggressive policy on protecting gays in the military, you might say: "Now, for many—probably even most—people in this class, the issue of gays in the military seems irrelevant. You're not gay, right? So, why worry? Well, there are plenty of reasons to worry. If the military can dictate sexual lifestyle, then it can dictate other aspects of lifestyle as well. If the military drives out gays 'who tell,' then it's weakening civil rights in this country as well as closing employment doors to about ten percent of our population. If the military drives out gays, it prejudices the remaining military personnel against them. Even those of you who are straight, therefore, should have important social and legal questions on your mind. Your life's not directly affected by the 'don't ask, don't tell' policy, but you sacrifice little or nothing by trying to help a marginalized group in society find self-respect and legal standing in this country."

Maintaining Self Identity When Facing Difference

Most of the time, however, you're probably not willing to surrender your self identity, your own life experiences and culture, to others. So, then you're in a pickle: how can you be true to yourself even while managing to work effectively with others?

One technique you can use is to recognize your similarities with others even while maintaining a separation of yourself from them. This is what the British statesman, Lord Chatham (William Pitt the Elder), did in 1777 when trying to convince the British House of Lords to withdraw German mercenaries from the American colonies. Among other things he said "If I were an American, as I am an Englishman, while a foreign troop was landed in my country, I never would lay down my arms—never—never—never!"[15] Notice how Lord Chatham wanted to make sure that other lords did not think he had an American soul; he kept his British identity separate from that of the people he was defending. He was an American advocate without taking on an American identity. Identity also can become a complicated issue when speakers see themselves as having multiple identities coming from multiple cultures that sometimes seem to conflict. So, speaking to the 1996 Republican National Convention, Mary Fisher had a potential identity problem: she had AIDS and was speaking as an AIDS advocate, yet to an audience in which the more conservative members especially wanted little to do with AIDS patients and with federal programs for help. Fisher phrased the potential identity problem early in the speech: "I mean to live, and to die, as a Republican. But I also live, and will die, in the AIDS community—a community hungry for the evidence of [political] leadership and desperate for hope." To make use of that distinction—and to overcome it—Fisher chose to strip away the conservative political culture of her listeners in order to demand their action: "The question is not political. It's a human question, sharpened by suffering and death, and it demands a moral response." She then could argue, by the end of her speech,

Speaking of ... *ethics*

Considering Cultural Practices

There may well be times when you run into cultural tenets or practices that you don't understand or that you find unappealing. Then what?

1. Suppose you're an African American who runs into a white person discussing the "Bell Curve," the research that suggests African Americans are intellectually inferior to whites and hence unable to achieve as much success as whites. How tolerant can and should you be of that opinion? Is it possible to approach such a person openly on the matter of race, intelligence, and success?

2. As a woman, you have a boss who regularly puts his arm around your shoulders while telling you that he's glad you're here and that the company wants to do everything it can to help you grow and prosper. You don't like the paternalism and even the sexual innuendo suggested by that arm on your body, though you have no reason to believe it's an aggressive move on his part. What can you say?

3. You're giving a speech on children's rights. In your audience are many international students from Arab countries that practice the circumcision of teenaged boys—a ritual you find revolting. Can you handle this issue reasonably for the Arab students as a question of children's rights?

The relationships between your personal feelings or moral standards and the cultural practices of your listeners can lead to serious ethical dilemmas. You must learn to think through them before opening your mouth in public.

that political action should be undertaken, not for ideological reasons, but for social and cultural ones. Hugging a 12-year-old African American girl, Heidia, who was born with AIDS, Fisher concluded her speech in this way:

> *The day may come when AIDS will have its way with me, when I can no longer lift my sons to see the future or bend down to kiss away the pain. At that moment Max and Zack will become the community's children more than my own, and we will be judged not through the eyes of politics but through the eyes of children. I may lose my own battle with AIDS, but if you would embrace moral courage tonight and embrace my children when I'm gone, then you and Heidia and I would together have won a greater battle, because we would have achieved integrity.[16]*

To find ways of affirming your own self, your own *ethos*, while also recognizing and complimenting your listeners' sense of self, is a search you will continue throughout your lifetime when you speak publicly. To find ways of achieving unity through social diversity is a central challenge to all who would inform and persuade others. You'll often find yourself saying such things as:

✔ "Well, now, I'm not a Mexican American, but I think I can understand something of the community's concern about racial stereotyping in the film *La Bamba* because . . . ."

✔ "The underclass in this country deserve more than a pat on the head, a dime in the tin cup, and a little contribution to your local Salvation Army shelter, though the financial support obviously is needed. The underclass deserves your attention— your attention to its social and psychological as well as economic needs. You may not be poor, but your life is directly affected by your relationships to this segment of society."

✔ "Consider the daily life of a football player during the season. You may think that the idea of the 'student-athlete' is a crock, yet, for football players every fall, it's a lifestyle they've got to learn to handle if they're going to survive both football and classes. They need, not your jealousy and disdain, but your understanding and personal support."

One final point: just as you'll often maintain your own identity in the face of different others, so also will you want to urge others to act from a conviction that their own cultural identities provide the grounds for actions. Karl Marx began his treatise on the proletarian revolution with the call, "Workers of the World, Unite!" His very first sentence signaled his argument that workers as a class had to take control of their own destinies because certainly the other classes of society weren't serving worker interests. In the 1960s, the phrase "Sisterhood is powerful" likewise was a call to recognize that gender needed to be taken into explicit consideration in social, economic, and political relationships and that gender could be the basis for empowerment. Similarly, the rallies of the 1960s around notions of "Black power" and "Black is beautiful" asserted that race was a positive, not negative, attribute of people. So, you occasionally will affirm not only your own but also others' identities as the bases of thought and action.

This is *not* to say that you always will be accepting of the lifestyle choices of others. There will be times when you find it important to confront the socially dangerous and/or personally destructive behaviors of, say, a drug-head or an alcoholic. There may be lifestyle choices that others have made that don't appeal to you, and you may find it impossible to accept appeals for cultural consistency—appeals to male bonding or sisterhood, to your whiteness or brownness, to your youth or status as an elderly person. Some questions will transcend cultural practices in your mind and you'll be forced to assault them, as for example happens when most Americans are confronted by white supremacists. Even then, however, it's vitally important that you understand all you can about culture as lived, thought, and performed so that you can select confrontational strategies that have a chance of actually moving listeners to change their life patterns.

Throughout much of this book, you'll find us returning to questions of cultural life, multiculturalism, and the search for unity. We do not approach what is essentially the cross-cultural dimensions of social life for political reasons. While multiculturalism assuredly has strongly political dimensions, our focus on it is cultural, not political. If you don't understand that speakers must adapt to their listeners' cultures, you'll have great difficulty speaking to any but your own close circle of culturemates. Social life—and hence of public communication—is rooted in cultural practices.[17] It becomes your job to understand and adapt your public speaking strategies to those practices.

Assessing Your Progress

Chapter Summary

1. Culture is a social group's system of meanings.

2. Thinking about culture as lived puts an emphasis on demographic or social categories for classifying people into groups. Cultural diversity represents differences in systems of meaning possessed by different groups in a society. Multiculturalism is a recognition that a country possesses, not a unitary culture with several sub-cultures, but a series of co-cultures that interpenetrate yet are separate from each other.

3. Culture is also a way of thinking. An ideology is a system of thought that embodies social values and perceptual orientations to the world. Hegemony is a concept that defines relationships between more powerful and less powerful people that are maintained in part by complicity on the part of the less powerful people.

4. Culture also is performed. You can see culture only when it is embodied; embodiment is the process whereby ideas, attitudes, values, and social character are given corporeal existence in communication actions. Once you learn culturally significant behavior, then you enact culture when you speak; enactment is a communication process whereby a person behaves in a manner consonant with a society's cultural rules.

5. The central cultural challenge that public speakers face is this: can you respect individual difference and cultural diversity even while attempting to get a group of people to think alike and act together?

6. At least five primary strategies for communicating unity through diversity are available to public speakers: (a) recognizing diversity while calling for unity; (b) negotiating among diverse values; (c) accepting multiple paths to shared goals; (d) working through the lifestyle choices of others; and (e) maintaining self identity in the face of cultural difference.

Key Terms

co-cultures (p. 48)

cultural diversity (p. 47)

culture (p. 44)

culture as lived (p. 47)

culture as performed (p. 49)

culture as thought (p. 49)

embodiment (p. 49)

enactment (p. 49)

hegemony (p. 48)

ideology (p. 48)

multiculturalism (p. 47)

sub-cultures (p. 47)

Assessment Activities

1. Do a demographic profile of your speech classroom, having everyone anonymously record their sex, age, the economic status of their family, place of birth or home state, and ethnic background. Your instructor will tabulate the results and then distribute them to everyone. Write down the central idea or claim for your next speech, and ask yourself: in what ways should the cultural backgrounds of my listeners as seen in the demographic profile affect the ways I handle this idea or claim? Turn it in for your instructor's comments.

2. Take one of the following topics and, either by yourself or in class discussion, identify three or more valuative positions that might be held by ideologically liberal, conservative, and middle-of-the-road people. Then suggest at least two shared goals you think might be acceptable to all three groups. Work with one of the following topics:

   Undocumented (illegal) aliens

   Control and financing of public education

   Equal Rights Amendment

   Juvenile crime

   Environmental protection

References

1.   The classic essays on speaking and class membership are Gerry Philipsen, "Speaking 'Like a Man' in Teamsterville: Culture Patterns of Role Enactment in an Urban Neighborhood," *Quarterly Journal of Speech, 61* (1975): 13–22, and his "Places for Speaking in Teamsterville," *Quarterly Journal of Speech, 62* (1976): 16–25. Cf. D. N. Maltz and R. A. Borker, "A Cultural Approach to Male-Female Miscommunication," in *Language and Social Identity,* edited by J. J. Gumperz (Cambridge, England: Cambridge University Press, 1982), 196–216.

2.   For a discussion of co-cultures, see the introduction and essays in Alberto González, Marsha Houston, and Victoria Chen, eds., *Our Voices: Essays on Culture Ethnicity and Communication,* 2nd ed. (Los Angeles: Roxbury Press, 1996).

3.   For discussions of relationships between thought/speech and culture, see Donal Carbaugh, "'Soul' and 'Self': Soviet and American Cultures in Conversation," *Quarterly Journal of Speech, 79* (1993): 182–200; Randall A. Lake, "Between Myth and History: Enacting Time in Native American Protest Rhetoric," *Quarterly Journal of Speech, 77*

(1991): 123–151; and Alberto González, "'Participation' at WMEX-FM: Interventional Rhetoric of Ohio Mexican Americans," *Western Journal of Speech Communication, 53* (1989): 398–410.

4. On the naturalization of myths and ideologies in our lives, see the classic work by French cultural theorist Roland Barthes, *Mythologies* (London: Paladin, 1973).

5. For a summary of much work on ideology and hegemony, see the writings of John Fiske, e.g., *Television Culture* (New York: Methuen, 1987) and *Media Matters: Everyday Culture and Political Change* (Minneapolis: University of Minnesota Press, 1994).

6. For a study of a communication practice (graffiti) as a kind of embodiment, see Dwight Conquergood, "Homeboys and Hoods: Gang Communication and Cultural Space," in *Group Communication in Context: Studies of Natural Groups,* edited by Lawrence R. Frey (Hillsdale, N.J.: Lawrence Earlbaum Associates, 1994), 23–55.

7. For an interesting study of enactment, see Y. Griefat and Tamar Katriel, "Life Demands *Musayara:* Communication and Culture Among Arabs in Israel," in *Language, Communication, and Culture,* edited by Stella Ting-Toomey and Filipe Korzenny (Newbury Park, Calif.: Sage, 1989), 121–137.

8. E.g, the Western linear approach to idea development is quite different from the emotion- or pathos-centered approach in classical Chinese rhetorical practice. See Mary M. Garrett, "Pathos Reconsidered from the Perspective of Classsical Chinese Rhetorics," *Quarterly Journal of Speech, 79* (1993): 19–39. African Americans likewise draw from different cultural resources. See Patricia A. Sullivan, "Signification and African-American Rhetoric: A Case Study of Jesse Jackson's 'Common Ground and Common Sense' Speech," *Communication Quarterly, 42* (1993): 1–15.

9. For a full discussion of these ideas, see Dennis Brissett and Charles Edgley, eds., *Life As Theatre: A Dramaturgical Sourcebook,* 2nd. ed. (New York: Aldine de Gruyter, 1990).

10. Jesse Jackson, "Common Ground and Common Sense," *Vital Speeches of the Day, 54* (August 15, 1988). See note 8 for a discussion of the style of this speech. This is not to say that Jackson never got into trouble himself over an ethnic comment. For an analysis of his remarks about New York as "Hymietown," see William L. Starosta and L. Coleman, "Jesse Jackson's 'Hymietown' Apology: A Case Study of Interethnic Rhetorical Analysis," in *Interethnic Communication,* edited by Y. Y. Kim (Beverly Hills: Sage, 1986), 117–135.

11. Adapted from "How to Define 'Family Values,'" *USA Weekend,* August 9–11, 1996, 4–5. An expanded treatment of this and other issues dominating Campaign '96 is found in *Clarifying Issues '96* (New York: Public Agenda, 1996), a pamphlet prepared to help citizens match their own thoughts with those of candidates.

12. Henri Mann Morton, "Strength Through Cultural Diversity," keynote address at the Northwest's Colville and Okanogan National Forest conference on cultural diversity, March 23, 1989, reprinted in Bruce E. Gronbeck et al., *Principles and Types of Speech Communication,* 12th ed. (New York: Longman's, 1994), 327.

13. On lifestyle choices, see Victoria Chen, "*Mien Tze* at the Chinese Dinner Table: A Study of the Interactional Accomplishment of Face," *Research on Language and Social Interaction, 24* (1990/91): 109–140, and Shohana Blum-Kulka and Tamar Katriel, "Nicknaming Practices in Families: A Cross-Cultural Perspective," in *Cross-Cultural Interpersonal Communication,* edited by Stella Ting-Toomey and Filipe Korzenny (Newbury Park, Calif.: Sage, 1991), 58–78.

14. Ruth 1:16–17, Holy Bible, Revised Standard Version.

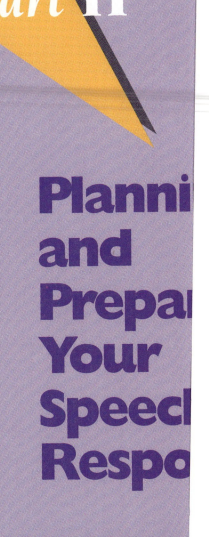

Part II

Planni
and
Prepa
Your
Speec
Respo

15. Lord Chatham, "The Attempt to Subju
reprinted in *The World's Best Orations From the E*
by David J. Brewer (St. Louis: Ferd. P. Kaiser, 189

16. Mary Fisher, address to the Republican N
transcription done from the C-SPAN broadcast o

17. This point is driven home in John C. Ham:
Heritage as Rhetorical Legacy: The Plan of De!
(1994): 53–70.

5 Understanding Your Audience

Every time a salesperson gets ready to call on a client, every time a lawyer prepares to address a jury, every time a teacher prepares a lecture, and every time you get ready to give a speech, audience analysis comes into play. Successful salespeople, lawyers, teachers, and speakers know that effective public speaking is audience-centered. You improve your chances of getting the desired response by tailoring your communication to your listeners—whether a client, a jury, a classroom, or an audience. People understand things in terms of their own experiences. To be most effective, you must analyze your listeners and select experiences common to them.

As you know by now, you need to interact with the people you are addressing. Because of the richness and diversity of the American population, you can't assume everyone thinks and acts exactly as you do. Think about your listeners as you select your speech topic, establish your purpose, and narrow your subject. Each of the remaining steps in speech preparation—selecting supporting materials, arranging the sequence of ideas, and developing introductions and conclusions—also requires that you keep your audience in mind. Your effectiveness as a speaker depends on your adapting to your listeners.

Obviously you can't address your speech to each person individually. But you can identify common features among your listeners. Think of your audience as an onion. You peel away one layer and find others. The most effective way to understand your audience may be to peel away as many layers as possible. Identifying those layers or characteristics is the key to audience analysis. Once you have determined the primary features of your listeners, you can begin to adapt your ideas to them. This chapter will discuss the demographic and psychological features of listeners, how to find out about your audience, and how to use what you learn. Let's first turn to demographic analysis.

Analyzing Your Audience Demographically

Demographic analysis is the study of observable characteristics in groups of people. In any audience, you can often observe traits that group members hold in common. You should determine your listeners' general age, gender, education, group membership, and cultural and ethnic background. Let's examine each of these factors individually.

Age

Are your listeners primarily young, middle-aged, or older? Does one age group seem to dominate a mixed audience? Is there a special relationship between age groups—parents and their children, for instance? Are your listeners your peers, or are you much younger or older?

Watch a nursery-school teacher talk to preschool children and you'll see how age gaps of 20 years or more can be overcome. Nursery school teachers know that they must adapt to their young listeners or risk chaos. They adapt partly by simplifying their vocabulary and shortening their sentences. If you've ever read a story to a child, you know another secret to engaging youngsters. You can command their attention through animation. If you talk like a wizard or a teapot or a mouse, you can see children's eyes widen. The point is this: even if your listeners are much different than you are, you can still engage them by recognizing what captures their attention. In this way, you are using audience analysis to make your message more effective.

Gender

Is your audience predominantly male or female, or is the group made up of both genders? Do your listeners maintain traditional gender roles, or do they assume different roles? Ted chose date rape as the topic for a classroom speech. He was concerned about the lack of information about date rape on his campus and wanted to provide his classmates with the facts. But two things bothered Ted. First, one of his friends asked him why he was giving a speech on this topic. To the friend, it seemed like date rape was an inappropriate topic for a male speaker. Ted was surprised at his friend's reaction but also wondered if others in his class would have the same thought. In addition, Ted realized that both men and women were members of his class. He wondered how he could interest everyone in the subject.

After some thought, Ted decided to handle the problem of gender by convincing his listeners that date rape is not an issue that affects just women. Since they all date, they should all be concerned. Ted would tell his listeners that he hadn't realized the extent of the problem until a good friend confided that she'd been raped by another student who offered to walk her back to her apartment after a party. In addition, Ted planned to present statistics showing the rising number of date rapes. In this way, he tackled the stereotype of the rapist as an unknown midnight assailant lurking in a dark alley. With this strategy, Ted was able to convince his classmates that date rape affected both men and women. They also wanted to listen to him because he was legitimately concerned about the problem. Ted's awareness of gender as a demographic variable allowed him to deal with his audience effectively.

Education

How much do your listeners already know about your subject? Does their experience allow them to learn about this subject easily and quickly? Obviously, people who have worked with a computer word-processing program, for example, will learn its new features more quickly than people who have not.

Knowing the educational background of your audience can guide you in your choice of language, kinds of supporting material, and organizational pattern. Assume that you are addressing the faculty senate as a student advocate of expanded student parking on campus. This audience will demand strong support for your arguments. You can express complex arguments in technical language. The general educational level of your listeners requires that you adapt your ideas and their development. However, when you are invited to speak to a local citizens' group about the proposal for expanded student parking, you will have to broaden your language, supporting material, and organization for a more diverse audience.

Group Membership

Do your listeners belong to groups that represent special attitudes or identifiable values? Are they part of a formal organization such as a church, chamber of commerce, or scouting group, or have they spontaneously come together? Can you pick out common traditions or practices within the organization? What is the cultural climate of the organization?

In some ways, Americans are joiners. We form churches, fan clubs, hobby organizations, health groups—the lists seem endless. You can find a group to join for almost any purpose. We come together to share common experiences, to solidify common values, and to express feelings. Often group members share demographic characteristics. For example, doctors, lawyers, and dentists join professional societies based on occupational similarities. Consumer advocacy groups and support groups are united by purpose. Members of labor unions hold jobs and economic welfare in common. Homeowners' groups share geographic features. Political parties and religious groups attract people who share common values. Tee ball clubs, high school reunions, and associations of retired persons unite people who are similar in age. Groups share similar interests and goals that can be identified readily. Identifying these common interests is an important element of assessing your audience, as the following example illustrates.

The city council in Abby's hometown wanted to build an incinerator for disposal of solid waste. Abby was against the incinerator project and, after voicing her opinions at a backyard barbecue, she found herself representing a grass-roots group of local homeowners. This group shared a common concern for their property values and the environmental safety of their neighborhood. Abby attended the next city council meeting to express the views of the neighborhood. After thinking about the city council's actions, she realized that the primary argument for the incinerator had been to save money. She told the council that more money could be saved by recycling household plastics, selling aluminum cans, and mulching grass clippings. Those simple steps would reduce the waste significantly and make the building of an incinerator unnecessary. Abby's clinching argument was to remind council members that several of them were up for reelection. Her arguments hit a nerve; the incinerator project was canceled. As members of a group, the city council was dependent on homeowners' approval for their jobs.

Cultural and Ethnic Background

Are members of your audience predominantly from particular cultural groups? Do your listeners share a special heritage? Can you identify common origins among listeners?

More and more, the United States is becoming a multiracial, multicultural society. Currently, over 25 percent of all Americans identify themselves as nonwhite. The number of nonwhites in this country is expected to grow rapidly in the next ten years. Many Americans celebrate their roots in other countries or cultures, and those strong cultural heritages may bear on your speechmaking experience. It is important to recognize the cultural and ethnic diversity of your listeners, as the following example shows.

Ed, a student in mass communication, was invited to talk about American media to a group of visiting students sponsored by the Japanese Youth Exchange Program. He realized that some of his examples would be familiar to his listeners. Many Japanese are avid sports fans, follow the Simpsons, and have fan clubs for American celebrities. The Japanese also enjoy their own programs. Considering this, Ed decided to investigate Japanese television more fully. He found many examples of high-quality programs. After reading some particularly interesting research on Japanese soap operas, Ed discovered "*Oshin,*" the daily serial drama rated highest among television programs in Japan. He read about the series, which dramatizes the life of an early twentieth-century heroine. The struggle of new ideas with traditional values is featured in most episodes, and Ed realized how conflict characterizes both Japanese and American soap operas. This recognition of the similarity in television programming gave Ed an idea for his speech. He decided to focus on conflict in soap opera programming and to use both American and Japanese programs as examples. The speech was a hit. Like Ed, you should recognize when the background of your audience influences the speech topic and its development.

Using Demographic Information Responsibly

The importance of demographic analysis does not lie in simply recognizing the variables present in an audience. This is just the first step. The key is to decide which of these demographic factors will affect your listeners' reception of your message. In other words, you must shape your message with your audience in mind.

Sometimes, several factors may affect your message. For example, if you've been asked to talk to a local kindergarten class about your baseball card collection, you must take age and education into consideration. You should adapt to your young listeners by using simplified concepts—talking about the number of hits rather than ERAs. You should also keep your talk brief to accommodate shorter attention spans. And, most importantly, you should involve children by using visual aids. Bring several cards for them to hold and examine.

If you were to talk about your baseball card collection to a group of local business owners, on the other hand, your message would be very different. The age and education of your listeners would still influence your message development, but since those demographic factors would be different, your message should be adapted to the changes. Since your listeners are older and better educated, they can understand more complex ideas. For example, you might focus on the investment potential of baseball card collections. As owners of businesses, their group membership suggests that they would be interested in the commercial aspects of your collection.

Speaking of . . . ethics

Using Audience Analysis Ethically

Marketers can often determine the underlying emotions and values that drive consumer choices using a process called "psychographics." This ability to understand consumer behavior based on demographic and psychological profiling gives marketers an impressive tool. It also gives rise to some ethical concerns. Consider the following uses of audience analysis:

1. Research suggests that many people who suffer from alcoholism feel deep social inadequacy and alienation. Advertisers often associate alcohol with social situations such as parties. Is this attempt to target alcoholics by tapping their need for companionship an ethical use of audience analysis?

2. Some fixed beliefs are **stereotypes**, the perception that all individuals in a group are the same. Is it appropriate for speakers to use stereotypes? For example, a speaker might say, "We all know the rich cheat on their taxes. Let's raise the tax rates in the higher income brackets to compensate." Or, "You can't trust him—he's a politician!"

3. Should advertisers of security devices such as pepper sprays, alarm systems, and handguns play on women's fears of rape and assault?

4. Tobacco companies target young people by offering inducements to purchase cigarettes, such as free gifts. Is this ethical?

For more information on psychographics, see: Rebecca Piirto, *Beyond Mind Games: The Marketing Power of Psychographics* (Ithaca, N.Y.: American Demographics Books, 1991).

Demographic analysis helps you to adapt your message to your listeners more effectively. You can better select and develop your key ideas if you know who is listening to your speech. Demographic analysis can also assist you in understanding your listeners by pinpointing the factors that are common among them.

Analyzing Your Audience Psychologically

Careful psychological analysis of your audience may provide clues about how they think. This is especially important if you intend to influence your listeners. Before you can hope to alter their thoughts or actions, you need to know what ideas they already hold.

To analyze your audience psychologically, identify what your listeners think and feel much as you would specify their demographic characteristics. We call this analysis **psychological profiling.** Beliefs, attitudes, and values are the key concepts in discussing the psychology of listeners. After we examine each of these concepts, we'll discuss ways you can use them to tailor your message to your listeners.

Beliefs

The first task of psychological profiling is understanding audiences' beliefs. **Beliefs** are convictions about what is true or false. They arise from first-hand experiences, from public opinion, from supporting evidence, from authorities, or even from blind faith. For example, you might believe "Calculus is a difficult course," based on your own experience. At the same time, you may also believe that calculus is important for your career because of what others have told you. And, you probably enrolled in college in the first place because your parents and high school teachers encouraged you to try college courses. Although each of these beliefs is held for different reasons, you consider each to be true.

Some beliefs can be supported by strong external evidence. These we call **facts.** When you say, "Research has proven that infant blue whales gain an average of ten pounds per day," you're very sure of that belief. While you may not know much about baby blue whales, you have confidence in the marine biologists who do. You hold facts with certainty because you have hard evidence to support them.

Other beliefs take the form of opinions. **Opinions** are personal beliefs that may not be supported by strong external evidence. You may think that all cats are nasty animals because you have been scratched by cats or because you are allergic to them. However, your experience is limited. Many people like cats. Normally, you signal to your listeners when your beliefs are opinions. You might say, "It's my opinion that cats are worthless creatures," or "In my opinion, cats are vicious." In this way, you are telling your listeners that your evidence to support your claims is limited. Thus, an opinion is a personal belief supported with less compelling external evidence than a fact.[1]

Since both facts and opinions are matters of belief, sometimes the difference between them is blurred. In colonial America, for instance, many people knew "for a fact" that regular bathing caused disease, just as their ancestors knew that the earth was flat and located at the center of the universe. If many people harbor similar opinions, those opinions may be taken for facts. It's important to recognize that opinions and facts are psychological constructs.

Beliefs are held with varying degrees of conviction. Some are relatively open to change, while others are fixed. Obviously, it is more difficult to change fixed beliefs than variable beliefs. **Fixed beliefs** are those that are highly resistant to change. They have been reinforced throughout a lifetime, making them central to one's thinking. Many early childhood beliefs, such as "Bad behavior will be punished," and "If you work hard, you'll succeed," are fixed. Some beliefs may harden in your mind and become resistant to change.

In contrast, **variable beliefs** are less well-anchored in your mind and experiences. You might enter college thinking you want to be a chemist; however, after an instructor praises your abilities in a composition class, you may consider becoming a writer. Then, you take a marketing class and find out that you're good at planning advertising campaigns. This self-discovery goes on as you take additional classes. Your beliefs about your talents change with your personal experiences; since your beliefs are still not firmly fixed, they may change again as you encounter new experiences.

Once you have investigated your audience's beliefs, how can you use this information? You need to determine which beliefs will help you and which are obstacles to be overcome. Pretend that you oppose granting rights to gay personnel in the military. You want to convince your classmates to accept your point of view. Immediately you recognize the swirling controversy centering on this subject, about which people hold many different facts and opinions. First, consider what your listeners believe to be true. If they accept that gays already serve in the military and have served with distinction, then you may have to convince them that the presence of gays is disruptive. On the other hand, if they think that the number of gays in the armed forces is negligible or that gay personnel do not make good soldiers, your job is much easier. Thus, determining your audience's beliefs will help you to focus your ideas.

Before you speak, it's also important to know which of your audience's beliefs are *fixed* (difficult to change) and which are *variable* (more easily altered). You can set more realistic expectations if you know that your listeners are unlikely to change their fixed beliefs, and you can concentrate on changing variable beliefs before you attack fixed beliefs. For example, consider trying to convince your classmates that education is a waste of time. Most likely, their belief that education is valuable is fixed and you'll have trouble changing it. On the other hand, you might have more luck getting them to change majors or take a class outside their majors. Their beliefs about which classes to take probably are variable.

Attitudes

The second goal of psychological profiling is to identify audience attitudes. **Attitudes** are tendencies to respond positively or negatively to people, objects, or ideas. Attitudes express our individual preferences and feelings such as, "I like my public speaking class," "Classical music is better than rap music," and "Cleveland is a beautiful city." In other words, they are emotionally weighted.

Attitudes often influence our behavior. One dramatic example of the strength of attitudes occurred when the Coca-Cola Corporation introduced new Coke, a refigured formula, with disastrous results. Although extensive blind taste tests indicated that people preferred new Coke's flavor, consumers reacted negatively because of their loyalty to the classic formula. Their attitudes controlled their purchasing behavior, and the corporation wisely "reintroduced" Coca-Cola Classic.

As a speaker, you should consider the dominant attitudes of your listeners. Audiences may have attitudes toward you, your speech subject, and your speech purpose. Your listeners may think you know a lot about your topic, and they may be interested in learning more. This is an ideal situation. However, if they think you're not very credible and they resist learning more, you must deal with their attitudes. For example, if a speaker tells you that you can earn extra money in your spare time by selling magazine subscriptions, you

TABLE 5.1 Beliefs and Attitudes
Beliefs and attitudes are psychological constructs held by individuals or by groups.

Beliefs	*Attitudes*
Seat belts save lives.	Fastening my seat belt takes too much time.
Vegetables contain important minerals and vitamins.	Broccoli tastes good.
My grandparents came from Mexico City.	I love my grandfather.

People's attitudes can vary dramatically. Powerful attitudes often come into play in our everyday lives.

may have several reactions. The thought of extra income from a part-time job is enticing. At the same time, you suspect that it might be a scam and you feel uncomfortable because you don't know the speaker well. These attitudes toward the speech topic, purpose, and speaker will undoubtedly influence your final decision about selling subscriptions.

Values

The third component of psychological profiling is understanding audience values. **Values** are the basic concepts organizing one's orientation to life. They underlie an individual's particular attitudes and beliefs. For many Americans, life, freedom, family, and honesty are basic values. These are deeply ingrained and enduring; as a result, they are very resistant to change. Imagine trying to convince a friend to renounce American citi-

FIGURE 5.1   Belief, Attitude, and Value Clusters

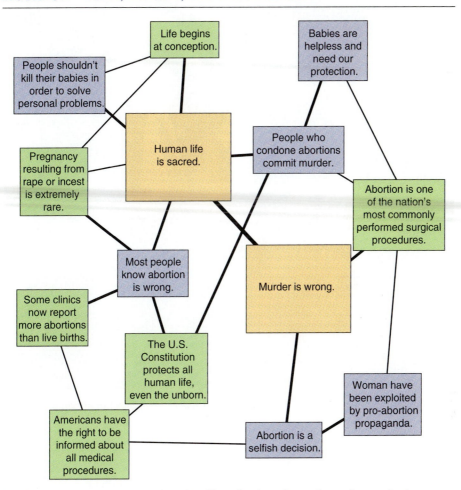

Beliefs, attitudes, and values are interdependent. They often form clusters that reinforce each other.

zenship. No matter how noble your cause, you will probably meet powerful resistance because you are attacking fundamental values.

Values are more basic than beliefs or attitudes because they represent broad categories that may motivate attitudes and beliefs. Values serve as the foundations for the beliefs and attitudes that cluster around them (see Figure 5.1). For example, a person may hold a value such as, "Human life is sacred." That value can be expressed in multiple attitudes including "Abortion is wrong" or "Mercy killing is immoral." That value may also be expressed in beliefs such as, "A fetus should be treated as a human being," "Most Americans are opposed to abortion rights legislation," or "Religious authority ought to be respected on questions of morality."

Values, then, underlie an individual's particular attitudes and beliefs. Former Representative Barbara Jordan, the first African-American woman to give the keynote address

Values serve to motivate people to action. Political change is often based upon shared value orientations.

at the Democratic National Convention, identified basic values that her audience shared. Among them, she listed "equality for all and privileges for none."[2] Her speech is highly regarded because she highlighted *common ground*—shared values that organized and influenced the beliefs and attitudes of her listeners.

Discovering Demographic and Psychological Factors

Now that you understand which demographic and psychological factors are important to consider when developing a speech, you should think about how you're going to discover this information. You may already know the answer: you can ask your listeners for their opinions and you can observe them and draw inferences from your observations. Let's look at each option.

Surveying Your Listeners

Often, the best source of information about your audience is your listeners themselves. Ask them. You may not have the services of a professional pollster, but you can conduct informal interviews with members of the group or develop a more formal survey to assess their beliefs, attitudes, and values.

Suppose you are concerned about the rapidly rising number of sexually transmitted diseases among local teenagers. As the parent of a teenager, you are convinced that every effort should be made in the schools to halt this alarming trend, including making condoms available to all students. If you intend to convince the school board to take action on this issue, you need to know how the members of the board currently feel about the issue. Your plan is clear: you talk to the members of the board individually and find out.

However, you may also have to convince the local Parent-Teacher Association to support your plan. This presents an entirely different problem since there are thousands of parents in your school district. Even if you spent hours on the phone, you still probably couldn't interview every parent in the district. Your alternative is to talk to parents active in the organization or call them randomly to get an accurate profile of their views.

In each case, the questions you will ask are basic. You want action, so it's clear that you will ask how they would vote on the issue. It's also important to know whether they'll vote at all, so you will need to find out whether they regularly attend meetings. Finally, you need to understand why they feel the way they do about the issue. In this way, if you have an opportunity to talk about the issue, you'll have the basic points of conflict already identified.

Observing Your Listeners

Sometimes you don't have direct access to members of your audience. If this is the case, then you must rely on indirect observation and inference for your audience analysis. Occasionally you'll have public statements, earlier conversations, voting behaviors, purchasing decisions, and other information on which to base your analysis. At other times, you will have to rely on indirect information from others.

If you aren't closely tied to the group you will address, you'll want to: (1) think through your personal experiences with identifiable groups in the audience; (2) talk with program chairpersons and others who can tell you who is in the audience and something about their interests; and (3) ask speakers who have addressed this or similar audiences what you can expect. Keep in mind that these strategies provide limited information. You can supplement this information by attending a few meetings of the group yourself or reading the constitution of or other literature about the group. Don't forget to check the Internet. Many groups maintain home pages and you can gain information from them. In combination, these observations will help you to adjust your speech to your listeners.

Finally, you can consult published sources that provide demographic and survey information on broad segments of our society. Opinion polls, market surveys, political profiles, and demographic shifts are all available in your library in sources such as *Statistical Abstract of the United States, Survey of Current Business, Business Conditions Digest, Bureau of Labor Statistics News, Statistics of Income Bulletin,* and *Facts on File.*

Using Your Psychological Profile

After you have developed a profile of your audience's beliefs, attitudes, and values, how can you use this information? Understanding your audience's beliefs, attitudes, and values will help you to make decisions about three aspects of your speech: your ideas, your supporting materials, and your phrasing. Your psychological profile can help you:

1. *Frame your ideas.* For example, if your audience believes childhood is a critical time of development, you can move from this belief to recruit volunteers for a day-care co-op. If they value family life, you can touch on this theme to solidify their commitment. On the other hand, if your audience is apathetic about childhood development, you must establish the critical nature of the early years of child development before you can hope to persuade them to support a co-op.

2. *Choose your supporting materials.* If your audience analysis shows that your listeners consider statistics to be factual, you should use scientific studies or numerical data in your speech. On the other hand, if your audience believes in the divine inspiration of the Bible, you can cite biblical testimony to sway them.

3. *Phrase your ideas.* You can choose your words to reflect the intensity of your audience's convictions. If your listeners are ready to picket a local video rental store, then your language should show the urgency of immediate action. Demand action now. On the other hand, if they are reluctant to take up placards, then you should use less forceful words.

Responsible Use of Audience Analysis in Speech Preparation

Audience analysis helps you search for clues to the way your listeners think and act. Identifying the demographic and psychological characteristics of your listeners is an important step toward good communication. Using these characteristics helps you to discover what might affect the audience's acceptance of you and your ideas. When you understand your listeners, you can plan your speech so that they can better understand it. Let's focus on how audience analysis helps you prepare to speak through audience targeting and audience segmentation.

As you consider your reasons for speaking, you need to determine what you can realistically expect to accomplish with your particular audience in the time you have available. Analysis of your audience helps you develop your speaking purpose, your goals, and the appeals you will use.

Developing Your Purposes

Suppose you have a part-time job with your college's Career Planning and Placement Office; you know enough about its operations and have enough personal interest in it to want to speak about career planning and placement to a variety of listeners. What you've discovered about different audiences should help you to determine appropriate, specific purposes for each. If you were to talk to a group of incoming students, for example, you would know that they probably:

✓ Know little about the functions of a career planning and placement office (have few beliefs in this area, none of which are fixed).

✓ Are predisposed to look favorably on career planning and placement (have a positive attitude toward the subject).

✓ Are more concerned with such short-term issues as getting an adviser, registering, and learning about basic degree requirements than they are with long-range matters such as finding jobs (are motivated by practical values).

✓ See you as an authoritative speaker and, consequently, are willing to listen to you (have a positive attitude toward the speaker).

Given these audience considerations, you would probably provide basic rather than detailed information about career planning and placement. You might phrase your specific purpose as follows: "To brief incoming students on the range of services offered by the Career Planning and Placement Office." This orientation will include a brief description of each service and a general appeal to your audience to use these services to make some curricular decisions.

If you spoke to a group of graduating college seniors on the same subject, you would address the audience differently. You would discover that they:

✓ Are familiar with the Career Planning and Placement Office through roommates and friends who have used it (have beliefs that are fixed).

✓ Have strong positive feelings about career planning and placement because they are hoping to use such services to find jobs when they graduate (have a positive attitude toward the subject).

✓ Tend to think education has prepared them to "earn a decent living" (have a practical perspective on the topic).

✓ May view you as an unqualified speaker on this subject, especially if you aren't a senior or aren't employed full-time (have a negative attitude toward the speaker).

Given these factors, you should offer specific details in some areas. You might describe the special features of the office rather than simply outlining its general duties. Your listeners need to know the *how;* they already know the *what.* You could reassure them that the office successfully places many students and point out that the process is more successful when students allow ample time for resume development, job searching, and interviewing. You could demonstrate your expertise by talking about career possibilities across a variety of fields—especially if you know what fields are represented in the group you are addressing. You might phrase your specific purpose as follows: "To inform graduating seniors about Midstate University's philosophy of career planning and placement, about ways that the office can help students find employment, and about specific types of information and assistance that the office provides to students." Audience analysis will help you to shape your specific purposes and determine which are most appropriate to your listeners.

Developing Your Goals

As a speaker, ask your listeners to accomplish only what is within their capacity. You can often discover your listeners' potential for action through an audience analysis. Demographic factors will tell you about the channels of action available to your listeners. Voters can cast their ballots in elections, parents can teach their children, consumers can boycott products, and many people can contribute money. You can use the psychological factors that you discover through audience analysis to stimulate listeners' motivations to act.

You can also determine ranges of authority through an audience analysis, especially through analysis of demographic factors. For example, in speaking with a local school's Parent-Teacher Association about instituting an after-school program of foreign language and culture instruction, you're addressing an audience made up of school administrators, teachers, and parents. Each of these groups has certain powers to act. School administrators can seek funding from the school board; teachers can volunteer

Speaking of . . . *skills*

Handling Hostile Audiences

How do you gain a positive response from people who disagree with you? While it is unreasonable to expect to convert every member of a hostile audience, you can improve your chances of getting them to listen with the following strategies:

1. *Establish goodwill.* Let them know you are concerned about the issues or problems you're discussing.
2. *Start with areas of agreement.* Develop some common ground before you launch into controversial territory.
3. *Offer principles of judgment.* Determine the basis on which you and your listeners can evaluate ideas.
4. *Develop positive credibility.* If your listeners respect you, they are less likely to reject your ideas.
5. *Use experts and supporting material to which your audience will respond.* Choose your supporting material with your audience in mind.
6. *Disarm your listeners with humor.* Mutual laughter establishes positive rapport.
7. *Use a multisided presentation.* Recognize more than one perspective on the issues.

Above all, be realistic when addressing a hostile audience. Remember that the more strongly an audience opposes your position, the less change you can reasonably expect to occur.

For more information, see: Herbert Simons, *Persuasion* (New York: Random House, 1986), pp. 150–160.

instructional time; and parents can petition the school board, enroll their children, and volunteer to help with the program. Your speech could include these specific goals for each group of listeners.

Be realistic about the degree of change you can expect from your listeners. How intensely can you motivate an audience to react to a topic? If your listeners are strongly opposed to downtown renovation, a single speech—no matter how eloquent—will probably not reverse their opinions. One attempt may only neutralize some of their objections. This is a more realistic goal for a single speech than completely reversing opinions.

How much action can you expect after your speech? If your prespeech analysis indicates that your listeners vehemently oppose nuclear power plants in your area, you may be able to recruit many of them to work long hours picketing, lobbying, and participating in telephone marathons. However, if they moderately oppose nuclear facilities, you might ask for a small monetary donation rather than an actual time commitment. Audience analysis should help you to set more realistic communication goals.

Developing Your Appeals

So far, we've focused on how audience analysis helps you to target your audience as a group. Keep in mind that no matter how close together people are seated in the room, they are still individuals. Sometimes you can approach each listener individually. However, such communication is time-consuming and inefficient when you're dealing with matters of broad public concern.

You can use an approach called **audience segmentation** to divide your audience into a series of subgroups or "target populations." A typical college audience, for example, might be segmented by academic standing (freshmen through seniors), by academic major (art through zoology), by classroom performance (A+ to F), or even by extracurricular activity (ROTC, SADD, Young Republicans, Pi Kappa Delta). You can direct main ideas to each of these subgroups.

Suppose you were to give a speech to members of a local community club, urging them to fund a scholarship. Your initial segmenting of the audience might tell you that the club is composed of social service personnel, educators, and business people. By thinking of the club as segmented into these subgroups, you should be in a position to offer each subgroup some reasons to support your proposal. For example, you might appeal to social service workers by saying: "The social-team concept means that working with everyone is necessary for the improvement of the community." And, for educators in your audience, you would state: "By denying education to capable students, we neglect to tap into one of the most important resources of our community—young people." Finally, for business people, you would declare: "Well-educated citizens contribute more to the financial resources of the community as investors, property owners, and heads of households."

You can see how each statement is directed to segments of your audience. These main ideas implicitly refer to the commitment of social services to helping people from all strata of life, to educators' beliefs and attitudes that youth are a national resource, and to business leaders' commitment to financial responsibility and success.

Understanding your audience is a key step in speech preparation. To become a competent speaker, you must make many decisions about your topic, specific purposes, and phrasing for central ideas and main ideas. Demographic and psychological analyses of audience members will help you to make these decisions. If you learn all you can about your listeners and use relevant information to plan your speech, you'll improve your chances for success.

A Sample Audience Analysis

In this chapter we have surveyed various factors that you will consider as you analyze your audience and occasion. If you work systematically, these choices will become clearer. Suppose you want your local city council to adopt a program in which drug addicts can exchange used hypodermic needles for clean ones. You think it will help prevent the spread of AIDS (acquired immunodeficiency syndrome) among drug addicts. You might prepare the following analysis of your audience as you plan your speech:

I. *General Description of the Audience:* The city council is comprised of 15 members elected to office by local districts. The city manager and mayor also attend council meetings. Citizens sometimes attend and speak at council meetings.

II. *Demographic Analysis:*

A. *Age:* Most of the council members are between 45 and 65.

B. *Gender:* The council is composed of 12 men and 3 women. The mayor and city manager are men.

C. *Education:* All but four of the council members have finished high school; several completed B.A. degrees in various fields, including political science, pharmacy, nursing, home economics, and accounting. Two health professionals on the council are familiar with disease history and control.

D. *Group Membership:* All listeners are politically active and registered voters. Although they do not necessarily share party affiliation, they all value participation in the democratic process.

E. *Cultural and Ethnic Background:* Ethnic background is mixed, but predominantly African American, European, and Hispanic.

III. *Psychological Profile:*

A. *Factual Beliefs:* Anyone who contracts AIDS will die of it. In spite of promising new research, there is no cure for AIDS.

B. *Opinions:* Most consider AIDS to be a problem associated with particular groups, including homosexual males, hemophiliacs, and intravenous-drug users.

C. *Attitudes:* Members of the council probably were surprised by the recent news of the AIDS death of a prominent community resident. They probably do not consider themselves likely victims.

D. *Values:* They are committed to the democratic process and take pride in political involvement at the community and state levels. They see themselves as common people—"the heart of America"—fulfilling the American dream. Council members often point to community progress in civil rights issues, general educational reforms, and high voter turnout during elections.

With this prespeech audience analysis completed, you have a better idea of how to frame your speech. From your analysis you conclude that the council may initially resist your needle exchange proposal because they think that AIDS affects only a small number of people who engage in high-risk behaviors. They may believe that most citizens are not at risk. Realizing this, you can choose among several approaches:

1. Stress the listeners' commitment to the welfare of the community and nation, their belief in the democratic process, and their belief in the rights of citizens in minority groups. Encourage their feelings of pride in previous civic accomplishments and challenge them to face the AIDS crisis. In other words, show them that it is in their best interests to confront and discuss unpopular issues for the well-being of the entire community.

2. Make it clear that this is not simply a moral issue. While recognizing the importance of traditional national values, also stress the practical importance of treating disease, regardless of moral issues. Use projections of future infection rates to em-

phasize that everyone's health may be affected if the disease is allowed, through ignorance or neglect, to spread unchecked.

3. Point out that other communities have used needle exchange programs with success.
   Emphasize predictions of future infection affecting broader populations. Overcome
   audience apathy and hostility by encouraging members to discuss the disease further.

4. Ask the council to sponsor an open forum for continued attention to the issue,
   rather than demanding immediate commitments or political action.

5. Recognize the group's excellent record in community projects. Stress the far-sight-
   edness of the council on other difficult issues. Point out that, in a democracy, fair
   play requires that each side be given equal time and consideration before anyone
   reaches a final decision. Aim the bulk of the speech at gaining approval for open-
   minded discussions.

As you can see, when you understand your listeners it's much easier to tailor a specific
message for them. You are more likely to develop an effective speech when you first consider the demographic and psychological characteristics of your listeners.

Assessing Your Progress

Chapter Summary

1. Public speaking is audience-centered.

2. The primary goal of audience analysis is to discover the demographic and psychological characteristics of your listeners that are relevant to your speech purposes and ideas.

3. Demographic analysis is the study of audience characteristics such as age, gender,
   education, group membership, and cultural and ethnic backgrounds.

4. Psychological profiling seeks to identify the beliefs, attitudes, and values of audience members.

5. Beliefs are convictions about what is true or false.

6. Beliefs may be facts or opinions, fixed or variable.

7. Attitudes are tendencies to respond positively or negatively to people, objects, or ideas.

8. Values are basic concepts that provide standards for life.

9. Audience analysis allows you to identify audience subgroups for more effective selection of main ideas.

Key Terms

attitudes (p. 71)

audience segmentation (p. 79)

beliefs (p. 70)

demographic analysis (p. 66)

facts (p. 70)

fixed beliefs (p. 70)

opinions (p. 70)

psychological profiling (p. 69)

stereotypes (p. 69)

values (p. 72)

variable beliefs (p. 70)

Assessment Activities

1. Choose the text of a speech from this textbook, from *Vital Speeches of the Day* (or another anthology of speeches), or from a newspaper, such as the *New York Times*. Identify statements of fact and opinion in the speech. Determine the speaker's attitudes and values from statements in the speech. Develop a profile of the audience and assess the effectiveness of the speech for this group of listeners.

2. Gather some magazine advertisements and bring them to class. As a class or in groups, share your advertisements. Speculate about the audiences for which they were intended. To what attitudes are the advertisers trying to appeal? Are they trying to create beliefs? What tactics do they use? How effective do you think these tactics are?

3. In a group or individually, pretend you are the chief speech writer for each of the individuals listed below. Decide which audience subgroups you will need to address. What values, attitudes, and beliefs are they likely to hold? What can you say in your speech to engage their attention and support?

   a. The president of the United States, addressing the nation on primetime television concerning the latest international diplomatic development.

   b. The president of your student government, welcoming first-year students to campus at the beginning of the academic year.

   c. A defense lawyer, conducting closing arguments in a murder trial.

   d. A ninth-grade teacher, cautioning a class about the use of illegal drugs.

References

1. For more discussion, see: David L. Bender (ed.), *American Values* (San Diego, Calif.: Greenhaven Press, 1989); Milton M. Rokeach, *Beliefs, Attitudes, and Values: A Theory of Organization and Change* (San Francisco: Jossey-Bass, 1968); and Rokeach, *The Nature of Human Values* (New York: Collier-Macmillan, Free Press, 1973).

2. See Wayne Thompson, "Barbara Jordan's Keynote Address: Fulfilling Dual and Conflicting Purposes," *Central States Speech Journal, 30* (1979): 272–277.

6 Finding Supporting Materials

You are living in a communications revolution. You have at your disposal the miracles that result from the harnessing of electricity: the computer chip, television, satellites, fax machines and electronic mail, and digital sound reproduction. Electronically, you can access and experience wildly diverse people, places, and events all over the world. You can now retrieve more data than at any other time in history. In a few minutes through the Internet alone, you can find a weather forecast for Beijing, a map of Rio de Janeiro, and the latest headline news.

You have access to staggering amounts of information. To conquer this glut of data, you need to know where to look for the information that you need. This chapter explores the challenge of finding and assembling the materials relevant to your speeches, your audiences, and the speech occasions.

Finding supporting materials should be a purposeful, targeted search, not an aimless bibliographical spree in the library or on the Internet. You must develop some sense of the supporting materials you will need, of the location of those materials, and of efficient ways to record the information you find. You will also need to know how to use supporting materials ethically. In this chapter we won't deal with these matters exhaustively, because your own libraries will have their own particular ways of organizing and handling materials. However, we do hope to get you off to a good start.

Determining the Kinds of Supporting Materials You'll Need

To guide your choice of supporting materials, you need to consider your main topic, your audience, and the ideas you intend to discussion. Thinking about these elements should help you decide what kind of supporting materials you will need. Consider the following critical questions to guide the selection of supporting materials before you begin your search process.

1. *What support does your topic require?* Specific topics require certain sorts of supporting materials. It's obvious that you wouldn't use the same kind of supporting material to describe your experience swimming with dolphins as you would to report your kennel club's financial status. The rational requirements of your speech topic should suggest the appropriate forms of supporting material.

   Consider another example: if you tell your listeners that tuition has increased, you need to show how much. This topic demands statistics that show a trend of rising tuition. The statistics provide a general picture and develop the scope of the problem. You might add testimony, examples, and comparisons and contrasts to depict details and to develop audience interest.

2. *What does your audience need to know?* No matter what forms of support you choose, merely citing the findings of research is clearly not enough. You also need to think about what your audience already knows and what they need to know. Your search for supporting materials should reflect your listeners' needs.

   If you give a speech on skin cancer, your audience is probably most interested in their chances of getting it. They may be unaware that certain practices, like the use of tanning beds, increase the risk of getting skin cancer and they probably don't know about the latest treatment methods. These are certainly things you will want to find out as you search for supporting material on this topic.

Speaking of . . . skills

How Much Is Enough?

Have you ever found yourself wondering, "How much supporting material should I use in my speech?" While there's no absolute rule governing the number or kind of supporting materials, you need enough support to establish your points. This varies according to the quality and kind of supporting materials. Here are some guidelines:

1. *Complex or abstract ideas are enhanced by concrete supporting materials such as visuals aids and specific examples.* A speech on chaos theory would be clarified by a graph or an example from daily life.
2. *Controversial points require a lot of authoritative evidence.* This means that a speech for raising income taxes would benefit from statistics, budget trend information, and well-respected testimony.
3. *Speakers with low credibility need more supporting material than speakers with high credibility.* If you plan to speak on educational reform for the next century but your only experience has been as a student, you should use a lot of supporting material.
4. *If your topic is abstract or distant from your listeners' experiences, use concrete supporting material to establish identification with listeners.* A speech on life in a space station doesn't come alive until you insert specific details and concrete examples.
5. *If your audience's attention or comprehension is low, use more examples.* Enliven a speech on accounting procedures with a story or a specific instance.

3. *Which form of support will be most effective for your topic?* As you conduct your research, you should realize that you will discover many forms of support. However, different forms of supporting material accomplish different results. Explanations, comparisons, and statistics will help you develop the topic so your listeners can better understand it. Examples and testimony will lend interest to the topic. In an introduction to a speech on fire alarms, you might use an example of a local house fire to stimulate audience interest and then, in the body of the speech, use statistics to establish the importance of installing fire alarms.

4. *How objective is your supporting material?* To read and think critically, you must be able to distinguish among sources of information. One way to differentiate is to distinguish between what historians call **primary sources** (eyewitness/first-hand accounts) and **secondary sources** (accounts based on other sources of information). The diary of a pioneer woman crossing the Great Plains in 1822 would be considered a primary source, since she herself recorded her experiences. The history of the westward movement based on many accounts of pioneers is a secondary source. Both are subject to biases. Obviously, the pioneer woman may not have had a "typical" experience, or her own personal prejudices may have influenced what she recorded. The same may be true of the historian. Furthermore, sometimes the sources an historian works from color the resulting history.

This initial thinking about your topic: (a) helps you decide what supporting materials your topic requires, (b) guides your selection of supporting materials in light of your audience demands, (c) determines which forms of supporting material are most effective for your topic, and (d) indicates what supporting material will be most objective.

Sources of Supporting Materials

Where can you find the kinds of supporting materials we've been discussing? A wide range of sources are available to you from computerized searches, printed materials, and interviews with experts. Let's examine the possibilities.

Computerized Database Searches

Working your way through the electronic world of information takes a few skills and some planning, but the results are well worth the effort. At most schools in the country and through an increasing number of inexpensive commercial services, you can access mountains of information with relative ease. You can search your library electronically, surf the Internet, and upload information from CD-ROMs. Let's explore the possibilities.

The Electronic Card Catalog Most colleges and universities either have or will soon install a computerized search system for their holdings. If you have access to such a system, it should be your first stop. For example, the University of Iowa uses the Oasis system, popular among larger research libraries. It allows you to search Iowa's card catalog and holdings of consortium libraries, the Humanities and Social Sciences Indexes, and Psychological Abstracts. Your library probably has a comparable system.

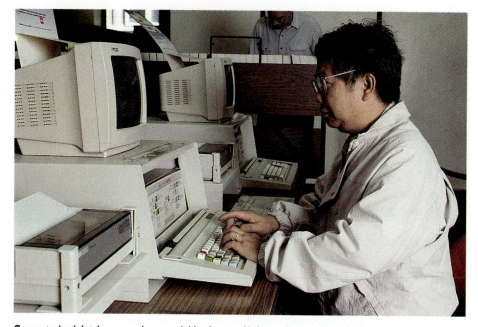

Computerized database searches can yield volumes of information rapidly and efficiently.

Suppose you want to do a speech on the 1991 Persian Gulf War. Searching with the phrase "Persian Gulf War" can turn up 402 entries—far too many to use. Specifying a subtopic such as "Press Coverage" yields eleven books: six on press coverage in general, three dealing specifically with U.S. coverage, one on coverage in Great Britain, and another on the war and public opinion. This is a more manageable list of materials. Take time to look at user information or the online help menu to make sure that you use the electronic card catalog with maximum efficiency. It will help you narrow your search through precise specification of topic or through subcategorization.

Specialized Databases Your library undoubtedly subscribes to one or more computerized databases. These work much like printed indexes—only much more quickly and thoroughly. Electronic databases are usually updated regularly, also making them more timely than printed indexes. The average university library probably has access to nearly 200 data files such as ERIC, BIOSIS, PsychInfo, AGRICOLA, Datrex, and MEDLINE. Computerized searches can be invaluable tools for research on speech topics.

To conduct a computerized database search intelligently, pick the database likely to have the information that you want. With the help of a reference librarian and the descriptive material on the databases, you'll know to go to ERIC (Educational Resources Information Center) if you want scholarly and educational papers written by humanities professors and to MEDLINE if you can make use of psychological and scientific studies of diseases and other medical problems. LEXUS-NEXUS will give you access to a staggering number of public and commercial information sources.

Be smart when picking key words for searches. Computerized searches can give you too much information if you select a broad category such as *television*. If you narrow and coordinate key words, you're more likely to get usable material. So, if you're interested in violence in children's television programming, coordinating the key words *television* and *violence* will narrow your search.

CD-ROM Searches   We're living through a great explosion in the use of the CD-ROM—a technological device that uses the CD as a storage vehicle for computer data. CDs hold much more information than computer disks and so are used to store and to retrieve data from multiple volumes. Check the holdings of your local library. Many offer on CD-ROMs sources like the *New York Times Index, The Oxford English Dictionary, The Modern Language Association Indexes, Encyclopaedia Britannica,* perhaps even the tables of contents to all communication journals. As more and more databases become available on CD-ROM, you'll be able to link electronically with the actual articles you want.

The Internet   If you have access to a personal computer and modem, you can search other online public services through the Internet. You can reach the World Wide Web, BRS/After Dark, CompuServe, Prodigy, Dow Jones News/Retrieval, Network News, WAIS/Wide Area Information Service, and other general databases that will give you a wealth of general information, news events, economic indicators, and discussion groups.

With the click of a mouse or a tap of an "enter" key, you can access unlimited information sources. We do not have the space here to teach you how to surf the 'Net. You may wish to work from books such as *The Internet for Dummies* or complete packages like the *Internet Starter Kit.* Better yet, sign up for a short course at your school or local library. And, if you join one of the private, for-profit services—America Online, Prodigy, CompuServe, or more localized services—you'll find many helpful tips right on your computer screen. Your college or university may also subscribe to such services.

By now, you probably cannot tune into a sports broadcast, a news program, or even a primetime television show without being told that you can use a "www." command to get to its "home page"—ESPNET's sports scores for the day, CNN International's informational background on big stories, *USA Today* online, National Public Radio's discussion group, or propaganda put out by the Republican and Democratic parties. You soon discover you can go to Mississippi State University for the Internet Movie Database, to SCREENsite for links between the Library of Congress and directories on film and television resources, to the Harvard-MIT-Tufts consortium on negotiation and conflict resolution, to the University of Maryland's site of resources and simulations for high school students, to state and federal government sources through ".gov" locations. Discovering how to draw on such information will make your speech preparation time not only well spent but even fun.

In any search, you want to maximize your efficiency. There are some special considerations that apply to electronic database searches. Keep these things in mind when you conduct such a search:

1. Evaluate the expertise of the source, because anyone with a modem and some basic understanding of how to get online can post messages on the Internet. Not everyone knows what they're talking about, so be sure to check the accuracy of the information you discover with other sources before you use it.

2. Make your search relevant to your topic. Set limits on your search. It's easy to get side-tracked. You'll discover thousands of fascinating ideas, meet people on-line, and become enchanted by the sheer capacity of the computer databases. You might start looking for information about the U.S. legal code, and three hours later realize

that you have read about UFO hot spots, popular underground rock bands, the Oneida Indian Tribe, an Eskimo art exhibit, and Greek mythology. The Internet is addictive. Time melts away as you sit in front of the terminal, so stick to your original search.

3. Consider the cost. Some commercial databases charge by the line and others by the hour. Either way, costs can mount rapidly. If you're not careful, your speech can end up as an expensive endeavor.

4. While online services all provide access to the Internet, it's a good idea to try out several since they offer different search features and include different databases. For example, the World Wide Web allows you to enter government documents, CompuServe offers tax services and forms, Microsoft Network features information from NBC News, Prodigy offers a wide variety of educational guides, and America Online provides an Electronic University Network. These are just a few of the options. Undoubtedly, there will continue to be rapid change in what's available. That's why you need to explore the Internet and become familiar with all its features.

As you tap into the Internet, there are other concerns as well, such as the frustration of trying to get online during peak user periods. Don't procrastinate. Give yourself plenty of time to get online and find your information. In addition, be careful about the files you download. It's possible to corrupt your computer files with a virus picked up from the Internet. There are many other issues concerning censorship, personal privacy and safety, and the security of financial transactions that take place on the Internet. But, for now, you're set to get started.

Print Materials

The most common source of supporting materials is the printed word: newspapers, magazines, pamphlets, and books. Through the careful use of a library, and with the help of reference librarians, you can discover an almost overwhelming amount of materials relevant to your speech subject and purpose.

Newspapers   Newspapers are obviously a useful source of information about events of current interest. Moreover, their feature stories and accounts of unusual happenings provide a storehouse of interesting illustrations and examples. You must be careful, of course, not to accept as true everything printed in a newspaper, since the haste with which news must be gathered sometimes makes complete accuracy difficult. Your school or city library undoubtedly keeps on file copies of one or two highly reliable papers, such as the *New York Times, The Observer,* the *Wall Street Journal,* or the *Christian Science Monitor,* as well as the leading newspapers of your state or region. Through the *New York Times Index,* you can locate the paper's accounts of people and events from 1913 to the present. Another useful and well-indexed source of information on current happenings is *Facts on File,* issued weekly since 1940. You can use it to find exact dates and information on very recent events.

Magazines   The average university library subscribes to hundreds of magazines and journals. Some, such as *Time, Newsweek,* and *U.S. News & World Report,* summarize weekly events. *Omni* and *Harper's* are representative of monthly publications that cover a wide range of subjects of both passing and lasting importance. *The Nation, Vital Speeches* of the Day, Fortune, Washington Monthly, and The New Republic, among other magazines, contain comment on current political, social, and economic questions. More specialized magazines include Popular Science, Scientific American, Ebony, Sports Illustrated, Field and Stream, Ms., Better Homes and Gardens, Byte, Today's Health, National Geographic, and The Smithsonian.

This list is, of course, just the beginning—there are hundreds of periodicals available covering thousands of subjects. To find a specific kind of information, use the Readers' Guide to Periodical Literature, which indexes most of the magazines you'll want to consult in preparing a speech. Or, if you'd like more sophisticated material, consult the Social Sciences Index and the Humanities Index, now computerized in most libraries. Similar indexes are available for publications from technical fields and professional societies; a reference librarian can show you how to use them.

Yearbooks and Encyclopedias The most reliable source of comprehensive data is the Statistical Abstracts of the United States, which covers a wide variety of subjects ranging from weather records and birth rates to steel production and election results. Information on Academy Award Winners, world records in various areas, and the "bests" and "worsts" of almost anything can be found in the World Almanac, The People's Almanac, The Guinness Book of World Records, The Book of Lists, and Information Please. Encyclopedias, such as the Encyclopaedia Britannica and Encyclopedia Americana, attempt to cover the entire field of human knowledge and are valuable chiefly as initial reference sources or for background reading. Refer to them for important scientific, geographical, literary, or historical facts; for bibliographies of authoritative books on a subject; and for supplemental information.

Documents and Reports Various government agencies—state, national, and international—as well as many independent organizations publish reports on special subjects. The most frequently consulted governmental publications are the hearings and recommendations of congressional committees on the publications of the U.S. Department of Health and Human Services or Department of Commerce. Reports on issues related to agriculture, business, government, engineering, and scientific experimentation are published by many state universities. Such endowed groups as the Carnegie, Rockefeller, and Ford Foundations and such special interest groups as the Foreign Policy Association, the Brookings Institution, the League of Women Voters, Common Cause, and the U.S. Chamber of Commerce also publish reports and pamphlets. Though by no means a complete list, The Vertical File Index serves as a guide to some of these materials.

Books Most subjects suitable for a speech have been written about in books. As a guide to these books, use the subject-matter headings in the card catalog of local libraries. Generally, you will find authoritative books in your school library and more popularized treatments in your city's public library. You can now access the card catalog via computer in many libraries. This often makes your search more efficient and productive.

Biographies The Dictionary of National Biography, the Dictionary of American Biography, Who's Who, Who's Who in America, Current Biography, and more specialized works organized by field contain biographical sketches especially useful in locating facts about famous people and in documenting the qualifications of authorities whose testimony you may quote.

Radio and Television Broadcasts

Lectures, discussions, and the formal public addresses of leaders in government, business, education, and religion are frequently broadcast over radio or television. Many of these talks are later printed by the stations or organizations that sponsor them. Usually, as in the case of CBS's *Meet the Press* or National Public Radio's *All Things Considered,* copies of broadcasts may be obtained for a small fee. Other broadcast content, such as national news broadcasts, is indexed by Vanderbilt University; your library may subscribe to that index, which is helpful in reconstructing a series of events. There are also computer databases that track media programs.

If manuscripts or transcripts are not available, you may take careful notes from videotaped or audiotaped programs. Be exact! Just as you must quote printed sources accurately and honestly, so, too, you are ethically obligated to give a person full credit for their radio and television remarks.

Obviously, you won't have to investigate all of these sources of materials for every speech you make. The key concept is relevance: go to the sources that will yield materials relevant to your topic. You are more likely to find historical statistics in print materials than in a television program or to find a viewpoint on a local problem in an interview than in a computer search. Think as you select sources of materials to investigate and then carry out the search carefully. If you do, you'll find the materials to make your speech authoritative and interesting.

Interviews

When looking for material, many of us forget the easiest and most logical way to start—by asking questions. The goal of an **informational interview** is to obtain answers to specific questions. In interviewing someone, you seek answers that can be woven into the text of your speech. Interviews increase your understanding of a topic so that you will avoid misinforming your audience, drawing incorrect inferences from information, and convoluting technical ideas. Your interviewee may be a content expert or someone who has had personal experience with the issues you wish to discuss. If you're addressing the topic of black holes, who is better qualified to help you than a physicist? If you're explaining the construction of a concrete boat, you might contact a local civil engineer for assistance. If you wish to discuss anorexia nervosa, you might interview a person who has suffered through the disorder. Interviews can provide compelling illustrations of human experiences. (See the box on p. 91).

Recording Information

When you find the information you've been looking for, you'll need a system for recording it. First, record the source citation completely. You'll need this information when you cite the source during your speech. Note the title of the book or article, author, and publication data including the place, publisher, and date of publication. Include the volume number if you're citing a journal article. It's helpful to record the call number or location of the source just in case you need to consult the information again.

Sometimes it's easiest to make photocopies of materials. However, if you take notes, you may find that notecards are more flexible than a notebook because they can be shuf-

Speaking of . . . skills

Conducting an Interview

You need to observe these general guidelines in planning an informational interview:

1. *Decide on your specific purpose.* What do you hope to learn from the interview? Can the person you are interviewing provide precise information from a unique perspective? Determine what you would like to glean from the interview and communicate that purpose directly to the person you plan to interview.

2. *Structure the interview in advance.* Plan your questions in advance so that you have a clear idea of *what* to ask *when.* The interview may not follow your list exactly, so you'll need to remain flexible and free to deviate from your interview plan to clarify or elaborate on a previous response. Begin the interview by setting limits on what will be covered during the session. End the interview by recapping the main ideas and expressing your appreciation.

3. *Remember that interviews are interactive processes.* Adept interviewers should be good listeners. You should listen carefully to what is said and accurately interpret the significance of those comments. There is a definite pattern of "turn-taking" in interviews that allows plenty of opportunity to clarify remarks and opinions.

4. *A good interviewer builds a sense of mutual respect and trust.* Feelings of trust and respect are created by revealing your own motivation, by getting the person to talk, and by expressing sympathy and understanding. Good communication skills and a well-thought-out set of questions build rapport in interview situations. You should always follow up the interview with a note or letter expressing your appreciation for the person's shared time and expertise.

fied by topic area or type of support. If you do use a notebook, try to record each item on half of each page. There are two reasons to do this: First, since most of your information won't fill a page, you will save paper. Second, cutting the sheets in half will make it easier to sort your data or to adopt a classification scheme and record information in accordance with particular themes or subpoints of your speech.

When recording information, place the appropriate subject headings at the top of your notecards and complete source citations at the bottom. This way, the notecards can be classified by general subject (top right heading) and by specific information presented (top left heading). (See Figure 6.1.)

Using Source Material Responsibly

Now that we've discussed locating and generating material for your speeches, we come to a major ethical issue—plagiarism. **Plagiarism** is defined as "the unacknowledged inclusion of someone else's words, ideas, or data as one's own."[1] One of the saddest things an instructor has to do is cite a student for plagiarism. In speech classes, students occasionally take material from a source they've read and present it as their own. Many speech teachers and members of audiences habitually scan the library periodicals section. Even if

FIGURE 6.1   A Sample Notecard

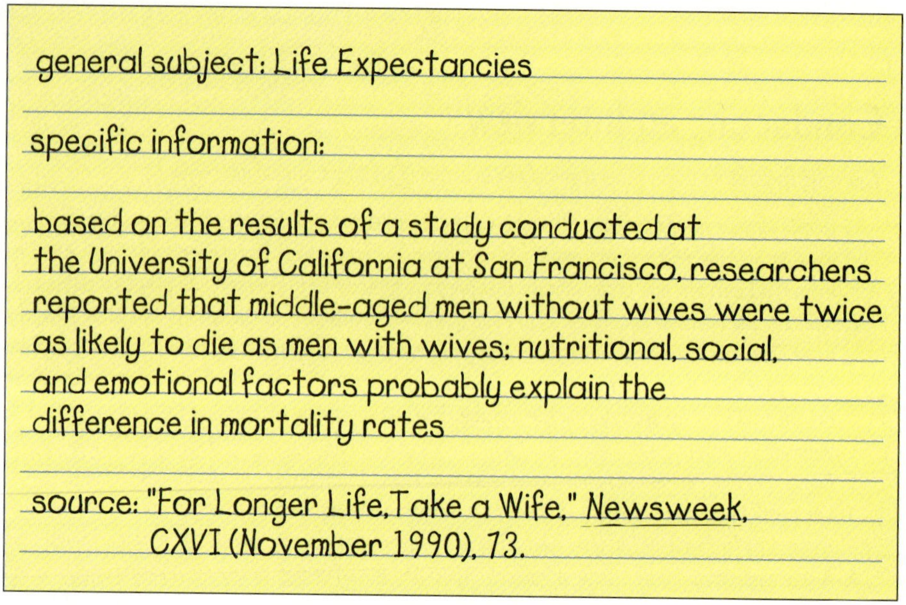

general subject: Life Expectancies

specific information:

based on the results of a study conducted at
the University of California at San Francisco, researchers
reported that middle-aged men without wives were twice
as likely to die as men with wives; nutritional, social,
and emotional factors probably explain the
difference in mortality rates

source: "For Longer Life, Take a Wife," Newsweek,
        CXVI (November 1990), 73.

You can use a notecard format like this to record information for later use.

listeners have not read the article, it soon becomes apparent that something is wrong: the wording differs from the way the person usually talks, the style is more typical of written than spoken English, or the speech is a patchwork of eloquent and awkward phrasing. In addition, the organizational pattern of the speech may lack a well-formulated introduction or conclusion or be one not normally used by speakers. Often, too, the person who plagiarizes an article reads it aloud badly—another sign that something is wrong.

Plagiarism is not, however, simply undocumented verbatim quotation. It also includes (a) undocumented paraphrases of others' ideas and (b) undocumented use of others' main ideas. For example, you are guilty of plagiarism if you paraphrase a movie review from *Newsweek* without acknowledging that staff critic David Ansen had those insights or if you use economic predictions without giving credit to *Business Week*.

Suppose you ran across the following idea while reading Neil Postman's *Amusing Ourselves to Death: Public Discourse in the Age of Show Business*[2]:

> *The television commercial is not at all about the character of products to be consumed. It is about the character of the consumers of products. Images of movie stars and famous athletes, of serene lakes and macho fishing trips, of elegant dinners and romantic interludes, of happy families packing their station wagons for a picnic in the country—these tell nothing about the products being sold. But they tell everything about the fears, fancies and dreams of those who might buy them. What the advertiser needs to know is not what is right about the product but what is wrong about the buyer. And so, the balance of business expenditures shifts from product research to market research. The television commercial has oriented business away from making*

Speaking of . . . ethics

What Is the Ethical Response?

1. You can't find exactly the right testimony from an expert to prove a point you want to make in a speech. Is it okay to make up a quote to use if you know it will result in a better grade on your speech?
2. Should you rip out a page from a magazine in the library if it contradicts something you plan to say in your speech? If the page is missing, nobody will know about the contradiction.
3. If you are a spokesperson for a company, is it okay to suppress facts about the side effects of a new fat free product? What if side effects aren't fatal and the product will let thousands of people lose weight?
4. If you can sell more life insurance when you exaggerate the death benefits, should you do it? What if your job depends on increasing your monthly sales? Is it okay to distort facts to keep your job?
5. Should you post a message on the Internet that you know isn't supported by facts? What if it's just a joke?
6. Should you deliberately conceal the source of a fact because you know it's not credible? What about attributing the fact to another, more credible source?

products of value and toward making consumers feel valuable, which means that the business of business has now become pseudo-therapy. The consumer is a patient assured by psycho-dramas.

Imagine that you wanted to make this point in a speech on the changing role of electronic advertising. Of course, you want to avoid plagiarism. Here are some ways you could use the ideas ethically:

1. *Verbatim quotation of a passage.* Simply read the passage aloud word for word. To avoid plagiarism, say, "Neil Postman, in his 1985 book *Amusing Ourselves to Death: Public Discourse in the Age of Show Business,* said this about the nature of television advertisements: [then quote the paragraph]."

2. *Paraphrasing of the main ideas:* Summarize the author's ideas in your own words: "We've all grown up with television advertising, and most of the time we endure it without giving it much thought. In his book *Amusing Ourselves to Death: Public Discourse in the Age of Show Business,* Neil Postman makes the point that instead of selling us on the virtues of a product, advertisers sell us our own fears and dreams. Advertisements are more about us than about the products being sold."

3. *Partial quotation of phrases:* Quote a brief passage and summarize the rest of the author's ideas in your own words: "Postman suggests that the shift from product research to market research indicates a shift in emphasis away from the product being sold and to the consumer. He says that business now focuses on making the consumer feel better through, quote 'pseudo-therapy. The consumer is a patient assured by psycho-dramas.'" Be sure to pause and say "quote" to indicate when you are quoting the author's words.

Plagiarism is easy to avoid if you take reasonable care. Moreover, by citing such authorities as Postman, who are well educated and experienced, you add their credibility to yours. Avoid plagiarism to keep from being expelled from the class or even from your school. Avoid it for positive reasons as well: to improve your ethos by associating your thinking with that of experts.

Assessing Your Progress

Chapter Summary

1. Your search for supporting materials should be purposeful; you should attempt to assemble materials relevant to your speeches, your audiences, and the occasions on which you're speaking.

2. To plan your search, you should consider: (a) the rational requirements of the topic, (b) the audience demands, (c) the power to prove generally associated with various kinds of supporting materials, and (d) the objectivity of your sources.

3. In executing your searches, you'll want to know how to conduct a computerized search and how to locate printed materials (newspapers, yearbooks and encyclopedias, documents and reports, books, and biographies) as well as radio and television broadcasts.

4. You can interview experts to obtain specific information.

5. You need to record information carefully and in a form you can use easily.

6. You must also remember to use source material ethically, avoiding plagiarism.

Key Terms

informational interview (p. 90)   primary sources (p. 85)

plagiarism (p. 91)   secondary sources (p. 85)

Assessment Activities

1. Select a major problem, incident, or celebration that has appeared in the news recently. Examine a story or article written about it in several of the following: the *New York Times, Christian Science Monitor, USA Today, Time, Newsweek, The New Republic,* and either the *Wall Street Journal* or *Business Week.* In a column from each source, note specifically what major facts, people, incidents, and examples or illustrations are included and what conclusions are drawn. Evaluate the differences among the sources you consulted. How are their differences related to their readership? What does this exercise teach you about the biases or viewpoints of sources?

2. Your instructor will divide your class into groups. Each group will locate a source for each topic on the list provided. Write down the page numbers where the material can be found. Compare your list with those of other groups. What sources did you discover? Did you miss any important sources of information?

Weekly summary of current national news

Brief sketch of the accomplishments of Margaret Chase Smith

Description of gene splicing

Text of John F. Kennedy's inaugural address

Daily summary of stock prices

Origin of the word *rhetoric*

Critical commentary on Allan Bloom's *The Closing of the American Mind*

Current status of national legislation on interstate transportation of horses for slaughter

3. Plan an interview of a celebrity or famous person. First, find out about the person by conducting a library search. Then, develop your interview questions. You might consider interviewing political leaders such as Margaret Thatcher, Ross Perot, or Nelson Mandela. Or, you could choose controversial social figures like Dr. Jack Kevorkian, Patricia Ireland, Madalyn Murray O'Hair, or Oliver North. What questions will you ask? Why? What is the best method for recording answers during the interview?

4. Consider the following sources for a speech on breast cancer. Which are primary and which are secondary sources? When would you use each?

   1. A summary of breast cancer research from 1983 to 1993 in an American medical journal.

   2. Your aunt's account of her mastectomy.

   3. A local newspaper article on the seven warning signs of cancer.

   4. A book titled *Surviving Cancer Surgery*.

   5. The meeting notes of a local cancer support group.

   6. A radio commentary on the importance of annual mammograms.

   7. A journal written by a cancer specialist who underwent breast cancer treatment.

   8. A U.S. government study evaluating the success of various treatments for breast cancer.

References

1. Louisiana State University, "Academic Honesty and Dishonesty," adapted from LSU's Code of Student Conduct, 1981.

2. Neil Postman, *Amusing Ourselves to Death: Public Discourse in the Age of Show Business* (New York: Viking Penguin, 1985), 128.

7 Using Supporting Materials

As you put your speeches together, you will need to consider the information you've assembled. The functions of supporting materials are to clarify, amplify, or justify the ideas that you're offering to your listeners. Just as a plant needs sun, water, and soil to bring it to life and sustain its growth, the ideas in a speech need supporting materials to thrive. If you're telling your classmates about local career opportunities, you'll need examples of those jobs and information about how to apply for them. If you're arguing that "The Olympic Games have become too commercialized," you must authoritatively define "commercialized" and provide statistical and illustrative materials to support your contention. If you don't provide such materials, you're wasting your time as well as that of your listeners.

Devoting careful thought to how you will use your supporting materials before you assemble your speech will pay off in efficient use of your preparation time, in confidence that your ideas are well supported, and in self-assurance when you approach the audience. This chapter seeks to provide some of the critical thinking skills you need to use supporting materials to earn audience acceptance of your ideas. First, we'll examine the functions and forms of supporting materials. Then, we'll suggest some ways of using these materials.

Functions of Supporting Materials

As you choose supporting materials for your speech, or as you listen to others speak, you should be conscious of how the supporting material clarifies, amplifies, and strengthens the ideas. Explanations, examples, and statistics are especially helpful in clarifying ideas. These materials allow you to present information that simplifies an idea for an audience, and they're useful when your listeners have little background or knowledge about the topic or when the subject matter is complex.

When your audience has only minimal knowledge of a concept, you should use explanations, comparisons, illustrations, and statistical magnitudes and trends to help you amplify the idea. These forms of support expand on it so that your audience can better examine the concept.

To strengthen or lend credibility to a point, you can use factual illustrations, specific instances, statistics, and testimony. These forms strengthen the idea by making it vivid and believable.

While there is no absolute rule about how each kind of supporting material functions, there is general agreement about what supporting materials accomplish in your speech. Here are some guidelines for choosing your supporting materials:

1. Complex and abstract ideas benefit from the use of specific information. Use examples (illustrations, narratives, or specific instances) to make complex or abstract ideas clearer. Compare the relationship of subatomic particles to balls on a billiard table, for instance. Specific examples (illustrations, narratives, or specific instances) provide more vivid details and make ideas more immediate. Because of this, they can stimulate your listeners' enthusiasm for complex or abstract material.

2. If your idea is controversial or if members of your audience are hostile, use supporting material such as statistics, explanations, and testimony. If you are trying to get management to accept a union, for example, you will certainly need credible supporting material. When there is disagreement among experts on the issue, you will need an abundance of supporting material.

3. Supporting materials can enhance your credibility as a speaker. While your listeners may question your ability to understand the complex nature of the federal budget deficit, they will respect authorities on the subject. They will also probably be reluctant to question supporting material such as statistical information. You should always use supporting materials when you are not an expert or when your status is lower than that of your listeners.

4. Supporting materials provide audience members with ammunition for later discussions. When you ask for a raise, you are more likely to get it by providing information about your job performance. Your supervisor can use this information in defending your raise to others. If you are asking your listeners to make sacrifices or to accept ideas that are unfamiliar to them, use plenty of supporting material. It provides the reassurance they need to take a risk and embrace a new thought.

5. Generally, examples create human interest, while statistics provide reasonable proof. Listeners tend to respond subjectively to narratives. On the other hand, their response to statistics is often more detached and objective. In a speech on street children in Brasilia, you would establish the significance of the problem by providing statistics. But, you would involve your listeners by telling them about the danger and hunger suffered by Emilio, who lives on the streets.

Forms of Supporting Materials

The supporting materials used to clarify, amplify, or justify your ideas can be divided into five categories: (1) *explanations,* (2) *comparisons and contrasts,* (3) *examples,* (4) *statistics,* and (5) *testimony* (see Figure 7.1).

FIGURE 7.1   The Forms of Supporting Materials

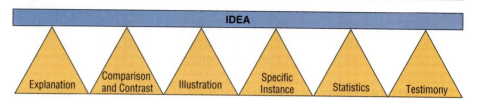

The supporting materials used to clarify, amplify, or justify your central ideas or claims are explanation, comparison and contrast, examples, statistics, and testimony. What should you consider as you choose supporting material?

Explanations

An **explanation** is a description that makes a term, concept, process, or proposal clear or acceptable. Explanations tell *what, how,* or *why,* and they are useful in showing the relationship between a whole and its parts. They also may give meaning to a difficult-to-envision concept.

Robert Lutz, president of Chrysler Corporation, wanted to explain inconsistencies in U.S. tariff rules and the unfair advantage they gave some Japanese auto exports to the United States. Here's the explanation he offered Cal-Berkeley students:

> *Let me tell you . . . the story of multipurpose vehicles, or "MPV's" for short. An MPV is a vehicle like, say, the Toyota 4-Runner sport utility. A funny thing happens to a 4-Runner when it's imported into this country. Four U.S. regulators all look it over. The fellow from the Environmental Protection Agency inspects and declares that it is "a truck," and will therefore only have to meet the emission standards for U.S. trucks, which are not as strict as those for cars. Behind him is the man from the National Highway Safety Administration, who certifies that it is indeed a truck so it won't have to have the same safety devices as a car. And then comes the inspector from the Department of Transportation, who also agrees that the vehicle is a truck so it won't have to meet the higher fuel economy requirements of a car. But then comes the fourth inspector. He's from the U.S. Customs Service. He looks at the 4-Runner and says, "Nope, this isn't a truck at all; it's a car!" And that means it pays a duty of only two-point-five percent instead of the 25 percent duty on trucks.*
>
> *Now what's going on here? Well, back in February of 1989, after intense lobbying by Japanese automakers, the U.S. Treasury Department, in a virtually unprecedented decision, overruled its own Customs Service and reclassified Japanese sport utilities and minivans from trucks to cars. It was, as President Clinton himself put it in a press conference last month, a "$300-million-dollar-a-year freebie to the Japanese for no apparent reason."[1]*

Notice the way this explanation works. Mr. Lutz sets up the four regulators, follows a Japanese MPV through them, offers the explanation, and then brings the audience up to date with a reference to President Clinton. He doesn't waste time with irrelevant details about the inspections, because he wants to keep our attention focused on the switch in definition.

Although explanations are good ways to clarify ideas, they shouldn't be too long or complicated and they shouldn't have to carry the weight of the argument. A much shorter, but still striking explanation is provided by Bessie Delany. Descendants of slave, Native American, and white settlers, Bessie explained why she and her sister Sadie lived long, productive lives in spite of racial discrimination: "When people ask me how we've lived past one hundred, I say, 'Honey, we never married. We never had husbands to worry us to death!'"[2]

Comparisons and Contrasts

Comparisons and contrasts are useful verbal devices for clarifying ideas—to make them distinctive and focused. Pointing out similarities and differences helps listeners comprehend your ideas and opinions.

Comparisons **Comparisons** connect something already known or believed with ideas a speaker wishes to have understood or accepted. Comparisons, therefore, stress similarities; they create analogies. During the darkest days of the Civil War, when critics attacked the administration's policies, Lincoln answered them by comparing the plight of the government with that of the famous tightrope walker, Blondin, attempting to cross Niagara Falls:

> *Gentlemen, I want you to suppose a case for a moment. Suppose that all the property you were worth was in gold, and you had put it in the hands of Blondin, the famous rope-walker, to carry across the Niagara Falls on a tightrope. Would you shake the rope while he was passing over it, or keep shouting to him, "Blondin, stoop a little more! Go a little faster!"? No, I am sure you would not. You would hold your breath as well as your tongue, and keep your hands off until he was safely over. Now the government is in the same situation. It is carrying an immense weight across a stormy ocean. Untold treasures are in its hands. It is doing the best it can. Don't badger it! Just keep still, and it will get you safely over.*

Contrasts **Contrasts** help to clarify complex situations and processes by focusing on differences. A speaker explaining arena football would want to contrast it with the more familiar rules governing interscholastic football. To clarify the severity of the 1996 Southwestern drought, the news networks contrasted average rainfall for normal summers with the current rainfall. Contrasts can be used not only to clarify unfamiliar or complex problems, but also to strengthen the arguments that you wish to advance. H. Ross Perot spoke at the Reform Party Nominating Convention in 1996. He used this contrast to show why private enterprise works better than government: "In business, you can promote people based on their performance. In politics, you get promoted based on your acting ability."[3]

Mr. Perot's contrast is startling, but serves as clear support for his central idea that a business leader should be the next president of the United States. Helping an audience reason along with you by visualizing differences is an excellent strategy for getting them to accept your ideas.

Comparisons and Contrasts Used in Combination You can use comparisons and contrasts together to double your audience's ability to see. For example, a student speaker focused on the messages in cartoons. To help his listeners understand how cartoons provide commentary, he compared and contrasted *Rocky and Bullwinkle* with *Beavis and Butthead*. He said:

Both cartoons have stirred up considerable public controversy. In the 1960s, some people boycotted Rocky and Bullwinkle *just as some refuse to watch* Beavis and Butthead *today. There are major differences, however.* Rocky and Bullwinkle *episodes pitted the pair against Boris and Natasha mimicking the Cold War conflict between the U.S. and the Soviet Union.* Beavis and Butthead, *on the other hand, avoid political commentary while focusing on the struggle of the main characters with adolescence.*

Whenever using comparisons and contrasts, try to make sure that at least one of the items is familiar to listeners. Comparing arena football and interscholastic football will make no sense to an Irish fan, who probably doesn't know anything about either one. You'd have to compare and contrast arena football and European soccer to clarify the arena game for her.

Examples

Examples can be powerful ways to involve an audience in your topic because they make abstract or general ideas easier to comprehend. If the example describes a concept, condition, or circumstance, it's called an **illustration;** if it's in story form, it's a **narrative.** A list of undeveloped illustrations are **specific instances.**

Some examples are hypothetical (made up) while others are factual—recitations of events that actually happened or persons, places, and things that actually exist. If you were giving a speech on why home-owners should move into apartments, you might narrate a "typical" home-owners' day: a leaky faucet to fix, a lawn to mow, real estate taxes to pay, and the neighbor's dog in the flower garden. Although not all of these occurred in the same day, asking listeners to imagine what life would be like if they *did* would help you to convey the care-free life of an apartment dweller.

Speaking of . . . *skills*

Choosing Supporting Materials

Recent research compared qualitative and quantitative supporting material. Qualitative supporting material includes examples, anecdotes, and analogies such as "a friend of mine was in a car crash and a seatbelt saved her." Quantitative supporting materials are statistical or numerical information such as "a recent investigation found the people are 50% more likely to be injured if they are not wearing a seatbelt."

The research found that both qualitative and quantitative supporting material are equally effective in changing attitudes initially. However, qualitative supporting materials worked much better over time. There are two reasons that qualitative supporting materials strengthen long-term attitude change:

1. Qualitative supporting materials are more vivid and the impact of vivid images is greater than that of numbers.
2. We can more easily remember qualitative supporting materials than numerical information.

See: Dean C. Kozoleas, "A Comparison of the Persuasive Effectiveness of Qualitative versus Quantitative Evidence," *Communication Quarterly,* 41 (1993): 40–50.

For many audiences, fact-based examples are more potent. President Ronald Reagan was famous for his reliance on homey little narratives. Hillary Rodham Clinton was equally successful using them in her travels around the country in search of a better health care system. Here's one of them:

> Dr. Rob Barrinson, one of the practicing physicians who spent hours and hours work-ing with us while also maintaining his practice, told us recently of an experience that he had as one of many. He admitted an emergency room patient named Jeff. Jeff suf-fered from cirrhosis of the liver. Dr. Barrinson put him in the hospital and within 24 hours received a call from Jeff's insurance company. The insurance company wanted to know exactly how many days Jeff would be in the hospital and why. Dr. Barrinson replied that he couldn't predict the precise length of stay. A few days later the insur-ance company called back and questioned whether Jeff would need surgery. Again, Dr. Barrinson said he wasn't yet sure.
>
> And what was Dr. Barrinson's reward for his honesty and his professionalism? He was placed on the insurance company's "special exemptions" list. You know, that's a list of troublesome doctors who make the insurance company wait a few days or a few weeks to determine the bottom line on a particular patient. From that point on, the insurance company called Dr. Barrinson six times in two weeks. Each time, he had to be summoned away from a patient to take the call. Each time, he spoke to a different insurance company representative. Each time, he repeated the same story. Each time, his role as the physician was subverted. And each time, the treatment of the patient was impeded.
>
> Dr. Barrinson and you know that medicine, the art of healing, doesn't work that way. There is no master checklist that can be administered by some faceless bureau-crat that can tell you what you need to do on an hourly basis to take care of your pa-tients; and, frankly, I wouldn't want to be one of your patients if there were."[4]

Specific instances are lists or groups of undeveloped illustrations or examples. Usu-ally, they are piled one on the other to drive the speaker's point home. They're undevel-oped because their power comes from cumulative effort rather than vivid detail. You can get away with using a single specific instance if all you need is a quick example, for in-stance: "You're all familiar with the windows in this classroom, but you might not have noticed their actual construction. I want to talk about those windows—those double-glazed, low-emissivity, gas-filled windows—and how the use of such windows con-tributes to reduced energy consumption on campus and in your life."

More often, though, speakers pile them up to help establish a point. In the famous passage in his declaration of war, Franklin Delano Roosevelt listed the nations attacked by the Japanese Imperial forces. More recently, Mary Fisher spoke at the Republican Na-tional Convention about AIDS. She said to the delegates: "[T]he AIDS virus is not a po-litical creature. It does not care whether you are Democrat or Republican, it does not ask whether you are Black or White, male or female, gay or straight, young or old."

She continued by adding details to the series of specific instances:

> Tonight, I represent an AIDS community whose members have been reluctantly drawn from every segment of American society. Though I am White, and a mother, I am one with a Black infant struggling with tubes in a Philadelphia hospital. Though I am female, and contracted this disease in marriage, and enjoy the warm support of

my family, I am one with the lonely gay man sheltering a flickering candle from the cold wind of his family's rejection.[5]

With these accumulated instances, Ms. Fisher demonstrated to her listeners the impact of the disease on all Americans.

Choosing Examples Three considerations should be kept in mind when selecting illustrations, narratives, and specific instances, whether hypothetical or factual:

1. Is the example clearly related to the idea it's intended to support? If the connection is difficult to show, it won't accomplish its goal. If your hypothetical story about a typical night in a dorm is more attractive than repellent for some listeners, you're in trouble!

2. Is it a fair example? An audience can be quick to notice unusual circumstances in an illustration or story; exceptional cases are seldom convincing. Having parachutists landing on your dorm roof in your story, for example, would stretch the credulity of your listeners.

3. Is it vivid and impressive in detail? Be sure your extended examples are pointed, fair, and visual.

Mrs. Clinton's narrative met all three of these criteria, especially the third one. She also was very good at drawing lessons or conclusions from her story.

Statistics

Statistics are numbers that show relationships between or among phenomena—relationships that can emphasize size or magnitude, describe subclasses or parts (segments), or establish trends. By reducing large masses of information into generalized categories, statistics clarify situations, substantiate potentially disputable central ideas, and make complex aspects of the world clear to your listeners.

Magnitudes We often use statistics to describe a situation or to sketch its scope or seriousness; that is, its size or **magnitude.** Especially if one statistical description of the size of a problem is piled up on others, the effect on listeners can be strong. Notice how the former U.S. Surgeon General Antonia Novello used multiple statistical descriptions of magnitude while urging citizens to think of violence as a community health problem:

> *Violence is a legitimate public health concern. It is your challenge—and mine. My friends, it is no small problem that: homicidal violence is now the leading cause of death among our youth; and that, in fact, every 14 hours a child younger than 5 is murdered. Firearms are now involved in one in every four deaths among 15- to 24-year-olds. And it is no small problem that domestic violence—along with child abuse and the abuse of the elderly—is found in every community and one-fourth of all American families; and up to six often married couples. Domestic violence today is the second most common cause of injury to women overall, and the leading cause of injuries to women ages 15 to 44. It is more common than automobile accidents, muggings, and rapes combined?[6]*

Not all uses of magnitudes, of course, need such piling up of instances. Simple, hard-hitting magnitudes sometimes work even better. For example, Brenda Theriault of the

Statistical-supporting material can be enhanced when it is represented visually. Your audience can see the relationships you are talking about.

University of Maine, arguing that there is "very little nutritional value in a hamburger, chocolate shake, and fries," simply noted that "of the 1,123 calories in this meal, there are 15 calories of carbohydrates, 35 calories of protein, and 1,073 calories of fat."[7] These were all the numbers the listeners needed in order to understand the nutrition in a typical fast-food meal.

Segments   Statistics also are used to isolate the parts of a problem or to show aspects of a problem caused by separate factors; parts or aspects can be treated as statistical **segments.** In discussing the sources of income for a college or university, for example, you'd probably segment the income by percentages coming from tuition and fees, state and federal money, gifts and contributions, special fees such as tickets, and miscellaneous sources. Then you'd be in a position to talk reasonably about next year's proposed tuition hike. A student speaker used survey results in this fashion to show how people shop on the World Wide Web:

In 1996, people spent a total of $518 million dollars on products and services they found via the Web. Computer products sales comprised 27% of this total and travel

Speaking of ... ethics

The Numbers Game

The rise of science in this century has been accompanied by the rise of numerical data—and its public exhibition. By now you've been told by one poll that the public favors a liberalization of abortion laws two-to-one but by another poll that the public favors tightening abortion laws by an equal percentage. You know that four out of five dentists surveyed recommend a particular brand of toothpaste. You've heard that a brand of cigarettes has the lowest level of tar and nicotine—from more than one manufacturer. As both listener and speaker, you have to make some ethical calls when encountering such data:

1. Contradictory polls such as the ones on abortion often result when questions are asked in slanted ways. "Do parents have to right to know when their underaged kids seek a dangerous abortion?" tends to encourage a positive answer, while "Ought women have the right to control their own bodies without external interference from others?" also encourages a positive answer—but one in favor of a very different public policy than the first. Questions can be loaded in favor of opposing public policies. You're wise to consider the actual questions when evaluating poll results.

2. Who were those "four out of five dentists surveyed"? Is it moral to cite statistics without reviewing how they were gathered and calculated?

3. If your favorite brand of cigarettes is one of five brands that all have the same low tar and nicotine content, technically, of course, yours has the lowest—and so do the other four brands. Is it moral, however, to claim your brand is "the lowest" or must you say that it is "one of the lowest"?

It's easy to fiddle with numbers: to round up or down, to compare only parts rather than wholes, to ignore key details that would properly contextualize information for listeners. It's easy, but if you play fast and loose with numbers, you might get caught. Learn to play the numbers game honestly so as to protect your reputation.

another 2.43%, making up over half of all Web sales. The remainder of the sales is divided almost equally among adult entertainment, general entertainment, food/drink, gifts/flowers, and apparel.[8]

As this example illustrates, the most important value of statistics doesn't lie in the numbers themselves but in how you interpret and use them. In using statistical data, always ask and answer the question, "What do these numbers mean or demonstrate?" In this case, it's clear that computer products and travel dominate Web site sales.

Trends Statistics often are used to point out **trends,** or indicators that tell us about the past, the present, and the future. The comparison of statistical data across time allows you to say that a particular phenomenon is increasing or decreasing (see Table 7.1). If you were arguing for stricter controls on chewing tobacco, you might cite U.S. Department of Agriculture statistics revealing that chewing tobacco use is up from 30 million pounds in 1981 to over 50 million pounds in 1991.[9] This upward trend suggests that something should be done to control smokeless tobacco. You could make your case even stronger by citing a corresponding upward trend in cancers of the lips, gums, and tongue.

TABLE 7.1 Types of Statistics

In a speech to inform, a speaker might use three types of statistics to describe students at Central University. What other forms of supporting material could complement these numbers?

Magnitudes	Segments	Trends
"Three fourths of all Central University students come from the state."	"Sixty percent of all Central University students major in business; 25 percent are humanities majors; the remaining 15 percent are in fine arts."	"Since 1975, enrollment at Central University has increased by 20 percent every five years."

An interesting use of a trend argument is found in testimony given to the U.S. House Subcommittee on Human Resources by Hortense Hunn, Executive Director of the California Preschool Services Department in San Bernardino County. She laid out what she considered to be a trend in spending on the Head Start program:

> There are numerous official fact sheets documenting Head Start's growth and development since its inception in 1965. I do not intend to reiterate the litany of glowing statistics which are readily available; suffice it to say that the National Head Start Program has grown from an "embryonic" program enrolling 561,000 children for about $96 million in the summer of 1965 to an "adolescent" program serving over 721,000 children and families for $1.7 billion in this year."[10]

Notice the cleverness with which Ms. Hunn framed her argument: she talked about "glowing statistics" in order to tell her audience to see them favorably; she used metaphors of maturation ("embryonic," "adolescent") to subtly project the need for further growth in Head Start (to "adulthood"); and she emphasized Head Start's direct service to children rather than its general family-services orientation, given that appeals to children usually are successful with listeners.

Using Statistics When you use statistics to indicate magnitude, to divide phenomena into segments, or to describe trends, help your listeners by softening the numbers:

1. *Translate difficult-to-comprehend numbers into more immediately understandable terms.* In a speech on the mounting problem of solid waste, Carl Hall illustrated the immensity of 130 million tons of garbage by explaining that trucks loaded with that amount would extend from coast to coast three abreast.[11]

2. *Don't be afraid to round off complicated numbers.* "Nearly 400,000" is easier for listeners to comprehend than "396,456"; "just over 33 percent" or, better yet, "approximately one third" is preferable to "33.4 percent."

3. *Use visual materials to clarify complicated statistical trends or summaries whenever possible.* Use a computer-generated graph; hand out a photocopied sheet of numbers; prepare a chart in advance. Such aids will allow you to concentrate on explaining the significance of the numbers rather than on making sure the audience hears and remembers them.

4. *Use statistics fairly.* Arguing that professional women's salaries increased 12.4 percent last year may sound impressive to listeners until they realize that women are still paid about a third less than men for equivalent work. In other words, provide fair contexts for your numerical data and comparisons.

Testimony

When you cite the opinions or conclusions of others, you're using **testimony.** Sometimes testimony merely adds weight or impressiveness to an idea, as when you quote Mahatma Gandhi or a clever turn of a phrase by your favorite author. At other times, it lends credibility to an assertion, especially when it comes from expert witnesses. When Janice Payan addressed the Adelante Mujer Conference, she used testimony in another way. She cited her favorite poem as a source of inspiration for her listeners. She urged them to seek success as she quoted the poet: "I wish someone has taught me long ago, How to touch mountains."[12]

Testimony should relate to the ideas you are discussing and should strengthen them. When you choose quotations to use in your speech, they should accomplish more than simply amplifying or illustrating an idea. Testimony also should satisfy four more specific criteria:

1. The person quoted should be qualified, by training and experience, to speak on the topic being discussed. Athletes are more credible talking about sports equipment or exercise programs than they are endorsing breakfast food or local furniture stores.

2. Whenever possible, the authority's statement should be based on firsthand knowledge. A Florida farmer is not an authority on an Idaho drought unless or he or she has personally observed the conditions.

3. The judgment expressed shouldn't be unduly influenced by personal interest. Asking a political opponent to comment on the current president's performance will likely yield a self-interested answer.

4. The listeners should perceive the person quoted to be an actual authority. An archbishop may be accepted as an authority by a Roman Catholic audience but perhaps not by Protestant or Hindu listeners. When citing testimony, don't use big names simply because they're well known. The best testimony comes from subject-matter experts whose qualifications your listeners recognize.

Finally, always acknowledge the source of an idea or particular phrasing. Avoid **plagiarism**—claiming someone else's ideas, information, or phraseology as your own. Plagiarism is stealing. Give your source credit for the material, and give yourself credit for having taken the time to do the research. (See "Using Source Material Responsibly" in Chapter 6.)

Critical Thinking and the Use of Supporting Materials

Most of us, with some effort, can gather supporting materials. The hard part is using those materials well. The effective use of supporting materials is an exercise in **critical thinking**—assessing the reasonableness of the connections between your assertions and your supporting materials. As you prepare your speech, or when you listen to the speeches of others, you should practice critical thinking. You can start by asking yourself questions such as:

TABLE 7.2   Checklist for Supporting Materials

You should evaluate your supporting materials when you plan your speeches. Answer the questions on this checklist as you plan your supporting materials.

General Considerations

_____ 1. Have I included sufficient supporting material?
_____ 2. Are my supporting materials distributed throughout my speech?
_____ 3. Do I provide extra support for confusing or controversial ideas?
_____ 4. Are my supporting materials interesting and clear?
_____ 5. Do I adequately credit the sources of my supporting materials?

Explanations

_____ 1. Are my explanations short and direct?
_____ 2. Do I provide other forms of support in addition to explanations?

Comparisons and Contrasts

_____ 1. Is at least one of the items in a comparison or contrast familiar to my listeners?
_____ 2. Is the basis of the comparison clear?
_____ 3. Is the contrast distinct enough?

Examples

_____ 1. Is the illustration or narrative clearly related to the idea it's intended to support?
_____ 2. Is the illustration or narrative typical?
_____ 3. Is the illustration or narrative vivid and adequately detailed?
_____ 4. Have I provided enough specific instances?
_____ 5. Can listeners easily recognize or understand the instances I mention?

Statistics

_____ 1. Are my statistics easy to understand?
_____ 2. Have I rounded off complicated numbers?
_____ 3. Am I using statistics fairly?
_____ 4. Should I use visual materials to clarify complicated numbers?
_____ 5. Have I adequately interpreted the statistics I've cited for my listeners?

Testimony

_____ 1. Is the authority qualified to speak on the topic being discussed?
_____ 2. Is the authority's statement based on firsthand knowledge?
_____ 3. Is the authority's opinion subject to personal influence or bias?
_____ 4. Do my listeners know the authority's qualifications?
_____ 5. Will my listeners accept this person as an authority?

1. Is the speaker providing supporting material or is the idea simply asserted? An **assertion** is a statement made without corroborating support. For example, you could assert that "Americans are now more dependent than ever before on foreign sources of oil." A careful listener, however, will want to know why you made this statement. Do you have statistics to show a trend of increasing dependence on foreign oil? Did an expert reach this conclusion?

2. Is a qualified source of the supporting material cited? Some speakers will provide statistics and examples but fail to tell you whether they obtained those facts from a reliable source. Listen for sources. A speaker who lists *Webster's Dictionary* as the source of a definition of *habeas corpus* probably hasn't done enough research. *Black's Law Dictionary* is a more credible source.

3. Is the supporting material offered adequate? Has the speaker offered enough support for main ideas? Perhaps the speaker has found an isolated fact or statistic or opinion. Demand more than a single piece of supporting material, especially if the ideas are controversial or unusual. Scientists arguing for the existence of life on Mars provide analyses of mineral data and high-tech photography to reveal micro-fossils of once-living organisms on meteorites. However, until additional supporting material is available, some skeptics aren't convinced that life once existed on Earth's next-door neighbor.

4. Is the supporting material varied? Strong use of supporting material includes variety. While you may find an article that says everything you want, you shouldn't stop there. Find more support for your ideas. In your speech, you will want to cite a variety of evidence such as testimony, examples, and statistics. Active listeners will concentrate on the kinds of supporting material you use. So, ask yourself if you are offering enough varied supporting material for reasonable acceptance of your ideas.

5. Does the material cited support the speaker's ideas? Sometimes we get so caught up in a narrative that we forget to consider the point of it. Or, a rush of statistics will leave us gasping. Don't forget to question the link between the statistics and the ideas of the speech. For example, a speaker who cites a 10 percent increase in Ford truck sales and concludes that the auto industry is healthy, may be gravely mistaken. Ford truck sales are only one segment of a much larger industry.

By asking yourself if the supporting materials are present, well qualified, adequate, varied, and relevant, you'll be thinking critically about ideas rather than just blindly accepting them. As a speaker, you should ask these questions as you prepare your speech. As a listener, you should concentrate on how the speaker is using supporting materials. Test supporting materials to be sure that they contribute to the development of ideas. The two outlines that follow illustrate how supporting materials can be used.

Sample Outline for an Informative Speech

In the outline, note how the speaker has combined verbal and visual material to establish and develop the central idea. In this speech, the supporting material is used to amplify the idea.

The speaker establishes the comparison, an analogy, immediately upon starting the speech.

How We Breathe

I. The human breathing mechanism may be likened to a bellows, which expands to admit air and contracts to expel it.

  A. When we inhale, two things happen.

    1. Muscles attached to the collarbone and shoulder bones pull upward and slightly outward.

    2. Muscles in the abdominal wall relax, allowing the diaphragm—a sheet of muscle and tendon lying immediately below the lungs—to fall.

  B. This permits the spongy, porous lungs to expand.

    1. A vacuum is created.

    2. Air rushes in.

  C. When we exhale, two things happen.

    1. Gravity causes the rib cage to move downward.

    2. Muscles in the abdominal wall contract, squeezing the diaphragm upward.

  D. The space available to the lungs is thus reduced.

    1. The lungs are squeezed.

    2. Air is emitted.

  E. The similarity between the breathing mechanism and a bellows is represented in this diagram:

    [Show "How We Breathe" diagram.]

II. In summary, then, to remember how the human breathing mechanism works, think of a bellows.

  A. Just as increasing the size of the bellows bag allows air to rush in, so increasing the space available to the lungs allows them to admit air.

  B. Just as squeezing the bellows bag forces air out, so contracting the space the lungs can occupy forces air to be emitted.

The speaker might point to parts of the body as they're mentioned—collarbone, shoulder bones, abdominal wall, diaphragm.

An explanation reveals the function of the muscles.

Demonstrative movements also would be appreciated by the audience: a lifting of the shoulders and chest cavity when talking about inhalation, a dropping of the rib cage and abdominal wall when describing exhalation.

The summary compares a bellows to how the lungs work.

Sample Outline for a Problem-Solution Speech

Study the following outline. Notice that a variety of supporting materials are used to strengthen each of the points in the speech. Although the proof of a single point may not require as many different supporting materials as are used in this outline, the variety of support shows how a number of different forms can be combined in a speech.

The Heartbreak of Childhood Obesity

I. Childhood obesity is an increasing problem in our society.

  A. Michelle is a typical American child—15% overweight.

  B. U.S. Department of Health and Human Services survey reveals a 54% increase in childhood obesity between 1963 and 1993.

This speech starts with an illustration and trend statistics.

C. The prediction for the future is even more bleak.

D. After defining the nature of obesity, let's examine the causes of obesity in children, and investigate some solutions we can implement.

II. Obesity is defined as a positive energy balance.

A. This means that more energy is conserved than expended.

B. Over time, the excess energy is stored by the body in fat cells.

C. Approximately every 2500 extra calories become an extra pound of body weight.

III. There are three primary causes for childhood obesity.

A. Some children inherit the tendency to acquire extra weight.

1. Parents who are obese tend to have children who are also obese.

2. Experiments with mice have located genetic triggers for overeating.

3. The genetic predisposition to gain extra weight is a contributing factor in childhood obesity, according to experts.

B. Eating style also contributes to obesity.

1. Dr. Daniel A. Kirschenbaum, who specializes in childhood obesity, reports that obese children typically show a "high-density" eating style.

2. A "high-density" eating style refers to both the quantity and frequency of eating among children.

3. High-density eating is a behavior that contributes to obesity.

4. Emotional stress may trigger high-density eating style.

C. Television viewing is also a culprit among obese children.

1. Dr. Steven Gortmaker of Harvard University says that many children watch over 30 hours of television weekly.

2. Inactivity, including television watching, result in a positive energy balance and, over time, leads to obesity.

3. In addition, Dr. William Dietz of Tufts University, notes that children are influenced by television commercials for food high in sugar and fat.

IV. You can control weight gain in children with four steps.

A. Don't assume the child will grow out of it.

1. If your family has a history of weight problems, be alert for them in children.

2. Four out of five children can be helped if the problem is dealt with immediately.

3. Dealing with weight gain immediately will prevent psychological and medical problems later.

B. Monitor mealtimes.

1. To limit high-density eating style, do not permit between-meal snacks.

An explanation clarifies what is meant by obesity.

The problem of obesity is developed as a three-part explanation.

To develop the problem, the speaker provides a comparison with lab mice, testimony of Dr. Kirschenbaum and Dr. Dietz, an explanation of high-density eating style, magnitude statistics.

In the solution section, the speaker uses magnitude statistics, explanations, testimony, segment statistics, and examples.

2. Teaching children to consume food at a slower pace, according to Dr. William Johnson and Dr. Pater Stalonas, is also helpful.

3. It is easier on the child if the entire family switches to a low-fat diet.

C. Substitute other activities for television viewing.

1. Over 50% of obesity problems in children could be controlled more effectively if parents simply turned off the television set.

2. Encourage activity in the child.

a. Enroll the child in athletic activities like swimming or soccer.

b. Encourage walking to and from school; just a half hour of walking per day can correct a positive energy balance.

D. Join a support group for the parents of obese children.

1. Contact the World Service Office of Overeaters Anonymous.

2. Speak to a representative of our local community service organization.

V. Now that you understand the causes of childhood obesity and some of the solutions, it's time to act.

A. Think about the consequences if you don't act now.

1. Obesity in childhood predisposes a person to a lifetime of medical and psychological trouble.

2. Obesity contributes to 90% of the cases of Type II diabetes in later life; over half of the cases of cardiovascular disease; and immeasurable emotional distress.

B. According to Pam Webber of Overeaters Anonymous: "It's better to risk hurting a child's feelings today, than let them live a lifetime of unhappiness."

C. Remember Michelle? If her parents begin now, they can spare Michelle the bleak future faced by too many of our overweight American children.

The conclusion to the speech offers segment statistics and testimony, plus a reference to the introductory illustration.

Assessing Your Progress

Chapter Summary

1. Supporting materials clarify, amplify, or justify the speaker's ideas.

2. Explanations are descriptions that make a term, concept, process, or proposal clear or acceptable.

3. Comparisons and contrasts point out similarities and differences between things that are familiar and things that are not.

4. Examples are illustrations, narratives, or specific instances that provide specific details about ideas or statements you want listeners to accept.

5. Illustrations are detailed examples; narratives take story form; and specific instances are clusters of undeveloped examples. Some are hypothetical (fictional), and some are factual ("real").

6. Statistics are numbers that show relationships between or among phenomena. Some emphasize size or magnitude; some describe subclasses or segments; and some establish trends, or the directions in which matters are heading over time.

7. Testimony is made up of the opinions or conclusions of credible persons.

8. To effectively use forms of support, you must learn critical thinking skills to: (a) identify assertions; (b) listen for reliable sources; (c) demand adequate support for ideas; (d) offer varied supporting materials; and, (e) understand the relevance of supporting materials to ideas.

Key Terms

assertion (p. 107)

comparisons (p. 99)

contrasts (p. 99)

critical thinking (p. 106)

explanations (p. 98)

illustration (p. 100)

magnitudes (p. 102)

narrative (p. 100)

plagiarism (p. 106)

segments (p. 103)

specific instances (p. 100)

statistics (p. 102)

testimony (p. 106)

trends (p. 104)

Assessment Activities

1. Read one of the speeches in this textbook. Identify its forms of supporting material. How effective are those materials in supporting the central idea of the speech? How well do supporting materials seem to be adapted to the immediate audience? How might the speaker have improved his or her use of supporting material?

2. Write down a single point or one idea. Then, amplify it with an explanation, a comparison/contrast, an example, statistics, and testimony. Share your example with your classmates. Evaluate the effectiveness of each form of supporting material. Which support is most involving for listeners? Which is most convincing? Which establishes the scope of the idea?

3. Prepare an outline for a short speech proving a point. State the central idea; support it with statistical materials, a comparison/contrast, and an illustration; then restate the claim in other words. Submit the outline to your instructor for evaluation. You may be asked to deliver the speech later.

References

1.   Robert Lutz, "Managed Trade: Spring of Hope or Nuclear Winter?" *Vital Speeches of the Day, 59* (1 July 1993): 554.

2.   Sarah and A. Elizabeth Delany with Amy Hill Hearth, *Having Our Say: The Delany Sisters' First 100 Years* (New York: Kodansha International, 1993).

3. H. Ross Perot, CNN Coverage of the Reform Party Nominating Convention, Long Beach, Calif. (August 11, 1996).

4. Hillary Rodham Clinton, "Health Care—We Can Make a Difference," *Vital Speeches of the Day, 59* (15 July 1993): 583.

5. Mary Fisher, "A Whisper of AIDS," reprinted in *Women's Voices in Our Time,* edited by Victoria L. DeFrancisco and Marvin D. Jensen (Prospect Heights, Ill: Waveland Press, 1994).

6. Antonia Novello, "Your Parents, Your Community—Without Caring There Is No Hope," *Vital Speeches of the Day, 59* (15 July 1993): 591.

7. Brenda Theriault, "Fast Foods," speech given at the University of Maine, spring 1992.

8. John Simons, "The Web's Dirty Secret," *U.S. News & World Report* 121 (19 August 1996): 51.

9. Claire Smith, "Working to Strike Out Smokeless Tobacco," *The New York Times* (13 May 1996): B7.

10. Hortense Hunn, "Testimony Before House Subcommittee on Human Resources," 8 April 1993. *Oversight Hearing Regarding the Head Start Program,* House of Representatives Hearing, 103rd Congress (Washington, D.C.: U.S. Government Printing Office, 1993), 88.

11. Carl Hall, "A Heap of Trouble," *Winning Orations, 1977.*

12. Janice Payan, "Opportunities for Hispanic Women: It's Up to Us," *Vital Speeches of the Day, 56* (1 September 1990): 591.

8 Organizing and Outlining Your Speech

Think of the last shopping trip you made for groceries. How did you do it? Did you wander aimlessly around the store looking for something that you might need? If you shop this way, you probably get home and discover that you forgot something important. Giving a speech is somewhat like a shopping trip. If you don't plan and organize it, you're undoubtedly going to leave out something important. Like an efficient shopper, you can organize your speaking so that both you and your listener get the most out of it. We'll discuss how to choose the pattern of organization and outline your speech. Let's begin with developing a speech plan.

Developing Your Speech Plan

Approaching your speech in a organized manner is important for several reasons. Just as you waste time wandering around a store if you don't have a shopping list, you appear to be less efficient if you give a disorganized speech. The result can be chaotic. There are five reasons to organize your speeches. First, your listeners don't learn as much because there is no obvious pattern for organizing the new material you present. You can't expect them to organize it first and then learn it. So good organization leads to better comprehension.

In addition, an organized speech is easier for you to present. The ideas fit together more logically and even if you forgot a phrase or two, the speech will still flow naturally because the ideas hold it together. Third, you will appear more credible when you give an organized speech. Your listeners will trust that you have prepared well and will be more likely to believe what you say.

There is also some evidence to suggest that well-organized speeches add to their persuasiveness. You can see why—if listeners trust your preparation and don't have to strain to understand the message, they are more likely to be impressed by your message. Finally, good organization lowers the frustration level for everyone—you and your listeners. This is reason enough to practice developing clear and effective organization in your speaking.

Developing Your Central Idea

The first step in planning your organization begins when you choose your central idea. Wording a central idea is essential to the planning of your speech because it determines the way you develop the whole talk—your main points, the information you include, the organization you'll present, and the ways you'll link your points.

Phrasing a central idea is especially critical, because the words you select limit the scope of your speech and control your relationship with your audience. For example, each of the following central ideas expresses a different focus and relationship with listeners:

1. "You can conserve energy by recycling aluminum cans, walking to classes, and using lower-wattage light bulbs at home."

2. "The development of the computer chip began twenty years ago and continues today."

3. "If our city builds a new parking garage, it will dangerously strain city finances."

These three central ideas establish very different parameters for developing a speech. The first offers three tangible actions a listener can take to save energy. The scope of the speech is limited to practical solutions. It also establishes listener involvement and responsibility in implementing the solution. The second topic, on the other hand, suggests a historical perspective that less directly involves the audience. Finally, the speaker who proposes the third topic is preparing to develop an argument.

In each case, the phrasing of the central idea determines the main features of the speech. This, in turn, should help you determine which organizational pattern is best for your speech.

Choosing Your Organizational Plan

To help you further, here are some clear general guidelines for organizing your speech. After you have identified your central idea, ask these questions to determine what you're looking for in an organizational pattern.

1. *Is the plan of my speech easy for my listeners to recognize?* You can eliminate frustration among your listeners if you give them a clear and simple plan to follow. Their attention can be riveted on you and your ideas rather than on puzzling out the direction of your speech. The result should be successful for both you and your listeners because they can remember clear ideas longer.

2. *Does my organizational pattern provide for adequate coverage of the material?* You must use a pattern that will complement your ideas and their supporting materials—one that will clarify your central idea. Phrasing your central idea will help you determine what you should include in your speech. This, in turn, will save time as you undertake your research.

3. *What structure is best adapted to my audience's needs?* Keep your audience in mind—what they know, expect, and need. If your listeners have never heard of

bioremediation, then you need to develop your speech on this topic in a very different way than if they are environmental scientists. You can't ignore your listeners' need to process information efficiently. That means beginning with what they already know.

4. *How can I make the speech move steadily forward toward a satisfying finish?* Listeners became increasingly frustrated when speeches don't seem to be developing. They need a sense of forward motion—of moving through a series of main points toward a clear destination. Backtracking slows down the momentum of the speech, giving it a stop-and-start progression rather than a smooth forward flow. You'll also enhance the sense of forward motion with internal summaries and forecasts, as well as transitions and physical movement to indicate progression.

Once you've planned your central idea and answered basic questions about the plan of your speech, you're ready to choose the type of arrangement.

Types of Organization

As we use the term here, **organization** is the order or sequence of ideas in a pattern that suggests their relationship to each other. There are four general categories of organization for speeches that arise from the demands of the topic: chronological, spatial, causal, and topical. We will add special audience-centered patterns later.

Chronological Patterns

Chronological patterns trace the order of events in a time sequence. This arrangement of ideas is useful when your goal is to give listeners a strong sense of development or motion. When using a chronological sequence, you begin at a point in time and move forward or backward to some concluding point. Where you start and end will depend on the central idea you're working with. For example, you might describe how to prepare an elegant cinnamon pear tart beginning with preparation of the crust and ending with baking instructions. The results wouldn't be the same if you presented the instructions in another order.

Suppose you wanted to trace the evolution of modern flight either from the Wright brothers or from Russia's launching of *Sputnik* in 1957. The beginning of the chronology depends on your goal. Are you trying to tell the whole story of aviation or the more specific story of space flight? Similarly, suppose you wanted to argue that children acquire language much earlier than previously thought. You would need to begin tracing language acquisition even before the child's first vocalizations.

Spatial Patterns

In the **spatial pattern,** the major points of the speech are organized in terms of their location, that is, their physical proximity to or direction from each other. A speech on the movement of weather systems from the north and south across the United States would fit such a pattern. If you conduct a tour of your campus or describe the states in the Russian confederation or the constellations in the Southern hemisphere, you would probably use a spatial pattern. Consider another example:

I. Volcanoes are one of the natural forces constantly at work changing the face of the earth.

II. The sheer power and beauty of nature evident in volcanoes should motivate you to see them. Suppose you wanted to take trip to view volcanoes:

    A. Start at Mt. St. Helens in the state of Washington (1991 eruption).

    B. Journey to the Aleutian Islands off the Alaskan coast to Mt. Akutan (1990 eruption).

    C. Cross the Pacific to Japan to Mt. Asama (1991 eruption).

    D. Drop down to Sumatra to find Mt. Kerinci (1987 eruption).

    E. Head west to Zaire in Africa to Mt. Nyamuragira (1988 eruption).

    F. Then to Italy's Etna (1990 eruption), Iceland's Hekla (1991 eruption), and home again.

III. Even if the whole trip's expensive, a visit to any of these active volcanoes could be the trip of a lifetime.[1]

Causal Patterns

Causal patterns of speech organization move either: (a) from an analysis of present causes to a prediction of future effects or (b) from present conditions to their apparent causes. Causal patterns give listeners a sense of physical coherence because ideas are developed in relationship to each other. Causal patterns assume that one event results from or causes another. When using a *cause-effect pattern,* you might first point to the increasing cost of attending college, and then argue that one of its effects is reduced enrollments. Or, using an *effect-cause pattern,* you could note that the estimated one percent decrease in college enrollments in 1992 was the result, at least in part, of the increasing costs. Compare the following two outlines:

I. Colleges and universities across the United States are raising tuition.

II. The effect of these tuition increases is to limit enrollments.

    A. Middle-income students are squeezed by tuition increases.

    B. Financially disadvantaged students often must drop out.

    C. Eventually, only the rich will be able to attend colleges and universities.

I. We can make higher education available to all capable students, if we provide financial assistance.

II. Financial assistance will enable many middle-income and financially disadvantaged students to attend colleges and universities.

    A. One primary source of funding is federal assistance in the form of student loans and grants.

    B. A second source of financial help is tax relief for the families of college and university students.

Notice that the first outline uses a cause-effect pattern; the second uses an effect-cause pattern. Adapt your speech to the situation by beginning with ideas that are better known to audience members; then proceed to the lesser-known facets of the problem. Use cause-effect if listeners are better acquainted with the cause; use effect-cause if the opposite is true.

Topical Patterns

Some speeches on familiar topics are best organized in terms of subject-matter divisions that have become standardized. Sports strategy is divided into offense and defense; kinds of courts into municipal, county, state, and federal jurisdictions; and types of trees into deciduous and evergreen categories. **Topical patterns** are most useful for speeches that list aspects of persons, places, things, or processes. Occasionally, a speaker tries to list all aspects of the topic. More often, however, a partial listing of the primary or most interesting aspects is sufficient. For example, suppose you wanted to give a speech to a general audience about stress. The following outline shows how you could organize the speech topically:

I. Symptoms of stress

II. Types of stress inducers

    A. Physical stress

    B. Emotional stress

III. Methods of stress reduction

    A. Relaxation techniques

    B. Meditation

    C. Exercise

Topical patterns are among the most popular and easiest to use. If you plan to list only certain aspects of the topic, take care to explain your choices. So, if someone asks, "Why didn't you talk about biofeedback as a means of reducing stress?" you could answer, "I focused on the three most common approaches to stress reduction and I wanted to present simple techniques that everyone could apply immediately."

The types of speech organization discussed so far—narrative, spatial, causal, and topical—are determined principally by the subject matter. While the audience is not ignored by the organizational pattern, it's the subject that usually suggests the pattern of organization.

Audience-Centered Patterns of Organization

At times, audience-oriented patterns of organization will more effectively arrange your material. These special patterns often work well because they're based on the listeners' needs. You should probably ask several questions to determine if an audience-oriented pattern of organization will work for you: (a) Can I introduce a new idea by comparing it to something my listeners already know? (b) How would a person approach this idea for the first time? (c) What are common, recurring questions about this topic? (d) Am I presenting a solution to a problem? or, (e) Can I eliminate all but one alternative solution to a question or problem? If you've answered "yes" to any of these questions, you might consider organizing your speech based on your listener's needs.

We'll examine five special patterns of organization: familiarity-acceptance order, inquiry order, question-answer order, problem-solution order, and elimination order.

Familiarity-Acceptance Order

Familiarity-acceptance order begins with what the audience knows or believes (the familiar) and moves on to new or challenging ideas (the unfamiliar). In an informative speech on quarks, you can begin with what the audience already knows about molecules and then introduce the new information on the subatomic particles called *quarks.*

Persuasive speeches based on accepted audience values are very well suited to skeptical or hostile audiences, especially when your reasoning is valid and your conclusions sound. When you meet these standards, your audience can't reject your claim without denying the underlying facts or values that they already accept.

Here are the main points from a persuasive speech outline using familiarity-acceptance order:

I. How many of us here are married or plan on getting married sometime in the future?

II. Marriage is an important social institution because it publicly expresses the love and commitment of two people for each other.

III. Homosexual marriages should be allowed.

    A. Public recognition would discourage discrimination and violence directed toward homosexuals.

    B. Homosexuals would be allowed to participate in employee benefit plans now reserved for heterosexual married partners.

    C. Legal sanctions involving spouses such as property inheritance and hospital visitation would become inclusive.

Even if you don't agree with the conclusions of this speaker, it is more difficult to reject the central idea of the speech because the speaker began with something you probably accept and then moved to the more controversial part of the speech.

Inquiry Order

Inquiry order provides a step-by-step explanation of how you acquired the information or reached the conclusion. Scientists carefully describe their research procedures in order to demonstrate the reliability of their findings. Similarly, if you want to persuade your neighbors to plant a new variety of oak tree, you could recount how you studied the varieties that seemed to be dying in your neighborhood, investigated possible choices, and searched for new varieties until the kind you now advocate emerged as the best.

Inquiry order has a double advantage. First, it displays all facts and possibilities for the audience. Second, it enables listeners to judge for themselves the worth of the information or policy being presented as it unfolds.

Question-Answer Order

Question-answer order raises and answers listeners' questions. First, you must determine which questions are most likely to arise in your listeners' minds. Then you need to develop your speech to answer each key question in a way that favors your conclusion. For example, when you buy a new car, you want to know about its principal features, the available options, its mileage, and its cost. When first learning about a new bond issue, listeners wonder how it will affect their taxes or government services. By structuring your speech to address these questions, you can maintain audience interest and involvement.

Problem-Solution Order

When you advocate changes in action or thought, your main points may fall naturally into a **problem-solution order.** First, you establish the existence of the problem. If your listeners are already aware of the problem, you can remind them of the primary issues. For example, if your listeners walk or ride bicycles to classes, they'll be unaware that there aren't enough parking spaces on campus; but if they drive automobiles, they'll be quite familiar with the parking shortage. You also need to depict the problem in a way that will help your listeners perceive it in the same way that you do. For example, your listeners may tolerate the parking shortage as a simple inconvenience of college life. You will need to show them that there is no reason to accept a parking shortage.

Once you've established that a problem exists, you must propose a solution to it. Your solution should be workable and practical. It would be silly to suggest that a multi-million-dollar parking complex be built if financing isn't available or if the parking complex still wouldn't accommodate enough automobiles. However, a car-pooling or busing system would be less expensive and limit the number of cars on campus.

Elimination Order

When your cassette player doesn't work, you probably systematically search for what's wrong: Are the batteries fresh? Is the pause switch off? Does the pickup spool turn? Is the tape box jammed? Just so, with **elimination order,** you first survey all the available solutions and courses of action that can reasonably be pursued. Then, proceeding systematically, you eliminate each of the possibilities until only one remains.

Elimination order is well suited to persuasive speeches. If you want student government to bring a special performer to campus, you might show that all other suggested entertainers are booked up, too expensive, or lack widespread appeal. In this way, you lead the members of student government to agree with the choice you advocate.

To use elimination order effectively, you first must make an inclusive survey of options. If you overlook obvious choices, your listeners won't be convinced by your analysis. Second, you must make the options mutually exclusive; otherwise, your listeners may choose more than one. Consider this example in which the speaker makes only one alternative seem the best:

I. Three options have been proposed.
  A. Jeep Grand Cherokee
  B. Ford Explorer
  C. Isuzu Trooper
II. The first two options should be eliminated.
  A. The Jeep Grand Cherokee is so popular that you get less for your money than you do with the others.
  B. The Ford Explorer is the newest of the three, and, feature for feature, the most expensive.

III. The Trooper is therefore the best way to go.
  A. It has the same features as the others for less money.
  B. It's been around long enough to have a solid history of customer care and good repair.

Of course, the elimination order works best if listeners agree with the criteria you've suggested for judgment. If cost is no object, the Grand Cherokee or Explorer still will be considered. Or, someone might object that while the Explorer is a comparatively new model, Ford Motor Company has a long history in the United States. Study your listeners to make sure the criteria for elimination are acceptable to them.

Outlining Your Speech

Once you have determined the type of organization you will use to arrange your ideas, you should record them in an outline. Outlining is an important tool for a speaker for two reasons:

1. *Testing.* An outline allows you to see your ideas. When you outline a speech, you can discover what ideas you've overemphasized to the exclusion or underdevelopment of others. Your outline is a testing device.

2. *Guiding.* When you're actually delivering a speech, an outline is the preferred form of notes for many, perhaps even most, speakers. A good speaking outline shows you where you've been, where you are, and where you want to get before you sit down. You even can include in your outline special speaking directions to yourself ("show map here"; "emphasize this idea").

To profit from both the testing and guiding aspects of outlines, you must learn to build complete, solid structures. Two types of outlines are most helpful for speakers. You can benefit from a rough outline as you plan your speech. And you need to develop an outline to help you present your speech. So, we'll discuss some strategies for developing the rough outline (a testing device) and a speaking outline (a guiding device).

Types of Outlines

You should develop your outline, as well as the speech it represents, gradually through a series of stages. Your outline will become increasingly complex as the ideas in your speech evolve and as you move the speech closer to its final form. But then, once you're ready to speak, the outline becomes simplified again. For the purposes of the public speaker, the rough outline and the speaking outlines are most important because they govern the discovery of ideas and the presentation of them. So, we'll concentrate on these.

Developing a Rough Outline A *rough outline* establishes the topic of your speech, clarifies your purpose, and identifies a reasonable number of subtopics. Suppose your instructor has assigned an informative speech on a subject that interests you. You

You identify a reasonable number of topics, arrange them, and amplify the ideas of your speech as you construct your rough outline.

decide to talk about drunk driving because a close friend was recently injured by an intoxicated driver. Your broad topic area, then, is drunk driving.

In the six to eight minutes you have to speak, you obviously can't cover such a broad topic adequately. After considering your audience and your time limit, you decide to focus your presentation on two organizations, Mothers Against Drunk Driving (MADD) and Students Against Drunk Driving (SADD).

As you think about narrowing your topic further, you jot down some possible ideas. You continue to narrow your list until your final ideas include the following:

1. Founders of MADD and SADD.
2. Accomplishments of the two organizations.
3. Reasons the organizations were deemed necessary.
4. Goals of MADD and SADD.
5. Action steps taken by MADD and SADD.
6. Ways your listeners can get involved.

Then, help your listeners to follow your thinking by clustering similar ideas. Experiment with several possible clusters before you decide on the best way to arrange your ideas.

Your next step is to consider the best pattern of organization for these topics. A chronological pattern would enable you to organize the history of MADD and SADD, but it would not allow you to discuss ways your listeners could help. Either cause-effect or effect-cause would work well if your primary purpose were to persuade. However, this is an informative speech, and you don't want to talk about the organizations only as the causes of reducing alcohol-related accidents.

In considering the audience-centered patterns, you decide that an inquiry order might work. You discard it, however, when you realize that you don't know enough about audience members' questions to use this organizational pattern effectively. After examining

Speaking of . . . *skills*

Memory and Organization

Research on organization and memory has shown that taking some specific outlining steps will help you and your listeners remember what you're talking about:

1. *The magic numbers.* In a classic study, Miller concluded that there is a limit to the number of items a person can easily recall—seven, plus or minus two. More recent research has suggested that a more manageable number of items is five, plus or minus two. Limit the number of points you make to from three to seven (preferably in the three-to-five range).

2. *Chunking.* But what if you want to include a lot more information? The answer: "chunk it." Divide the information into chunks or groups. Listeners are much more likely to remember five chunks of information than 17 separate points.

3. *Map your movement.* As we've suggested throughout this chapter, mapping your ideas helps your listeners to follow your speech. An audience can't read your speaking outline so you have to give them a verbal map of your ideas. You can signal your most important ideas ("I have three main points.") and subordinated ideas ("There are two advantages of my first argument."). Letting an audience see, by means of your language, the coordinated or equal relationships among your main ideas will help keep listeners from getting lost.

4. *Mnemonics.* Mnemonics help you remember ideas. When you learned "Thirty days hath September, April, June, and November . . . ," you learned an easily recalled ditty that in turn helped you to remember which months had 30 and which had 31 days. Speakers, too, can sometimes find a mnemonic to help listeners remember: for example, the three-R's of conserving resources ("Recycle," "Reduce," and "Re-use") or the ABC sequence ("airwaves," "breathing," "compression") for cardiopulmonary resuscitation taught in CPR classes.

For Further Reading: G. Mandler, "Organization and Memory," in *Human Memory: Basic Principles*, edited by Gordon Bower (New York: Academic Press, 1977), 310–354. See also Mandler's articles in C. R. Puff, ed., *Memory Organization and Structure* (New York: Academic Press, 1979), 303–319. G. A. Miller, "The Magic Number Seven, Plus or Minus Two: Some Limits on Our Capacity for Processing Information." *Psychological Review, 63* (1956): 81–97.

the alternatives, you finally settle on a topical pattern. A topical pattern allows you to present three clusters of information:

1. *Background of MADD and SADD:* information about the founders, why the organizations were founded.

2. *Description of MADD and SADD:* goals, steps in action plans, results.

3. *Local work of MADD and SADD:* the ways in which parents work with their teenagers and with local media to accomplish MADD and SADD goals.

As you subdivide your three clusters of information, you develop the following general outline:

I. Background of MADD and SADD

   A. Information about the founders

    B. Reasons the organizations were founded

  II. Description of the organizations

    A. Their goals

    B. The action steps they take

    C. Their accomplishments so far

  III. Applications of their work on a local level

    A. "Project Graduation"

    B. Parent-student contracts

    C. Local public service announcements

A **rough outline** identifies your topic, provides a reasonable number of subtopics, and reveals a method for organizing and developing your speech. Notice that you've arranged both the main points and subpoints topically. A word of warning: *You should make sure that the speech doesn't turn into a "string of beads" that fails to differentiate between one topic and the next.* With topical outlines, always figure out a way to make the topics cohere, hold together.

The next step in preparing an outline is to phrase your main headings as precisely as possible. Then you can begin to develop each heading by adding subordinate ideas. As you develop your outline, you'll begin to see what kinds of information and supporting materials you need to find.

Developing a Speaking Outline Of course, your rough outline would be maddening to use when you're actually delivering your speech. It would be too detailed to manage from a lectern; you'd probably be tempted to read to your listeners because it would include so many details. If you did that, you'd lose your conversational tone. Therefore, you need to compress your rough outline into a more useful form. A **speaking outline** uses key words or phrases to jog your memory when you deliver your speech. It is a short, practical form to use while delivering your speech (see Figure 8.1). The actual method you use to create your speaking outline will depend on your personal preference; some people like to work with small pieces of paper, others with notecards. Whatever your choice, however, your speaking outline should be unobtrusive. Large notebook pages will distract your listeners from what you have to say. There are five things to keep in mind as you prepare your speaking outline:

1. Note most points with only a key word or phrase—a word or two should be enough to trigger your memory, especially if you've practiced the speech adequately.

2. Write out fully the ideas that must be stated precisely, such as people's names or statistical information or exact quotations.

3. Include directions for delivery such as "SHOW POSTER."

4. Find methods of emphasis that will easily catch your eye, show the relationship of ideas, and jog your memory during your speech delivery. You might use capital letters, underlining, indentation, dashes, and highlighting with colored markers to emphasize important ideas.

5. Use your speaking outline during your practice sessions so that you are familiar with it when you give your speech.

FIGURE 8.1   Sample Speaking Outline (on Notecards)

FRIENDS DON'T LET FRIENDS DRIVE DRUNK
I. Background
    A. MADD: 1980. Candy Lightner
    B. SADD: her other daughter for hi-school kids
II. Description
    A. Goals
        1. public agitation (gov't. officials, letters to editor,
            task forces, all for little money)
        2. expose deficiencies in current legis. & control
           a. tougher laws state by state (STATISTICS)
           b. pressure judges (JUDGE NORTON, SANDERS, HANKS)
           c. more arrests (STATISTICS)
        3. public education
           a. more consciousness
           b. media attention

    B. MADD's action steps
        1. goals (what community needs most)
        2. educate organizers
        3. set research priorities (arrest records,
            conviction rates, PSA's, prom nights)
        4. formulate plans of action
        5. go public! (note on Simons's *Understanding Persuasion*)

    C. Results
        1. 320 MADD chapters by 1984
        2. 600,000 volunteers
        3. State laws changing
           a. 1982: 25 states, 30 pieces of legis.
           b. Congress: drinking age to 21
           c. Florida, red bumper sticker, CONVICTED DUI
        4. fatalities down (statistics)
        5. popularity of low-alc beer: wines, coolers

    III. Local projects
        A. contracts
        B. prom night (Operation Graduation)
        C. PSA's and publicity
           1. MADD TV ads
             a. after drunk driving
             b. sober group member
             c. host/guest—*Friends don't let friends d.d.*
           2. SADD projects
             a. school posters (SHOW POSTER)**
             b. non-alc party kits
             c. ads

Guidelines for Preparing Outlines

The amount of detail that you include in an outline will depend on your subject, on the speaking situation, and on your previous experience in speech preparation. New subject matter, unique speaking contexts, and limited prior speaking experience all indicate the need for a detailed outline. Your instructor may even require a full-content outline to help you develop the content of your speech. Under any circumstances, a good outline should meet these basic requirements.

1. Each unit in the outline should contain one main idea. If two or three ideas merge under one subpoint, your audience will lose direction and become confused. Suppose you are outlining a speech advocating that Athens, Greece, should be the permanent site for the Olympic Games. You include the following subpoint: "Also, the costs are prohibitive, and returning the games to their homeland would place renewed emphasis on their original purpose." Notice that this point combines two separate ideas about costs and the games' purpose. This can be confusing to your listeners. It would be more effective to separate the ideas and develop them as individual points. You could do it this way:

   a. Costs for building new sites in new locations every four years are becoming prohibitive.

   b. Returning the games to their homeland would place renewed emphasis on their original purpose.

2. Less important ideas in the outline should be subordinate to more important ones. Subordinate ideas are indented in an outline, and they are marked with subordinate symbols. Doing a good job with subordination helps you know what to emphasize when you're speaking. Proper subordination lets the main arguments stand out and the evidence cleanly relate to those arguments. Consider the following example:

I. The cost of medical care has skyrocketed.
   A. *Hospital charges* are high.
      1. A private room may cost more than $1,500 a day.
      2. Operating room fees may amount to tens of thousands of dollars.
      3. X-rays and laboratory tests incur extra expenses.
   B. *Doctors' charges* constantly go up.
      1. Complicated operations cost several thousand dollars.
      2. Office calls usually cost between $25 and $100.
   C. *Drugs* are expensive.
      1. Most antibiotics cost $2 to $3 per dose.
      2. The cost of nonprescription drugs has mounted.

3. Phrase your main points effectively. You can help your listeners to understand your message better if you are concise, choose vivid language, and use parallel structure.

   Be concise. Choose your words carefully. State your main points as briefly as you can without distorting their meaning. Crisp, clear, straightforward statements are easier to grasp than rambling, vague, complex declarations. Say, "Get regular exercise," not "Regular exercise, considering age and physical conditioning, lends itself to improved physiological functioning."

   Use vivid language. Whenever possible, state your main points in evocative words and phrases. Drab, colorless statements are easily forgotten; punchy lines grab attention. Phrase your main points so they'll appeal directly to the concerns of your listeners. Instead of saying, "We should take immediate action to reduce the costs of higher education," say, "Cut tuition now!"

Finally, use parallel structure. In a speech, your listeners have only one chance to catch what you're saying; parallelism in sentence structure helps them do so. The repetition of a key phrase aids the listener in remembering this series: "Cope with cold and flu season by washing your hands, getting enough sleep, and taking vitamin C. Wash your hands to destroy the viruses. Get enough sleep to reduce physical stress. Take vitamin C to fortify your body." Notice in this series that the most important phrases are repeated. Such parallelism will help your listeners grasp and remember the major ideas in your speech.

Assessing Your Progress

Chapter Summary

1. An organized speech is: (a) easier for listeners to comprehend, (b) easier to present, (c) perceived as more credible, (d) often more persuasive, and (e) lowers both speaker and listener frustration.

2. A well-developed central idea helps determine the best organizational pattern for a speech.

3. Organization is the sequence of ideas in a pattern that suggests their relationship to each other.

4. Four types of organization are: chronological, spatial, causal (effect-cause and cause-effect), and topical.

5. Audience-centered organizational patterns include familiarity-acceptance, inquiry, question-answer, problem-solution, and elimination order.

6. Speakers use outlines for testing their ideas and guiding their oral presentation of those ideas.

7. Rough outlines test ideas; speaking outlines guide ideas.

8. Guidelines for outlining include: (a) each unit should contain only one idea, (b) less important ideas should be subordinate to more important ones, (c) main ideas should be phrased effectively.

9. When phrasing main points, be concise, use vivid language, make your statements immediate, and use parallel structure.

Key Terms

causal pattern (p. 117)

chronological pattern (p. 116)

elimination order (p. 120)

familiarity-acceptance order (p. 119)

inquiry order (p. 119)

organization (p. 116)

problem-solution order (p. 120)

question-answer order (p. 119)

rough outline (p. 124)

spatial pattern (p. 116)

speaking outline (p. 124)

topical pattern (p. 118)

Assessment Activities

1. For each of the following topics, suggest two ways that materials might be organized. Consider which of the two would be more effective:

   a. Directions for driving in snow.

   b. The evolution of stereophonic sound.

   c. A rationale for including women in combat.

   d. The effect that the influx of tourists from the West will have on Russia.

   e. A description of the proposed route for a highway bypass.

2. Bring a short magazine or newspaper article and a photocopy of it to class. Cut the photocopy into separate paragraphs or sentences. Ask a classmate to assemble the separated paragraphs or sentences into a coherent story. Compare your classmate's results to the original article.

3. For a speech entitled "The Investigator as a Resource," discussing why a lawyer may want to hire a private detective on a case-by-case basis, rearrange the following points and subpoints in proper outline form:

   a. Investigative services can save the lawyer time.

   b. Investigative reports indicate areas the lawyer should concentrate on to build a case.

   c. It is advantageous for a lawyer to employ an investigator on a case-by-case basis.

   d. The investigator performs two basic services.

   e. Known witnesses must be interviewed and other witnesses identified.

   f. The detective examines reports from the FBI and other governmental and private agencies and evaluates them for reliability and to determine what must be done.

   g. The investigator examines, collects, preserves, and analyzes physical evidence.

   h. The investigator compiles information in an effort to reconstruct an incident.

   i. Lawyers may need detective assistance only occasionally, on especially critical cases.

   j. Investigative reports can be used in out-of-court settlements.

References

1. The data in this outline were taken from *The World Almanac and Book of Facts 1992* (New York: World Almanac, 1991), 529–530.

9

Beginning and Ending Your Speech

Just as aerobics instructors begin with warm-ups and end with cool-downs, so must you systematically prepare your audience to encounter new ideas and then take them back to their own worlds at the end of your speech. Your success in getting a listener's attention is partly due to how well you package your speech ideas with a powerful introduction and conclusion. Well-prepared introductions and conclusions allow you to develop a relationship with your listeners by orienting them to your ideas and then reinforcing them at the end. The introduction and conclusion signal clearly when your speech starts and ends so as to prevent confusion among your listeners.

Introductions and conclusions are not trivial aspects of public speaking. Introductions form first impressions that can affect your listeners' perceptions of the remainder of the speech. Conclusions give you one last opportunity to reinforce your main ideas and leave a lasting impression. In fact, people most often remember what they first hear or see (the **primacy effect**) and what they most recently have seen or heard (the **recency effect**). That is why introductions and conclusions require special effort when you prepare your speeches.

In this chapter, we'll review ways to capture and sustain listeners' attention, examine the purposes of introductions and conclusions, and suggest various strategies for beginning and ending speeches.

Capturing and Holding Attention

When you listen to your favorite album, you can block out the rest of the world. Sometimes, you can pay attention so completely that it seems like only minutes instead of hours have passed. **Attention** is the ability to focus on one element in a given perceptual field. When attention is secured, competing elements in the perceptual field fade and, for all practical purposes, cease to exist. That explains why everything else disappears when you are listening to your favorite album.

Watch an audience, and you'll quickly realize that listeners' attention can drift away from the message. Their attention ebbs and flows as listeners think about last night, the 90-degree heat, or paying the rent on time. Unless you capture listeners' attention in your introduction and maintain it throughout your speech, your message will be lost.

How can you capture and hold the attention of your listeners when giving a speech? Your ideas can be presented in nine ways that have high attention value. These factors of attention can be used anywhere in your speech. You can exploit them in your introduction or conclusion. It's also a good idea to distribute them throughout the body of your speech to stimulate your listeners to follow your ideas closely. The **factors of attention** are: activity, reality, proximity, familiarity, novelty, suspense, conflict, humor, and the vital (see Figure 9.1).

Activity

Suppose you've got two TV sets side by side. On one set, two Senate aides discuss solvency projections for the Social Security system. On the other, there's a high-speed cops-and-robbers car chase, replete with flying debris, collisions, and a fiery conclusion. Which set are you likely to watch? Similarly, a speaker can heighten activity by being sure to:

Choose active verbs. Raced, tore, shot through, slammed, ripped, slashed, catapulted, flew, flashed—most of these are simple verbs, but they depict activity.

Select dynamic stories. Use illustrations that depict action, that tell fast-moving stories. Propel your story forward, and your audience will stay with you.

Use short segments. Keep your speech moving—it will seem to drag if one point is expanded while other points are skimmed over.

Reality

The earliest words you learned were names for tangible objects such as *mommy, cookie,* and *truck.* While the ability to abstract—to generalize—is one of the marks of human intelligence, don't lose your audience by becoming too abstract. Refer to specific events,

FIGURE 9.1   The Factors of Attention

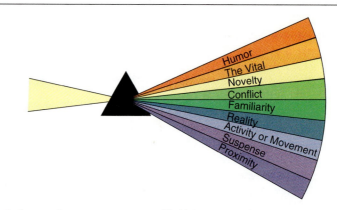

You can use the factors of attention to capture and hold the interest of your listeners.

persons, and places. For example, when we referred to "tangible objects," an abstract phrase, we gave you three real examples: *mommy*, *cookie*, and *truck*. Concrete words have more force than general references.

Proximity

Proximity means *nearness;* we usually notice things that closely surround us. A direct reference to a person in the audience, a nearby object or place, an incident that has just occurred, or the immediate occasion helps you to command attention. The following introduction uses proximity to engage the listeners:

> *Do you realize how much fast food students consume? Within four blocks of this classroom are nine restaurants, including McDonald's, Wendy's, Cracker Barrel, Domino's Pizza, Kentucky Fried Chicken, and Best Steak House. Two of the others are local submarine shops. Even the student union runs a fast-food counter. Should we start wondering what our lunch habits are doing to our nutrition—to our bodies and our minds?*

Familiarity

References to the familiar are attention-sustaining, especially in the face of new or strange ideas. The familiar is comfortable. People drive the same route to work, children sing the same songs over and over, and you've probably watched your favorite movie more than once. Stories about George Washington, Abraham Lincoln, and Martin Luther King, Jr., get repeated on occasions when cultural memories are used to guide decisions. How many times have you heard speakers repeat John F. Kennedy's famous phrase, "Ask not what your country can do for you; ask what you can do for your country"? We like the reassurance that such familiarity provides.

Novelty

Novel happenings, dramatic incidents, or unusual developments attract attention. Look at the tabloid newspaper headlines next time you're in the grocery checkout line: "Grandmother Gives Birth to Quadruplets," "Elizabeth Taylor to Marry Martian," "Elvis Sighted at Amusement Park." These bizarre stories catch our attention. References to size and contrast work well to create novelty.

When using novelty, blending the familiar and the novel, the old and the new, often yields the best results. Otherwise, you risk stretching the credulity of your listeners, as do those supermarket tabloids. To stimulate interest in the evolving nature of the self-defense plea in criminal courts, you might cite recent, highly publicized trials in which alleged victims claim self-defense in response to years of physical or mental abuse. Citing specific cases, such as the Menendez brothers' murder of their parents, provokes interest through novelty.

Suspense

Much of the appeal in mystery stories arises because we don't know how they will end. Films such as *Pulp Fiction* and *The Birdcage* have enough unusual twists to hold audiences spellbound. You, too, can use uncertainty in your speeches by pointing to puzzling relationships or unpredictable forces. Introduce suspense into the stories you tell, building up to a surprising climax. Hint that you'll divulge valuable information later: "Stay with me through this speech, because by the end you'll learn how to cut your book bill in half every semester."

Conflict

Controversy grabs attention. Soap operas are fraught with love, hate, violence, passion, and power struggles. Conflict, like suspense, suggests uncertainty; like activity, it's dynamic. The next time you hear the news, listen for conflict. Newscasters often portray natural phenomena, such as floods, as nature's assaults on human beings. Sportscasters describe athletes as "battling the odds." And even weather forecasters talk about "surviving Arctic blasts of frigid air." The concept of struggle brings the sense of urgency to the day's events.

In your speeches, you can create conflict among ideas, such as the competing theories regarding the extinction of dinosaurs. You can present opposing viewpoints among experts. You can emphasize, for example, the conflicts inherent in the struggles of individuals fighting the system, confronting the forces of nature, or facing the ravages of disease. When your ideas are cast as controversies or conflicts, they become dramatic and engaging.

Humor

Listeners usually pay attention when they're enjoying themselves. Humor can unite you and your audience by relaxing everyone and providing a change of pace. When using humor to capture and hold attention, remember to stick close to your central idea by choosing humor that is relevant. Be sure to use only humorous stories that are in good taste, and so avoid offending members of your audience. Comedian Bill Cosby met both of these requirements when he poked fun at a University of South Carolina graduating class. In his commencement speech, Cosby reminded his listeners:

> *All across the United States of America, people are graduating. And they are hearing so many guest speakers tell them that they are going forth. As a parent I am concerned as to whether or not you know where 'Forth' is. Let me put it to you this way: We have paved a road—the one to the house was already paved. 'Forth' is not back home.*[1]

The Vital

The phrase, *the vital,* was coined by Alan Monroe, the original author of this textbook, to reflect our tendency to be concerned with things that immediately benefit us. We pay attention to matters that affect our health, reputation, property, or employment. When a speaker says, "Students who take internships while in college find jobs after graduation three times as fast as those who don't," you're likely to pay attention—getting a job is vital to you. Appealing to *the vital,* therefore, is a matter of personalizing the speech for a particular audience—making it as relevant to their concrete circumstances as possible.

There are nine different ways to stimulate attention: activity, reality, proximity, familiarity, novelty, suspense, conflict, humor, and the vital. Use these attention-getters to grab and maintain your listeners' attention throughout your speech. They give your speech sparkle and spunk, they reach out to your listeners, and they help your listeners follow and remember your speech.

Beginning Your Speech

The beginning of a speech must gain the listeners' attention, secure goodwill and respect for the speaker, and prepare the audience for the discussion to follow.

As we have already suggested, you can use the factors of attention to engage your listeners during the beginning moments of your speech. When your audience is prepared to listen, your ideas will have their greatest impact. By weaving the factors of attention throughout the remainder of your speech, you can turn initial interest into sustained attention.

In many situations, your own reputation or the chairperson's introduction will help to generate goodwill. You can also refer to your own experience with the topic to boost your credibility. You gain additional respect from your listeners when you share your background research with them.

However, there may be times when your audience is opposed to you or your topic. In these instances, it's important to deal with opposition openly so that you will receive a fair hearing. By commenting on the differences between your views and those of your listeners, you can let them know that you're aware of disagreements but are seeking areas of consensus.

When confronted by indifference, distrust, or skepticism, you must take steps early in the speech to change these attitudes so that your position will be received openly. Even if your listeners don't agree, you can often secure their respect for your honesty and integrity by dealing directly with them.

Finally, you can prepare your listeners for your speech by stating your purpose early. Audiences that are forced to guess the purpose of a speech soon lose interest. A preview of your ideas and speech structure will help your audience follow along.

Speaking of . . . ethics

Revealing Responsible Intentions

Consider this scenario. You are planning a speech in which you hope to persuade your listeners to donate money to your political caucus. Should you reveal your intention in your introduction?

While we generally are unaffected by the awareness that persuasion is intended, we strongly react to deception. Research suggests the worst effect on listeners will occur if you disguise your intent but it is discovered as you speak.

Other factors such as your listeners' initial attitudes also influence how they will respond to your intention. If your listeners are highly involved or strongly committed to an opposing view, they will be less inclined to listen to you if they know your goal is to persuade.

In every case, avoid the appearance of direct manipulation. You should say, "Let's investigate the options together," rather than "Today I'm going to persuade you to . . . ." Most of us like to think that we have free choice.

For further information, see: Richard Petty and John Cacioppo, "Effects of Forewarning, Cognitive Responding, and Resistance to Persuasion," *Journal of Personality and Social Psychology*, 35 (1970): 645–655.

An introduction that secures your audience's attention and goodwill and prepares them to listen lays a solid foundation for acceptance of the central idea of your speech. You can establish attention by presenting your ideas in ways that create interest. We will examine a number of established means for tailoring your introduction to achieve the best results.

Referring to the Subject or Occasion

If your audience already has a vital interest in your subject, you need only to state that subject before presenting your first main point. The speed and directness of this approach signals your eagerness to address your topic. Professor Russell J. Love used this approach when discussing rights for people with severe communication problems: "My talk tonight is concerned with the rights of the handicapped—particularly those people with severe communication disabilities. I will be presenting what I call a bill of rights for the severely communicatively disabled."[2]

Although such brevity and forthrightness may strike exactly the right note on some occasions, you should not begin all speeches this way. To a skeptical audience, a direct beginning may sound immodest or tactless; to an apathetic audience, it may sound dull or uninteresting. When listeners are receptive and friendly, however, immediate reference to the subject often produces an effective opening.

Instead of referring to your subject, you may sometimes want to refer to the occasion that has brought you and your audience together. This is especially true of a special occasion or when an important event has occurred. Franklin Delano Roosevelt began his declaration of war this way when he said: "Yesterday, December 7, 1941—a date which will live in infamy—the United States of America was suddenly and deliberately attacked by naval and air forces of the empire of Japan."[3] In this instance, the American people knew what had occurred; they wanted an immediate response.

More recently, a student found herself in the position of giving a speech on the same topic a preceding speaker presented. She adapted to the occasion with this reference: "A few minutes ago, Vlado gave us a bleak picture of the scope of teenage pregnancy. Since the problem is so serious, I'd like to spend additional time discussing it." This introduction does more than acknowledge the duplication of topic, it provides a reason for listeners to focus further attention on it.

Using a Personal Reference or Greeting

At times, a warm, personal greeting from a speaker or the remembrance of a previous visit to an audience or scene serves as an excellent starting point. Personal references are especially useful when a speaker is well known to the audience. In June 1990, Barbara Bush used a personal reference to a previous visit to Wellesley College as she addressed the senior class. She elaborated on her enthusiasm for the occasion when she added, "I had really looked forward to coming to Wellesley, I thought it was going to be fun; I never dreamt it would be this much fun. So thank you for that."[4]

Author Harvey MacKay combined his personal gratitude for being asked to speak to a Pennsylvania State University audience with realism. MacKay made the connection between himself and his audience with the common feelings they both shared:

> *I'm flattered to be here today, but not so flattered that I'm going to let it go to my head.
> . . . By the time you're my age ninety-nine out of a hundred will have completely for-*

FIGURE 9.2   Types of Introductions and Conclusions

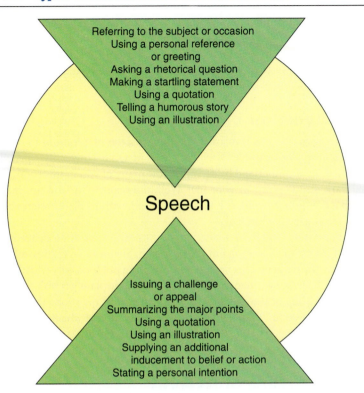

Referring to the subject or occasion
Using a personal reference
or greeting
Asking a rhetorical question
Making a startling statement
Using a quotation
Telling a humorous story
Using an illustration

Speech

Issuing a challenge
or appeal
Summarizing the major points
Using a quotation
Using an illustration
Supplying an additional
inducement to belief or action
Stating a personal intention

You can choose among different types of introductions and conclusions for your speeches. As you choose your introduction, ask yourself if it orients your audience to your purposes and ideas. When choosing a conclusion, ask if it summarizes your ideas and achieves closure.

> *gotten who spoke at your graduation. And, I can accept that. Because I can't remember the name of my commencement speaker either. What I do remember from graduation day is the way I felt: excited, scared and challenged. I was wondering what the world was like out there, and how I would manage to make an impact."*[5]

The way a personal reference introduction can be used to gain the attention of a hostile or skeptical audience is illustrated by a speech presented by Anson Mount, Manager of Public Affairs for *Playboy*, to the Christian Life Commission of the Southern Baptist Convention:

> *I am sure we are all aware of the seeming incongruity of a representative of* Playboy *magazine speaking to an assemblage of representatives of the Southern Baptist Convention. I was intrigued by the invitation when it came last fall, though I was not surprised. I am grateful for your genuine and warm hospitality, and I am flattered (though again not surprised) by the implication that I would have something to say that could have meaning to you people. Both* Playboy *and the Baptists have indeed been considering many of the same issues and ethical problems; and even if we have not arrived at the same conclusions, I am impressed and gratified by your openness and willingness to listen to our views.*[6]

If a personal reference is sincere and appropriate, it will establish goodwill as well as gain attention. Avoid extravagant, emotional statements, however, because listeners are quick to sense a lack of genuineness. At the other extreme, avoid apologizing. Don't say, "I don't know why I was picked to talk when others could have done it so much better" or, "Unaccustomed as I am to public speaking . . . ." Apologetic beginnings suggest that your audience needn't waste time listening. Be cordial, sincere, and modest, but establish your authority and maintain control of the situation.

Asking a Question

Another way to open a speech is to ask a question or series of questions to spark thinking about your subject. For example, Nicholas Fynn of Ohio University opened a speech about free-burning of timberland by saying: "How many of you in this room have visited a National Park at one point in your life? Well, the majority of you are in good company."[7] Such a question introduces a topic gently and, with its direct reference to the audience, tends to engage the listeners.

Rhetorical questions, those for which you do not expect direct audience response, are often used to forecast the development of the speech. Shannon Dyer of Southwest Baptist University in Missouri opened her speech by wondering out loud why whistleblowers didn't prevent the *Challenger* accident and the Union Carbide plant gas leak at Bhopal, India. She moved to the body of the speech with more rhetorical questions that previewed the main points of her speech: "Thus, let's examine the dilemma of whistleblowers. First, who are whistleblowers? Then, what is the high personal price for their warnings? And finally, how can we protect these citizens—the watchdogs of our nation's safety?"[8]

Making a Startling Statement

On certain occasions, you may choose to open a speech with what is known as the *shock technique,* making a startling statement of fact or opinion. This approach is especially useful when listeners are distracted, apathetic, or smug. It rivets their attention on your topic. For example, the Executive Director of the American Association of Retired Persons (AARP), after asking some rhetorical questions about health care, caught his listeners' attention with a series startling statements:

> *Given what we're spending on health care, we should have the best system in the world. But the reality is that we don't. Thirty-seven million Americans have no health insurance protection whatsoever, and millions more are underinsured. We are twentieth—that's right, twentieth—among the nations of the world in infant mortality. The death rate for our black newborn children rivals that of Third World countries. And poor children in America, like their brothers and sisters in Third World nations, receive neither immunizations nor basic dental care.*
>
> *Those statistics give us a sense of the scope of the problem. What they don't adequately portray is the human factor—the pain and the suffering. While terminally ill patients may have their lives extended in intensive care units—at tremendous cost—middle-age minority women die of preventable and treatable cancer, hypertension and diabetes.*[9]

Avoid overusing shock techniques. The technique can backfire if your listeners become angry when you threaten or disgust them.

Using a Quotation

A quotation may be an excellent means of introducing a speech, because it can prod listeners to think about something important and it often captures an appropriate emotional tone. When Agnar Pytte, President of Case Western Reserve University, spoke to the Cleveland City Club on the topic of political correctness and free speech, he opened his speech with a quotation: "As Benjamin Cardozo said: 'Freedom of expression is the indispensable condition of all our liberties.'"[10] Pytte continued by using Cardozo's statement to investigate the current debate over political correctness on college campuses. The opening quotation provided the groundwork by effectively piquing the interest of the audience and inviting listeners to further consider the impact of political correctness on free speech. Pytte could then proceed into a discussion of current examples of the political correctness debate, confident that his audience was paying attention.

Telling a Humorous Story

You can begin a speech by telling a funny story or relating a humorous experience. When doing so, however, observe the following three rules of communication:

1. Be sure that the story is at least amusing, if not funny; test it out on others before you actually deliver the speech. Be sure that you practice sufficiently so you can present the story naturally. And use the story to make a point instead of making it the center of your remarks. In other words, brevity is crucial.

2. Be sure that the story is relevant to your speech; if its subject matter or punch line is not directly related to you, your topic, or at least your next couple of sentences, the story will appear to be a mere gimmick.

3. Be sure that your story is in good taste; in a public gathering, an off-color or doubtful story violates accepted standards of social behavior and can undermine an audience's respect for you. You should avoid sexual, racist, antireligious, ageist, homophobic, and sexist humor.

All three of these rules were observed by George V. Grune, CEO of The Reader's Digest Association, Inc., as he delivered a commencement address to the Graduate School of Business at Rollins College:

> This morning I'd like to talk about global marketing and the opportunities it offers American business today—and each of you individually. I understand international marketing was a favorite subject for many of you, and I suspect earning a living is uppermost on your minds, considering the occasion we celebrate today.
>
> There is a story about a king who once called three wise men together and posed the same problem to each: "Our island is about to be inundated by a huge tidal wave. How would you advise the people?" The first man thought long and hard and then said, "Sire I would lead the people to the highest spot on the island and then set up an all-night prayer vigil."
>
> The second said, "Master, I would advise the people to eat, drink and be merry for it would be their last opportunity to do so." The third wise man said, "Your majesty, if I were you, I would immediately advise the people to do their best to learn how to live under water."

> *As you progress in your business career, you'll face many challenges that will test your ability to in effect "learn how to live under water." Those who adapt and find new solutions to complex issues will be the most successful. And nowhere is that more true than in the global arena.[11]*

After relating his anecdote, Grune was ready to talk about the treacherous, difficult challenges facing students of international marketing.

Using an Illustration

A real-life incident, a passage from a novel or short story, or a hypothetical illustration can also get a speech off to a good start. As with a humorous story, an illustration should be not only interesting to the audience but also relevant to your central idea. Deanna Sellnow, a student at North Dakota State University, used this technique to introduce a speech on private credit-reporting bureaus:

> *John Pontier, of Boise, Idaho, was turned down for insurance because a reporting agency informed the company that he and his wife were addicted to narcotics, and his Taco Bell franchise had been closed down by the health board when dog food had been found mixed in with the tacos. There was only one small problem. The information was made up. His wife was a practicing Mormon who didn't touch a drink, much less drugs, and the restaurant had never been cited for a health violation.[12]*

The existence of a problem with private credit-reporting bureaus is clear from this introduction. In addition, when listeners get involved with someone like John Pontier who has encountered the problem, they become more attentive. When this happens, the illustration can have a powerful impact.

Completing Your Introduction

You can use one of the approaches that we've discussed alone or you can combine two or more. You might open with a startling illustration or a humorous reference to the occasion, for example. No matter what type of introduction you use, you should have one purpose in mind: arousing the attention and winning the goodwill and respect of your listeners. Your introduction should be relevant to the purpose of your speech and should lead smoothly into the first of the major ideas that you wish to present; that is, your introduction should be an integral part of the speech. It should not be, for example, a funny story told merely to make an audience laugh; it should be thematically and tonally tied to the body of the speech.

Your introduction should also forecast the speech's development by means of a preview. The preview establishes your listeners' confidence in your organization, thus enhancing your credibility. It creates listener receptivity by providing a structure for you and your listeners to follow during the speech. Here are some examples of types of previews:

1. *Announce the organizational pattern.* You might say, "I'll develop the effects of the problem of alcoholism and then examine its causes" (causal pattern). "In demonstrating how to troubleshoot minor car problems, I'll consider three topics. I'll be talking about the electrical system, the fuel system, and the mechanical system" (topical order).

Speaking of . . . skills

How Long Should It Be?

According to a classic study, the average speaker spends about 10 percent of the total speech on the introduction and 5 percent on the conclusion. The introduction may increase to 13 percent in speeches designed to stimulate or inspire, such as sermons, dedications, or memorials. In practical terms, this means that you will probably take 1 minute to introduce a 10-minute speech and 30 seconds to conclude it.

Can you think of circumstances when you'd spend more time introducing or concluding your remarks? less time?

For the original study, see: Edd Miller, "Speech Introductions and Conclusions," *The Quarterly Journal of Speech, 32* (1946): 181–183.

2. *Use mnemonic devices.* Acronyms aid memory; for example, "I'm going to discuss the ABCs of jogging: **A**lways wear good shoes. **B**aby your feet. **C**all a podiatrist if problems develop."

3. *Employ alliteration.* Rely on sound similarities to create interest. For example: "My advice for finding someone to marry? Use the three A's—availability, attitude, and *amour.*"

4. *Use repetition.* Reinforce your message by repeating the main phrases. You can say, "We need to examine how tuition increases harm us, how tuition increases harm our parents, and most importantly, how tuition increases harm our state."

When effective, your introductory remarks will both establish a common ground of interest and understanding and provide a structure to guide your audience toward the conclusion that you intend to reach.

Ending Your Speech

Just as the introduction to your speech accomplishes specific purposes, so too does the conclusion. An effective conclusion should focus the attention of your audience on your central idea. If your speech has one dominant idea, you should restate it in a clear and forceful manner. If your speech is more complex, you may summarize the key points, or you may spell out the action or belief that these points suggest.

In addition to reinforcing the central idea, your conclusion should leave the audience in the proper mood. If you want your listeners to express vigorous enthusiasm, stimulate that feeling with your closing words. If you want them to reflect thoughtfully on what you have said, encourage a calm, meditative attitude. Decide whether the response you seek is a mood of serious determination or good humor, of warm sympathy or utter disgust, of thoughtful consideration or vigorous action. Then, end your speech in a way that will create that mood.

Finally, a good ending should convey a sense of completeness and finality. Listeners grow restless and annoyed when they think the speech is finished, only to hear the speaker ramble on. Avoid false endings. Tie the threads of thought together so that the pattern of your speech is brought clearly to completion.

Speakers employ many strategies to convey a sense of closure to their speeches. We will examine the conclusion techniques that are used regularly.

Issuing a Challenge

You may conclude your speech by issuing a challenge to your listeners, requesting support or action, or reminding them of their responsibilities. John E. Cleghorn, President of the Royal Bank of Canada, urged his audience to cultivate diversity in their businesses. He summarized the progress yet to be made in respecting individual differences, and then issued this challenge: "Our different linguistic, cultural and regional backgrounds constitute our greatest strength. Our challenge is to harness all the elements of our diversity to maintain and enhance the quality of life that we all cherish so much."[13]

Summarizing the Major Points or Ideas

In an informative speech, a summary allows the audience to pull together the main strands of information and to evaluate the significance of the speech. In a persuasive speech, a summary gives you a final opportunity to present, in brief form, the major points of your argument. For example, a student presented this summary of an informative speech on tornadoes:

> You've seen the swirling funnel clouds on the six o'clock news. They hit sometimes without much warning, leaving in their paths death and destruction. Now you should understand the formation of funnel clouds, the classification of tornadoes on the Fujita scale, and the high cost of tornadoes worldwide in lives and property. Once you understand the savage fury of tornadoes, you can better appreciate them. Tornadoes are one of nature's temper tantrums.

If the student's purpose had been to persuade his listeners to take certain precautions during a tornado alert, the summary of the speech might have sounded like this:

> The devastation left in the path of a tornado can be tremendous. To prevent you and your loved ones from becoming statistics on the six o'clock news, remember what I told you this afternoon. Seek shelter in basements, ditches, or other low areas. Stay away from glass and electric lines. And, remember the lesson of the Xenia, Ohio, disaster. Tornadoes often hit in clusters. Be sure the coast is clear before you leave your shelter. Don't be a statistic.

In each case, summarizing the main ideas of the speech gives the speaker another opportunity to reinforce the message. Information can be reiterated in the summary of an informative speech, or the major arguments or actions can be strengthened in the summary of a persuasive speech.

Using a Quotation

You can cite others' words to capture the spirit of your ideas in the conclusion of your speech. Quotations are often used to end speeches. Quoted prose, if the author is credible, may gather additional support for your central idea. Notice how Faye Wattleton, former

President of Planned Parenthood of America, was able to add the credibility of an influential historical figure to her plea for women's empowerment: "As Queen Victoria said, "I am not interested in the possibility of defeat." May each of us determine to never consider the possibility of defeat, but to press on until justice, equality, and liberty are ours."[14]

Poetry, too, may distill the essence of your message in uplifting language. Bishop Leontine Kelly concluded her speech celebrating the diversity of human talents with the words of a well-known Christian hymn: "How firm a foundation ye saints of the Lord, Is laid for your faith in God's excellent word."[15] The recognition of these familiar words probably inspired members of her audience.

Using an Illustration

Illustrations engage your listeners emotionally. If you use a concluding illustration, it can set the tone and direction of your final words. Your illustration should be both inclusive and conclusive—inclusive of the main focus or thrust of your speech and conclusive in tone and impact. Sometimes the same illustration can be used to tie together a whole speech. This is what Michael Twitchell, a student in a speaking contest, did when talking about the causes and effects of depression. Here's his opening:

> Have you ever felt like you were the little Dutch boy who stuck his finger in the leaking dike? You waited and waited but the help never came. The leak became worse and the water rushed around you and swept you away. As you fought the flood, gasping and choking for air, you realized that the flood was inside yourself. You were drowning and dying in your own mind. According to the American Journal of Psychiatry, as many as half the people in this room will be carried away by this devastating flood. What is this disaster? Mental depression.

Notice how Twitchell's concluding words reinforce the illustration used in his introduction:

> Let's go back to my illustration of the little Dutch boy. He was wise to take action and put his finger in the dike, preventing the flood. In the case of depression, each one of us must be like the little Dutch boy—willing to get involved and control the harmful effects of depression.[16]

Supplying an Additional Inducement to Belief or Action

Sometimes you may conclude a speech by quickly reviewing the principal ideas presented in the body and then supplying one or more additional reasons for endorsing the belief or taking the proposed action. In his speech, Michael Twitchell spoke at length about the devastating effects of depression. After proposing numerous reasons for people to get involved in the battle, Twitchell offered, in the conclusion to his speech, an additional inducement:

> Why should you really care? Why is it important? The depressed person may be someone you know—it could be you. If you know what is happening, you can always help. I wish I had known what depression was in March of 1978. You see, when I said David Twitchell could be my father, I was making a statement of fact. David is my father. I am his son. My family wasn't saved; perhaps now yours can be.[17]

Speakers sometimes indicate their personal intentions to take action. This is especially effective when the speaker is highly regarded by listeners or when immediate actions are urged.

Stating a Personal Intention

Stating your own intention to adopt the action or attitude you recommend in your speech is particularly effective when your prestige with the audience is high or when you have presented a concrete proposal requiring immediate action. By professing your intention to take immediate action, you and your ideas gain credibility. In the following example, a speaker sets himself up as a model for the actions he wants his listeners to take:

> Today I have illustrated how important healthy blood is to human survival and how blood banks work to ensure the possibility and availability of blood for each of us. It is not a coincidence that I speak on this vital topic on the same day that the local Red Cross Bloodmobile is visiting campus. I want to urge each of you to ensure your future and mine by stopping at the Student Center today or tomorrow to make your donation. The few minutes that it takes may add up to a lifetime for a person in need. To illustrate how firmly I believe in this opportunity to help, I'm going to the Student Center to give my donation as soon as this class is over. I invite any of you who feel this strongly to join me.

Regardless of the means you choose for closing your speech, remember that your conclusion should focus the attention of your listeners on the central theme you've developed. In addition, a good conclusion should be consistent with the mood or tenor of your speech and should convey a sense of completeness and finality.

Sample Outline for an Introduction and Conclusion

An introduction and conclusion for a classroom speech on MADD and SADD might take the following form. Notice that the speaker uses suspense in combination with startling statements to lead the audience into the subject. The conclusion combines a summary with a final illustration and a statement of personal intention.

Friends Don't Let Friends Drive Drunk

INTRODUCTION

I. Many of you have seen the "Black Gash," the Vietnam War Memorial in Washington, D.C.

   A. It contains the names of more than 40,000 Americans who gave their lives in Southeast Asia between 1961 and 1973.

   B. We averaged over 3000 war dead a year during that painful period.

II. Today, another enemy stalks Americans.

   A. The enemy kills, not 3000, but over 20,000 citizens every 12 months.

   B. The enemy is not hiding in jungles but can be found in every community in the country.

   C. The enemy kills, not with bayonets and bullets, but with bottles and bumpers.

III. Two organizations are trying to contain and finally destroy the killer.

   A. Every TV station in this town carries a public service ad that says "Friends Don't Let Friends Drive Drunk."

   B. In response to the menace of the drunk driver, two national organizations—Mothers Against Drunk Driving and Students Against Drunk Driving—have been formed and are working even in this community to make the streets safe for you and me.

   C. [Central idea] MADD and SADD are achieving their goals with your help.

   D. To help you understand what these familiar organizations do, first I'll tell you something about the founders of MADD and

SADD; then, I'll describe their operations; finally, I'll mention some of the ways community members get involved with them.

[Body]

CONCLUSION

I. Today, I've talked briefly about the Lightners and their goals for MADD and SADD, their organizational techniques, and ways in which you can get involved.

II. The work of MADD and SADD volunteers—even on our campus, where I'm sure you've seen their posters in the Student Center—is being carried out to keep you alive.

    A. You may not think you need to be involved; but remember: After midnight, one in every five or fewer drivers on the road is probably drunk: You could be involved whether you want to be or not.

    B. That certainly was the case with Julie Smeiser, a member of our sophomore class, who just last Friday was hit by a drunk driver when going home for the weekend.

III. If people don't take action, we could build a new "Black Gash"—this time for victims of drunks—every two years, and soon fill Washington, D.C., with monuments to needless suffering.

    A. Such monuments would be grim reminders of our unwillingness to respond to enemies at home with the same intensity with which we attacked enemies abroad.

    B. A better response would be to support actively groups such as MADD and SADD, who are attacking the enemy on several fronts at once in a war on motorized murder.

IV. If you're interested in learning more about SADD and MADD, stop by Room 324 in the Student Center tonight at 7:30 to hear the president of the local chapter of SADD talk about this year's activities. I'll be there; please join me.

Assessing Your Progress

Chapter Summary

1. You can capture and sustain your listeners' attention by using one or more of the nine factors of attention: activity, reality, proximity, familiarity, novelty, suspense, conflict, humor, and the vital.

2. Introductions should seize attention, secure goodwill, and prepare an audience for what you will be saying.

3. Types of introductions include referring to the subject or occasion, using a personal reference or greeting, asking a rhetorical question, making a startling statement of fact or opinion, using a quotation, telling a humorous story, and using an illustration.

4. In concluding your speech, you should attempt to focus the thoughts of your audience on your central theme, maintain the tenor of your speech, and convey a sense of finality.

5. Techniques for ending a speech include issuing a challenge or appeal, summarizing the major points or ideas, using a quotation, using an illustration, supplying an additional inducement to belief or action, and stating a personal intention.

Key Terms

attention (p. 129)

factors of attention (p. 130)

primacy effect (p. 129)

proximity (p. 131)

recency effect (p. 129)

Assessment Activities

1. In class groups, devise two introductory strategies for the following speakers to use in the situations noted. Share the introductions. Did they generate attention? Did they secure goodwill? Did they prepare the audience for the ideas in the speech?

   Marilyn Quayle at a pro-life conference

   Steven Spielberg at a radio broadcaster's conference

   Roger Staubach at a banquet sponsored by the Fellowship of Christian Athletes

   Janet Reno at a meeting of the Fraternal Order of Police

   Pope John Paul II at an interdenominational meeting of church leaders

2. Consult the Internet or an almanac to find out what famous events occurred on this date in history. Then, write an introduction for an informative speech to your classmates referring to the occasion. Ask your listeners if you secured their interest. Write an introduction for a persuasive speech to an alumni reunion. Evaluate the effectiveness of the introduction in establishing the purpose of the speech.

3. Participate in a chain of introductions and conclusions. One student will begin by suggesting a topic for a speech. A second student will suggest an appropriate introduction and conclusion and justify those choices. A third student will challenge those selections and propose alternative introductions and/or conclusions. Continue this discussion until everyone has participated. Which examples were most effective? Determine why they were effective.

References

1. Bill Cosby, "University of South Carolina Commencement Address," 1990, unpublished manuscript available from the author.

2. Russell J. Love, "The Barriers Come Tumbling Down," Harris-Hillman School Commencement, Nashville, Tenn. (21 May 1981). Reprinted by permission.

3. Franklin Delano Roosevelt, "War Message," in *American Voices: Significant Speeches in American History 1640-1945*, edited by James Andrews and David Zarefsky (New York: Longman, 1989), 476.

4. Barbara Bush, "Choice and Change," Wellesley College, 1 June 1990, manuscript available from the author.

5. Harvey MacKay, "How to Get a Job," *Vital Speeches of the Day, 57* (19 August 1991).

6. Anson Mount, Manager of Public Affairs for *Playboy* magazine, from a speech presented to the Christian Life Commission of the Southern Baptist Convention, in *Contemporary American Speeches,* 5th ed., edited by Wil A. Linkugel, et al. (Dubuque, Ia.: Kendall/Hunt, 1982).

7. Nicholas Fynn, "The Free Burn Fallacy," *Winning Orations 1989.* Reprinted by permission of Larry Schnoor, Executive Secretary, Interstate Oratorical Association, Mankato State University, Mankato, Minn.

8. Shannon Dyer, "The Dilemma of Whistleblowers," *Winning Orations 1989.* Reprinted by permission of Larry Schnoor, Executive Secretary, Interstate Oratorical Association, Mankato State University, Mankato, Minn.

9. Horace B. Deets, "Health Care for a Caring America: We Must Develop a Better System," *Vital Speeches of the Day, 55* (1 August 1989).

10. Agnar Pytte, "Political Correctness and Free Speech: Let the Ideas Come Forth," *Vital Speeches of the Day, 57* (1 September 1991).

11. George V. Grune, "Global Marketing: Global Opportunities," *Vital Speeches of the Day, 55* (15 July 1989).

12. Deanna Sellnow, "Have You Checked Lately?" *Winning Orations.* Reprinted by permission of Larry Schnoor, Executive Secretary, Interstate Oratorical Association, Mankato State University, Mankato, Minn.

13. John E. Cleghorn, "Diversity: The Key to Quality Business," *Vital Speeches of the Day, 59* (15 January 1993): 215.

14. Faye Wattleton, "Address at the Triennial Convention of the YWCA," reprinted in *Women's Voices in Our Time,* edited by Victoria L. DeFrancisco and Marvin D. Jensen (Prospect Heights, Ill.: Waveland Press, 1994), p. 134.

15. Bishop Leontine Kelly, "Celebrating the Diversity of Our Gifts," reprinted in *Women's Voices in Our Time,* edited by Victoria L. DeFrancisco and Marvin D. Jensen (Prospect Heights, Ill.: Waveland Press, 1994), p. 115.

16. Michael A. Twitchell, "The Flood Gates of the Mind," *Winning Orations.* Reprinted by permission of Larry Schnoor, Executive Secretary, Interstate Oratorical Association, Mankato State University, Mankato, Minn.

17. Twitchell, "The Flood Gates of the Mind."

Part III

Responsible Presentation

10 Wording Your Speech

Language functions on multiple levels. Language is a *referential, relational,* and *symbolic* medium of communication. As language points to aspects of the world, it is referential. When you label or name things like "dog," "tree," "cupcake," you are employing the referential nature of language. As you probably realize, young children learn the power of language as a referential tool early.

Language also has relational powers; it suggests associations between people. "Give me that cupcake" not only points to the cupcake, but also indicates that one person has the power or authority to command another person. When you use slang or jargon with friends, you are bonding through language. Some groups even use their own special languages that don't sound right when spoken by an outsider. It might sound odd, for example, to hear a your grandmother say, "That's a gnarly set of wheels, man."

And, language is symbolic. That means language can be disconnected from the concrete world and even focus our attention on nonreal (unicorns) and nonconcrete (democracy) entities. Whole empires of thought can be constructed out of language. When you speak, it's not enough to know the words; you must also understand how language reflects human relationships and shared senses of reality—your culture and thinking.

In the next three chapters, we'll turn our attention to the encoding or deciphering of messages. **Encoding** occurs when you put ideas into words and actions. This includes your choice of language, use of visual aids, and even bodily and vocal behaviors. In this chapter, we'll focus on selecting your speaking style, creating a speaking atmosphere, and using language strategically.

Selecting Your Style

Generally, spoken language is uncomplicated; it has to be since we use it every day—at the grocery store, over the back fence, around the supper table, and in the street. Usually,

Getting someone to see your point
of view often depends on strategic
rhetorical decisions.

public speakers mimic the conversational quality of everyday language because listeners prefer it. Most of the time when you speak, you will choose this oral style.

Oral style is informal and imprecise, typical of conversation. But some spoken language is complicated and formal; this is the type of language more closely resembling written work. **Written style** is formal and precise. It usually indicates a formal occasion or weighty topic. Consider the following examples of written and oral style:

Written Style	Oral Style
Remit the requested amount forthwith.	*Pay your bill.*
Will you be having anything else?	*Whutkinahgitcha?*
To avoid injury, keep hands away from the cutting surface.	*Don't touch the blade!*
Contact a service representative to register your dissatisfaction with the product.	*Call to complain.*

If you write out your whole speech before giving it, the result is likely to be stilted and stiff. It may sound more like an essay than a speech. For example, consider the following introduction:

I am most pleased that you could come this morning. I would like to use this opportunity to discuss with you a subject of inestimable importance to us all—the impact of inflationary spirals on students enrolled in institutions of higher education.

Translated into an oral style, a speaker would say:

Thanks for coming. I'd like to talk today about a problem for all of us—the rising cost of going to college.

Notice how much more natural the second version sounds. The first is wordy—filled with prepositional phrases, complex words, and formal sentences. The second contains shorter sentences and simpler vocabulary, and it addresses the audience directly.

For most speech occasions, you should cultivate an oral style. On rare, highly ceremonial occasions, you may decide to read from a prepared text. However, even then, you should strive for oral style.[1] There are four qualities that will help you develop a clear and effective oral style. Let's consider accuracy, simplicity, restatement, and coherence.

Accuracy

Careful word choice is an essential ingredient to effectively transmitting your meaning to an audience. Oral language is usually concrete and specific. If you tell a hardware store

Speaking of . . . *skills*

Oral Versus Written Style

How do you instantly recognize that a speaker has written out a speech? Inherently it sounds like it's been written. The speaker uses written rather than oral style. Here are some ways that oral style differs from written style:

1. The average sentence is shorter in oral communication.
2. You use fewer different words when you speak.
3. You also use a larger number of short words such as "it" and "the." In fact, fifty simple words constitute almost half of your speaking vocabulary.
4. You refer to people more often with words like "I," "you," "me," "our," and "us."
5. You use more qualifying words such as "much," "many," "a lot," and "most."
6. Your language choices are more informal and you use more contractions.

clerk, "I broke the dohickey on my hootenanny and I need a thingamajig to fix it," you'd better have the hootenanny in your hand or the clerk won't understand. When you speak, your goal is precision. You should leave no doubt about your meaning.

Since words are symbols that represent concepts or objects, your listener may attach a meaning to your words that's quite different from the one you intended. This misinterpretation becomes more likely as your words become more abstract. *Democracy,* for example, doesn't mean the same thing to a citizen in the suburbs as it does to a citizen in the ghetto. *Democracy* will elicit different meanings from Americans who belong to the Moral Majority than it will from those who belong to the American Socialist Party.

Students of General Semantics, the study of words or symbols and their relationships to reality, continually warn us that many errors in thinking and communication arise from treating words as if they were the actual conditions, processes, or objects. Words are not fixed and timeless in meaning, nor does everyone use them in exactly the same way.

To avoid vagueness, choose words that express the exact shade of meaning you wish to communicate. You might say that an object *shines,* but the object might also *glow, glitter, glisten, gleam, flare, blaze, glare, shimmer, glimmer, flicker, sparkle, flash,* and *beam.* Each word allows you to describe the object more precisely.

Simplicity

"Speak," said Lincoln, "so that the most lowly can understand you, and the rest will have no difficulty." Because electronic media reach audiences and cultures more varied than Lincoln could have imagined, you have even more reason to follow his advice today. Say *learn* rather than *ascertain, try* rather than *endeavor, use* rather than *utilize, help* rather than *facilitate.* Don't use a longer or less familiar word when a simple one is just as clear. Evangelist Billy Sunday illustrated the effectiveness of familiar words in this example:

> If a man were to take a piece of meat and smell it and look disgusted, and his little boy were to say, "What's the matter with it, Pop?" and he were to say, "It is undergoing a process of decomposition in the formation of new chemical compounds," the boy would be all in. But if the father were to say, "It's rotten," then the boy would understand and hold his nose. "Rotten" is a good Anglo-Saxon word, and you do not have to go to the dictionary to find out what it means.[2]

Simplicity doesn't mean *simplistic;* if you talk down to your audience, they will be insulted. Instead, speak directly using words that convey precise, concrete meanings.

Restatement

If accuracy and simplicity were your only criteria as a speaker, your messages might resemble a famous World War II bulletin: "Sighted sub, sank same." But, because words literally disappear into the atmosphere as soon as they're spoken, you don't have the writer's advantage when transmitting ideas to others. Instead, you must rely heavily on restatement. **Restatement** is the repetition of words, phrases, and ideas so as to clarify and reinforce them. The key here is not simply to repeat yourself, but to repeat or rephrase in order to advance the listeners' understanding or acceptance of an idea. Advertisers frequently depend on restatement to reinforce their point. For example, the jingle for a typical laundry soap might make the point this way: "Suds gets your clothes clean. Suds removes dirt, stains, and odors. Suds tackles the toughest cleaning jobs your kids bring home."

Restating an idea from a number of perspectives usually involves listing its components or redefining the basic concept. You can see this principle of reiteration at work in the following excerpt from Bill Clinton's speech to Georgetown University students in 1991:

> *To turn America around, we need a new approach founded on our most sacred principles as a nation, with a vision for the future. We need a New Covenant, a solemn agreement between the people and their government, to provide opportunity for everybody, inspire responsibility throughout our society, and restore a sense of community to this great nation. A New Covenant to take government back from the powerful interests and the bureaucracy, and give this country back to ordinary people.*
>
> *More than 200 years ago, the founders outlined our first social compact between government and the people, not just between lords and kings. More than a century ago, Abraham Lincoln gave his life to maintain the Union the compact created. Sixty years ago, Franklin Roosevelt renewed that promise with a New Deal that offered opportunity in return for hard work. Today we need to forge a New Covenant that will repair the damaged bond between the people and their government and restore our basic values—the notion that our country has a responsibility to help people get ahead, that citizens have not only the right but a responsibility to rise as far and as high as their talents and determination can take them, and that we're all in this together.[3]*

Notice Clinton's tactics here: first, he justifies the need for the concept. Then, he formally defines it ("a solemn agreement . . ."). Next, he indicates its functions. He then offers examples of previous covenants from American history, finally getting to "Today we need to forge . . . ," which allows him to offer more detail on what he sees as the functions of the New Covenant. These varied restatements thus serve as a structure for his developmental materials.

Restatement can help your listeners remember your ideas more readily. However, be careful of mindless repetition; too many restatements, especially of simple ideas, can be boring.

Coherence

Just as you must use restatement because people listening to you speak don't have the luxury of reviewing the points, you must signal where you're at in your speech because your listeners aren't able to perceive punctuation marks that might help them distinguish one idea from another as you speak. In order to be understood, oral communication requires **coherence,** or the logical connection of ideas. To achieve coherence, you should use forecasts or previews, summaries, and signposts.

Forecasts or *previews* provide clues to the overall speech structure. Previews are especially helpful in outlining the major topics of the speech. They precede the development of the body of the speech, usually forming part of the introduction. Consider the following examples:

> *Today I am going to talk about three aspects of family life—trust, love, and commitment.*

There are four major elements in developing a winning resume. We'll look at establishing your strengths, forming a positive impression, including sufficient detail, and developing an edge.

The history of the Vietnam War can be divided into two periods—the French involvement and the commitment of American troops.

Each of these forecasts provides a link between the introduction to the speech and the development of ideas in the body of the speech. A listener knows what to expect from each forecast. In a sense, you are providing a road map when you signal your speech structure in a forecast.

Final **summaries** are also important in providing coherence in your speech. It is your last chance to remind listeners of your main topics and leave them with a final impression of your speech. A final summary usually forms part of the conclusion and often parallels the forecast. For example, a final summary might look like this:

Today we talked about what constitutes a strong family life. Experts agree that there are three things that all families need—trust, love, and commitment.

When you sit down to apply for your first job, remember the four major elements in developing a winning resume. Think about establishing your strengths, forming a positive impression, including sufficient detail, and developing an edge.

The history of the Vietnam War has been divided into two periods—the French involvement and the commitment of American troops.

Notice that all three examples of final summaries parallel the forecast for the speech. They are direct, clear, and remind the listener of the primary structure of the speech.

In addition to forecasts and summaries, you must use *signposts* or *transitions*—linking phrases that move an audience from one idea to another. Signposts or transitions are words or phrases—such as *first, next,* or *as a result*—that help listeners follow the movement of your ideas. Signposts such as "the history of this invention begins in . . ." also provide clues to the overall message structure. The following are useful signposts:

- ✓ *In the first place. . . . The second point is . . . .*
- ✓ *In addition to. . . . notice that . . . .*
- ✓ *Now look at it from a different angle:. . . .*
- ✓ *You must keep these three things in mind in order to understand the importance of the fourth:. . . .*
- ✓ *What was the result?*
- ✓ *Turning now to . . . .*

The preceding signposts are neutral: they tell an audience that another idea is coming but don't indicate whether it's similar, different, or more important. You can improve the coherence of your speeches by indicating the precise relationships among ideas. Those relationships include parallel/hierarchical, similar/different, and coordinate/subordinate relationships. Here are some examples:

Parallel: Not only . . . but also . . . .

Hierarchical: More important than these . . . .

Different: In contrast . . . .

Similar: Similar to this . . . .

Coordinated: One must consider X, Y, and Z . . . .

Subordinated: On the next level is . . . .

Forecasts, summaries, and signposts are important to your audience. Forecasts and summaries give listeners an overall sense of your entire message; if listeners can easily see the structure, they'll better understand and remember your speech. The signposts lead your listeners step by step through the speech, signaling specific relationships between and among ideas.

Creating an Atmosphere

You cultivate the atmosphere of the speaking occasion largely through your speaking style. In a graduation speech or an awards banquet address, you want to encourage the personal reflection of your listeners; but at a fraternity gathering or holiday celebration, you want to create a social, interactive atmosphere.

Sometimes the atmosphere of the occasion dictates what speaking style should be used. You don't expect a light, humorous speaking style during a funeral. Even so, sometimes a minister, priest, or rabbi will tell a funny story about the deceased. Yet the overall tone of a funeral eulogy should be solemn. In contrast, a speech after a football victory, election win, or successful fund drive is seldom somber. Victory speeches are times for celebration and unity.

The speaking **atmosphere** is the mind-set or mental attitude that you attempt to create in your audience. A serious speaker urging graduating seniors to remember the most important things in life might say, "Rank your values and live by them." That same idea expressed by actor Alan Alda sounded more humorous:

> *We live in a time that seems to be split about its values. In fact it seems to be schizophrenic.*
>
> *For instance, if you pick up a magazine like* Psychology Today, *you're liable to see an article like "White Collar Crime: It's More Widespread than You Think." Then in the back of the magazine they'll print an advertisement that says, "We'll write your doctoral thesis for 25 bucks." You see how values are eroding? I mean, a doctoral thesis ought to go for at least a C-note.*[4]

How do you generate an atmosphere or mood in your listeners? The answer depends on the speaking situation, your speech purpose, and your listeners' expectations. You can adjust the intensity of your speech and manage the appropriateness of your language to communicate a relationship with your listeners.

Intensity

You can communicate your feelings about ideas and objects through word choices. You can communicate your attitude toward your subject by choosing words that show how you feel. This, in turn, suggests how you expect your listeners to react to the subject. In one way, you are demonstrating their response through your language choices. For example, consider these attitudinally weighted terms:

Highly Positive	Relatively Neutral	Highly Negative
Savior	G.I.	Enemy
Patriot	Soldier	Baby-killer
Freedom fighter	Combatant	Foreign devil

These nine terms are organized by their intensity, ranging from the highly positive *savior* to the highly negative *foreign devil*. Notice the religious connotations present in the extreme examples of language intensity. Such terms have obviously potent associations with deeply held beliefs.

How intense should your language be? Communication scholar John Waite Bowers suggested a useful rule of thumb: let your language be, roughly, one step more intense than the position or attitude held by your audience.[5] For example, if your audience is already committed to your negative position on tax reform, then you can choose intensely negative words, such as *regressive* and *stifling*. If your audience is uncommitted, you should opt for comparatively neutral words, such as *burdensome*. And, if your audience is in favor of tax changes, you can use still less negative words, such as *unfair*, so as to avoid turning them off and to encourage them to keep an open mind. Intense language can generate intense reactions, but only if you match your word choices to your listeners' attitudes.

Appropriateness

Your language should be appropriate to the speech topic and situation. Solemn occasions call for restrained and dignified language; joyful occasions call for informal and lively word choices. The language used at the christening of a baby wouldn't work at a pep rally, and vice versa. Suit your language to the atmosphere of the occasion.

Informal Language   Make sure that your language is appropriate to your audience. Before you use informal language, check to see who's listening. Informal language, including slang, quickly goes out of style. *Gee whiz, wow, good grief, hip, cool, far out, homeboy, awesome,* and *radical* became popular at different times. *Far out* would sound silly in a speech to your peers, and *gnarly* would sound ridiculous to an audience of senior citizens. As you work through your speech, consider your language choices as inherent elements in developing the tone of your speech.

Gender-Neutral Language   Words can communicate values or attitudes to your listeners. They also suggest relationships between you and your audience. Gender-linked words, particularly nouns and pronouns, require special attention. **Gender-linked words** are those that directly or indirectly identify males or females—*policeman, washerwoman, poet,* and *poetess*. Pronouns such as *he* and *she* and adjectives such as *his* and *her* are obviously gender-linked words. **Gender-neutral words** do not directly or indirectly denote males or females—*chairperson, police officer,* or *firefighter*.

Since the 1960s and the advent of the women's movement, consciousness of gendered language has gradually surfaced. The question of whether language use affects culture

Speaking of . . . *ethics*

Doublespeak

Advertisers and politicians are often accused of using words that deceive or mislead. Think of any recent advertising or political campaign. *Liberal*, for instance, was once a positive label. In the recent campaigns, the word became associated with negative attributes. It has come to connote the big spender—someone who wastes public energy and tax dollars on unrealistic schemes.

You can probably identify hundreds of words or phrases used to disguise facts. The Reagan and Clinton administrations didn't want to raise taxes but pursued *revenue enhancement* through *user fees*. People below the poverty line are *fiscal underachievers*. Nuclear weapons are labeled *radiation enhancement devices* and *peacekeepers*. And the 1984 invasion of Grenada was officially a *predawn vertical insertion*. Some language usage makes the unpleasant seem good and the positive appear negative. Language can shield us from the reality it represents.

Such name calling is by no means limited to politicians. Advertisers market *new and improved* products. We're tantalized with *real faux pearls* and *genuine imitation leather*. Advertisers exploit our health consciousness with *low-cholesterol* and *high-fiber* ingredients. Take a few moments to think about the following uses of language:

1. Suppose that you notice biased language in an article you're reading to research a speech topic. Should you cite the article as supporting material in your speech?
2. You genuinely believe in your recommendations for solving the problems you outline in a speech and you want to convince your listeners to sign a petition for change. Is it fair to use scare tactics or to tell them that they've got only one day left to act when in fact there's more time?
3. Should you ever use racy, obscene, or questionable language during a speech? Does it affect the relationship you establish with your listeners?
4. Is it ever fair to call people who aren't present *crooks* or attach similar labels to them?
5. Do you think language can obscure our understanding of reality? Under what circumstances do you think this happens? Should anything be done to make language more honest? What can you do to accomplish this?

and socialization still is being debated. However, as a speaker you must be careful not to alienate your audience or to propagate stereotypes unconsciously through your use of language. In addition to avoiding most gender-linked words, you've got to handle two more problems:

1. *Inaccurately excluding members of one sex.* Some uses of gendered pronouns inaccurately reflect social-occupational conditions in the world: "A nurse sees *her* patients eight hours a day, but a doctor sees *his* for only ten minutes." Many women are doctors, just as many men are nurses. Most audience members are aware of this and may be displeased if they feel that you're stereotyping roles in the medical profession.

2. *Stereotyping male and female psychological or social characteristics.* "Real men never cry." "A woman's place is in the home." "The Marines are looking for a few good men." "Sugar 'n spice 'n everything nice—that's what little girls are made of." Falling back on these stereotypes gets speakers into trouble with audiences, both male and female. In these days of raised consciousness, audiences are insulted to

hear such misinformed assertions. In addition, these stereotypes conceal the potential in individuals whose talents are not limited by their gender.

These problem areas demand your attention. A speaker who habitually uses sexist language is guilty of ignoring important speaking conventions that have taken shape over the past several decades. How can you avoid sexist language? Here are four easy ways:

1. *Speak in the plural.* Say, "Bankers are often. . . . They face . . . ." This tactic is often sufficient to make your language gender-neutral.

2. *Say "he or she" when you must use a singular subject.* Say, "A student majoring in business is required to sign up for an internship. He or she can . . . ." This strategy works well as long as you don't overdo it. If you find yourself cluttering sentences with "he or she," switch to the plural.

3. *Remove gender inflections.* It's painless to say *firefighter* instead of *fireman*, *chair* or *chairperson* instead of *chairman*, and *tailor* instead of *seamstress*. Gender inflections can usually be removed without affecting your speech.

4. *Use gender-specific pronouns for gender-specific processes, people, or activities.* It is acceptable to talk about a mother as *her* or a current or former president of the United States as *him*. Men do not naturally bear children, and a woman has not yet been elected to the White House.

Ultimately, the search for gender-neutral idioms is an affirmation of mutual respect and a recognition of equal worth and the essential dignity of individuals. Gender differences are important in many aspects of life, but when they dominate public talk, they're ideologically oppressive. Be gender neutral in public talk to remove barriers to effective communication.[6]

Selecting an appropriate style is a matter of assessing yourself, your audience, the situation or context, and your speaking purposes. A thorough assessment of these variables will help you to select an appropriate style.

In summary, wording your speech demands careful thought about the clarity of your language use, the persuasive force lying behind words, and the overall sense of tone or style that results from choosing language with particular characteristics. In the world of international diplomacy, a wrong word can cause a breakdown in negotiations. In your world, it can produce confusion, misunderstanding, or even disgust. Take time to shape your oral language as carefully as you shape your ideas.

Using Language Strategically

Developing an effective oral speaking style is important. You will also, however, want to tap more directly into the powers of language—the powers to alter people's minds and move them to action. To accomplish those goals, you need to use oral language strategically. We will focus on three of the most common language strategies: definitions, imagery, and metaphor.

Definitions

Audience members need to understand the fundamental concepts of your speech. You can't expect them to understand your ideas if your language is unfamiliar. As a speaker, you have several options when working to define unfamiliar or difficult concepts.

Definitions help you to grasp concepts. Contextual definitions are used in specific contexts.

You're most familiar with a **dictionary definition,** which categorizes an object or concept and specifies its characteristics: "An orange is a *fruit* (category) that is *round, orange in color,* and a member of the *citrus family* (characteristics)." Dictionary definitions sometimes help you to learn unfamiliar words, but they don't help an audience very much. If you do use dictionary definitions, go to specialized dictionaries. You certainly wouldn't depend on *Webster's Third International Dictionary* to define *foreclosure* or *liability* for a presentation on real estate law. For this technical application, sources such as *Black's Law Dictionary* and *Guide to American Law* are more highly respected.

Occasionally, a word has so many meanings that you have to choose one. If that's the case, use a **stipulative definition** to orient your listeners to your subject matter. A stipulative definition designates the way a word will be used in a certain context. You might say, "By *rich* I mean, . . ." or you might use an expert's stipulative definition such as this one from former President Jimmy Carter:

> *Who is rich? I'm not talking about bank accounts. . . . A rich person is someone with a home and a modicum of education and a chance for at least a job and who believes that if you make a decision that it'll have some effect at least in your own life, and who believes that the police and the judges are on your side. These are the rich people.[7]*

You can further clarify a term or concept by telling your audience how you are *not* going to use the concept—by using a **negative definition.** So, Chicago police Sergeant Bruce Talbot defined "gateway drug" in this manner:

> *[F]or adolescents, cigarette smoking is a gateway drug to illicit drugs such as marijuana and crack cocaine. By gateway drug I do not mean just that cigarettes are the first drug young people encounter, alcohol is. But unlike alcohol, which is first experienced in a*

social ritual such as church or an important family event, cigarettes are the first drug minors buy themselves and use secretly outside the family and social institutions.[8]

Defining negatively can clear away possible misconceptions. Using a negative definition along with a stipulative definition, as did Sergeant Talbot, allows you to treat a commonplace phenomenon in a different way.

Sometimes you can reinforce an idea by telling your listeners where a word came from. One way to do this is by using an **etymological definition.** An etymological definition is the derivation of a single word; we offered an example of this in Chapter 1, tracing the word *communication* back to its Latin origins.

One of the best ways to define is by an **exemplar definition,** especially if the concept is unfamiliar or technical. Exemplar definitions are familiar examples. You might tell your listeners, "Each day, most of you stroll past the Old Capitol on your way to classes. That building is a perfect example of what I want to talk about today—Georgian architecture." Be careful to use in your definition only those examples that are familiar to your audience members.

A **contextual definition** tells listeners how a word is used in a specific situation. So, Professor Jonathan Mann was arguing that AIDS and other new diseases are changing our understanding of health—not as individuals but as a society. He captures that change by defining the word *solidarity* in terms of health:

> [S]olidarity describes a central concept in this emerging perspective on health, individuals, and society. The AIDS pandemic has taught us a great deal about tolerance and nondiscrimination, a refusal to separate the condition of the few from the fate of the many. Solidarity arises when people realize that excessive differences among people make the entire system unstable. Charity is individual; solidarity is inherently social, concerned with social justice, and therefore also economic and political.[9]

Still another means of making technical or abstract notions easier to understand is the **analogical definition.** An analogy compares a process or event that is unknown with known ones, as in, "Hospitals and labs use cryogenic tanks, which work much like large thermos bottles, to freeze tissue samples, blood, and other organic matter." By referring to what is familiar, the analogical definition can make the unfamiliar much easier to grasp. But the speaker must be sure that the analogy fits.

The points here are simple but important: (1) You have many different kinds of definitions to choose from when working with unfamiliar or difficult concepts. (2) Select definitional strategies that make sense for your subject matter, your audience, and your purposes.

Imagery

People grasp their world through the senses of sight, smell, hearing, taste, and touch. To intensify listeners' experiences, you can appeal to these senses. The senses through which you reach your listeners *directly* are the visual and the auditory. Listeners can see you, your facial expressions, your movements, and your visual aids, and they can hear what you say (see Figure 10.1).

You can stimulate your listeners' senses *indirectly* by using language to recall images they have previously experienced. **Imagery** consists of sets of sensory pictures evoked in the imagination through language. The language of imagery is divided into seven types,

FIGURE 10.1   The Types of Imagery

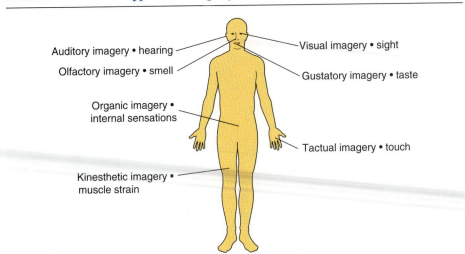

Auditory imagery • hearing

Olfactory imagery • smell

Organic imagery • internal sensations

Kinesthetic imagery • muscle strain

Visual imagery • sight

Gustatory imagery • taste

Tactual imagery • touch

Speakers can stimulate their listeners' senses indirectly through language which triggers sensations.

each related to the particular sensation that it seeks to evoke: visual (sight), auditory (hearing), gustatory (taste), olfactory (smell), tactile (touch), kinesthetic (muscle strain), and organic (internal sensations).

Visual Imagery *Visual imagery* describes optical stimuli. Try to make your audience see the objects or situations that you're describing. Mention size, shape, color, and movement. Recount events in vivid visual language. Consider the conclusion from a speech by former Federal Communications Commissioner Newton N. Minow to the Gannett Foundation Media Center in 1991. He envisioned a past event, a look at primitive TV in 1938, to reintroduce some timeless problems. He played off the "vision" of television as well as the imagery of light (or dark, in the case of the Gulf War of 1991). *Vision* became a wonderfully ambiguous word referring both to light and to what we learn to see in the world:

> *I commend some extraordinary words to the new generation. E. B. White sat in a darkened room in 1938 to see the beginning of television, an experimental electronic box that projected images in the room. Once he saw it, Mr. White wrote:*
>
> *"We shall stand or fall by television, of that I am sure. I believe television is going to be the test of the modern world, and that in this new opportunity to see beyond the range of our vision, we shall discover either a new and unbearable disturbance to the general peace, or a saving radiance in the sky."*
>
> *That radiance falls unevenly today. It is still a dim light in education. It has not fulfilled its potential for children. It has neglected the needs of public television. And in the electoral process it has cast a dark shadow.*
>
> *This year, television has enabled us to see Patriot missiles destroy Scud missiles above the Persian Gulf. Will television in the next thirty years be a Scud or a Patriot? A new generation now has the chance to put the vision back into television, to travel from the wasteland to the promised land, and to make television a saving radiance in the sky.[10]*

Image-evoking language can recreate experiences for others.

Auditory Imagery   To create auditory imagery, use words that describe sounds. Auditory imagery can project your listeners into a scene by helping them hear noises. Author Tom Wolfe described a demolition derby by recounting the chant of the crowd as it joined in the countdown, the explosion of sound as two dozen cars started off in second gear, and finally "the unmistakable tympany of automobiles colliding and cheap-gauge sheet metal buckling."[11]

Gustatory Imagery   Gustatory imagery depicts sensations of taste. Sometimes you may even be able to help your audience taste what you're describing. Mention its saltiness, sweetness, sourness, or spiciness. Remember that foods have texture as well as taste. While demonstrating how to make popcorn, you might mention the crispness of the kernels, the oily sweetness of melted butter, and the grittiness of salt. Such descriptions allow your listeners to participate in the experience through their imaginations.

Olfactory Imagery   Olfactory imagery describes sensations of smell. Help your audience smell the odors connected with the situation you describe. Smell is a powerful sense because it normally triggers a flood of associated images. You can stimulate this process by describing the odor or by comparing the odor with more familiar ones. Elspeth Huxley remembered her childhood trek to Kenya at the turn of the century by recalling its smells:

> *It was the smell of travel in those days, in fact the smell of Africa—dry, peppery yet rich and deep, with an undertone of native body smeared with fat and red ochre and giving out a ripe, partly rancid odour which nauseated some Europeans when they*

first encountered it but which I, for one, grew to enjoy. This was the smell of the Kikuyu, who were mainly vegetarian. The smell of tribes from the Victoria Nyanza basin, who were meat-eaters and sometimes cannibals, was quite different; much stronger and more musky, almost acrid, and, to me, much less pleasant. No doubt we smelt just as strong and odd to Africans, but of course we were fewer in numbers, and more spread out.[12]

Tactile Imagery   Tactile imagery is based on the sensations that come to us through physical contact with external objects. In particular, tactile imagery gives sensations of texture and shape, pressure, and heat or cold. Let your audience feel how rough or smooth, dry or wet, or slimy or sticky modeling clay is (texture and shape). Let them sense the pressure of physical force on their bodies, the weight of a heavy laundry bag, the pinch of jogging shoes, the blast of a high wind on their faces (pressure).

Sensations of heat or cold are aroused by thermal imagery. General Douglas MacArthur's great speech to the Cadets of West Point on "duty, honor, and country" used vivid examples of tactile imagery as he described soldiers of the past,

bending under soggy pack on many a weary march, from dripping dusk to drizzly dawn, slogging ankle deep through mire of shell-pocked roads; to form grimly for the attack, blue-lipped, covered with sludge and mud, chilled by the wind and rain, driving home to their objective, and for many, to the judgment seat of God.[13]

Kinesthetic Imagery   Kinesthetic imagery describes the sensations associated with muscle strain and neuromuscular movement. Let your listeners experience for themselves the agonies and joys of marathon racing—the muscle cramps, the constricted chest, the struggle for air—and the magical serenity of getting a second wind and gliding effortlessly toward the finish line.

Organic Imagery   Hunger, dizziness, nausea—these are organic images. Organic imagery captures internal feelings or sensations. There are times when an experience is not complete without the description of inner feelings. The sensation of dizziness as a mountain climber struggles through the rarified mountain air to reach the summit is one example. Another is the way the bottom drops out of your stomach when a small plane tips sharply, then rights itself. Since such imagery is powerful, you shouldn't offend your audience by overdoing it. Develop the rhetorical sensitivity required to create vividness without making the resultant image gruesome, disgusting, or grotesque.

The seven types of imagery we have considered—visual, auditory, gustatory, olfactory, tactile, kinesthetic, and organic—open new levels of awareness that help listeners experience your message. Different people respond to different kinds of imagery, so you should insert several types of imagery in your speeches. In the following example, note how the speaker combines various sensory appeals to arouse listener interest and reaction:

The strangler struck in Donora, Pennsylvania, in October of 1948. A thick fog billowed through the streets enveloping everything in thick sheets of dirty moisture and a greasy black coating. As Tuesday faded into Saturday, the fumes from the big steel mills shrouded the outlines of the landscape. One could barely see across the narrow streets. Traffic stopped. Men lost their way returning from the mills. Walking through the streets, even for a few moments, caused eyes to water and burn. The thick fumes grabbed at the throat and created a choking sensation. The air acquired a sickening bittersweet smell, nearly a taste. Death was in the air.[14]

In this example, college student Charles Schaillol uses vivid, descriptive phrases to affect the senses of his listeners—visual: "thick sheets of dirty moisture"; organic: "eyes to water and burn"; and olfactory, gustatory: "sickening bittersweet smell, nearly a taste."

To be effective, such illustrations must appear plausible. The language must convey a realistic impression that the situation described could happen. The speaker who describes the strangler that struck Donora offers a plausible account of the event. More important, he does so in a fashion that arouses feelings. His listeners wouldn't have shared the experience if he had simply said, "Air pollution was the cause of death in Donora."

Metaphor

Images created by appealing to the senses are often the result of metaphors. A **metaphor** is the comparison of two dissimilar things. Charles Schaillol's description of fog as "thick sheets of dirty moisture" is one example. Scholar Michael Osborn notes that the metaphor should "result in an intuitive flash of recognition that surprises or fascinates the hearer."[15] Furthermore, good metaphors extend our knowledge or increase our awareness of a person, object, or event. When they're fresh or vivid, they can be powerful aids in evoking feelings. For example, referring to a table's "legs" is a metaphor, but it's boring. It's much more interesting to say, "Balanced on four toothpicks, the antique table swayed under its heavy burden."

Metaphors drawn from everyday experiences provide wide audience appeal. In the following speech, Martin Luther King, Jr., relied on our experiences of light and darkness:

With this faith in the future, with this determined struggle, we will be able to emerge from the bleak and desolate midnight of man's inhumanity to man, into the bright and glittering daybreak of freedom and justice.[16]

This basic light-dark metaphor allowed King to suggest (a) sharp contrasts between inhumanity and freedom and (b) the inevitability of social progress as "daybreak" follows "midnight." The metaphor communicated King's beliefs about justice and injustice and urged others to action. Words are not neutral pipelines for thought. Words not only reflect the world outside your mind, but also, as critic Kenneth Burke suggests, help *shape* our perceptions of people, events, and social contexts. Language has a potent effect on people's willingness to believe, to feel, and to act.

Sample Speech

William Faulkner (1897–1962) presented the following speech on December 10, 1950, as he accepted the Nobel Prize for Literature. His listeners might have expected a speech filled with the kind of pessimism so characteristic of his novels. Instead, he greeted them with a stirring challenge to improve humankind.

Notice in particular Faulkner's use of language. Although known for the tortured sentences in his novels, he expresses his ideas clearly and simply in his speech. His style suggests a written speech, yet his use of organic imagery and powerful metaphors keep the speech alive. The atmosphere is generally serious, befitting the occasion. You might expect a Nobel Prize winner to talk about himself, but Faulkner did just the opposite. He stressed his craft, writing, and the commitment necessary to practice that craft; this material emphasis led naturally to an essentially propositional rather than narrative form. More than 40 years ago, William Faulkner offered a speech that is as relevant today as it was in 1950.

On Accepting the Nobel Prize for Literature William Faulkner[17]

I feel that this award was not made to me as a man, but to my work—a life's work in the agony and sweat of the human spirit, not for glory and least of all for profit, but to create out of the materials of the human spirit something which did not exist before. So this award is only mine in trust. It will not be difficult to find a dedication for the money part of it commensurate with the purpose and significance of its origin. But I would like to do the same with the acclaim too, by using this moment as a pinnacle from which I might be listened to by the young men and women already dedicated to the same anguish and travail, among whom is already that one who will some day stand here where I am standing./1

Our tragedy today is a general and universal physical fear so long sustained by now that we can even bear it. There are no longer problems of the spirit. There is only the question: When will I be blown up? Because of this, the young man or woman writing today has forgotten the problems of the human heart in conflict with itself which alone can make good writing because only that is worth writing about, worth the agony and the sweat./2

He must learn them again. He must teach himself that the basest of all things is to be afraid; and, teaching himself that, forget it forever, leaving no room in his workshop for anything but the old verities and truths of the heart, the old universal truths lacking which any story is ephemeral and doomed—love and honor and pity and pride and compassion and sacrifice. Until he does so, he labors under a curse. He writes not of love but of lust, of defeats in which nobody loses anything of value, of victories without hope and, worst of all, without pity or compassion. His griefs grieve on no universal bones, leaving no scars. He writes not of the heart but of the glands./3

Until he relearns these things, he will write as though he stood among and watched the end of man. I decline to accept the end of man. It is easy enough to say that man is immortal simply because he will endure: that

Faulkner establishes a series of contrasts built around a "not this . . . but this" construction to deflect attention from himself to his work. The contrasts sharpen the points he'll make throughout the speech; it's the art, not the artist, that counts; creating art is extraordinarily hard work; we can't write out of fear but out of the need to elevate the soul and spirit of humanity.

He frames his whole speech as an address to young writers.

When he addresses the issue of the bomb and our fear of it, he attacks that fear immediately. First, he suggests the presence of the fear and then via restatement comes back to it in the next three sentences. Second, he continues the linguistic contrasts between fear and spirit, human heart in conflict and the agony and the sweat.

Faulkner expands this central idea via a series of literal and metaphorical contrasts. Read these sentences aloud to capture the pounding rhythm that guides them: love versus lust, defeats versus victories, value and hope versus pity and compassion. Body metaphors complete the paragraph.

Faulkner concludes with a flood of imagery: images are auditory ("the last ding-dong of doom," "his puny inexhaustible voice," and "the poet's voice"); visual ("the last worthless rock hanging tideless in the last red and dying evening"); tactile ("the pillars" that provide support for people to "endure and prevail"); and organic ("lifting his heart").

The restatement of vocabulary, the intertwining of images and exhortations, the affirmation of life in the face of atomic devastation, and, of course, the sheer presence of Faulkner himself combine to make this one of the two or three greatest Nobel Prize speeches ever given.

when the last ding-dong of doom has clanged and faded from the last worthless rock hanging tideless in the last red and drying evening, that even then there will still be one more sound: that of his puny inexhaustible voice, still talking. I refuse to accept this. I believe that man will not merely endure: he will prevail. He is immortal, not because he alone among creatures has an inexhaustible voice, but because he has a soul, a spirit capable of compassion and sacrifice and endurance. The poet's, the writer's, duty is to write about these things. It is his privilege to help man endure by lifting his heart, by reminding him of the courage and honor and hope and pride and compassion and pity and sacrifice which have been the glory of his past. The poet's voice need not merely be the record of man, it can be one of the props, the pillars to help him endure and prevail./4

Assessing Your Progress

Chapter Summary

1. Language functions on referential, relational, and symbolic levels.

2. Encoding occurs when you put ideas into words and actions.

3. Successful speeches generally are characterized by oral style that is typical of conversation.

4. You can cultivate oral style through accurate word choice, simple phrasing, restatement, and signaling coherent speech structure.

5. The intensity and appropriateness of language can be altered to contribute to the atmosphere in a speaking situation.

6. Rhetorical strategies are word and phrase choices intended to control the impact of the speech. Three of the most common are definition, imagery, and metaphor.

7. Speakers can define unfamiliar or difficult concepts in multiple ways, via dictionary, stipulative, negative, etymological, exemplar, contextual, and analogical definitions.

8. Imagery consists of word pictures created in the imagination through language. There are seven types of images: visual, auditory, gustatory, olfactory, tactile, kinesthetic, and organic sensations.

9. Metaphor is the comparison of two dissimilar things.

Key Terms

analogical definition (p. 160)

atmosphere (p. 155)

coherence (p. 153)

contextual definition (p. 160)

dictionary definition (p. 159)

encoding (p. 149)

etymological definition (p. 160)

exemplar definition (p. 160)

forecast (p. 153)

gender-linked words (p. 156)

gender-neutral words (p. 156)

imagery (p. 160)

metaphor (p. 164)

negative definition (p. 159)

oral style (p. 150)

restatement (p. 152)

signposts (p. 154)

stipulative definition (p. 159)

summary (p. 154)

written style (p. 150)

Assessment Activities

1. Choose one of the items listed below and describe it, using the seven kinds of imagery to create an involving portrait for your listeners. How many kinds of imagery did you use? Which was most effective for your listeners?

   One of the scenes in your favorite movies.

   A tropical plant.

   A breakfast food.

   A complicated machine.

   The oldest building on campus.

2. Find a complicated message (e.g., an insurance policy, an agreement for a credit card or a loan, income tax instructions, or a difficult passage from a book). Rewrite it in simple, yet accurate language. Bring a copies of both messages to class. Present both versions of the material to your classmates. Which was most effective? Why?

3. Read one of the sample speeches in this textbook. Identify the methods the speaker uses to make the language effective. Were the speaker's word choices effective? Did the speaker choose an appropriate style? What rhetorical strategies can you discover in the speech?

References

1.   For a summary of several technical studies distinguishing between oral and written styles, and for a discussion of sixteen characteristics of oral style, see John F. Wilson and Carroll C. Arnold, *Public Speaking as a Liberal Art*, 5th ed. (Boston: Allyn and Bacon, 1983), 227–229.

2.   Quoted in John R. Pelsma, *Essentials of Speech* (New York: Crowell, Collier, and Macmillan, 1934), 193.

3.   William J. Clinton, "The New Covenant," in *Representative American Speeches, 1991–1992*, edited by Owen Peterson (New York: H. W. Wilson Co., 1992), 52–53.

4. Alan Alda, "A Reel Doctor's Advice to Some Real Doctors," in Stephen E. Lucas, *The Art of Public Speaking* (New York: Random House, 1983), 364.

5. John Waite Bowers, "Language and Argument," in *Perspectives on Argumentation,* edited by G. R. Miller and T. R. Nilsen (Glenview, Ill.: Scott, Foresman, 1966), 168–172.

6. There are many studies of gender and communication. For overviews, see H. M. Hacker, "Blabbermouths and Claims: Sex Differences in Self-Disclosure in Same-Sex and Cross-Sex Friendship Dyads," *Psychology of Women Quarterly, 5* (1981): 385–401; Judith C. Pearson, *Gender and Communication* (Dubuque, Ia.: Wm. C. Brown, 1985); Barbara Bate, *Communication and the Sexes* (New York: Harper & Row, 1987); Lea P. Stewart, Pamela J. Cooper, and Sheryl A. Friedly, *Communication Between the Sexes: Sex Differences and Sex-Role Stereotypes* (Scottsdale, Ariz.: Gorsuch Scarisbrick, 1986); and Carole Spitzack and Kathryn Carter, "Women in Communication Studies: A Typology of Revision," *Quarterly Journal of Speech, 73* (1987): 401–423.

7. James E. Carter, "Excellence Comes from a Repository That Doesn't Change," *Vital Speeches of the Day, 59* (1 July 1993), 548.

8. Bruce Talbot, "Statement," Hearings before Senate Committee on Commerce, Science, and Transportation, *Tobacco Product Education and Health Promotion Act of 1991, S. 1088,* 14 November 1991, 102nd Congress (Washington, D.C.: U.S. Government Printing Office, 1991), 77.

9. Jonathan Mann, "Global AIDS: Revolution, Paradigm, and Solidarity," *Representative American Speeches, 1990–1991,* edited by Owen Peterson (New York: H. W. Wilson Co., 1991), 88.

10. Newton N. Minow, "How Vast the Wasteland Now?" in *Representative American Speeches, 1991–1992,* edited by Owen Peterson (New York: H. W. Wilson Co., 1992), 169.

11. A selection from Tom Wolfe, *The Kandy-Kolored Tangerine-Flake Streamline Baby* (Thomas K. Wolfe, Jr., 1965). Reprinted by permission of Farrar, Straus and Giroux, Inc. and International Creative Management.

12. Elspeth Huxley, *The Flame Trees of Thika: Memories of an African Childhood* (London: Chatto & Windus, 1959), 4.

13. Excerpt from Douglas MacArthur, "Duty, Honor and Country," *The Dolphin Book of Speeches,* edited by George W. Hibbit (George W. Hibbit, 1965). Reprinted by permission of Doubleday & Company, Inc.

14. From Charles Schaillol, "The Strangler," *Winning Orations.* Reprinted by permission of Larry Schnoor, Executive Secretary, Interstate Oratorical Association, Concordia College, Moorhead, Minn.

15. Michael Osborn, *Orientations to Rhetorical Style* (Chicago: Science Research Associates, 1976), 10.

16. From Martin Luther King, Jr., "Love, Law and Civil Disobedience" (Martin Luther King, Jr., 1963). Reprinted by permission of Joan Daves.

17. William Faulkner, "On Accepting the Nobel Prize for Literature," *The Faulkner Reader* (New York: Random House, 1954).

11 Delivering Your Speech

If you're struggling with the physical aspects of delivering your speeches, you're in good company. Many famous speakers have had to overcome severe delivery problems before becoming effective speakers. Abraham Lincoln suffered from extreme speech fright; Eleanor Roosevelt was awkward and clumsy; John F. Kennedy had a strong dialect and repetitive gestures; Helen Keller was blind and deaf. These speakers realized that success depends not only on careful planning before the speech but also on effective presentation. They each worked hard to develop the oral delivery skills that heightened the impact of their ideas.

You must be aware that you communicate with your entire body—your face, your gestures, your voice, and your posture. Your voice and bodily movements—the *aural and visual channels of communication*—help to transmit your feelings and attitudes about yourself, your audience, and your topic. You may see speakers who approach the lectern dragging their feet and fussing with their notes. Their attitudes are abundantly clear even before they utter their first words. Unwittingly, these speakers establish audience predispositions that work against them. Even if their ideas are important, those ideas are overshadowed by distracting nonverbal communication.

If you've heard a recording or seen a video of Martin Luther King, Jr., giving his "I Have a Dream" speech, you can appreciate the dramatic difference between hearing him speak and merely reading a copy of the speech. The same is true of Jesse Jackson, Camille Paglia, Rush Limbaugh, Colin Powell, Ann Richards, and Susan Molinari. Oral presentation can add fire to the message. Orality's great strength—its edge—comes from the personal presence established by your voice and your physical presence.

Your speech will gain strength and vitality if it's presented well. To help you achieve this objective, we'll discuss three important aspects of presentation: selecting the method of presentation, using your voice to communicate, and using your body to communicate.

Selecting the Method of Presentation

How should you present your speech? Your choice will be based on several criteria, including the type of speaking occasion, the purpose of your speech, your audience analysis, and your own strengths and weaknesses as a speaker. Attention to these considerations will help you to decide whether your method of presentation should be impromptu, memorized, read from a manuscript, or extemporized.

The Impromptu Speech

An **impromptu speech** is delivered on the spur of the moment, without preparation. The ability to speak off the cuff is useful in an emergency, but you should avoid impromptu speeches whenever possible, because they produce unpredictable outcomes. In an impromptu speech, you must rely entirely on previous knowledge and skill. You might be asked in the middle of a sorority meeting, for example, to give a progress report on your pledge committee. Or, you might be called on in class to summarize the ideas in a paper you turned in last week.

For best results when speaking on an impromptu basis, try to focus on a single idea, carefully relating all details connected to that idea. If you relay the plans for the annual pledge-week open house or the central thesis of your paper, you'll be more likely to stay on track. Sticking with a single idea will keep you from rambling incoherently.

The Memorized Speech

On rare occasions, you may write out your speech and commit it to memory. When notecards or a TelePrompTer cannot be used, it may be acceptable for you to give a **memorized speech.** When making a toast at your parents' twenty-fifth wedding anniversary, for example, you probably wouldn't want to speak from notecards. Some speakers, such as comedians, deliver their remarks from memory to free their hands to mimic the movements of the character they are playing.

Speakers who use memorized presentations are usually most effective when they write their speeches to sound like informal and conversational speech rather than formal, written essays. Remember that with a memorized speech, you'll have difficulty responding to audience feedback. Since the words of the speech are predetermined, you can't easily adjust them as the speech progresses.

The Manuscript Speech

A **manuscript speech** is written out beforehand and then read from a manuscript or TelePrompTer. By using TelePrompTers, speakers can appear to be looking at television viewers while they're really reading their manuscripts projected onto clear sheets of Plexiglas. When extremely careful wording is required, the manuscript speech is appropriate. When the president addresses Congress, for example, a slip of the tongue could misdirect domestic or foreign policies. Many radio and television speeches are read from manuscripts because of the strict time limits imposed by broadcasting schedules.

The Extemporaneous Speech

Most speeches that you'll deliver will be extemporaneous. An **extemporaneous speech** is one that is prepared in advance and presented from abbreviated notes. Most of the advice in this textbook pertains to extemporaneous speaking. Extemporaneous speeches are nearly as polished as memorized ones, but they are more vigorous, flexible, and spontaneous.

Before giving an extemporaneous speech, you must plan and prepare a detailed outline and speaking notecards. Then, working from the notecards, you practice the speech aloud, using your own words to communicate the ideas. Your expressions differ somewhat each time you deliver the speech. Your notes, however, regulate the order of ideas. With this approach, you gain control of the material and also preserve your spontaneity of expression. Good preparation is the key to extemporaneous speaking. Otherwise, your speech may resemble an impromptu speech; in fact, the terms *impromptu* and *extemporaneous* are often confused.

While you may use all four types of speech presentation for different occasions during your lifetime, extemporaneous speaking is the most important. Extemporaneous speaking displays your enthusiasm for speaking and the sincerity of your ideas. In order to develop your skills as an extemporaneous speaker, you will need to learn to use both your voice and your body to communicate with your listeners.

Using Your Voice to Communicate

Your voice is an instrument that helps convey the meaning of language. Since preliterate times, when all cultures were oral, voice has been the primary connector between people. Sounds flow among people, integrating them, creating a sense of identification, of community.[1] Although you've been speaking for years, you've probably not tapped the full potential of your voice—its power to connect you with others. You'll need to take time to practice in order to achieve your vocal potential, just as you would to master any instrument. The suggestions in this section will help you to get started.

You communicate your enthusiasm to your listeners through your voice. By learning about the characteristics of vocal quality, you can make your ideas more interesting. Listen to a stock market reporter rattle off the daily industrial averages. Every word might be intelligible, but the reporter's vocal expression may be so repetitive and monotonous that the ideas seem unexciting. Then, listen to Al Michaels doing a play-by-play of a football game or Dick Vitale covering a basketball game. The excitement of their broadcasts depends largely on their voices.

Our society prizes one essential vocal quality above all others—a sense of "conversationality."[2] The conversational speaker creates a sense of two-way, interpersonal relationship, even when behind a lectern. The best hosts of afternoon talk shows or evening newscasts speak as though they're engaging each listener in a personal conversation. Speakers who've developed a conversational quality—Geraldo Rivera, Oprah Winfrey, Dick Cavett, Joan Lunden, and Regis Philbin, for example—have recognized that they're talking *with*, not *at*, an audience.

The Effective Speaking Voice

Successful speakers use their voices to shape their ideas and emotionally color their messages. A flexible speaking voice possesses intelligibility, variety, and understandable stress patterns.

Intelligibility *Intelligibility* refers to the ease with which a listener can understand what you're saying. It depends on loudness, rate, enunciation, and pronunciation. Most of the time, inadequate articulation, a rapid speaking rate, or soft volume is acceptable because you know the people you're talking with and because you're probably only 3 to 5 feet from them. In public speaking, however, you may be addressing people you don't know, often from 25 feet or more away. When speaking in public, you have to work on making yourself intelligible:

1. *Adjust your volume.* Probably the most important single factor in intelligibility is how loudly you speak. Volume is related to the *distance* between you and your listeners and the amount of *noise* that is present. You must realize that your own voice sounds louder to you than it does to your listeners. Obviously, you need to project your voice by increasing your volume if you're speaking in an auditorium filled with several hundred people. However, you shouldn't forget that a corresponding reduction in volume is also required when your listeners are only a few feet away. The amount of surrounding noise with which you must compete also has an effect on your volume. (See Figure 11.1.) Increase your volume to counter a distraction.

FIGURE 11.1 Loudness Levels

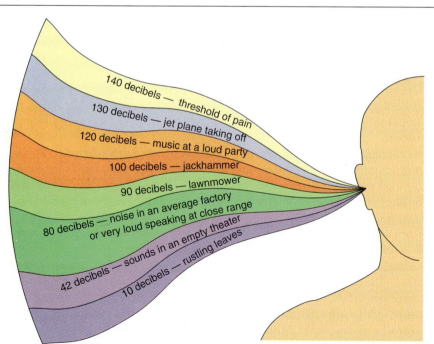

140 decibels — threshold of pain
130 decibels — jet plane taking off
120 decibels — music at a loud party
100 decibels — jackhammer
90 decibels — lawnmower
80 decibels — noise in an average factory or very loud speaking at close range
42 decibels — sounds in an empty theater
10 decibels — rustling leaves

As you can see, noise varies considerably. You should adjust your volume when you speak to a "quiet" audience as well as if you are competing with a lawnmower outside the building.

2. *Control your rate.* **Rate** is the number of words spoken per minute. In animated conversation, you may jabber along at 200 to 250 words per minute. This rate is typical of people raised in the North, Midwest, or West. As words tumble out of your mouth in informal conversations, they're usually intelligible because they don't have to travel far. In large auditoriums or outdoors, though, rapid delivery can impede intelligibility. Echoes sometimes distort or destroy sounds in rooms; ventilation fans interfere with sound. In the outdoors, words seem to vanish into the open air.

   When addressing larger audiences, cut your rate by a third or more. Obviously you don't go around timing your speaking rate, but you can remind yourself of potential rate problems as you prepare to speak. Get feedback from your instructors and classmates regarding your speaking rate.

3. *Enunciate clearly.* **Enunciation** refers to the crispness and precision with which you form words. Good enunciation is the clear and distinct utterance of syllables and words. Most of us are "lip lazy" in normal conversation. We slur sounds, drop syllables, and skip over the beginnings and endings of words. This laziness may not inhibit communication between friends, but it can seriously undermine a speaker's intelligibility.

   When speaking publicly, force yourself to say *going* instead of *go-in, just* instead of *jist,* and *government* instead of *guvment.* You will need to open your mouth wider and force your lips and tongue to form the consonants firmly. If you're having trouble enunciating clearly, ask your instructor for some exercises to improve your performance. (See "Speaking of . . . Skills: Vocal Exercises.")

4. *Meet standards of pronunciation.* To be intelligible, you must form sounds carefully and meet audience expectations regarding acceptable pronunciation. Even if your words aren't garbled, any peculiarity of pronunciation is sure to be noticed by some listeners. Your different pronunciation may distract your listeners and undermine your credibility as a speaker.

A **dialect** is language use—including vocabulary, grammar, and pronunciation—unique to a particular group or region. Your pronunciation and grammatical or syntactical arrangement of words determine your dialect. You may have a foreign accent, a southern or northern dialect, a Vietnamese pitch pattern, a New England twang, or a Hispanic trill. A clash of dialects can result in confusion and frustration for both speaker and listener. Audiences can make negative judgments about the speaker's credibility—that is, the speaker's education, reliability, responsibility, and capacity for leadership—based solely on dialect.[3] Paralinguists call these judgments *vocal stereotypes.*[4] Wary of vocal stereotypes, many news anchors have adopted a midwestern American dialect, a manner of speaking that is widely accepted across the country. Many speakers become bilingual, using their own dialects when facing local audiences but switching to midwestern American when addressing more varied audiences. When you speak, you'll have to decide whether you should use the grammar, vocabulary, and vocal patterns of middle America.

Variety   As you move from conversations with friends to the enlarged context of public speaking, you may discover that listeners accuse you of monotony of pitch or rate. When speaking in a large public setting, you should compensate for the greater distance that sounds have to travel by varying certain characteristics of your voice. Variety is produced by changes in rate, pitch, stress, and pauses.

1. *Vary your rate.* Earlier, we discussed the rate at which we normally speak. Alter your speaking rate to match your ideas. Slow down to emphasize your own thoughtfulness or quicken the pace when your ideas are emotionally charged. Observe, for example, how Larry King varies his speaking rate from caller to caller or how an evangelist changes pace regularly. A varied rate keeps an audience's attention riveted to the speech.

2. *Change your pitch.* **Pitch** is the frequency of sound waves in a particular sound. Three aspects of pitch—level, range, and variation—are relevant to effective vocal communication. Your everyday pitch level—whether it is habitually in the soprano, alto, tenor, baritone, or bass range—is adequate for most of your daily communication needs.

   The key to successful control of pitch depends on understanding the importance of **pitch variation.** As a general rule, use higher pitches to communicate excitement and lower pitches to create a sense of control or solemnity. Adjust the pitch to fit the emotion.

Stress   A third aspect of vocal behavior is stress. **Stress** is the way in which sounds, syllables, and words are accented. Without vocal stress, you'd sound like a computer. Vocal stress is achieved in two ways—through vocal emphasis and through the judicious use of pauses.

Use Vocal Emphasis   **Emphasis** is the way that you accent or attack words. You create emphasis principally through increased volume, changes in pitch, or variations in rate. Emphasis can affect the meanings of your sentences. Notice how the meaning of "Jane's taking Tom out for pizza tonight" varies with changes in word emphasis:

1. "JANE's taking Tom out for pizza tonight." (Jane, not Alyshia or Shani, is taking Tom out.)

2. "Jane's taking TOM out for pizza tonight." (She's not taking out Olan or Christopher.)

3. "Jane's taking Tom OUT for pizza tonight." (They're not staying home as usual.)

4. "Jane's taking Tom out for PIZZA tonight." (They're not having seafood or hamburgers.)

5. "Jane's taking Tom out for pizza TONIGHT." (They're going out tonight, not tomorrow or next weekend.)

A lack of vocal stress not only gives the impression that you are bored but also causes misunderstandings of your meaning. Changes in rate can also be used to add emphasis. Relatively simple changes can emphasize where you are in an outline: "My s-e-c-o-n-d point is . . . ." Several changes in rate can indicate the relationship among ideas. Consider the following example:

> *We are a country faced with . . . [moderate rate] financial deficits, racial tensions, an energy crunch, a crisis of morality, environmental depletion, government waste . . . [fast rate], and - a - stif - ling - na - tion - al - debt [slow rate].*

The ideas pick up speed through the accelerating list of problems but then come to an emphatic halt with the speaker's main concern, the national debt. Such variations in rate emphasize for an audience what is and what isn't especially important to the speech. If you want to emphasize the many demands on their time faced by parents, you could relate a list of daily activities at increasingly rapid rate. By the end of the list, your listeners would probably feel some of the stress facing parents.

Use Helpful Pauses   Pauses are the intervals of silence between or within words, phrases, or sentences. When placed immediately before a key idea or before the climax of a story, they can create suspense: "And the winner is [pause]!" When placed after a major point, pauses can add emphasis, as in: "And who on this campus earns more than the president of the university? The football coach [pause]!" Inserted at the proper moment, a dramatic pause can express feelings more forcefully than words. Clearly, silence can be a highly effective communicative tool if used intelligently and sparingly and if not embarrassingly prolonged.

Sometimes, speakers fill silences in their discourse with sounds: *um, ah, er, well-ah, you-know,* and other meaningless fillers. Undoubtedly, you've heard speakers say, "Today, ah, er, I would like, you know, to speak to you, um, about a pressing, well-uh, like, a pressing problem facing this, uh, campus." Such vocal intrusions convey feelings of hesitancy and a lack of confidence. Make a concerted effort to remove these intrusions from your speech. Also avoid too many pauses and those that seem artificial, because you to be appear manipulative or overrehearsed.

On the other hand, don't be afraid of silences. Pauses allow you to stress important ideas, such as the punch line in a story or argument. Pauses also intensify the involvement of listeners in emotional situations, such as when Barbara Walters or William F. Buckley, Jr., pause for reflection during an interview.

Practicing Vocal Control

Your vocal qualities are of prime importance in determining the impression you make on an audience. While you can't completely control your vocal qualities, you can be alert to their effects on your listeners. Keep your repertoire of vocal qualities in mind as you decide how to express key ideas for an audience.

Don't assume that you'll be able to master in a day all of the vocal skills we have described. Take your time to review and digest the ideas presented. Above all, *practice aloud.* Record yourself on tape and then listen to the way you're conveying ideas. Ask your instructor to provide exercises designed to make your vocal instrument more flexible. When you're able to control your voice and make it respond to your desires, you'll have a great deal more control over your effect on listeners. Before any vocal skill can sound natural and be effective with listeners, it must become so automatic that it will work with little conscious effort. Once your voice responds flexibly in the enlarged context of public speaking, you'll be able to achieve the sense of conversationality so highly valued in our society.

Using Your Body to Communicate

Just as your voice communicates and shapes meanings through the aural channel, your physical behavior carries messages through the visual channel. You can use both the aural and visual channels to create a better understanding of your presentation. To help you

Vocal Exercises

If you are concerned about improving your vocal control, these exercises can be helpful. Here's a sample of what you can do:

1. *Breath control.* Say the entire alphabet, using only one breath. As you practice, try saying it more and more slowly so as to improve your control of exhalation.

2. *Control of pitch.* Sing "low, low, low, low," dropping one note of the musical scale each time you sing the word until you reach the lowest tone you can produce. Then sing your way back up the scale. Now sing "high, high, high, high," going up the scale to the highest note you can reach. Sing your way back down. Go up and down, trying to sense the notes you're most comfortable with—your so-called optimum pitch. Give most of your speeches around your optimum pitch.

3. *Articulatory control.* Pronounce each of the following word groups, making sure that each word can be distinguished from the others. Have someone check your accuracy: jest, gist, just; thin, think, thing; roost, roosts, ghost, ghosts; began, begun, begin; wish, which, witch; affect, effect; twin, twain, twine. Or try the following tongue twisters:

The sixth sheik's sixth sheep's sick.

Three gray geese in the green grass grazing; gray were the geese and green was the grazing.

Barry, the baby bunny's born by the blue box beating rubber baby buggy bumpers.

explore the ways of enhancing your use of the visual channel, we'll examine the speaker's physical behavior.

Dimensions of Nonverbal Communication

While some use the phrase *nonverbal communication* to refer to all aspects of interpersonal interaction that are nonlinguistic, we'll focus the discussion here on physical behavior in communication settings. In recent years, research has reemphasized the important role of physical behavior in effective oral communication.[5] Basically, three generalizations about nonverbal communication should guide your speechmaking:

1. *Speakers reveal and reflect their emotional states through their nonverbal behaviors.* Your listeners read your feelings toward yourself, your topic, and your audience from your facial expressions. Consider the contrast between a speaker who walks briskly to the front of the room, head held high, and one who shuffles, head bowed and arms hanging limply. Communication scholar Dale G. Leathers summarized a good deal of research on nonverbal communication processes: "Feelings and emotions are more accurately exchanged by nonverbal than verbal means. . . . The nonverbal portion of communication conveys meanings and intentions that are relatively free from deception, distortion, and confusion."[6]

2. *The speaker's nonverbal cues enrich or elaborate the message that comes through words.* You can use physical movement to reinforce the ideas of your speech. The words "We must do either *this* or *that*" can be illustrated with appropriate arm-and-hand gestures. Taking a few steps to one side tells an audience that you're moving from one argument to another. A smile enhances your comment on how happy you are to be there, just as a solemn face reinforces the dignity of a wedding.

3. *Nonverbal messages form a reciprocal interaction between speaker and listener.* Listeners frown, smile, shift nervously in their seats, and engage in many types of nonverbal behavior. The physical presence of listeners and the natural tendency of human beings to mirror each other when they're close together mean that nonverbal behavior is a social bonding mechanism. For this chapter, though, we'll concentrate on the speaker's control of physical behavior in four areas: *proxemics, movement and stance, facial expressions,* and *gestures*.

Proxemics   Proxemics is the use of space by human beings. Two components of proxemics, physical arrangement and distance, are especially relevant to public speakers. *Physical arrangements* include the layout of the room in which you're speaking, the presence or absence of a lectern, the seating plan, the location of chalkboards and similar aids, and any physical barriers between you and your audience. *Distance* refers to the extent or degree of separation between you and your audience.[7]

Both of these components have a bearing on the message you communicate publicly. Typical speaking situations involve a speaker facing a seated audience. Objects in the physical space—the lectern, a table, several flags—tend to set the speaker apart from the listeners. This setting apart is both *physical* and *psychological*. Literally as well as figuratively, objects can stand in the way of open communication. If you're trying to create a more informal atmosphere, you should reduce the physical barriers in the setting. You might stand beside or in front of the lectern instead of behind it. In very informal settings, you might even sit on the front edge of a table while talking.

So, what influences your use of physical space?

1. *The formality of the occasion.* The more solemn or formal the occasion, the more barriers will be used; on highly formal occasions, speakers may even speak from an elevated platform or stage.

2. *The nature of the material.* Extensive quoted material or statistical evidence may require you to use a lectern; the use of visual aids often demands such equipment as an easel, a VCR, or an overhead projector.

3. *Your personal preference.* You may feel more at ease speaking from behind rather than in front of the lectern.

The distance component of proxemics adds a second set of considerations. In most situations, you'll be talking at what anthropologist Edward T. Hall has termed a "public distance"—12 feet or more from your listeners.[8] (See Figure 11.2.) To communicate with people at that distance, you obviously can't rely on your normal speaking voice or subtle changes in posture or movement. Instead, you must compensate for the distance by using larger gestures, broader shifts of your body, and increased vocal energy. By contrast, you should lower your vocal volume and restrict the breadth of your gestures when addressing a few individuals at a closer distance. If you don't, you'll probably notice them backing away from you.

FIGURE 11.2 Classification of Interhuman Distance

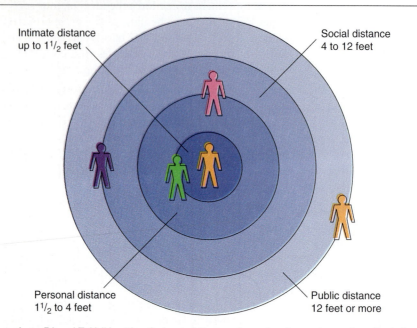

Intimate distance
up to 1½ feet

Social distance
4 to 12 feet

Personal distance
1½ to 4 feet

Public distance
12 feet or more

Anthropologist Edward T. Hall has identified typical distances for various human interactions. Typically, public speaking occurs within social distance and public distance.

Movement and Stance The ways you move and stand provide a second set of bodily cues for your audience. **Movement** includes physical shifts from place to place; **posture** refers to the relative relaxation or rigidity and vertical position of the body. Movements and posture can communicate ideas about yourself to an audience. The speaker who stands stiffly and erectly may, without uttering a word, be saying, "This is a formal occasion" or "I'm tense, even afraid, of this audience." The speaker who leans forward, physically reaching out to the audience, often is saying silently, "I'm interested in you. I want you to understand and accept my ideas." The speaker who sits casually on the front edge of a table and assumes a relaxed posture may suggest informality and readiness to engage in a dialogue with listeners.

Movements and postural adjustments regulate communication. As a public speaker, you can, for instance, move from one end of a table to the other to indicate a change in topic; or you can accomplish the same purpose by changing your posture. At other times, you can move toward your audience when making an especially important point. In each case, you're using your body to reinforce transitions in your subject or to emphasize a matter of special concern.

But keep in mind that your posture and movements can also work against you. Aimless and continuous pacing is distracting. Nervous bouncing or swaying makes listeners seasick, and an excessively erect stance increases tension in listeners. Your movements should be purposeful and enhance the meaning of your words. Stance and movement can help your communicative effort and produce the impressions of self-assurance and control that you want to exhibit.

Movement and stance can communicate ideas about you to others around you.

Facial Expressions   When you speak, your facial expressions function in a number of ways. First, they express your feelings. What researchers Paul Ekman and Wallace V. Friesen call *affect displays* are communicated to an audience through the face. **Affect displays** are facial signals of emotion that an audience perceives when scanning your face to see how you feel about yourself and how you feel about them.[9]

Second, facial changes provide listeners with cues that help them interpret the contents of your message. Are you being ironic or satirical? Are you sure of your conclusions? Is this a harsh or pleasant message? Researchers tell us that a high percentage of the information conveyed in a typical message is communicated nonverbally. Psychologist Albert Mehrabian has devised a formula to account for the emotional impact of the different components of a speaker's message. Words, he says, contribute 7 percent, vocal elements 38 percent, and facial expression 55 percent.[10] From this formula, you can see how important the dimensions of delivery are in communication, particularly your voice and facial expressions. In fact, some internet users have devised a set of symbols called "emoticons" to give expression to their computer messages.

Third, the "display" elements of your face—your eyes, especially—establish a visual bond between you and your listeners. Our culture values eye contact. The speaker who looks people square in the eye is likely to be perceived as earnest, sincere, forthright, and self-assured. In other words, regular eye contact with your listeners helps establish your credibility. Speakers who look at the floor, who read from notes, or who deliver speeches to the back wall sever the visual bond with their audiences and lose credibility.

Of course, you can't control your face completely, which is probably why listeners search it so carefully for clues to your feelings. You can, however, make sure that your facial messages don't contradict your verbal ones: when you're uttering angry words, your face should be communicating anger; when you're pleading with your listeners, your eyes should be engaging them intently. In short, let your face mirror your feelings. That's one of the reasons it's there!

Gestures   Gestures are purposeful movements of the head, shoulders, arms, hands, and other areas of the body that support and illustrate the ideas you're expressing. Fidgeting with your clothing and notecards and playing with your hair aren't purposeful gestures. They distract from the ideas you're communicating. The effective public speaker commonly uses three kinds of purposeful gestures:

1. *Conventional gestures* are physical movements that are symbols with specific meanings assigned by custom or convention. These gestures *condense* ideas: they are shorthand expressions of things or ideas that would require many words to describe fully. A speaker can use the raised-hand "stop" gesture to interrupt listeners who are drawing premature conclusions or the "V for victory" sign when congratulating them for jobs well done.

2. *Descriptive gestures* are physical movements that describe the idea to be communicated. Speakers often depict the size, shape, or location of an object by movements

Descriptive gestures depict size, shape, or location.

of the hands and arms; that is, they draw pictures for listeners. You might indicate the size of a box by drawing it in the air with a finger or raise an arm to indicate someone's height.

3. *Indicators* are movements of the hands, arms, or other parts of the body that express feelings. Speakers throw up their arms when disgusted, pound the lectern when angry, shrug their shoulders when puzzled, or point a threatening finger when issuing a warning. Such gestures communicate emotions to your listeners and encourage similar responses in them. Your facial expressions and other body cues usually reinforce such gestures.[11]

You can improve your gestures through practice. As you practice, you'll obtain better results by keeping in mind that the effectiveness of gestures is affected by relaxation, vigor and definiteness, and proper timing.

First, if your muscles are tense, your movements will be stiff and your gestures awkward. You should make a conscious effort to relax your muscles before you start to speak. You might warm up by taking a few steps, shrugging your shoulders, flexing your muscles, or breathing deeply.

Second, good gestures are natural and animated. They communicate the dynamism associated with speaker credibility. You should put enough force into your gestures to show your conviction and enthusiasm. Avoid exaggerated or repetitive gestures such as pounding the table or chopping the air to emphasize minor ideas in your speech. Vary the nature of your gestures as the ideas in your speech demand.

Third, timing is crucial to effective gestures. The *stroke* of a gesture—that is, the shake of a fist or the movement of a finger—should fall *on* or slightly before the point the gesture emphasizes. Just try making a gesture after the word or phrase it was intended to reinforce has already been spoken. It appears ridiculous. Practice making gestures until they're habitual, and then use them spontaneously as the impulse arises.

Adapting Nonverbal Behavior to Your Presentations

You can gain more effective control of your physical behavior by learning how to orchestrate your gestures and other movements. You can make some conscious decisions about

Speaking of . . . apprehension

Breathe Through Your Fears

You can adapt some of the breathing techniques from yoga and meditation to help you control the physical stress that inhibits movement and vocal quality. Here's a simple, but effective exercise to try:

1. Breathe in slowly, counting to 6 (one-one thousand, two one-thousand, etc.).
2. Hold your breath for a count of 3.
3. Exhale slowly counting to 6.

Repeat this exercise before you practice your speech. Then, use it again to prepare for the delivery of your speech.

how you will use your body together with the other channels of communication to communicate effectively.

1. *Signal your relationship with your audience through proxemics.* If you're comfortable behind a lectern, use it; however, keep in mind that it's a potential barrier between you and your listeners. If you want your whole body to be visible to the audience but you feel the need to have your notes at eye level, stand beside the lectern and arrange your notecards on it. If you want to relax your body, sit behind a table or desk; but compensate for the resulting loss of action by increasing your volume. If you feel relaxed and want to be open to your audience, stand in front of a table or desk. Learn to be yourself while speaking publicly.

   Consider your listeners' needs as well. The farther you are from them, the more important it is for them to have a clear view of you, the harder you must work to project your words, and the broader your physical movements must be. The speaker who crouches behind a lectern in an auditorium of 300 people soon loses contact. Think of large lecture classes you've attended or outdoor political rallies you've witnessed. Recall the delivery patterns that worked effectively in such situations. Put them to work for you.

2. *Adapt the physical setting to your communicative needs.* If you're going to use visual aids—such as a chalkboard, flipchart, or working model—remove the tables, chairs, and other objects that might obstruct your audience's view. Increase intimacy by arranging chairs in a small circle or stress formality by using a lectern.

3. *Adapt your gestures and movement to the size of the audience.* Keeping in mind what Hall noted about public distance in communication, you should realize that subtle changes of facial expression or small hand movements can't be seen clearly in large rooms or auditoriums. Although many auditoriums have a raised platform and a slanted floor to make you more visible, you should adjust to the distance between yourself and your audience by making your movements and gestures larger.

4. *Establish eye contact with your audience, looking specific individuals in the eye.* Your head should not be in constant motion; *continuously* does not imply rhythmic, nonstop machine-gun movement. Rather, take all your listeners into your field of vision periodically; establish firm visual bonds with individuals occasionally. Such bonds enhance your credibility and keep your auditors' attention riveted to you.

   Some speakers identify three audience members—one to the left, one in the middle, and one to the right—and make sure they regularly move from one to the other of them. For those who don't have trouble moving from side to side, another technique is to do the same thing from front to back, especially if the audience isn't too big. Making sure that you are achieving even momentary eye contact with specific listeners in different parts of the audience creates the sense of visual bonding that you want.

5. *Use your body to communicate your feelings.* When you're angry, don't be afraid to gesture vigorously. When you're expressing tenderness, let that message come across your relaxed face. In other words, when you communicate publicly, use the same emotional indicators as you do when you talk to individuals on a one-to-one basis.

Many of the gestures we use have culturally defined meanings. These are called conventional gestures.

6. *Regulate the pace of your presentation and control transitions with bodily movement.* Shift your weight as your speech moves from one idea to another. Move more when you're speaking more rapidly. Reduce bodily action and gestures accordingly when you're slowing down to emphasize particular ideas.

7. *Finally, use your full repertoire of gestures.* You probably do this in everyday conversation without even thinking about it; recreate that behavior when addressing an audience. Physical readiness is the key. Keep your hands and arms free and loose so that you can call them into action easily, quickly, and naturally. Let your hands rest comfortably at your sides, relaxed but ready. Then, as you unfold the ideas of your speech, use descriptive gestures to indicate size, shape, or relationships, making sure the movements are large enough to be seen in the back row. Use conventional gestures also to give visual dimension to your spoken ideas. Keep in mind that there is no right number of gestures to use. However, as you practice, think of the kinds of bodily and gestural actions that complement your message and purpose.

Selecting the appropriate method of presentation and using your voice and body productively will enhance your chances of gaining support for your ideas. *Practice* is the key to the effective use of these nonverbal elements. Through practice, you'll have an opportunity to see how your voice and body complement or detract from your ideas. The more you prepare and practice, the more confident you'll feel about presenting the speech and the more comfortable you'll be. Remember that the nonverbal channel of communication creates meaning for your audience.

Assessing Your Progress

Chapter Summary

1. Every speaker should effectively use the aural and visual channels of communication.

2. Begin with an appropriate method of presentation—impromptu, memorized, manuscript, or extemporaneous delivery. Your choice will be based on the type of

speaking occasion, the seriousness and purpose of your speech, your audience analysis, and your own strengths and weaknesses as a speaker.

3. Regardless of the method of presentation, a good voice enables you to make your message clearer. A flexible speaking voice has intelligibility, variety, and understandable stress patterns.

4. Volume, rate, enunciation, and pronunciation interact to affect intelligibility.

5. Different standards of pronunciation create regional differences known as *dialects.*

6. Changes in rate, pitch, and stress and pauses create variety in presentation and help eliminate monotonous delivery.

7. Three generalizations about nonverbal communication are significant: (a) speakers reveal and reflect their emotional states through their nonverbal behaviors; (b) nonverbal cues enrich or elaborate the speaker's message; and (c) nonverbal messages form an interaction between speaker and listener.

8. Speakers knowledgeable about the effects of proxemics can use space to create physical and psychological intimacy or distance. A speaker's movement and posture regulate communication.

9. Facial expressions communicate feelings, provide important cues to meaning, establish a visual bond with listeners, and establish speaker credibility.

10. Gestures enhance listener response to messages if the gestures are relaxed, definite, and properly timed.

11. Speakers commonly use conventional gestures, descriptive gestures, and indicators.

Key Terms

affect displays (p. 179)	memorized speech (p. 170)
dialect (p. 173)	movement (p. 178)
emphasis (p. 174)	pitch (p. 174)
enunciation (p. 173)	pitch variation (p. 174)
extemporaneous speech (p. 171)	posture (p. 178)
gesture (p. 180)	proxemics (p. 177)
impromptu speech (p. 170)	rate (p. 173)
manuscript speech (p. 170)	stress (p. 174)

Assessment Activities

1. Divide the class into teams and play charades. For rules, see David Jauner, "Charades as a Teaching Device," *Speech Teacher, 20* (1971): 302. A game of charades will help you to focus on the nonverbal elements of communication. Identify conventional gestures, facial expressions, and movement that clarify messages during the game.

2. Form small task groups. Appoint a member of the group to record ideas and then think of as many situations as possible in which each of the four methods of speak-

ing would be used. Choose a reporter to convey the group's examples to the class. How many of the situations do you think you will encounter? Which situations are tied to success in a career?

3. Choose a selection from a poetry anthology and practice reading it aloud. As you read, change your volume, rate, pitch and emphasis, and use pauses. Practice reading the poem in several ways to heighten different emotions or to emphasize different interpretations. Record your reading of the poem on tape and play it back to evaluate it, or ask a friend to listen and offer suggestions.

References

1. For a fascinating discussion of oral speech's communal powers—of its "psychodynamics"—see Chapter 3 of Walter J. Ong, *Orality and Literacy: The Technologizing of the Word* (London: Methuen, 1982).

2. Thomas Frentz, "Rhetorical Conversation, Time, and Moral Action," *Quarterly Journal of Speech, 71* (1985): 1–18.

3. Mark Knapp, *Essentials of Nonverbal Communication* (New York: Holt, Rinehart & Winston, 1980).

4. Klaus R. Scherer, H. London, and Garret Wolf, "The Voice of Competence: Paralinguistic Cues and Audience Evaluation," *Journal of Research in Personality, 7* (1973): 31–44; Jitendra Thakerer and Howard Giles, "They Are—So They Spoke: Noncontent Speech Stereotypes," *Language and Communication, 1* (1981): 255–261; Peter A. Andersen, Myron W. Lustig, and Janis F. Andersen, "Regional Patterns of Communication in the United States: A Theoretical Perspective," *Communication Monographs, 54* (1987): 128–144.

5. Much of the foundational research is summarized in Mark L. Knapp and Judith Hall, *Nonverbal Communication in Human Interaction*, 3rd ed. (New York: Holt, Rinehart & Winston, 1982).

6. Dale G. Leathers, *Nonverbal Communication Systems* (Boston: Allyn & Bacon, 1975), 4–5.

7. For a fuller discussion, see Leathers, 52–59.

8. Hall divides interhuman communication distances into four segments: *intimate distance,* up to $1\frac{1}{2}$ feet apart; *personal distance,* $1\frac{1}{2}$ to 4 feet; *social distance,* 4 to 12 feet; and *public distance,* 12 feet or more. With these distinctions, he has carefully noted how people's eye contact, tone of voice, and ability to touch and observe change from one distance to another. See Edward T. Hall, *The Hidden Dimension* (New York: Doubleday, 1969), chap. 10.

9. Paul Ekman, *Emotion in the Human Face,* 2nd ed. (Cambridge: Cambridge University Press, 1982).

10. Robert Rivlin and Karen Gravelle, *Deciphering the Senses: The Expanding World of Human Perception* (New York: Simon & Schuster, 1984), 98. Such numbers, of course, are only formulaic estimates and are important only as proportions of each other.

11. For a more complete system of classifying gestures, see Paul Ekman and Wallace V. Friesen, "Hand Movements," *Journal of Communication, 22* (1972): 360.

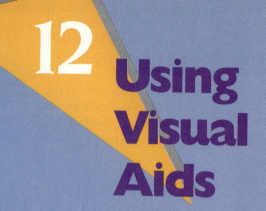

12 Using Visual Aids

You live in what has been called the "ocularcentric century."[1] While the Western world, in a sense, always has been eye-centered, and while "seeing is believing" is an aphorism with a long history, your era illustrates a depth of commitment to seeing that is unparalleled in world history. Television, film, transparencies, VCRs and videotape, videodiscs, the CD-ROM and related digital technologies, overhead and opaque projectors, billboards, poster art, banners trailing from airplanes, sidewalk tables with samples from a store's "today only" sale—your environment is plastered with images from an amazing range of sources. Entire companies—from famous media studios down to small-town graphics production shops in basements—exist because of your willingness to pay for good pieces of visual rhetoric.

From the time you participated in "show and tell" in elementary school, you've offered eye-centered presentations to others, using **visual aids** in your communication efforts. Your physical presence in front of an audience makes a powerful visual statement, and your use of visual aids can make visual communication an essential part of the speech transaction. For these reasons, it's important for you to learn more about visual aids.

Research on visual media, learning, and attitude change has given us a lot of information about the impact of visual aids on audiences.[2] Experienced speakers have offered additional advice. In this chapter, we'll combine what we've learned from social-scientific research with wisdom from the professionals. First, we'll focus on the functions of visual aids; then we'll examine the various types of visual aids and explore ways to use them effectively.

The Functions of Visual Aids

Visual aids are illustrative and persuasive materials that rely primarily on sight. Visual materials enhance your presentation in two ways: (a) they aid listener comprehension and memory, and (b) they add persuasive impact to your message.

Comprehension and Memory

The old saying "A picture's worth a thousand words" seems especially true if the picture adds information that's easily understood visually. We understand ideas better and remember them longer if we see them as well as hear them. Research has demonstrated that bar graphs are especially effective at making statistical information more accessible to listeners. Charts and human-interest visuals, such as photographs, have proven to help listeners process and retain data.[3] Even simple pictures have had significant effects on children's recall and comprehension during storytelling.[4] Visuals can be immensely valuable if your purpose is to inform or teach an audience. Visuals make information easier to understand, retain, and recall.

Persuasion

In addition to enhancing comprehension and memory, visuals can heighten the persuasive impact of your ideas because they engage listeners actively in the communicative exchange. Lawyers, for example, aware of the dramatic persuasive effects of visuals, often include visual evidence such as photographs of injuries or diagrams of crime scenes in their cases in order to sway the opinions of juries. Some lawyers even have experimented with the use of video technology to create dramatic portrayals of events in order to influence jury decisions; for example, by showing the dangerous traffic flow of an intersection in a vehicular homicide case.

Undeniably, your credibility and your persuasiveness are enhanced by good visuals.[5] By satisfying the "show-me" attitude prevalent among listeners, visual materials provide a crucial means of meeting listener expectations.[6]

Types of Visual Support

There are many different types of visual materials. Depending on your speech topic and purpose, you may choose one or several types of visual support. We will discuss each type and examine specific approaches to using it to supplement your oral presentations.

Actual Objects

You can often bring to a presentation the actual objects you're discussing. Live animals or plants can, under some circumstances, be used to enhance your speeches. If your speech explores the care and feeding of iguanas, you can reinforce your ideas by bringing to the speech an iguana in a properly equipped cage. Describing the differences between two varieties of soybeans may be easier if you demonstrate the differences with real plants. Discretion and common sense will help make such visuals work *for* you rather than *against* you. You might be stretching your luck, for example, by bringing a real mule into the classroom to demonstrate saddling techniques or by bringing an untrained cat to show off the virtues of clumping litter.

Using the **actual object** should focus audience attention on your speech, not serve as a distraction. A speech about boogie board skiing is enhanced by a display of the essential equipment. A speech about how to repair holes in a plaster wall is clarified by showing pieces of plaster board at the various stages. Cooking demonstrations are enlivened with samples prepared before the presentation, since you usually doesn't have time to perform the actual work during the speech.

You can use your own body to add concreteness and vitality to your presentation. You might, for example, demonstrate warm-up exercises, macarena steps, or tennis strokes during your speech. Remember to control the experience. Make sure that everyone, even people in the back rows, can see you. Demonstrate stretching exercises on a sturdy table-top rather than on the floor. Slow the tempo of a tennis stroke so that the audience can see any intricate action and subtle movements. One advantage of properly controlled visual action is that with it you can control the audience's attention to your demonstration. You also should dress appropriately. A physical therapy major might add credibility by wearing a uniform when demonstrating CPR, and an aerobics instructor can wear a leotard and tights. Of course, the clothing should not substitute for a clearly visible demonstration of CPR or aerobics.

Photographs and Slides

Photographs can often be a good substitute for the real thing. Photographs can give the audience a visual sense of your topic. For example, photos can illustrate fire damage to ravaged homes or show the contours of a wooded field threatened by a new shopping mall. Make sure that your audience is able to see details from a distance. You can enlarge photos or use slides so that people can see them more easily. Avoid passing small photos through the audience, because such activity is disruptive. The purpose of a visual aid is to draw the attention of all members of the audience simultaneously.

Like photographs, slides (35-mm transparencies) allow you to depict color, shape, texture, and relationships. It is also easier to show many slides than many photographs. If you're showing off the Padre Islands as a good place to go for spring break, you may use slides to show your audience the buildings and landscape of both islands. If you're giving a speech on the history of magic lanterns, you can use slides to show various styles in operation. If you're speaking against the construction of a river reservoir, you can enhance your persuasiveness by showing slides of the whitewater that will be disrupted by the dam. If you're discussing stylistic differences among famous artists, you may wish to show slides of art works from the neoclassical and baroque periods.

Using slides requires sure practice in handling equipment. It also requires some forethought about the setup of the presentation. Have you loaded the slides in the cartridge correctly? Will you speak from the front of the room or from next to the projector? Will your voice carry over the noise of the projector? Do you know how to change the projection lamp? Did you bring along a spare bulb just in case? Will you need an extension cord? Do you know how to remove a jammed slide? Attention to small, seemingly inconsequential details like these will make a major difference in how smoothly the presentation goes. If you operate on the assumption that whatever can go wrong will, you'll be prepared to solve most problems.

Videotapes and Films

Videotapes and films let you put action into pictures. Videotaped segments from several current sitcoms can dramatically reinforce your claim that minorities are underrepresented in comedy-centered television. Two or three videotaped political ads can help you

Representations convey information in various ways. For instance, a photograph of an inline skate (*top*) gives an audience a realistic but complicated view of the object, whereas an abstract representation, such as a diagram (*bottom right*), strips away unnecessary details to illustrate the parts of the object more clearly. Also abstract yet highly visible, an action shot (*bottom left*) provides a feeling of a three-dimensional image of the object, allowing a speaker to point out its parts and discuss its functions.

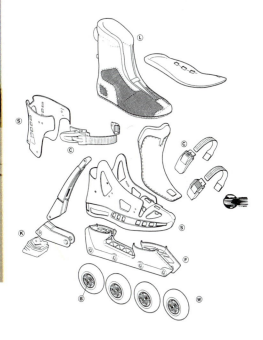

illustrate methods for savaging opponents. As with all projection equipment, familiarity with the operation of a videocassette recorder or film projector ensures a smooth presentation. Make sure that you can operate the equipment properly and quickly. Delays increase your nervousness and detract from your presentation.

Chalkboard Drawings

Chalkboard drawings are especially valuable when you need a quick illustration or want to show something step by step. By drawing each step as you discuss it, you can center the audience's attention on your major points. Coaches often use this approach when showing players how to execute particular plays. Time sequences also can be sketched on a chalkboard. To visually represent the history of the civil rights movement in the United States, you can create a timeline that illustrates key events, such as the arrival of the first slaves in Jamestown, the Emancipation Proclamation, and the 1965 Voting Rights Act.

Whether or not you use drawings will depend on the formality of the situation. If you're brainstorming ideas for building renovation with a prospective client, quick sketches may suffice. However, if you're meeting with the client's board of directors, the same rough drawings will be inadequate. The board will expect a polished presentation, complete with a professionally prepared prospectus. Similarly, chalkboard drawings may be sufficient to explain the photovoltaics of solar power to a group of classmates, but when presenting those data as part of a science fair project, you need refined visual support materials. Most of the time, the care with which you prepare these visuals will convey to your audience an attitude of either indifference or concern.

Overhead Projections

You can use an overhead projector just as you would use a chalkboard, to illustrate points as you talk. However, an overhead projector offers some advantages over a chalkboard: you can turn it off when you've made your point, thus removing a distracting image that you'll be competing with if it stays around. Another advantage is that you can uncover one part of the overhead screen at a time, keeping the remainder covered so as to control the flow of information. Finally, you can prepare overheads before the speech, giving them a more professional appearance than chalkboard drawings; hence, they dominate corporate talks. During the speech you can point to them or add to them to emphasize your claims.

When you're using either a chalkboard or an overhead projector, be aware of your technique. First, make your drawings large enough so that the audience can see them. Second, continue to talk to the audience as you draw; this will mean alternately looking at the board and the people. Don't let your listeners' attention drift away while drawing. They'll also get bored if you talk to the chalkboard or to the light source. Third, be sure to stand so that you don't block the audience's view of your visuals. Fourth, when you're through talking about the illustration, erase it or turn off the projector—kill the competing message source.

Graphs

Graphs show relationships among various parts of a whole or between variables across time. Graphs are especially effective for representing numerical data. There are several types of graphs:

FIGURE 12.1 Bar Graph

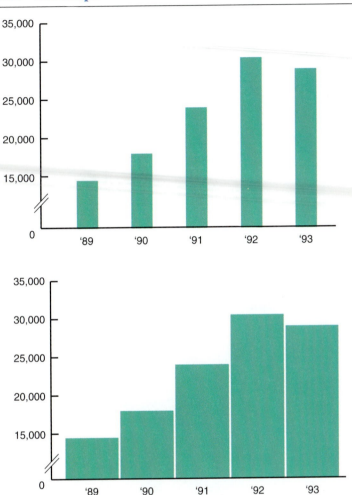

Bar graphs illustrate relationships. Changing the space and size of bars can affect the visual message.

1. **Bar graphs** show the relationships between two or more sets of figures (see Figure 12.1). Research has demonstrated that plain bar graphs are the most effective method for displaying statistical comparisons,[7] perhaps because bar graphs represent numbers in a visual form. If you were illustrating the difference among male and female incomes in various fields, you'd probably use a bar graph.

2. **Line graphs** show relationships between two or more variables, usually over time (see Figure 12.2). If you interested in showing popular support for Bill Clinton, Bob Dole, and Ross Perot, 1991 through 1996, you'd use a line graph.

3. **Pie graphs** show percentages by dividing a circle into the proportions being represented (see Figure 12.3). A speaker raising funds for a local hospice could use a pie graph to show how much of its income was spent on administration, nursing care,

FIGURE 12.2 Line Graph

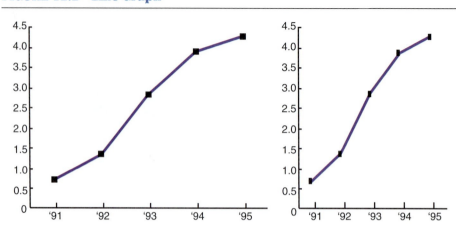

Line graphs can reveal relationships, but they can also deceive the unwary. These graphs show the same data but use different spacing along the axes to change the visual image, with the second version making the increase in hotel prices seem much greater. *Source:* Smith Travel Research, as reported in *USA Today,* October 27, 1995, B1.

FIGURE 12.3 Pie Graph

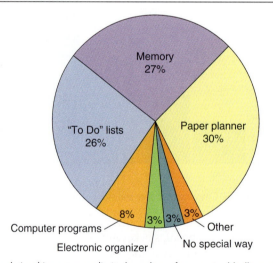

Pie graphs dramatize relationships among a limited number of segments. Ideally, a pie graph should have from two to five segments, never more than eight. This one compares seven different methods people use as organizational reminders. *Source:* Opinion Research Corporation for Fuji Computer Products, as reported in *USA Today,* October 27, 1995, B1.

other kinds of support, drugs, and equipment for terminally ill patients. City managers use pie graphs to show citizens what proportion of their tax dollars go to municipal services, administration, education, recreation, and law enforcement.

FIGURE 12.4 Pictograph

Have smoke
detector
96%

Battery
powered
76%

Don't check
batteries regularly
23%

Think batteries
are dead
8%

Speakers with artistic skills can create interesting visual aids, such as the graphic representation of the status of battery-powered smoke detectors. The pictures enhance the argument that people need to do more than merely install smoke detectors. *Source:* Angus Reid Group for American Sensors, as reported in *USA Today,* October 27, 1995, A1.

4. **Pictographs** function like bar graphs but use symbols instead of bars to represent size and numbers (see Figure 12.4). A representation of U.S., Canadian and Russian grain exports might use a miniature drawing of a wheat shock or an ear of corn to represent 100,000 bushels; this representation would allow a viewer to see at a glance the disparity among the exports of three countries. You can easily create pictographs with computer clip art.

Your choice of bar, line, pie, or pictorial graphs will depend on the subject and the nature of the relationship you wish to convey. A pie graph, for example, can neither easily illustrate discrepancies between two groups nor show change over time. Bar and line graphs don't easily show the total amount being represented.

Regardless of the type of graph you choose, when you're preparing them, you must be very careful not to distort your information. A bar graph can create a misleading impression of the difference between two items if one bar is short and wide while the other is long and narrow. Line graphs can portray very different trends if the units of measurement are not the same for each time period. You can avoid misrepresenting information by using consistent measurements in your graphs and by using a computer to generate your graphs.

Charts and Tables

Charts and tables condense large blocks of information into a single picture. **Tables** present information in parallel columns while **charts** can take a number of varied forms. The Periodical Table of Elements and the tax tables published in the 1040 U.S. tax form are two common charts you've probably seen. If not too complicated, charts and tables work well in technical speeches. So, if you discuss various contributions to the operation of the United Nations, you can break down the contributions of, say, ten countries to five of the major agencies of the U.N. If you want to show why the United States has such trouble establishing a consistent energy policy, your presentation will be much easier to follow if your listeners have a federal organizational chart for reference.

There are two special types of charts: **flipcharts** unveil ideas one at a time on separate sheets; **flowcharts** show relationships among ideas or facts on a single sheet. Both flipcharts and flowcharts may include drawings or photos. If you present successive ideas with a flipchart, you'll focus audience attention on specific parts of your speech. In a speech on fighting in the Gulf War of 1991, you could use a separate chart for each week of the engagement. If you presented the entire six weeks on one chart, the chart would become cluttered and your audience might stray from your explanation to read the entire chart. You could also use separate charts to focus on specific assaults by different countries.

You can use a flowchart to indicate the chronological stages of a process; for example, a flowchart will allow audiences to visualize the stages of a presidential campaign or the process of making processed seafood (e.g., "krab"). You can also use a flowchart to show relationships among ideas or interdependent actions, such as the competition between conservative and liberal views of "family values." And, of course, you're familiar with organizational flowcharts used by groups to show the relationships among members of the group. In a speech on the passage of a legislative bill, a flowchart would clarify each step of the process.

As long as the information is not too complex or lengthy, tables and charts may be used to indicate changes over time and to rank or list items and their costs, frequency of use, or relative importance. Tables and charts should be designed so that they can be seen and so that they convey data simply and clearly. Too much information will force the audience to concentrate more on the visual support than on your oral explanation. For example, a dense chart, showing all the major and minor offices of your college, may simply overwhelm listeners as they try to follow your explanation. If the organization is too complex, you may want to develop a series of charts, each one focusing on a smaller unit of information.

Models

Models can be very attractive to listeners. **Models** are reduced or enlarged scale replicas of real objects. Architects construct models of new projects to show clients. You can use models of genes to accompany your explanation of the genome project. As with other visual aids, models need to be manageable and visible to the audience. You can increase listener interest if you use a model that comes apart so that different pieces can be examined. Be sure to practice removing and replacing the parts before your speech.

Strategies for Selecting and Using Visual Aids

Your decision about which visual aids will work best for you should be based on four considerations: (a) the characteristics of the audience and occasion, (b) the communicative potential of various visual materials, (c) your ability to integrate verbal and visual materials effectively, and (d) the potential of computer-generated visual materials.

Consider the Audience and Occasion

Think about the folks you're talking to when deciding on visuals. Do you need to bring a map of the United States to an audience of college students when discussing the movement of contagious diseases in this country? If you're going to discuss a volleyball team's offensive and defensive formations, should you provide diagrams for your listeners? Can you expect an audience to understand the administrative structure of the federal bureaucracy without providing an organizational chart?

How can you answer those questions? It may be quite difficult, for example, to decide what your classmates know about governmental structures or what Rotary Club members know about football plays. Probably the best thing you can do is to do a little first-hand interviewing by speaking with several of your potential listeners ahead of time. In other words, before making any final decisions about visual supporting materials, do as much audience research as you possibly can.

As part of your preparation for using visuals, take into account the speaking occasion. Certain occasions demand certain types of visual support materials. The district manager who presents a report of projected future profits to the central office without a printed

Speaking of . . .   skills

Using Visual Aids in Business

It's wise to use visual aids when developing a professional presentation for a client or business meeting. Research has shown that visual aids are effective tools for three reasons. First, visual aids can make your presentation more persuasive. Second, they enhance your audience's estimate of your credibility and appearance of professionalism. Third, presenters using visual aids require less meeting time to achieve their results. Overall, it makes good sense to incorporate visual aids in your presentations. Observe some simple rules:

1. *Prepare a professional look.* The business world by now absolutely expects professional-looking visuals: desktop computer-generated overheads, high-quality slides, folders with eye-catching paper, power-point computer projections, and so on. Sloppy work will kill you.

2. *Always make something to take away.* Large businesses, especially, run on team meetings and project presentation sessions—often, more than one a day. Give the folks coming to your presentation something to take away, so that they can remember your work. Summarize the main dimensions of the problem and your proposed solutions; hand out your business card with phone, fax, and e-mail numbers; popular these days is a computer disk with images and important materials on it, given how cheap disks are now.

3. Know the equipment before you start. Know how to run the particular VCR or computer projector in the room you're using. Try out the slide projector. Make sure you know where the switch for the power screen is. Fumbling because you don't know which remote runs the VCR and which the sound system will make you look less than professional.

These rules apply, with varying degrees of harshness, to your presentations in any other setting as well.

handout or diagram will probably find his or her credibility questioned. The military adviser who calls for governmental expenditures for new weapons without offering pictures or drawings of the proposed weapons and printed technical data on their operation is not likely to be a convincing advocate. A basketball coach without a chalkboard may succeed only in confusing team members at half-time. Plan ahead to supply the visual media demanded by the situation. If the speaking occasion doesn't appear to require certain visual supports, analyze the occasion further for different visual possibilities. Use your imagination. Be innovative. Don't overlook opportunities to make your speech more meaningful, more exciting, and more interesting for your listeners.

Consider the Communicative Potential of Various Visual Aids

Use a little common sense when preparing visuals; then about what each kind is especially good for. In general, pictorial or photographic visuals can make an audience *feel* the way you do. For example, you can use slides, movies, sketches, or photographs of your travels in western Colorado to accompany your speech on high plateaus. Such visual aids stimulate your audience to share in the awe and tortured beauty that you experienced. If you show slides of civilian victims in Bosnia-Herzogovina, you are likely to gain an emotional response. Such a response can maximize your efforts to persuade your listeners.

Visuals containing descriptive or written materials, on the other hand, can help an audience *think* the way you do. For example, models, diagrams, charts, and graphs about the population and economy of Mediterranean area may persuade your listeners to conclude that the United States should send more foreign aid to Turkey. A timeline representing ethnic conflicts in Eastern Europe can help your listeners understand the historical context of contemporary fighting in the region. Such visual aids encourage understanding and thought rather than emotional responses.

Integrate Verbal and Visual Materials Effectively

To be effective, your visual aids should complement your spoken message. Visuals should save time, enhance the impact of your speech, clarify complex relations, and generally enliven your presentation. Consider the following suggestions for getting the maximum benefit from your visuals:

1. *Use color to create interest.* Use contrasting colors (red on white, black on yellow) to highlight information in an organizational chart or to differentiate segments of a pie graph or bars in a bar graph. As a rule, color commands attention better than black and white.

2. *Keep visual aids clear and simple.* This is especially important for charts and other graphic devices. Make essential information stand out clearly from the background. Let simplicity guide your preparation.

3. *Make your visuals large enough to be seen easily.* Listeners get frustrated when they must lean forward and squint in order to see detail in a visual aid. Make your figures and lettering large enough so that everyone can see them. Follow the example of John Hancock who, when signing the Declaration of Independence in 1776, wrote his name large enough to "be seen by the King of England without his glasses."

Speaking of . . . ethics

Can pictures lie?

Can pictures lie? Aren't they each worth a thousand words? Isn't seeing believing? Isn't showing better than telling? Not necessarily—especially in today's visually centered world. Consider:

- Hopes of finding American soldiers missing in action in Vietnam (MIAs) were briefly inspired by photos that seemed to show the Americans holding signs that displayed current dates. Those pictures turned out to have been faked.
- During the 1992 campaign, political action committees (PACs) ran ads that showed Bill Clinton holding hands in victory with Ted Kennedy on the Democratic Convention stage. What the PAC had done was morphed a picture of Kennedy's head on Vice President Al Gore's body.
- During the 1988 campaign, another PAC ran an ad whose text included these words: "As governor, Michael Dukakis vetoed mandatory sentences for drug dealers. He vetoed the death penalty. His revolving-door prison policy gave weekend furloughs to first-degree murderers not eligible for parole. While out, many committed other crimes like kidnapping and rape. And many are still at large. Now Michael Dukakis says he wants to do for America what he's done for Massachusetts." The pictures accompanying those statements showed: (1) the sun setting over a prison with guards in the watchtowers; (2) a revolving gate where prisoners, many representing minorities, presumably were being let out as quickly as they were being put in; and, (3) guards standing watch over empty prisons at night—when crime increases.

Thanks to digital editing, you now can easily add to or subtract from pictures, printing the altered photos so cleanly that the forgery is almost impossible to detect. Pictures can be altered to "say" something that isn't true. Or, they can add images that transform the meanings of words. The visual dimension can be helpful to both speaker and audience when it is used in morally defensible ways. It can be destructive of the truth when it's not.

4. *Make your visuals neat.* Draw neatly, spell correctly, make lines proportional, and make letters symmetrical. Such advice may seem unnecessary, but too often beginning speakers throw together visual materials at the last minute. They forget that their visual aids also contribute to audiences' assessment of their credibility. Misspelled words and sloppy graphs will lower listeners' estimation of your competence.

5. *Decide how to handle your visual aids in advance.* Decide on a visual aid and practice with it well in advance, especially for demonstration speeches. Suppose you want to show your listeners that anyone can change a tube even on a rear wheel without screwing up the chain and gear-shifting mechanisms. Do you bring in a whole bike? (Probably.) Do you actually change a tube on that bike? (Probably not—takes too long for the assigned length of the speech.) So, do you bring another wheel and change a tube on that? (Yup.) Do you demonstrate how to put the wheel back on the bike? (In part. Unlock the rear wheel on the bike you brought along, take the chain off the sprocket, slacken the cables, then put the chain back on and show them how to adjust the cables. Then show them a chart recording the process step

by step.) In thinking through how much of the process you can demonstrate in the available time, you can figure out how to handle actual objects and other visuals.

6. *Compensate orally for any distraction your visual aid may create.* Remember that you're always competing with other message sources for your listeners' attention. Listeners may find the visual aid so intriguing that they miss part of your message. You can partially compensate for any potential distraction by building repetition into your speech. By repeating your main ideas you give your listeners several chances to follow your thoughts. As added insurance, you also might keep your visual aid out of sight until you need to use it.

7. *Coordinate slides, films, overhead projections, or videotapes with your verbal message.* Mechanical or electronic messages can easily distract your listeners. You need to talk louder and move vigorously when using a machine to communicate, or you need to show the film or slides either *before* or *after* you comment on their content. Whatever strategy you choose, make sure that your visual materials are well integrated into your oral presentation. That is, use transitions that integrate your visual aids with the speech. If you are using a chart, you might say, "This chart shows you what I've been saying about the growing season for different varieties of tomatoes." Also indicate where you obtained the information represented on the chart and summarize the information before you go on to your next idea.

8. *Hand your listeners a copy of the materials you wish them to reflect on after your speech.* If you're making recommendations to the tenants association office, provide copies of your proposal for their subsequent action. Or if you're reporting the results of a survey, your listeners will better digest the key statistics if you give each audience member a copy of them. Few people can recall the seven warning signs of cancer, but they might keep a wallet-sized list handy if you order enough for the whole class from the American Cancer Society. Of course, don't duplicate your entire speech. Select only those items with lasting value.

These suggestions should enable you to take advantage of visual communication. Good visual aids don't detract from your message. Instead, they illustrate and empower your ideas, and add a dimension—seeing—that your audiences are used to processing when thinking about feelings and ideas.

Evaluate Computer-Generated Visual Materials

You can tap into the digital world of computer graphics when you prepare your visual aids. While you may not be able to produce visuals similar to the action shots that accompanying a televised football game, you can still use readily available computer-generated visual materials. Computers are very effective when processing numerical data and converting them into bar, line, and pie graphs; you can scan in images and even morph them for humorous effects; with a modem and a phone line, you can put a class online to a Web site halfway across the globe. As with other types of visual aids, you should choose the computer graphics that fit your purpose, physical setting, and audience needs. Here are some suggestions for ways to use such materials:

1. *Use computer graphics to create an atmosphere.* It's easy to make computer banners with block lettering and pictures. Hang a banner in the front of the room to set a

Well-executed computer graphics can be photographed and converted into a transparency (slide) or directly projected from a table designed for that purpose.

mood or establish a theme. For example, a student urging her classmates to get involved in a United Way fund-raising drive created a banner with the campaign slogan, "Thanks to you, it works for all of us." Initially, the banner captured attention; during the speech the banner reinforced the theme. Or, if you're going to talk about negative political advertising and can get online, go to www.dnc.org to see what the Democratic National Committee's saying about Republican leaders and policies. That certainly will draw your listeners right into the center of your topic.

2. *Enlarge small computer-generated diagrams.* Most computer diagrams are too small to be seen easily by an audience. You can shoot a 35-mm slide right off your screen so that you can project it. Or, if you have access to a computer-projection table, images you've stored on a disk can be projected directly.

3. *Enhance the computer-generated image in other ways.* Suppose you print off some images or tables on the usual black-and-white printer. Use markers to color pie graphs or to darken the lines of a line graph. Use press-on letters to make headings for your graphs. Mixing media in such ways can give your presentations a professional look even if you're not working with color printers or computer projectors. If you have access to the right technology, you can create three-dimensional images of buildings, machines, or the human body.

The world of electrified sight and sound sometimes seems far, far away from the antiquated world of person-to-person public speaking. Perhaps, but if you learn to integrate personal talk and audiovisual presentation, you'll find that your ability to reach and stir audiences has been enhanced. Working an audience across channels—verbal, visual, acoustic—allows you to complicate messages and yet give them a powerful presence that informs and persuades listeners who've been raised on sight and sound. Expertly hooking up talk and visualizations will pay off.

Assessing Your Progress

Chapter Summary

1. Visual aids as a discrete mode, or channel, of communication can aid listener comprehension and memory and add persuasive impact to a speech.

2. There are many types of visual aids: actual objects, photographs and slides, videotapes and films, chalkboard drawings, graphs, charts, and models.

3. Types of graphs include bar, line, pie, and pictographs.

4. Flipcharts unveil ideas one at a time; flowcharts show the entire process on a single sheet.

5. In selecting and using visual aids, consider the audience and the occasion, examine the communicative potential of various visual aids, find ways to integrate verbal and visual materials effectively, and find ways to effectively use computer graphics.

Key Terms

actual objects (p. 187)   line graphs (p. 191)

bar graphs (p. 191)   models (p. 194)

charts (p. 193)   pictographs (p. 193)

flipcharts (p. 194)   pie graphs (p. 191)

flowcharts (p. 194)   tables (p.193)

graphs (p. 190)   visual aids (p. 196)

Assessment Activities

1. Plan a short speech explaining or demonstrating a complex process. Choose two different types of visual aids and ask the class to evaluate their effectiveness. You might consider the following processes:

    a. The procedure for gene splicing.

    b. The judicial process for bringing a class-action suit.

    c. The layout of bird-feeding stations.

    d. The procedure for rotating automobile tires.

    e. The usual patterns for movements of high- and low-pressure weather systems.

    f. A method for downloading Internet images into a computer's hard drive.

2. Work in small groups to develop at least three different types of visual aids for three of the following topics. A representative of each group will report to the class as a whole, telling about or showing the proposed visual aids.

a. How to play an autoharp.

b. How to splint a broken arm or leg.

c. How to build large, complex sand castles or snow sculptures.

d. How to store firewood outdoors.

e. How to cut your grocery bill.

f. How to replace a washer in a drippy faucet.

3. Videotape a home shopping or a how-to-do-it show and play the videotape in class. Evaluate the use of visual aids in the show. Were they easily seen? Did they demand attention? Did the speaker use the visual aids effectively? What would have made the use of visual aids more effective? Alternatively, write up a one-page description and evaluation for assessment by your class instructor.

References

1. Ocular = eye; centric = centered. See Jacques Ellul, *The Humiliation of the Word*, translated by Joyce Main Hanks (Grand Rapids, Mich.: William B. Eerdmans, 1985); Chris Jenks, ed., *Visual Culture* (New York: Routledge, 1995).

2. A good summary of research into multiple aspects of visual discourse can be found in Paul Messaris, *Visual Literacy: Image, Mind, & Reality* (Boulder, Colo.: Westview Press, 1994). Cf. Larry Raymond, *Reinventing Communication: A Guide to Using Visual Language for Planning, Problem Solving, and Reengineering* (Milwaukee: ASQC Quality Press, 1994).

3. William J. Seiler, "The Effects of Visual Materials on Attitudes, Credibility, and Retention," *Communication Monographs, 38* (1971): 331–334.

4. Joel R. Levin and Alan M. Lesgold, "On Pictures in Prose," *Educational Communication and Technology Journal, 26* (1978): 233–244. Cf. Marilyn J. Haring and Maurine A. Fry, "Effect of Pictures on Children's Comprehension of Written Text," *Educational Communication and Technology Journal, 27* (1979): 185–190.

5. For more specific conclusions regarding the effects of various kinds of visual materials, see James Benjamin and Raymie E. McKerrow, *Business and Professional Communication* (New York: Longman, 1994), 175–179.

6. The best statement on the rationale for visuals we know of is Edgar B. Wycoff, "Why Visuals?" *AV Communication, 11* (1977): 39, 59.

7. See G. D. Feliciano, R. D. Powers, and B. E. Kearle, "The Presentation of Statistical Information," *AV Communication Review, 11* (1963): 32–39; M. D. Vernon, "Presenting Information in Diagrams," *AV Communication Review, 1* (1953): 147–158; and L. V. Peterson and Wilbur Schramm, "How Accurately Are Different Kinds of Graphs Read?" *AV Communication Review, 2* (1955): 178–189.

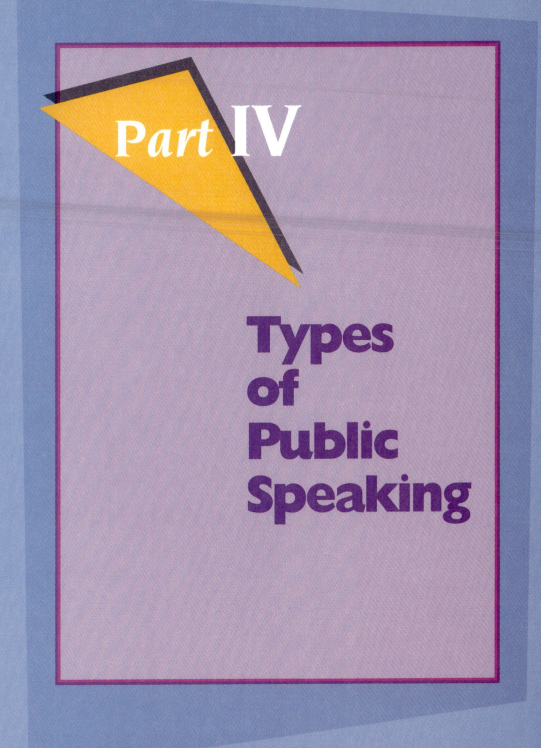

Part IV

Types of Public Speaking

13 Speeches to Inform

Reaching your audience is what public speaking is all about. You can talk until day turns into night and then keep talking until the Morning Star rises in the southwest, but if you don't reach your audience, you can forget it. Your listeners are awash in bits and pieces of facts, in the drone of "information radio," in digitized data. You've got to find ways to grab them by the scruff of their psychological necks and the seat of their psychological pants, get them to sit up and take notice, and then package facts and ideas in ways that they can understand and remember. That's what informative speaking is all about.

- ✓ What does it mean to inform an audience? Surely it's more than giving them piles of facts. What's it about?

- ✓ In how many ways can you inform an audience? What kinds of speeches are informative?

- ✓ What special challenges does the informative speaker face? How can you meet those challenges successfully, especially in a world where different groups of people have different data bases?

These are some of the questions we'll investigate in this chapter.

Facts, Knowledge, and the Information Age

Our society almost worships facts. A staggering amount of information is available to us, particularly because of such technological developments as electronic media, photostatic printing, miniaturized circuitry, fax machines, and computerized data storage and retrieval systems. Jumping onto the World Wide Web via America Online, Compuserve, MCIAccess or your school's mainframe computer puts you on the information superhighway, which has more lanes than the Santa Monica Freeway. The entire Indiana University library

TABLE 13.1 Milestones in American Baseball	
Year	**Event**
1845	First baseball club (Knickerbocker Baseball Club of New York) organized
1849	First uniform is adopted by the Knickerbockers
1857	National Organization of Baseball Players—the first association—is founded
1862	First enclosed baseball park (Union Grounds, Brooklyn) is built
1869	First salaried team (Cincinnati Red Stockings) goes 65–0 for the year
1871	First professional league (National Association of Professional Baseball Players) is formed
1876	The National League is established
1877	First minor league (International Association) is organized
1901	The American League is established

is available online, as are huge collections of words, pictures, and sounds from around the world. Detective Joe Friday from the old Dragnet series would never dare say "Just the facts, Ma'am" today, for he'd immediately be drown in data.

By themselves, mere facts tell us nothing. **Information** is but a collection of factoids until human beings shape, interpret, and act on it. Public speakers often serve as interpreters of information. They are called on to assemble, package, and present information to other human beings—to turn information into knowledge. To actually create **knowledge**—information that has been given human significance—you have to relate it to people's interests, needs, curiosities, and orientations to the world.

So, consider the information presented in Table 13.1.[1] There it is—a collection of information, of data. To give this assemblage of facts significance to people, you have to attach these factoids to a mental framework, like the story of the growing professionalization of baseball in the nineteenth century. Then, these references to the coming of teams, uniforms and other identity marks, the professionalization of the players through pay and players' organizations, the formation of a two-tiered system with feeder clubs in minor leagues taking over talent development, the coming of enclosed parks to guarantee income from fans, and the organization of leagues to control play and access to the sport all make sense. This is how bits of information are converted into knowledge.

One theme will be sounded again and again in this chapter: "mere information" is useless until you put it together in ways that make it clear and relevant to others. Informative speeches clarify facts and ideas for audiences. Without clarification or interpretation, information is meaningless. The informative speaker's job is to adapt data and ideas to human needs. In this chapter, we'll discuss various types of informative speeches, outline the essential features of informative talks, and then review some ways of structuring each type of informative speech.

Types of Informative Speeches

Informative speeches take many forms depending on the situation, the level of knowledge possessed by listeners, and your own abilities as a presenter of data. Four of these forms—speeches of definition, instructions and demonstrations, oral reports, and lectures—occur so frequently, however, that they merit special attention. They represent four common ways in which people package information to meet the needs of others.

Speeches of Definition

"Mommy, what's a 'nerd'?" "Professor Martinez, what's the difference between a 'Web site' and a 'home page'?" "Chantel, before I take you on as a realtor, I want to know what a 'joint agency' is." You've been asking questions like these all of your life. A speech of definition doesn't just offer a dictionary definition. Rather, a **speech of definition** seeks to define concepts or processes in ways that make them relevant to listeners. Once 5-year-old Sarah knows what a nerd is, she'll know she has a human relations problem; once you know what kind of Web site a home page is, you'll know whether you want to build one or not; and once you know that a joint agency can represent both you and a seller or buyer, you'll have the information you need to know whether that's good or bad for your situation.

Instructions and Demonstrations

Throughout your life, you've heard classroom instructions, job instructions, and instructions for the performance of special tasks. Not only have you gone through many "tell" sessions but you've also had people "show" you how to execute actions—how to sort various kinds of paper for recycling, how to manage a counter at a fast foods shop, how to set corner posts for a picket fence. Generally, **instructions** are verbal communications that explain processes, while **demonstrations** verbally and nonverbally explain and illustrate those processes. Both involve the serial presentation of information, usually in steps or phases. Both require clarity because your listeners are expected to learn or reproduce these steps themselves.

Oral Reports

An **oral report** is a speech that arranges and interprets information gathered in response to a request made by a group. Academic reports, committee reports, and executive reports are examples of oral reports. Scientists and other scholars announce their research findings in oral reports at professional conventions. Committees in business, industry, and government carry out special tasks and then present oral reports to their parent organizations or constituencies. Board chairpersons present annual oral reports to the stockholders on the past year's activities. You may have been asked to present a report on possible spring trips for an organization.

Lectures

Lectures increase the audience's understanding of a particular field of knowledge or activity. They usually involve explanations and definitions. For instance, a business executive might define "total quality management" and go on to show how such a style can make the company work better; a historian might tell a group of students what sociocultural forces converged to create the American Revolution; and a social worker could lecture an audience of government officials on the local impact the 1996 federal welfare reform package.

You'll likely be called upon often to give informative talks on the job.

Essential Qualities of Informative Speeches

Your goal as an informative speaker is to make it easy for your listeners to retain new information. There are five things you can do to ensure that your listeners remember what you say. You should strive for clarity, the association of new ideas with familiar ones, packaging or clustering of ideas, strong visualization, and motivational appeal.

Clarity

Informative speeches achieve maximum clarity when listeners can follow and understand what the speaker is saying. Clarity is largely the result of two factors: effective organization and the careful selection of words.

Achieving Clarity through Effective Organization

Limit Your Points   Confine your speech to three or four principal ideas, grouping whatever facts or ideas you wish to consider under these main headings. Even if you know a tremendous amount about your subject matter, remember that you can't make everyone an expert with a single speech.

Use Transitions to Show Relationships among Ideas   Word your transitions carefully. Make sure to indicate the relationship of the upcoming point to the rest of your ideas. You might say, "Second, you must prepare the chair for caning by cleaning out the groove and cane holes"; "The introduction of color to television sports in 1964 was fol-

Speaking of . . . skills

Choosing a Topic

If you're searching for informative speech topics, you can develop possible topics by brainstorming (see Chapter 2) or you can develop your ideas from standard subject areas. Consider these subject areas as you generate your own informative speech topics:

1. *People.* We're all curious about the lives of others. Build on this curiosity by focusing on someone you know, someone you admire, or someone unique. You might investigate the lives of the Wright brothers or Blanche Scott, the first American woman to fly. Or what about famous people like Bill Cosby or Clara Barton? Perhaps villians like Rasputin or John Dillinger fascinate you.

2. *Places.* This might be an opportunity to talk about a place you've visited or would like to visit—a city, museum, park, or another country. Cities like Rome or your hometown, museums like the Louvre or the local football hall of fame, parks like the Everglades or your favorite state park, and countries like Tanzania or Argentina can be intriguing speech topics.

3. *Things.* The possibilities are endless. Begin with what you already know. You could talk about your baseball card collection, the architectural style of your neighbor's house, or your uncle's antique automobile.

4. *Events.* Famous occurrences make good speech topics. There are recent events like political elections, the bombing of the World Trade Center, the floods caused by the Mississippi River, or the conflict in Bosnia-Herzegovina. In addition, you might talk about historical events such as famous battles, unusual discoveries, natural disasters, or memorable celebrations.

5. *Ideas.* Theories, principles, concepts, theologies, and traditions can make excellent informative speeches. You could explain the traditions of Taoism, the theory of relativity, the principles of capitalism, the concept of aging, or the funereal doctrines of Catholicism.

6. *Procedures.* Descriptions of processes can be fascinating. Your listeners may have wondered how watches work, what enables microwave ovens to cook food, or how ballets are choreographed.

lowed by an equally important technology, the slow-motion camera"; "To test these hypotheses, we set up the following experiment." Such transitions allow listeners to follow you from point to point.

Keep Your Speech Moving Forward Rather than jumping back and forth between ideas, charging ahead, and then backtracking, develop a positive forward direction. Move from basic ideas to more complex ones, from background data to current research, or from historical incidents to current events.

Achieving Clarity through Word Choice The second factor in achieving clarity is being understood. You can develop understanding through careful selection of your words. For a fuller development of the use of language, see Chapter 10. For now, think about the following ways to achieve clarity.

Keep Your Vocabulary Precise, Accurate—Not Too Technical In telling someone how to finish off a basement room, you might be tempted to say, "Next, take one of these long sticks and cut it off in this funny-looking gizmo with a saw in it and try to make the corners match." An accurate vocabulary will help your listeners remember what supplies and tools to get when they approach the same project: "This is a ceiling molding; it goes around the room between the wall and the ceiling to cover the seams between the paneling and the ceiling tiles. You make the corners of the molding match by using a mitre box, which has grooves that allow you to cut 45-degree angles. Here's how you do it."

Simplify When Possible   If your speech on the operation of a dimmer switch sounds like it came out of the documentation for computer software, then it's too technical. An audience bogged down in unnecessary detail and complex vocabulary can become confused and bored. Include only as much technical vocabulary as you need.

Use Reiteration to Clarify Complex Ideas   Rephrasing helps to solidify ideas for those who didn't get them the first time. You might say, for example, "Unlike a terrestrial telescope, a celestial telescope is used for looking at moons, planets, and stars; that is, its mirrors and lenses are ground and arranged in such a way that it focuses on objects thousands of miles—not hundreds of feet—away from the observer." In this case, the idea is rephrased; the words aren't simply repeated.

Associating New Ideas with Familiar Ones

Audiences grasp new facts and ideas more readily when they can associate them with what they already know. In a speech to inform, try to connect the new with the old (see Figure 13.1). To do this, you need to know enough about your audience to choose relevant experiences, images, analogies, and metaphors to use in your speech.

Sometimes such associations are obvious. A college dean talking to an audience of manufacturers on the problems of higher education presented his ideas under the headings of raw material, casting, machining, polishing, and assembling. He translated his central ideas into an analogy that his audience, given their vocations, would understand. If you cannot think of any obvious associations, you may have to rely on common expe-

FIGURE 13.1   Association of New Ideas with Familiar Ones

Audiences grasp new concepts more quickly when those concepts are compared to things they already know. What familiar concepts could you use to explain molecules? gene splicing? inflation?

riences or images. For instance, you might explain the operation of a department store's pneumatic tube system by comparing it to sucking through a straw, or you could explain a cryogenic storage tank by comparing it to a thermos bottle.

Clustering Ideas

You can help listeners make sense out of your speech by providing them with a well-organized package of tightly clustered ideas. Research on memory and organization has demonstrated that the "magic number" of items we can remember is seven, plus or minus two; more recent research has suggested that the number is probably five, again plus or minus two.[2] This research suggests that you ought to group items of information under three, five, or seven headings or in three, five, or seven clusters. You might, for example, organize a lecture on the history of American television around developments in key decades—the 1950s, 1960s, 1970s, 1980s, and 1990s—rather than breaking it down year by year. College registration may be presented to freshmen as a five-step process: (a) secure registration materials, (b) review course offerings, (c) see an adviser, (d) fill out the registration materials, and (e) enter the information into the computer. The American Cancer Society has organized the most common symptoms of cancer into seven categories to help you remember them.

Mnemonic devices in your outline also can provide memory triggers. CPR instructors teach the ABCs of cardiopulmonary resuscitation: (a) clear the *airways,* (b) check the *breathing,* and (c) initiate chest *compressions.* A speaker giving a talk on the Great Lakes

Speaking of . . . *apprehension*

Information Overload

A nightmare that you might have one day goes something like this: you're in the library, getting together materials for a speech, when suddenly statistics, quotations, and examples start flying off the shelves. You're bombarded with supporting materials; it stacks up around you like urban garbage. You thought you'd be afraid only of too little information; in today's world, it's the information glut that scares you. What to do?

The frustration you can feel for having found too much information for your speech is real, and is in fact a problem. But you can handle it. Consider doing the following:

- *Sample it.* Even if you've found thirteen great examples, pick out only two or three of them. Use the ones you think are most relevant to the audience's needs and desires.
- *Rotate it.* Use some of the examples this time, and some other ones when talking to friends about the topic.
- *Table it.* If you have too much information to deliver orally, put some of it on a graph or table and either project it or hand it out to your listeners. That way, you won't have to recite all of the numbers, yet they won't go to waste.
- *Distribute it.* Lots of juicy quotations? Use them not only in the body of the speech as supporting materials, but also in the introduction to set the tone and in the conclusion to wrap up your ideas.

If you do a good job at finding supporting materials, you'll have much too much at your disposal. That's all right. Better than having too little. Be happy in the knowledge that the opposite problem is much, much worse.

can show listeners how to remember the names of the lakes by thinking of HOMES: Huron, Ontario, Michigan, Erie, and Superior. These memory devices also help you to remember the main points in your outline. Information forgotten is information lost; package your data and ideas in memorable clusters.

Relevant Visualizations

As we've been emphasizing, relevance is a key to speechmaking success. Using visualizations—recreations of events that people can "see"—can be a powerful technique for catching up an audience; if they can be made to see a process or event, they perhaps can be induced to project themselves mentally into it. So, for example, a student audience might know about the Vietnam War only through the mass media; that's where they had seen it, and thus references to movies and TV programs would be a good way for you to get into the topic. Word pictures help listeners into the world of your informative speech:

> *Picture this: You're walking down the Coleman Street in Collegeville, enjoying a sunny afternoon, when you come across a man who looks desperate, and says "Ca-oo-elp-mee-plee-plee-ahm-hafin', ahm-ahm-ahm-hafin'." What do you do? Is this person drunk? Crazy? Sick? In diabetic shock? Having a heart attack? Or maybe just someone participating in a psych experiment? How are you going to handle this situation? Well, in my speech today, I'm going to tell you how to handle it. Today, I want to talk to you about . . . .*

Notice that the speaker tries to depict a familiar locale and a plausible event in that locale, so as to set up a speech on the new kinds of first-aid training currently offered to students at her school. If she's successful in conveying a sense of fear, uncertainty, and mistrust, then she's likely going to have her listeners following the rest of her talk.

Motivating Your Audience

Finally, and perhaps most important, you must be able to motivate your audience to listen. Unfortunately, many people ignore this essential feature of good informative speeches. Many of us blithely assume that because we are interested in something, our audience also will want to hear about it. You may be fascinated by collecting American commemorative stamps, but your listeners may yawn through your entire speech unless you motivate them. You need to give them a reason to listen. To make them enthusiastic, you might explain how stamps reflect our heritage or you might tell them how competitions are held for stamp art.

Keep in mind what we've said about attention in Chapter 9. You can use the factors of attention to engage the members of your audience and to draw them into your speech.

Structuring Informative Speeches

Now that we've described the various types of informative speeches and examined their essential features, it's time to examine ways to structure each type. Of course, it's possible to use any of the organizational patterns we've described earlier, but some patterns are better suited to particular types than others.

Speaking of . . . ethics

Suppressing Information

If you do a good job of pre-speech research, you'll come across a tremendous amount of information. You'll know much more than you'll be able to fit into a 5- or 8-minute speech. So, you'll cut some. What kind? You'll be tempted to cut material that runs counter to what you want to argue. Is that ethical?

- You give a speech on the filth and disease associated with the processing of poultry in slaughterhouses. You know that the President signed a bill during the summer of 1996 for reforming poultry treatment in those plants. Should you mention it or not?
- Tuition jumped eight percent each of the past two years, though over the past ten years, tuition increases at your school have averaged four percent. Is it all right to deal with only the past two years in a speech on the need for more state monies into your state's higher education system?
- Ratings of TV shows are done in two ways: total number of households tuned in to a program, or percentage of the audience viewing a program at any given time. So, *The Late Show with David Letterman* isn't watched by a lot of households, but it easily has the highest percentage of program viewers in its time slot. So, in a speech on the popularity of the show, is it all right to quote only the percentage-of-audience figure while suppressing the actual number of viewing households?

A simple rule of thumb: assume someone will know the information you've suppressed, and then decide what you'd have to say if someone quoted the material you left out. That may get you out of your ethical dilemmas.

Speeches of Definition

Because one of your primary jobs in speeches of definition is to bring coherence and focus to information or concepts, structuring such speeches is a crucial activity.

Introduction   Because speeches of definition treat either unfamiliar or familiar concepts in a new light, their introductions must create curiosity and establish need in listeners. Creating curiosity is a special challenge in speeches on unfamiliar concepts since we're all tempted to say, "Well, if I've made it this far in life without knowing anything about quarks or double-entry bookkeeping or Library of Congress book coding, why should I bother with learning about these ideas now?" You need to make people wonder about the unknown. Use new information to attract attention and arouse curiosity.

Speeches of definition must also be attentive to the needs or wants of the audience. In other words, their introductions should include explicit statements that indicate how the information can affect the listeners, such as, "Understanding the coding system used by the Library of Congress will help you find books you're looking for faster and, as an additional payoff, show you how to find other books like the one you're looking for."

Body   Most speeches of definition use a topical pattern because such speeches usually describe various aspects of an object or idea. It seems natural, for example, to use a topical pattern for a speech on careers in television around such topics as careers in broadcast TV, careers in cable TV, and careers in industrial TV.

There are occasions when other patterns may serve your specific purpose even better than topical patterns. You might use an effect-cause pattern, for example, when preparing an informative speech on the laws of supply and demand. You could enumerate a series of effects with which people are already familiar—changing prices at the gas pumps—and then discuss the laws of supply and demand that account for such changes.

Conclusion   Conclusions for speeches of definition have two characteristics: (a) they usually include a summary of the main points, and (b) they often stress the ways in which people can apply the ideas that have been presented. For example, the speaker discussing diabetes could conclude by offering listeners the titles of books containing more information, the phone number of the American Diabetes Association, the local address of a clinic, or the meeting time and place of a diabetics support group.

A speech defining diabetes could be outlined in a topical pattern as follows. Note several characteristics of this speech:

1. The speaker tries early on to engage listeners' curiosity and to review listeners' personal needs. The use of a personal example is particularly good for this kind of speech.

2. The speaker offers statistics on diabetes early so that the audience knows that the disease is widespread and serious.

3. Three topics are previewed, then developed in the body of the speech to engage three aspects of listeners' thinking.

4. After offering a summary of the central idea, the speaker returns to the personal example, adding closure to the speech.

Instructions and Demonstrations

Flip through your television channels and you'll come across cooking demonstrations, home-improvement shows, sewing instructions, home shopping demonstrations, and painting lessons. Each presents the steps required to complete a project. Like successful educational television shows, instructions and demonstrations should break down a process or procedure into a series of steps. Each step should be easy to understand and to visualize.

Introduction   In some speaking situations, such as presentations in speech communication classrooms, listener attendance may not be voluntary. On these occasions, you'll have to pay special attention to motivational matters. If your audience has invited you to speak or is attending your talk voluntarily, you can assume listener interest. When giving instructions or offering a demonstration, you'll usually need to spend only a little time generating curiosity or motivating people to listen. After all, if you're instructing listeners in a new office procedure or giving a workshop on how to build an ice boat, they already have the prerequisite interest and motivation; otherwise they wouldn't have come. When your audience is already motivated to listen, you can concentrate your introduction on two other tasks.

1. *Preview your speech.* If you're going to take your listeners through the steps involved in refinishing a bookcase, give them an overall picture of the process before you start detailing each operation.

Practice coordinating verbal and visual materials while speaking so that you can do it smoothly and professionally.

2. *Encourage listeners to follow along.* Even though some of the steps may be difficult, urge everyone to listen. A process such as tombstone rubbing, for example, looks easier than it is: many people are tempted to quit listening and give up somewhere along the way. If, however, you forewarn them and promise them special help with the difficult techniques, they will be more likely to bear with you.

Body   As we suggested earlier, most speeches of demonstration and instruction follow a natural chronological or spatial pattern. Consequently, you usually will have little trouble organizing the body of a speech of demonstration or instruction. Your problems are more likely to be technical and may include the following:

1. *The problem of rate.* If you need to let a cream pie set and cool before building a top layer, what do you do? You can't just stand there and wait for cooling. Instead, you also have a cooled pie, ready for the next step. You also need to preplan some material for filling the time—perhaps additional background or a brief discussion of what problems can arise at this stage. Preplan your remarks carefully for those junctures so you can maintain your audience's attention.

2. *The problem of scale.* How can you show various embroidery stitches to an audience of 25? When dealing with minute operations, you often must increase the scale of operation. In this example, you could use a large piece of poster board or even a 3- by 4-foot piece of cloth stretched over a wooden frame. By using an oversized needle, yarn instead of thread, and stitches measured in inches instead of millimeters, you could easily make your techniques visible to all audience members. At the

other extreme, in a speech on how to make a homemade compost frame, you should work with a scaled-down model.

3. *The coordination of verbal and visual methods.* Both instructions and demonstrations usually demand that speakers "show" while "telling." To keep yourself from becoming flustered or confused, be sure to practice *doing* while *talking*—demonstrating your material while explaining aloud what you're doing. Decide where you'll stand when showing a slide so that the audience can see both you and the image; practice talking about your aerobic exercise positions while you're actually doing them; do a Web search for your speech in practice sessions so you'll be ready to do it for a real audience. If you don't, you'll inevitably get yourself into trouble in front of your listeners.

Conclusion   Conclusions for demonstration speeches usually have three parts:

1. *Summary.* Most audiences need this review, which reminds them to question procedures or ideas they don't understand.

2. *Encouragement.* People trying new processes or procedures usually get in trouble the first few times and need to be reassured that such trouble is predictable and can be overcome.

3. *Offer of help.* What sounded so simple in your talk may be much more complicated in execution. If possible, make yourself available for assistance: "As you fill out your application form, just raise your hand if you're unsure of anything and I'll be happy to help you." Or point to other sources of further information and assistance: "Here's the address of the U.S. Government Printing Office, whose pamphlet X1234 is available for only three dollars; it will give you more details"; "If you run into a problem fetching computer files that I haven't covered in this short orientation, just go over to Maria McFerson's desk, right over here. Maria's experienced in these matters and is always willing to help." Such statements not only offer help but assure your listeners that they won't be labeled as dimwitted if they actually have to ask for it.

Thinking through requirements of speeches of instruction and demonstration might result in a speaking outline like the one on page 000.

Oral Reports

Your principal strategy in an oral report must be to meet the audience's expectations with the information and the recommendations you present.

Introduction   An oral report is requested by a group, committee, or class; the audience, therefore, generally knows what it expects and why. As a result, in introducing oral reports, you need not spend much time motivating your listeners. Instead, you should concentrate on describing how you gathered and organized your information and pointing ahead to any action that your listeners are expected to take in light of your information. The key to a good introduction for an oral report is orientation—reviewing the past (your listeners' expectations and your preparations), the present (your goal now), and the future (your listeners' responsibilities once you are done). Remember that you're giving your report to your audience for a *purpose.*

Body   The principle for organizing the body of an oral report can be stated simply: select the organizational pattern best suited to your audience's needs. Have you been asked to provide your listeners with a history of a group or a problem? Use a chronological pattern. Do they want to know how a particular state of affairs came to be? Try a cause-effect format. Have you been asked to discuss an organizational structure for the group? A topical pattern will allow you to review the constitutional responsibilities of each officer. Note the use of a topical pattern in the sample outline that follows.

Sample Outline for an Oral Report

Report from the Massage Therapy Committee[5]

I. Our committee was asked to investigate different kinds of massage therapy and then to recommend a therapy program for our exercise club.

  A. We interviewed various kinds of massage therapists working in this area.

  B. Different committee members had massages done by each therapy so that we can talk more specifically about each technique.

II. We examined five kinds of massage therapy:

  A. Swedish massage is the most common in this area.

    1. Therapists use long strokes, kneading, and rubbing techniques on the outer layers of muscles on the surface of the whole body.

    2. This technique is especially useful for relaxation and improving circulation.

  B. Deep-tissue massage is one alternative to Swedish massage.

    1. Here, slow strokes with harder pressure are used.

    2. This technique is used primarily to relieve muscle tension.

  C. Neuromuscular or trigger-point therapy is practiced at several senior centers.

    1. Therapists use strong finger pressure at key trigger points, especially points of muscular tension.

    2. They are working on chronic pain, to break its cycles.

  D. Sports massage is available at many fitness centers.

    1. Specific groups of muscles are worked on with pressure and heating ointments.

    2. It attacks muscles spasms, tendinitis, and tenderness.

  E. Shiatsu (from Japan) and acupressure (from China) are growing in this area.

    1. Like acupressure, shiatsu and acupressure rely on pressure to unblock energy (called "qi" ["chi"]) flowing along pathways in the body.

The charge of the committee is stated.

The five options are reviewed by description and result.

2. These techniques are used for pain from headaches or chronic sources.

III. As we thought about the needs of our exercise group, we had the following thoughts:

A. The most common complaints from most of us are about tension and the chronic pain of growing older.

B. Some of you also wanted to learn some pain relief techniques that you could use by yourself at home.

C. Cost also is a consideration for many of you.

IV. Therefore, considering these factors, our committee recommends that two sorts of massage therapy be offered here.

A. A neuromuscular therapist should be asked in once a week to help those of us with chronic pain who want to learn some techniques we can use between visits to the therapist.

B. A Swedish masseur should be available at least every two weeks for rubdowns and relaxation from the cares of this world.

C. We also agreed that a list of therapists in this area, by kind of therapy, should be distributed to everyone.

D. I think we should thank the committee for its work, and its willingness to take your questions. Do you have any?

Evaluation begins by stating the criteria used.

The evaluation is offered positively (though the committee should be ready to indicate as well why it eliminated some approaches).

Final recommendations for action are provided.

Conclusion   Most oral reports end with a conclusion that mirrors the introduction. Mention again your report's purpose; review its main points; publicly thank committee members; and then either offer a motion to accept the committee recommendations, or—in the case of informative reports—request questions from the audience. Conclusions to reports, when done well, are quick, firm, efficient, and pointed.

Lectures

You'll find it's often difficult to engage an audience fully in a lecture—to get them interested in the topic and tuned in to the point of view you're taking. This problem should guide the way you structure the introductions, bodies, and conclusions of lectures.

Introduction   Introductions and conclusions can provide your greatest challenges when structuring lectures. It is particularly important in lectures to raise curiosity. How many of your classmates are wondering about the causes of the Crimean War at ten o'-clock in the morning? Who cares how the geography of the countryside shaped relations between the Balkan countries? How many of us want to know why the American experience in Vietnam still affects domestic politics? As was suggested in this chapter's opening vignette, you can earn your listeners' attention by relating your topic to something they are familiar with or interested in—in the case of the speech on Vietnam, the mass media. You should also include in your introduction a forecast of the lecture's structure.

TABLE 13.2 Checklist for Introductions and Conclusions to Informative Speeches

Speeches of Definition

_____ 1. Does my introduction create curiosity or entice my audience to listen?

_____ 2. Does my introduction include an explicit statement that shows my listeners how the information in my speech will affect them?

_____ 3. Does my conclusion summarize my main ideas?

_____ 4. Does my conclusion stress ways my listeners can apply the ideas I've discussed?

Instructions and Demonstrations

_____ 1. Does my introduction encourage everyone to listen?

_____ 2. Does my introduction pique listener curiosity?

_____ 3. Do I preview my main points in my introduction?

_____ 4. Do I summarize my main points in my conclusion?

_____ 5. Do I encourage listeners to try new procedures even though they may experience initial difficulty?

_____ 6. Do I tell my listeners where they can find help or information in the future?

Oral Reports

_____ 1. Do I remind my listeners of their request for information?

_____ 2. Do I describe the procedures I used for gathering information for this report?

_____ 3. Does my introduction include a forecast of subtopics?

_____ 4. Does my introduction suggest the action that will be recommended in the report?

_____ 5. Does my conclusion mention the main purpose of the report?

_____ 6. Does my conclusion review the main points of the report?

_____ 7. Do I recognize and thank committee members for their contributions?

_____ 8. Do I call for action on a motion or questions from my listeners?

Lectures

_____ 1. Does my introduction raise listeners' curiosity?

_____ 2. Do I forecast my main topics in my introduction?

_____ 3. Does my conclusion suggest implications of the information listeners have received or call for listeners' action?

Body   The key to most lectures lies in the way in which the speaker constructs a _viewpoint_ or _rationale_. Suppose that you wanted to explain the origins of U.S. involvement in Vietnam in the 1950s. You in fact could offer several explanations from varied viewpoints, depending on which story of that country and the war that you wanted to tell. You might want to tell the French story, and the defense (with U.S. help) of its stronghold, Dien Bien Phu, in what was then called Indochina. Or, could you talk about allied support of the French, including $3 billion from the United States, and its impact on Euro-American foreign policy. You might prefer the cultural story of Indochina, its split between Western capitalism and Catholicism in the south and Chinese communism and Buddhism in the north, leading to a clash of lifestyles supported by superpowers on both sides. The military story itself also would make an interesting lecture: the French holding the fort at Dien Bien Phu, absolutely convinced that it was invulnerable to a peasant army, only to find itself blown out in the siege of 1954. And, of course, the political story of Vietnam might also be told: the Cold War, the tension of Franco-American relations, SEATO (the South East Asia Treaty Organization), which committed the United States to defend east Asian countries against Communist aggression.[3]

All of these approaches are "correct," and each gives you a significant explanation about the importance of Vietnam to Western (including U.S.) interests as they were perceived at the time. If you tried to tell them all, you'd drive your audience crazy. A better strategy in most lectures, therefore, is to identify the viewpoint you'll take—"Let me tell you the story of American involvement in Vietnam from an economic [cultural/military/political] point of view. If we look at Vietnam in this way, we'll see that . . . ." Such a statement signals your viewpoint, recognizes that you're not trying to be exhaustive, and tells your listeners what to listen for. Help them keep the story straight.

Conclusion   Typically, the conclusion of a good lecture suggests additional implications or calls for particular actions. (See Table 13.2.) For example, if you've explained in a lecture how contagious diseases spread through geographical areas, you probably should conclude by discussing actions that listeners can take to break the contagion cycle. Or if you've reviewed the concept of children's rights to a parent-teacher organization, you might close by asking your listeners to consider what these rights should mean to them— how they should change their thinking and their behavior toward six-year-olds.

Sample Outline for a Speech of Definition

What Is Diabetes?[4]

INTRODUCTION

The speaker uses a vividly developed personal example to gain attention.

I. I never knew my grandmother. She was a talented artist; she raised six kids without all the modern conveniences like microwave ovens and electric clothes dryers; and my dad still talks about the time she foiled a would-be burglar by locking him in a broom closet until the police came. My grandmother had diabetes. It finally took her life. Now my sister has it. So do 16 million other Americans.

The scope of the problem is explained.

II. Diabetes threatens millions of lives, and it's one of nature's stealthiest diseases.

A motivation for listening is provided.

III. It's important to understand this disease because, more than likely, you or someone you know will eventually have to deal with it.

Supporting testimony shows the severity of the disease.

A. Diabetes is the third leading cause of death behind heart disease and cancer, according to the American Diabetes Association.

Listeners are warned that ignorance of the disease makes the problem worse.

B. Over one third of those suffering from the disease don't even know they have it. That simple knowledge could make the difference between a happy productive life and an early death.

C. Furthermore, diabetes is implicated in many other medical problems: it contributes to coronary heart disease; it accounts for 40 percent of all amputations and most cases of new blindness.

The scope of the problem is expanded by pointing out that other medical conditions are complicated by diabetes.

D. In the next few minutes, let's look at three things you should know about "the silent killer," diabetes—what it is, how it affects people, and how it can be controlled.

The three main ideas of the speech are previewed.

BODY

I. What diabetes is.

The first main point is stated.

A. Diabetes is a chronic disease of the endocrine system that affects your body's ability to deliver glucose to its cells.

Diabetes is defined in medical terms.

B. The symptoms of diabetes, according to Dr. Charles Kilo, are weight loss in spite of eating and drinking, constant hunger and thirst, frequent urination, and fatigue.

The symptoms of diabetes are explained.

II. How diabetes affects people.

The second main point is provided.

A. Type I diabetes occurs when your body cannot produce insulin, a substance that delivers glucose to your cells.

Type I diabetes is operationally defined.

1. Only 5 to 10 percent of all diabetics are Type I.

Who is affected by Type I is further explained.

2. This type, also known as *juvenile diabetes,* usually shows up in the first 20 years of life.

3. Type I diabetes can be passed on genetically but is also thought to be triggered by environmental agents such as viruses.

4. Type I diabetics must take insulin injections to treat the disease.

The treatment is revealed.

B. Type II diabetes occurs when your body produces insulin but fails to use it effectively.

Type II diabetes is operationally defined.

1. Of all diabetics, 90 to 95 percent have Type II.

Supporting statistics show the scope of this type.

2. This type usually shows up after a person turns 40.

3. It often affects people who are overweight; more women are affected than men.

Who is affected by Type II is further explained.

4. Insulin injections are sometimes used to treat the disease, though exercise, proper diet, and oral medications often are enough.

The treatment is revealed.

III. How to control diabetes.

The third main point is provided.

A. Type I diabetes cannot be cured, but it can be controlled.

The treatments for Type I are explained.

1. Patients must take insulin injections, usually several times a day.

2. Patients need to monitor their blood sugar levels by pricking a finger and testing a drop of blood.

3. According to *Science News,* several new treatments are available:

Supporting testimony is offered for new treatments.

a. One new device uses near-infrared beams to determine blood sugar level.

Near-infrared beams determine blood sugar levels.

New methods of delivering
insulin are outlined.

  b. Insulin can be taken through the nose or in pill form.
  c. Pancreatic transplants have been performed with limited
     success.
B. Type II diabetes can be controlled through life-style modifications.

The treatments for Type II
are explained.
Testimony supports the value
of weight loss.

  1. Usually these diabetics are required to lose weight by exercis-
     ing, according to Dr. JoAnn Manson.
  2. Changes in diet are also required.

Insulin-stimulating
medications are explained.

Insulin injections replace
unsuccessful behavior
modifications.

  3. Some people take oral medications that stimulate the release
     of insulin, decrease glucose production in the liver, and foster
     insulin activity.
  4. If these modifications fail, Type II diabetics must take insulin
     injections.

CONCLUSION

Listeners are reminded of the
definition of diabetes.

  I. Diabetes is a serious disease in which the body can no longer pro-
     duce or use insulin effectively.

The three main ideas of the
speech are reiterated.

  II. The two types of diabetes occur at different stages in life and re-
      quire different measures for control of the disease.

The speech reaches closure by
referring to the introductory
personal example.

  III. My grandmother lived with her diabetes for years but eventually lost
       her life to it. My sister has the advantages of new treatments and fu-
       ture research in her fight with diabetes.

Listeners are warned that
diabetes could affect them.

  IV. As we age, many of us will be among the 600,000 new diabetics each
      year. Through awareness, we can cope effectively with this silent
      killer.

Sample Outline for a Demonstration Speech

How to Build a Picket Fence

INTRODUCTION

Reference to a familiar sight
on campus.

  I. If you walk by the President's house on your way to class, you un-
     doubtedly have noticed the picket fence surrounding his backyard,
     providing him and his family with an open-yet-personalized backyard
     in which to escape the pressures of this school.

Social and personal motivation.

Working with a model to
make comprehension easier.

  II. Well, with a little time and patience, you can build a fence just like
      that for your or your parents' backyard. In four easy steps and with
      only a few tools, you can make a fence that will be the envy of your
      neighborhood and a monument to your talent.

  (SHOW MODEL)

BODY

I. First, you must lay out the fence.

   A. Measure the total perimeter (WORK WITH THE MODEL).

   B. Establish the location of corner posts and posts in between the corners.

Show examples.

      1. Posts should be placed no more than eight feet apart.

      2. Be sure to plan for a post on each side of any gates or trellises you want to include.

   C. Calculate the lengths of 2 by 4s you'll want to string between the posts.

      1. You'll need two 2 by 4s between each set of posts—one for the top rail, one for the bottom rail.

      2. Set distances between posts to be near the length of 2 by 4s as they're cut at the lumber yard—6', 7' 10" (studs), 8', 10', 12', or 16'.

         a. The cheapest rails you can buy are economy studs, though they're not always good enough for a nice fence.

         b. Some of the nicest rails you can make are cut out of cedar or pine treated with preservatives.

   D. Order your materials from the lumber yard.

      1. Order cedar or treated pine 4 by 4s for the corner posts long enough to stick 30" to 36" above ground and to go below the frostline in your area. Your lumber yard can help you with questions about the frostline.

      2. Order cedar or pine 2 by 4s.

      3. Roughsawn 1-by-4 cedar makes very nice pickets, though you should get pine if you plan on painting the fence.

      4. Buy enough ready-mix cement to put at least a quarter cubic foot of it around each post for stabililty.

         a. Ready-mix cement will allow you to mix it in a wheelbarrow or other container without having to order in sand and gravel.

         b. Your lumber yard will have a mixture of cement and gravel made for fence posts.

      5. Get 2-by-4 brackets into which you'll place the bottom railing (SHOW A BRACKET).

Show a 2-by-4 bracket so listeners know what to buy.

      6. Buy 16D nails for fastening the top 2 by 4s to the posts and 4D nails for fastening the brackets to the posts and the bottom 2 by 4s to the brackets.

      7. Purchase 1 5/8" deck screws to attach the pickets to the rails.

      8. I am handing out a diagram of the fence I laid out for my backyard, together with the materials order list, so you see more clearly what's happening.

Handout so listeners can remember.

E. With the materials picked up or delivered, you're ready to begin actual construction: setting posts, hanging the rails, and putting on the pickets.

II. The ugliest job is setting the posts.

A. Lay out the fence by stringing a line along its perimeter, using black magic marker to indicate where the posts will go; then dig.

B. Digging holes for the posts can be back-breaking work when the ground is as hard as it is around here.

1. If you're going to dig them by hand, borrow or rent both an augur posthole digger to cut the dirt, and a pinch-type digger to drag the dirt out of the holes (SHOW THE DIGGERS).

Show the tools.

2. Consider renting what's often called a "Little Beaver," a power augur for digging 6″ or 8″ holes.

a. If you're not used to exercise, get help.

b. Use it to dig holes about six inches deeper than you'll need them, so you can put rocks or sand in the bottom to help with drainage.

C. Next, cut the posts to the right length.

1. Put the posts into the holes on top of rocks and sand.

Draw post with wings (or show a slide).

2. Put wings on each post: two pieces of 1 by 3 or 1 by 4, one nailed parallel and one nailed perpendicular to the fence line (SHOW DIAGRAM OR SLIDE).

3. These wings will help you stablize the posts as they sit in the middle of the holes.

D. Then fill the rest of the holes.

1. Pour some rock around the bottom of each post.

2. Then add cement, to make a collar of at least a foot.

3. If you still have room in the hole, finish filling it with dirt and rock.

E. Allow the cement to set at least two days before returning to work.

1. You want the cement dried before pounding on the posts.

2. Also, you'll cut the tops off the posts to make them even, so a solid post is a must.

III. The third step is attaching the rails.

A. Measure the distance from center to center between the posts.

1. Cut rails that length.

2. Nail them flat on top of the posts with the 16D nails.

B. Then measure the distance between posts.

1. Measure down from the top of the posts about two feet and mark.

2. Nail a 2-by-4 bracket above that mark (SHOW BRACKET AGAIN).

3. Do the same on the next post, then cut a rail to run between the brackets.

      4. Slide the rail into place and nail it down with 4D nails.

   C. And that's all there is to rails!

IV. Now you're ready for the final step—the pickets.

   A. Cut one picket to be a pattern (SHOW A PICKET).

Show a sample picket.

      1. You can get three pickets out of a 12′ 1-by-4 board.

        a. If you cut the top of the picket at a diagonal, you'll have pickets just over four feet long.

        b. If you want to save a little money, you can cut three pickets out of a 10′ 1 by 4 for pickets a little under three-and-a-half feet tall.

      2. Rent or borrow a power deck screwdriver like this one (SHOW IT).

Show the tool and demonstrate it.

        a. Using a power deck screwdriver is fun and fast.

        b. Notice (DEMONSTRATING) how quickly I can screw a picket to a post.

Return to your model.

        c. If you space 1 by 4s about two-and-a-half inches apart, each picket will take up six inches, so it will be easy to calculate how many you need, say, in a six- or eight-foot span.

        d. You'll have to fiddle with the pickets a bit if you're not exactly six-and-a-half or eight feet between posts, but you can handle that.

CONCLUSION

I. And with that, except for gates and trellises, which would take another whole speech, you're done.

   A. With gates in place, you can keep a dog inside the fence.

   B. Even without them, you'll have a pleasant enclosure in which to grow flowers and vegetables, cut paths, place benches, and feed birds.

II. Picket fences make for all-American yards.

   A. Robert Frost wrote that "Good fences make good neighbors."

      1. While he was being ironic in that poem, "Mending Fence," his sentiment can be taken more positively than he meant it.

Use of poetry to inspire the listeners.

      2. Good fences can beautify neighborhoods and create pride in one's home.

   B. A good picket fence isn't a barrier to others, but rather an invitation to look, to admire, and to talk with your neighbors about what's growing inside.

      1. Just ask our President—the whole community participates in his backyard life because of that picket fence.

Offer a final inducement to act.

      2. You can offer the same invitation to others by following the four easy steps I've outlined on the handout I've given you—happy fencing!

Sample Speech

The following speech, "The Geisha," was delivered by Joyce Chapman when she was a freshman at Loop College, Chicago. It illustrates most of the virtues of a good informative speech: (1) it provides enough detail and explanations to be clear; (2) it works from familiar images of geishas, adding new ideas and information in such a way as to enlarge listeners' frames of reference; (3) its topical organization pattern is easy to follow; and, (4) it gives listeners reasons for listening.

The Geisha[6] Joyce Chapman

A personal reference establishes an immediate tie between Ms. Chapman and her topic.

As you may have already noticed from my facial features, I have Oriental blood in me and, as such, I am greatly interested in my Japanese heritage. One aspect of my heritage that fascinates me the most is the beautiful and adoring Geisha./1

Ms. Chapman works hard to bring the listeners—with their stereotyped views of Geishas—into the speech through comments many might have made and references to familiar films.

I recently asked some of my friends what they thought a Geisha was, and the comments I received were quite astonishing. For example, one friend said, "She is a woman who walks around in a hut." A second friend was certain that a Geisha was, "A woman who massages men for money and it involves her in other physical activities." Finally, I received this response, "She gives baths to men and walks on their backs." Well, needless to say, I was rather surprised and offended by their comments. I soon discovered that the majority of my friends perceived the Geisha with similar attitudes. One of them argued, "It's not my fault, because that is the way I've seen them on TV." In many ways my friend was correct. His misconception of the Geisha was not his fault, for she is often portrayed by American film producers and directors as: a prostitute, as in the movie, *The Barbarian and the Geisha,* a streetwalker, as seen in the TV series, "Kung Fu," or as a showgirl with a gimmick, as performed in the play, *Flower Drum Song.*/2

A Geisha is neither a prostitute, streetwalker, nor showgirl with a gimmick. She is a lovely Japanese woman who is a professional entertainer and hostess. She is cultivated with exquisite manners, truly a bird of a very different plumage./3

The central idea is stated clearly.
A transition moves the listeners easily from the introduction to the body of the speech via a forecast.

I would like to provide you with some insight to the Geisha, and, in the process perhaps, correct any misconception you may have. I will do this by discussing her history, training, and development.

The first section of the body of the speech is devoted to an orienting history that cleverly wipes away most of the negative stereotypes of the Geisha.

The Geisha has been in existence since 600 A.D., during the archaic time of the Yakamoto period. At that time the Japanese ruling class was very powerful and economically rich. The impoverished majority, however, had to struggle to survive. Starving fathers and their families had to sell their young daughters to the teahouses in order to get a few yen. The families hoped that the girls would have a better life in the teahouse than they would have had in their own miserable homes./5

During ancient times only high society could utilize the Geisha's talents because she was regarded as a status symbol, exclusively for the elite. As the Geisha became more popular, the common people developed their own imitations. These imitations were often crude and base, lacking sophistication and taste. When American GIs came home from World War II, they related descriptive accounts of their wild escapades with the Japanese Geisha. In essence, the GIs were only soliciting with common prostitutes. These bizarre stories helped create the wrong image of the Geisha./6

Today, it is extremely difficult to become a Geisha. A Japanese woman couldn't wake up one morning and decide, "I think I'll become a Geisha today." It's not that simple. It takes sixteen years to qualify./7

At the age of six a young girl would enter the Geisha training school and become a Jo-chu, which means housekeeper. The Jo-chu does not have any specific type of clothing, hairstyle, or make-up. Her duties basically consist of keeping the teahouse immaculately clean (for cleanliness is like a religion to the Japanese). She would also be responsible for making certain that the more advanced women would have everything available at their fingertips. It is not until the girl is sixteen and enters the Maiko stage that she concentrates less on domestic duties and channels more of her energies on creative and artistic endeavors./8

A nice transition moves Chapman to her second point on the rigors of Geisha training. She discusses the training in language technical enough to make listeners feel that they're learning interesting information but not so detailed as to be suffocating.

The Maiko girl, for example, is taught the classical Japanese dance, Kabuki. At first, the dance consists of tiny, timid steps to the left, to the right, backward and forward. As the years progress, she is taught the more difficult steps requiring syncopated movements to a fan./9

The Maiko is also introduced to the highly regarded art of floral arrangement. The Japanese take full advantage of the simplicity and gracefulness that can be achieved with a few flowers in a vase, or with a single flowering twig. There are three main styles: Seika, Moribana, and Nagerie. It takes at least three years to master this beautiful art./10

During the same three years, the Maiko is taught the ceremonious art of serving tea. The roots of these rituals go back to the thirteenth century, when Zen Buddhist monks in China drank tea during their devotions. These rituals were raised to a fine art by the Japanese tea masters, who set the standards for patterns of behavior throughout Japanese society. The tea ceremony is so intricate that it often takes four hours to perform and requires the use of over seventeen different utensils. The tea ceremony is far more than the social occasion it appears to be. To the Japanese, it serves as an island of serenity where one can refresh the senses and nourish the soul./11

One of the most important arts taught to the Geisha is that of conversation. She must master an elegant circuitous vocabulary flavored in Karyuki, the world of flowers and willows, of which she will be a part. Consequently, she must be capable of stimulating her client's mind as well as his esthetic pleasures./12

The third point of the speech—how a Geisha develops her skills in her actual work—is clearly introduced and then developed with specific instances and explanations.

Having completed her sixteen years of thorough training, at the age of twenty-two, she becomes a full-fledged Geisha. She can now serve her clients with duty, loyalty, and most important, a sense of dignity./13

The Geisha would be dressed in the ceremonial kimono, made of brocade and silk thread. It would be fastened with an obi, which is a sash around the waist and hung down the back. The length of the obi would indicate the girl's degree of development. For instance, in the Maiko stage the obi is longer and is shortened when she becomes a Geisha. Unlike the Maiko, who wears a gay, bright, and cheerful kimono, the Geisha is dressed in more subdued colors. Her make-up is the traditional white base, which gives her the look of white porcelain. The hair is shortened and adorned with beautiful, delicate ornaments./14

As a full-fledged Geisha, she would probably acquire a rich patron who would assume her sizable debt to the Okiya, or training residence. This patron would help pay for her wardrobe, for each kimono can cost up to $12,000. The patron would generally provide her with financial security./15

The Geisha serves as a combination entertainer and companion. She may dance, sing, recite poetry, play musical instruments, or draw pictures for her guest. She might converse with them or listen sympathetically to their troubles. Amorous advances, however, are against the rules./16

So, as you can see the Geisha is a far cry from the back-rubbing, streetwalking, slick entertainer that was described by my friends. She is a beautiful, cultivated, sensitive, and refined woman./17

The conclusion is short and quick. Little more is needed in a speech that has offered clear explanations, though some speakers might want to refer back to the initial overview of negative stereotypes in order to remind the listeners how wrong such views are.

Assessing Your Progress

Chapter Summary

1. Speeches to inform include talks that seek to assemble, package, and interpret raw data, information, or ideas, so as to create knowledge in listeners.

2. The four types of informative speeches are speeches of definition, instructions and demonstrations, oral reports, and lectures.

3. No matter what type of informative speech you're preparing, you should strive for five qualities: clarity; associating new ideas with familiar ones; clustering ideas to aid memory and comprehension; constructing relevant visualizations to aid in audience comprehension; and motivating your audience.

4. Each type of informative speech can be structured into introductions, bodies, and conclusions that maximize your ability to reach your audiences.

Key Terms

demonstrations (p. 207)

information (p. 206)

instructions (p. 207)

knowledge (p. 206)

lectures (p. 207)

oral report (p. 207)

speech of definition (p. 207)

Assessment Activities

1. In a concise written report, indicate and defend the type of arrangement (chronological sequence, spatial sequence, and so on) you think would be most suitable for an informative speech on the following subjects:

   a. The status of minority studies on campus.

   b. Recent developments in genetic engineering.

   c. Mayan excavations in Central America.

   d. Tax-free savings for retirement.

   e. How a chat room works.

   f. Censorship of video games.

   g. Diet fads of the 1980s and 1990s.

   h. Residential colleges in universities.

   i. Buying your first house.

   j. What life will be like in the year 2500.

2. Plan a two- to four-minute speech in which you will give instructions. For instance, you might explain how to calculate your tax liability in any given year, how to canvass for a political candidate, or how to make a group flight reservation. This exercise is basically descriptive, so limit yourself to using a single visual aid.

3. Describe an unusual place you have visited on a vacation—for example, a cathedral in a foreign city or a historical site. Deliver a four- or five-minute speech to the class, in which you describe this place as accurately and vividly as possible. Then ask the class to take a moment to envision this place. If possible, show them a picture of what you have described. How accurately were they able to picture the place? How might you have ensured a more accurate description? What restrictions did you feel without the use of visual aids?

References

1. This information taken from *Professional Baseball: The First 100 Years* (New York: Poretz-Ross Publishers, 1969).

2. For background on information packaging, see G. Mandler, "Organization and Memory," in *Human Memory: Basic Processes,* edited by Gordon Bower (New York: Academic Press, 1977), 310–354; Mandler's articles in C. R. Puff, ed., *Memory Organization and Structure* (New York: Academic Press, 1976); and the classic G. A. Miller, "The Magic Number Seven Plus or Minus Two: Some Limits on Our Capacity for Processing Information," *Psychological Review, 63* (1956): 81–97.

5. Information for this review was taken from *Modern Maturity,* September–October 1996, esp. p. 72.

3. For details on these stories, see David Halberstam, *The Fifties* (New York: Villard Books, 1993).

4. Information for this outline taken from Phyllis Barrier, "Diabetes: It Never Lets Up," *Nation's Business* (November 1992), 77; David Bradley, "Is a Pill on the Way for Diabetes?" *New Scientist* (27 June 1992), 17; C. Ezzell, "New Clues to Diabetes' Cause

and Treatment," *Science News* (21 December 1991), 406; Charles Kilo and Joseph R. Williamson, *Diabetes* (New York: John Wiley & Sons, 1987); Mark Schapiro, "A Shock to the System," *Health* (July–August 1991), 75–82; Carrie Smith, "Exercise Reduces Risk of Diabetes," *The Physician and Sportsmedicine* (November 1992), 19; John Travis, "Helping Diabetics Shed Pins and Needles," *Science News* (6 July 1991), 4; Janice A. Drass and Ann Peterson, "Type II Diabetes: Exploring Treatment Options," *American Journal of Nursing 96* (November 1996): 45–49; personal experience of one of the authors.

6. Joyce Chapman, "The Geisha," in Roselyn Schiff et al., *Communication Strategy: A Guide to Speech Preparation* (Glenview, Ill.: Scott, Foresman and Co., 1981). Used with permission of Longman Publishers.

14 Speeches to Persuade

You probably don't think about it, but you're bathed in persuasive appeals every day of your life. Billboards confront you on your way to school, posters call for your attention, teachers urge you to see their points of view, campus signs plead with you not to litter, and Burger King wants you to "Have It Your Way"—as long as it's a Whopper. Speaking publicly in order to persuade shares many features with other kinds of persuasion that we experience all the time.

The general purpose of persuasion is to change or reinforce attitudes or behaviors. The speaker who persuades makes a very different demand on the audience than does the speaker who informs. The informative speaker is satisfied when listeners understand what has been said. The persuader, however, attempts to influence the listener's thoughts or actions. The persuader may even plead with the audience to agree with or act on the speech. Occasionally, persuaders seek to reinforce ideas or actions that already exist in listeners. They may defend the status quo, urging rejection of proposed changes. Whatever the specific purpose, the general purpose of persuasion is to convince audiences.

To persuade audiences successfully, you must make them *want* to believe or act. When people are forced to accept beliefs, they may soon abandon them. So, two subsidiary purposes of persuasive speaking must be kept in mind: (a) to provide the audience with motives for believing, by appealing to their basic needs or desires and (b) to convince them that your recommendation will satisfy these desires. Consider the following story:

> Spring break was still two months away, though time was getting short. Meredith wanted to join some friends on the Cayman Islands, but how? She'd not only need her parents' permission, but she'd need a little cash as well. What appeals would reach them? "Everyone's doing it?" No, that didn't work last time. "I deserve a break after all of the hard work I've been doing this semester?" Not bad, but it wouldn't justify going to the Cayman Islands, exactly. Finally a thought occurred to Meredith. She went to her adviser, who agreed to help. Then she headed to a supper with her

We live in a world that runs on promotions and pitches—persuasion, in other words. What are some examples of persuasive advertising evident in this photo?

parents, and started to talk: "You know I want a nice spring break to end my college career. But, I know I'm in college mainly to learn and improve my knowledge of my field. I know how I can do both. I want to go with some of my friends to the Cayman Islands. While I'm there, I can gather some plant samples, climatological data, and pictures of the terrain. Then when I'm back I can do an independent study with my adviser on relationships between flora and island geography. I'll have fun, but also earn academic credit and have an independent project I can put into a portfolio when I go job hunting. What do you think?"

Meredith worked hard to find the right motive and to convince her parents that a trip to the islands would satisfy their desires as well as her own. Meredith's approach to fulfilling her desire for a great spring break was a classic exercise in audience analysis and verbal persuasion. She explored her experience in reaching this particular audience, considered its habitual grounds for granting her help and privilege, and kept on thinking about her parents until she figured out a way to satisfy both her desires and their expectations. Exchanges like this occur millions of times a day.

We'll begin this chapter with a discussion of motive needs and the motivational appeals that speakers can use to tap those needs. Then, we'll examine the motivated sequence, an organizational pattern that helps you to incorporate motivational appeals successfully into your speeches.

Changing Audiences' Minds and Actions

We'll make a distinction in this chapter that may help you to focus more particularly on techniques for successfully persuading others to think and act in particular ways. A **persuasive speech** we'll identify as one that seeks to change an audience's beliefs, attitudes, or values—to reorient their thinking in some significant way. An **actuative speech,** on the other hand, we'll discuss as one that seeks to alter people's actual behavior. So, a speech that asks listeners to think of alcoholism as a disease rather than a social disgrace would be a persuasive speech; one that asks them to intervene in the lives of friends who drink too much, to get them treatment, is an actuative speech. The distinction is not especially important except in one respect: you need to realize that it's one thing to convince people to change their minds, but quite another to get them to act upon that conviction.

✓ "Sure I believe in blood banks, but, ah, well, like I'm too busy to go to the blood mobile today, OK?"

✓ "Sure I believe that cafeteria workers are being ripped off, but, ah, support a union? I couldn't do that. I haven't got time for any more organizations/I'm too broke to pay union dues/they're just a bunch of outside agitators/I can't risk my job/etc."

The key to success in both persuasive and actuative speeches is motivation: Can you find ways to tap into the audience's motivations so as to change thought and behavior? To answer that question, we need to talk about needs and desires, motives and motivational appeals, and motivationally sound structures for persuasive and actuative speeches.

Analyzing the Needs and Desires of Listeners

Begin with the simple assumption that people's thoughts and actions are related their needs (things that are missing and yet perceived as necessary to their lives) and desires

Society could not function were not citizens able to convince each other to take or avoid collective actions.

Speaking of . . . *skills*

Persuading the Diverse Audience

As we noted in the opening to Chapter 4, one of the most difficult tasks a speaker faces is trying to convince a diversified audience to act together. How can you get racially diversified, bi-gendered, class-stratified audiences of young and old people to work in harmony?

The advice offered in that chapter bears repeating (and re-reading if necessary):

- recognize diversity even while calling for unity
- show that particular values are held in common even if they're operationalized differently by various groups of people
- encourage different paths to a goal they all can share
- exhort people to adjust some of their own lifestyle choices for the greater good of all
- assure people that they can maintain their self-identity even when working with people of different values, lifestyles, and cultures

All of this is good advice, *but can you actually execute it? How?* Well, the bottom line is courage: the courage to recognize difference in explicit ways, to force people to confront and deal with their differences, and to make joint progress on problems caused by those very differences. If you are willing to tackle diversity problems in public speech, the following sorts of topics could be brought up:

1. *Gender differences:* Males as well as females should be talking about solutions to date rape.
2. *Racial differences:* Whites as well as blacks should be reading W. E. B. DeBois and Louis Farrahkan, and using them as authorities in speeches.
3. *Age differences:* The young as well as the old should be interrogating examples of deplorable living conditions in state nursing homes.
4. *Class issues:* Rich as well as poor need to know how ghetto-ization has developed across Europe and the United States, examining both its positive and negative cultural effects.

Without the courage to bridge cultural gaps in public talk, we'll remain divided from each other, eternally suspicious and uninformed, silently reproducing divisions, incapable of working across our cultural gaps when the situation demands it.

(things that are hoped for as ends in themselves or means to new achievements). Generally speaking, therefore, a sense of **need** arises out of a perceived lack, and a sense of **desire,** from a hope to improve one's life. So, you need to eat (hunger being a sense of a lack of nourishment), but you desire pizza (a preferred kind of food, not necessary but nonetheless hoped for).

The first step in constructing persuasive and actuative speeches thus begins with an attempt to assess needs and desires: (1) *What* do these people think they lack and *what* do they think would improve their lives in positive ways? (2) *How* can I use those needs and desires to construct a successful persuasive or actuative speech?

Turning Needs and Desires into Motivational Appeals

Needs and desires, of course, are psychological constructs—perceptions people have of themselves, their plight in life, their fantasies, their nightmares. Insofar as these perceptions drive people to think and act in particular ways, they are usefully thought of as motive needs. A **motive need** is an impulse to satisfy a psychological-social want or a biological urge. Such needs may arise from physiological considerations—pain, lack of food, or surroundings that are too hot or cold—or they may come about for sociocultural reasons, such as when you feel left out of a group or wonder whether your peers like you. If you feel the need deeply, your feelings may compel you to do something about your situation. You might eat, adjust the thermostat, or join a group. In each situation, you will have been motivated to act.

Once you recognize the power of motive needs to propel human action, you may ask, "How can I identify and satisfy these needs in a speech? How can I use these basic needs, wants, and desires as the basis for effective public communication?" The answer to both of these questions is, "With the use of motivational appeals." A **motivational appeal** is either (a) a visualization of a desire and a method for satisfying it or (b) an assertion that an entity, idea, or course of action holds the key to fulfilling a particular motive need.

Suppose that you want to borrow a friend's car. How do you prepare to ask? Usually, you create scenarios in your mind. In these scenarios, you try out various motivation appeals: "Should I mention how far it is to walk? [*appeal to sympathy*] What about a reminder of the time I loaned my friend something? [*appeal to previous affiliation*] Should I ease my friend's fears by stressing my safe driving record?" [*appeal to previous success*] By examining the alternatives, you assemble a group of motivational appeals and organize them into narratives that serve as prods to action.

At other times, you may create motivational appeals through verbal labeling or **attribution.**[1]

Suppose you have some strained muscles in your back, but avoid going to a massage therapy business because you think of massages as lascivious, immoral, a bad substitute for real medicine, and much too expensive for your college student budget. Finally, a friend convinces you to go for a Swedish massage. You discover that the massage has no sexual dimensions at all, that the therapist asks about the medical treatment you've been getting to make sure the massage is complementary to it, that you feel awfully good when it's over, and that it costs about half of what you expected. You decide that you've misconstrued massage therapy altogether. You set up a weekly massage schedule at least until your back is better.

What happened? You changed the attributes of *massage* in your mind. Instead of attributing negative terms, such as *debasing, immoral, nonscientific,* and *expensive* to *massage,* you began to attribute to it positive terms, such as *healing, beautiful, therapeutic,* and *valuable.* Your behavior eventually changed because you had begun to use different terms to label things. Motivational appeals may use language to activate desires in people.

Using Motivational Appeals

If you attempted to list the potential motivational appeals for every audience, you might never finish. The task is endless. Rather than trying to list each individual appeal, consider the general thrust of each motive cluster. A **motive cluster** is a group of individual

TABLE 14.1 Motive Clusters

Individual motivational appeals fall into clusters that share a common theme. Think of a current television advertisement and identify the motive clusters in it.

Affiliation	Achievement	Power
Companionship	Acquisition/saving	Aggression
Conformity	Success/display	Authority/dominance
Deference/dependence	Prestige	Defense
Sympathy/generosity	Pride	Fear
Loyalty	Adventure/change	Autonomy/independence
Tradition	Perseverance	
Reverence/worship	Creativity	
Sexual attraction	Curiosity	
	Personal enjoyment	

appeals that are grounded in the same fundamental human motivation. Table 14.1 shows the three motive clusters—affiliation, achievement, and power—as well as the motivational appeals within each cluster.[2] **Affiliation motives** include the desire to belong to a group or to be well liked or accepted. This cluster also includes love, conformity, dependence on others, sympathy toward others, and loyalty. **Achievement motives** are related to the intrinsic or extrinsic desire for success, adventure, creativity, and personal enjoyment. **Power motives** concern primarily the desire to exert influence over others.[3]

If you begin with this list, you'll be in a better position to choose those motivational appeals with the greatest relevance to your topic and audience. Remember this guideline as you make your choices: *motivational appeals work best when they are associated with the needs and desires of your listeners.* Analyze your audience and then choose your motivation appeals based on what you've learned about it.

The Affiliation Cluster Affiliation motives are dominated by a desire for acceptance or approval. They refer to a greater concern for promoting interpersonal bonds than for achieving personal success or individual power. A social desire to be part of a group is an affiliation motive. What follows are some examples of appeals to listeners' affiliation desires:

1. *Companionship and affiliation.* "Blood is thicker than water." We all need others—their presence, their touch, and their acceptance of who we are. In many ethnic groups, the appeal to affliation with people of like background ("blood") is even stronger than an appeal to self-satisfaction ("water") and danger. That's why we respond to appeals such as, "We care about you," "We're looking for a few good men," and "You're one of the brothers and must always remember who you are."

2. *Conformity.* "AARP—It's For People Like You." So goes one of the primary advertising slogans of the American Association for Retired People; you'll join if you feel you share enough characteristics with other over-50 folks to want to belong to a multimillion-member social club and lobby. As well, ads for soft drinks work to convince you that "your kind of person" drinks Coke, Mountain Dew, or Pepsi. "The Pepsi Generation" explicitly stressed conformity, and the "You've got the

right one, baby" campaign always shows groups of people approving Ray Charles's endorsement of that cola. At times, people's need to belong becomes so strong that they feel psychological pressure because of their social, ethnic, gender, or class identification to act on the bases of group, rather than personal judgment.

3. *Deference/dependence.* "Nine out of ten doctors recommend . . . ." We defer to wisdom, experience, or expertise that surpasses our own. Testimony of experts to whom listeners might defer is a successful form of supporting material.

4. *Sympathy/generosity.* "You could be the parent this child has never known for a dollar a day." Such appeals appear in magazine ads asking you to support efforts to save children around the world through financial foster-parenting. All charitable appeals to give and appeals to self-sacrifice in the name of the "common good" assume that your social self—the part of you that bonds with others—will overcome your private self, the self-centered part of you. "Reach out and touch someone," "Give that others might live," and "Contribute today to help us 'Take Back the Night'" are appeals that form the heart of many actuative speeches.

5. *Loyalty.* "The camaraderie becomes something that you carry the rest of your life with those individuals. Sometimes you never get a chance to see those individuals again, but in your heart you know you'd do anything for them because they did that for you in a situation which could have gotten them killed."[4] With these words, Vietnam veteran Ron Mitscher tried to describe the loyalty he felt to his fellow soliders—to other members of "the Brotherhood." Speakers often ask listeners to be loyal to family, friends, organizations, states, geographical regions, or their nation.

6. *Tradition.* "Always for them: duty, honor, country. Always their blood, and sweat and tears, as they saw the way and the light."[5] When General Douglas MacArthur wanted to symbolically unite West Point cadets to yesterday's soldiers, he appealed to tradition—the values that mark the entrance arch to the Academy. The past is stationary, stable; we use it to guide us into the unknown future—hence its great rhetorical strength.

7. *Reverence or worship.* "But in a larger sense we cannot dedicate, we cannot consecrate, we cannot hallow this ground. The brave men, living and dead, who struggled here, have consecrated it far above our power to add or detract."[6] With these words, President Abraham Lincoln invoked a sense of reverence for the dead of both the North and South after the bloody battle of Gettysburg, Pennsylvania. In doing so, he recognized our inferiority to others, to institutions, to nature, and to deities who humble us in their magnitude and eternity. Reverence can take three forms: hero worship, reverence for institutions, and divine worship. As a speaker, you have relatively little power to make your listeners revere you or your words; however, you can appeal to their reverence for ideas, people, or institutions.

8. *Sexual attraction.* "Don't Be Such a Good Boy." With that campaign, the men's cologne Drakkar Noir used an appeal that has sold you deodorant, hair rinse and spray, beer and liquor, automobiles, blue jeans—and men's grooming products. Sex sells. As your consciousness of gender roles is raised, you may find blatantly sexual appeals objectionable. However, few sexual appeals are blatant; you'll notice

that at the core they most often are appealing to people's desire to be attractive to a social group. Most of us respond positively to messages that promise to enhance our personal physical and psychological attractiveness to others.

The Achievement Cluster   Achievement motives concern an individual's desire to attain goals, to excel in certain behaviors or activities, or to obtain prestige or success. The following appeals to achievement motives can pull a person toward the accomplishment of a particular goal:

1. *Acquisition/saving.* "Earn good money now in our new Checking-Plus accounts!" We live in an era of investment clubs, Supplemental Retirement Accounts (SRAs), and more financial advisers than bankers. *Reward* is the name of the game, and its lure is strong. By describing material rewards in social, spiritual, or personal terms, you can also appeal to other motives at the same time as you appeal to achievement motives. So, appeals to buy U.S. Saving Bonds not only promise reward but visualize you as part of a great American tradition—an affiliative appeal.

2. *Success/display.* "Hear the Radio That Woke Up An Entire Industry [Bose—Better Sound Through Research]." "Sisterhood is powerful." Appeals such as these depend on people's interest in making a mark, in developing or actualizing themselves, in being associated with something as successful as a Bose sound system, or in succeeding in the company of others like yourself.

3. *Prestige.* "L'Oreal—Because you're worth it!" Ads for luxury automobiles, designer clothes, and expensive personal grooming products make use of this appeal to your sense of worth—to your place in a community or within a power structure. Ownership of material goods carries with it status. An appeal to listeners' desire for prestige should take into account their desire for affiliation. For example, driving an expensive foreign car identifies one as a member of an elite group.

4. *Pride.* "Be proud of America. Support the troops." So far as appeals to pride are concerned, the 1991 Gulf War was a high point for many Americans. Over 80 percent of them supported President Bush's conduct of that operation; the appeal was strong. Such appeals tighten our loyalties to groups and—when coupled with appeals to adventure, creativity, or independence—move us to greater personal exertion. The appeal to pride can be especially powerful when made to audience members in terms of class (appeals to "the working class"), race (appeals to "Black pride"), gender (appeals to "the working mother"), sexual orientation (appeals to "gay and lesbian lifestyles"), or disability (appeals to "students with learning disabilities").

5. *Adventure/change.* "The Polo Sport Arena: A place to test yourself and your environment," says the clothing manufacturer. "Join the Navy and see the world," says the local recruiter. The human soul yearns for release, swells at the prospect of risk. Participating in adventure is a way that people validate their own worth.

6. *Perseverance.* "It's not the size of the dog in the fight but the size of the fight in the dog." Pieces of conventional wisdom like this saying recognize that change does not come easily and that individuals must be taught to be patient; disappointments must not be allowed to halt projects. Visualizing what the future will bring is an effective strategy in motivating people to persevere. "We shall overcome" and "For a better tomorrow" appeal to perseverance.

7. *Creativity.* "Draw me." Ads that say "Draw me," urging you to draw a duck or a face to earn a scholarship for a correspondence art course, and cookbooks that promise you'll become a gourmet chef appeal to your need to be creative.

8. *Curiosity.* "Will the Internet bring an end to business computing as we know it?" asks the Microsoft Corporation in one of its ads designed to engage corporate executives. Children open alarm clocks to find out where the tick is, adults crowd the sidewalks to gaze at a celebrity, and executives poke around to see what they've got to do to stay ahead of the game. Appeals to curiosity launch exploration, scholarship, experimentation—and enrollment in the Peace Corps.

9. *Personal enjoyment.* "Give your eyes something to scream about," says an ad for three-dimensional graphics; S3 Incorporated's ad melds your visual and vocal capabililties in screams of pleasure—"Because you want 3D so real it screams." Perhaps the most totally self-centered appeal is the appeal to pleasure. The promise of personal comfort and luxury, the aesthetic enjoyment of meditation, recreation and rest resulting from exercise, relief from home and work restraints among people with similar cultural backgrounds, and just plain fun, if believed, will move many in your audience to act.

The Power Cluster Humans seek to dominate and control others, either physically or psychologically. Appeals to power motives often are the most potent motivational appeals you can make. Although the use of power motives can be terribly manipulative, it need not be. By appealing to people's sense of social and moral responsibility, as well as to the power motives described below, you can urge people to use power in positive ways:

1. *Aggression.* "We have not raised armies with ambitious designs of separating from Great Britain and establishing independent States. We fight not for glory or for conquest. We exhibit to mankind the remarkable spectacle of a people attacked by unprovoked enemies, without any imputation or even suspicion of offense."[7] Thus did John Dickinson, the "Pennsylvania Farmer" as he called himself, urge the colonists to fight back against the British in the summer of 1775. Humans tend to form territorial or hierarchical groups and societies. The human urge to claim rights and territory is the foundation for appeals to personal and social competition; it's been one of the bases for the cultural revolutions of the last half-century. No one wants to lose. That's why advertisers tell you to "get ahead of the crowd" or "beat your competition to the punch."

2. *Authority/dominance.* "If the FDA [Food and Drug Administration] will not protect us, we must protect ourselves."[8] When Samantha Hubbard built that argument in a speech attacking the irradiation of food, she was appealing to our natural desire to dominate our environment before it dominates us. Aggressive people can win in competition. Even McGruff, the crime-fighting dog featured in public service announcements who says "Take a bite out of crime," appeals to the desire to dominate.

3. *Defense.* "If I were an American, as I am an Englishman, while a foreign troop was landed in my country, I never would lay down my arms—never—never—never."[9] In encouraging England to get out of America in 1777, former prime minister William Pitt recognized the power of an appeal to a defensive position. The line between attack and self-defense may seem a thin one at times, yet it's important to

Advertisters change motivational appeals when aiming at different segments of society.

maintain it. It's seldom socially acceptable to attack someone else. A socially acceptable way to raise people's fighting spirit for a public cause is to appeal to the need for defense; President Bush worked hard in 1991 to portray the U.S. role in the Persian Gulf as one of defense rather than offense. The appeal is linked to power in terms of listeners' ability to exert authority over their collective needs through the defense of vital interests.

4. *Fear.* "Friends don't let friends drive drunk." This slogan of the Mothers Against Drunk Driving (MADD) campaign makes double use of fear appeal: it appeals to

Speaking of . . . ethics

Using Fear Appeals

Among the most potent appeals to audiences are fear appeals. Research suggests fear appeals are so powerful that they actually can interfere with a listener's ability to process information critically. However, research indicates that fear appeals retain their effectiveness over extended periods of time.

Sometimes fear appeals are used for laudable goals, such as the Juvenile Awareness program at New Jersey's Rahway State Prison (the basis of the 1977 television special "Scared Straight"). In this program, deliquent youths are introduced to convicts who describe the horrors of prison life. Results suggest that the program helps deter young people from further delinquent activity. However, fear appeals are always accompanied by the potential for misuse. Think about the following applications of your classroom speaking. What would you do if you were the speaker? Why?

1. You are planning a persuasive speech to convince your audience that war is morally wrong. You are totally committed to peace and believe that anything you can do to maintain peace in this world is your moral obligation; therefore, you exaggerate some of the facts about recent world conflicts to frighten your audience about the results of war.

2. You give a speech on the increase of date rape on college campuses. In order to convince your audience that date rape is wrong and extremely common, you create scenarios that appeal to the fears of your listeners. Your scenarios are so vivid that several of your listeners, who are rape survivors, are visibly overcome with emotion. One of the listeners is so upset that she must leave the classroom during your speech. Everyone in the audience sees her leave.

3. You feel very strongly that the college president is wrong to continue investing college money in countries where torture and imprisonment without trial are legal. You present a persuasive speech in which you appeal to your audience's fears by suggesting that the college president is actually propagating torture and corrupting the values of U.S. citizens to the point that someday torture and imprisonment without trial might be legal in the United States. Your listeners become so incensed, as a result of your speech, that they march to the president's house and set his car on fire.

4. You are preparing to give a speech on hate crimes in the United States and you want to make sure that you have your audience's attention before you begin. Therefore, you decide to present the details of a series of grisly murders committed in your town by a psychopath—even though these murders were not motivated by hate but by mental illness and so they aren't examples of hate crimes.

your fear of not being a true friend as well as to your fear of accidents involving drunk drivers. People have many fears—of failure, of death, of speechmaking, of inadequacy. Look at the ads: "Will we be able to give our kids what our parents gave us?" (Equitable Insurance), "Ring around the collar!" (Wisk detergent), "American Express: don't leave home without it." Fear can drive people to achievement and bravery or to hatred and butchery. Use fear appeals cautiously (see the "Speaking of . . . Ethics: Using Fear Appeals" box).

5. *Autonomy/independence.* "Free should the scholar be—free and brave. Free even to the definition of freedom, 'without any hindrance that does not arise out of his own

constitution.'"[10] When Ralph Waldo Emerson spoke these words a century and a half ago, he was working hard to convince American intellectuals to separate themselves from European thinkers. You also hear this appeal: "Be your own person; don't follow the crowd." Appeals to "follow your own heart" and "stand on your own two feet" draw their force from our struggles to stand apart from one another.

You may have noticed that some of the appeals we've just described seem to contradict each other. For example, fear seems to oppose adventure; sympathy and conformity seem to work against independence. Remember that human beings are changeable creatures, who at different times may pursue quite different goals and thus who can be reached in many different kinds of verbalizations of their wants and desires. The clusters we've described aren't all inclusive;[11] but, this discussion is enough to get you started into your work on persuasion.

Using Motivational Appeals

In practice, motivational appeals are seldom used alone; speakers usually combine them. Suppose you were selecting a new mountain bike. What factors would influence your decision? One would be price (*saving*); a second certainly would be performance (*adventure*); another might be comfort and appearance (*personal enjoyment*); a fourth probably would be European styling (*prestige*) or uniqueness (*independence*). These factors combined would add up to *pride* of ownership. Some of these influences, of course, would be stronger than others; some might conflict. But all of them probably would affect your choice. You would base your decision to buy the bike on the strongest of the appeals.

Because motivational appeals are interdependent, it's a good idea to coordinate them. You should select three or four appeals that are related and that target segments of your audience. When you work from cluster appeals, you tap multiple dimensions of your listeners' lives.

Review your appeals for their pertinence and consistency. After all, you don't want to describe the *adventure* of spelunking (cave exploration) so vividly that you create a sense of *fear*. Conflicting appeals are counterproductive. Examine the following series of main headings for a speech given by a tourist agency representative urging students to take a summer trip to Europe

1. The three-week tour is being offered for the low price of $2,500 (*acquisition and savings*).
2. There will be a minimum of supervision and regimentation (*independence*).
3. You'll be traveling with friends and fellow students (*companionship*).
4. We'll take you to places the adult-oriented tours never get (*curiosity*).

In the complete presentation, this representative also emphasized the educational value of the experience (*self-advancement*) and said that a special mountain-climbing expedition would be arranged (*adventure*). Notice how the speaker targeted student audiences.

One final piece of general advice: inconspicuous appeals work best. Avoid saying, "I want you to *imitate* Jones, the successful honors student" or "If you give to the Russian democracy fund, we'll print your name in the newspapers so that your *reputation* as a caring person will be known to everybody." People rarely admit, even to themselves, that they act on the basis of self-centered motivations—greed, imitation, personal pride, and fear. Be subtle when using these appeals. For example, you might encourage listeners to imitate the actions of well-known people by saying, "Habitat for Humanity counts among its volunteers the former president and First Lady, Jimmy and Rosalynn Carter."

Organizing Persuasive Speeches: The Motivated Sequence

Now it's time to think about organizing your appeals into a whole speech. As we've suggested, an important consideration in structuring appeals is your listeners' psychological tendencies—ways in which individuals' own motivations and circumstances favor certain ways of structuring ideas. You must learn to sequence supporting materials and motivational appeals to form a useful organizational pattern for speeches as a whole. Since 1935, the most popular such pattern has been called **Monroe's motivated sequence** (see Figure 14.1).[12] We will devote the rest of this chapter to it.

The motivated sequence ties problems and solutions to human motives. The motivated sequence for the presentation of verbal materials is composed of five basic steps:

1. *Attention.* Create interest and desire.

2. *Need.* Develop the problem by analyzing wrongs in the world and by relating them to the individual's interests, wants, or desires.

3. *Satisfaction.* Propose a plan of action that will alleviate the problem and satisfy the individual's interests, wants, or desires.

4. *Visualization.* Depict the world as it will look if the plan is put into action.

5. *Action.* Call for personal commitments and deeds.

Structuring Actuative Speeches

The motivated sequence provides an ideal blueprint for urging an audience to take action. That's what it was designed for—since it was used originally as the basis for sales presentations. Let's look first at some ways that you might use Monroe's sequence to structure actuative speeches.

Step 1: Getting Attention You must wake up and engage your listeners at the very beginning of your speech if you hope to get them to move. Remember that startling statements, illustrations, questions, and other factors can focus attention on your message. You can't persuade an audience unless you have its attention.

Step 2: Showing the Need: Describing the Problem Once you've captured the attention of your listeners, you're ready to explain why change is needed. To do this, you must show that a definite problem exists. You must point out, through facts and figures, just how bad the present situation is: "Last month our Littleton plant produced only 2000 carburetors rather than the 3000 scheduled. If we don't increase production, we'll have to shut down our main assembly line at Denver. That will cost the company over $1,000,000 and put 158 people out of work."

In its full form, a need or problem step has four parts:

FIGURE 14.1   The Motivated Sequence

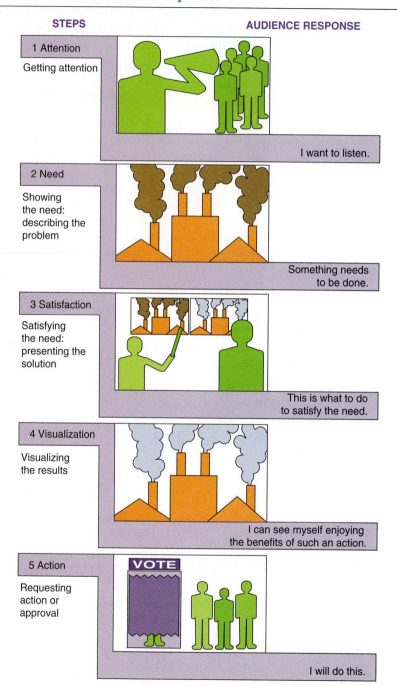

Notice how the audience should respond to each step of the motivated sequence.

1. *Statement.* Give a definite, concise statement of the problem.

2. *Illustration.* Give one or more examples explaining and clarifying the problem.

3. *Ramification.* Offer additional examples, statistical data, testimony, and other forms of support showing the extent and seriousness of the problem.

4. *Pointing.* Offer an explanation of how the problem directly affects the listener.

Statement and *pointing* should always be present, but the inclusion of *illustration* and *ramification* will depend on the amount of detail required to convince the audience. Whether you use the complete development or only part of it, the *need* step is critical in your speech. Here your subject is first tied to the needs and desires of your listeners.

Step 3: Satisfying the Need: Presenting the Solution   The solution or satisfaction step urges the adoption of a policy. Its goal is to get your listeners to agree that the program you propose is the correct one. Therefore, this step consists of presenting your proposed solution to the problem and proving that this solution is practical and desirable.

Five items are usually contained in a fully developed satisfaction step:

1. *Statement.* State the attitude, belief, or action you wish the audience to adopt. This is a statement of action: "We need to adopt an incentive system for our Littleton carburetor plant."

2. *Explanation.* Make sure that your proposal is understood. Visual aids such as charts and diagrams can be very useful here. In our example, you would define the incentive system: "By *incentive system,* I mean that workers at the Littleton plant should be paid by the actual number of carburetors completed rather than the hours worked."

3. *Theoretical demonstration.* Show how your proposed solution meets the need. For example, you could say, "Worker productivity will rise because workers are paid not just for putting in time but for completing carburetors."

4. *Reference to practical experience.* Supply examples to prove that the proposal has worked effectively where it has been tried. Facts, figures, and the testimony of experts support your contention: "Production at our New Albany plant increased by 42 percent after we instituted this compensation schedule."

5. *Meeting objections.* Forestall opposition by answering any objections that might be raised against the proposal. You might counter the objections of the labor union by arguing, "Increased plant productivity will allow us to expand the medical benefits for plant workers."

Just as certain phases can sometimes be omitted from the need step, one or more of these phases can be left out of the satisfaction step. Also, the foregoing order does not always have to be followed exactly. Occasionally, you can best meet objections by answering them as they arise. In other situations, the theoretical demonstration and reference to practical experience can be combined. If the satisfaction step is developed properly, at its conclusion the audience will say, "Yes, you're right; this is a practical and desirable solution to the problem you identified."

Step 4: Visualizing the Results The function of the visualization step is to intensify desire. It should picture for the audience future conditions if your proposal is or is not adopted. In the visualization step, you ask your listeners to project themselves into the future. This projection can be accomplished in one of three ways: by (1) the *positive method,* (2) the *negative method,* or (3) the *method of contrast.*

1. *The positive method.* Describe how conditions will improve under your proposal. Make such a description vivid and concrete. Select a situation that you are quite sure will arise. Then picture your listeners actually enjoying the conditions your proposal will produce. For example, if plant productivity allows better medical benefits, describe the advantages for everyone—lower deductibles, dental care, free eye examinations, and hospice services.

2. *The negative method.* Describe conditions as they will be in the future if your proposal is *not* carried out. Picture for your audience the evils that will arise from failure to follow your advice. Select the most undesirable conditions and show how they will be aggravated if your proposal is rejected. Describe plant employees being laid off, losing their pension plan, and experiencing the trauma of finding new jobs in a tight market.

3. *The method of contrast.* Combine the two preceding methods. Use the negative approach first and then use the positive approach. In this way, the benefits of the proposal are contrasted with the disadvantages of the present system. The following illustration shows how a speaker, urging you to carefully plan all four years of college before starting your freshman year, might develop a visualization step by the method of contrast.

Suppose that you enter the university, as nearly a third of our students do, with little sense of educational interests and goals. In your first two semesters, you simply take a few required courses and pass your writing and speaking skills tests. In your second year, you start experimenting with some electives on the basis of friends' recommendations: "Take Speech 101 because it's easy"; "Take Photography 102 because it's cool"; "Take Art 103 because it's pretty"; "Take History 104 because I'm taking it"; "Take Astronomy 105 because the professor is neat." Now comes your junior year— you're nowhere near a major, and you're getting close to the three-quarter mark in your education. Your adviser nags you, your parents nag you, your friends nag you— you even get down on yourself. In your senior year, you sample some social work courses, finally discovering something you really like. Only then do you realize it will take three or four more semesters—if you're lucky—to complete a B.S.W. degree.

In contrast, suppose you—like another quarter of our entering students—seek career and personal advising early. You enroll for the no-credit "Careers and Vocational Choices" seminar in your first semester. While meeting your liberal arts requirements, you take classes in as many different departments as possible so as to get a broad sampling. Near the end of your sophomore year, you talk with people in both career planning and personal counseling, all the while trying courses in areas of possible interest. By your junior year, you get departmental advisers in two majors, find out you don't really like one as much as you thought, and then go only to the second after midyear. You then complete that major, taking a correspondence class to catch

*up because you were a little behind; but still you graduate with others who entered
college the year you did.*

*Careful planning, reasoning through choices, and rigorously analyzing your own
interests and talents—these are the actions that separate the completers from the com-
plainers at the end of your years here. So. . . . [Move into the action step at this point.]*

Whichever method you use—positive, negative, or contrast—remember that the visualization step must stand the test of reality. The conditions you picture must be vivid and
reflective of the world as listeners know it. Let your listeners actually see themselves enjoying the advantages or suffering the evils you describe. The more realistically you depict the situation, the more strongly your listeners will react.

Step 5: Requesting Action The function of the action step is to call for explicit
action. You can do this by offering a challenge or appeal, a special inducement, or a statement of personal intention. For examples, review the conclusions discussed in Chapter 9.
Your request for action should be short and intense enough to set your listeners's resolve
to act. Finish your speech firmly and sit down.

The motivated sequence is flexible. You can adapt it to various situations once you are
familiar with its basic pattern. Like cooks who alter good recipes to their personal tastes,
you can adjust the formula for particular occasions—changing the number of main
points from section to section, sometimes omitting restatement from the attention step,
sometimes omitting the positive or negative projections from the visualization step. *Like
any recipe, the motivated sequence is designed to give you a formula that fits many different
situations.*[13] It gives you an excellent pattern but does not remove the human element;
you still must think about your choices. Consider the choices made in the following outline of an actuative speech using the motivated sequence.

Sample Outline for an Actuative Speech

Numbers That Can Save Your Life[14]

Specific Purpose: To urge students to begin checking their blood pressure even while in school.

  I. Americans live in a maze of numbers:
      A. Your student ID number identifies you on the campus.
      B. Your telephone number lets others reach you.
      C. Your social security number follows you from near birth to death
         and after.
  II. A number most of you ignore, however, could kill you—your blood
      pressure.

Attention step: *The
speaker opens with
common, everyday
numbers to ease the
audience into the speech.*

Need step: *The speaker decides to attack the problem of hypertension by using multiple devices; statistics to quantify the enormity of the problem, expert testimony to add some emotional power to the numbers, and a good explanation of what happens to people with high blood pressure to make the problem seem real. A final piece of testimony is added to stir in a little more fear.*

A. According to the Department of Health and Human Services, this year 310,000 Americans will die from illnesses in which the major factor is hypertension.

B. Two million will suffer strokes, heart attacks, and kidney failure as a direct result of hypertension.

C. According to Dr. Theodore Cooper, Director of the Heart and Lung Institute, "Hypertension can be brought under control through proven treatment which is neither unduly hazardous, complicated or expensive."

D. Before this will sink in, you must understand what high blood pressure does to your body.

   1. When your blood pressure becomes too great for the arterial walls, it can tear a muscle; and if the artery breaks, you can die.

   2. High blood pressure can also result from fatty tissues, salts, and fluid build-ups that cause the arteries to narrow and the heart to work harder, until it stops.

E. Even worse, according to the National High Blood Pressure Council, "Half of those who have high blood pressure don't even know that they do. Of those who do, only half are being treated; only half again of those have their blood pressure under control. Patients and physicians alike just don't seem to take this condition seriously."

III. Thus, the public needs to be aware of these problems, health care must be improved, and hypertensives must learn that self-control is life.

A. Public service ads can keep the issue before the public.

B. Community- and business-supported hypertension clinics must be established at little or no cost to clients.

C. Individuals simply must monitor their own blood pressure regularly.

IV. The future of a significant proportion of our population depends on these programs.

A. Given the American diet, general lack of exercise, and tense lifestyles, heart attacks will claim more and more victims annually without these programs.

B. With such programs, our collective health will improve measurably.

   1. Drs. Andrea Foote and John Erfurt have established a Worker Health Program, which was tested at four different sites and which allowed 92 percent of the hypertensives at those job sites to control their blood pressure.

   2. The Hypertensive Education Program in Michigan and Connecticut is cutting the insurance rates in those states.

   3. In 1970, Savannah, Georgia, had the infamous title, "Stroke Capital of the World"; but today, with 14 permanent blood pressure reading stations and special clinics, the stroke rate has been cut in half.

Satisfaction step: *The speaker puts forward a three-layered solution: a national mass-media assault, a community-based solution, and steps listeners can take.*

Visualization step: *The speaker goes with both negative and positive visualization. The negative visualization of more heart attacks is fueled by fear and is complemented nicely by a positive visualization arising from specific instances of successful programs.*

V. Even now, in your prime, it's time for you to develop good health maintenance habits.

 A. You could be one of America's 11 million people with high blood pressure and not even know it.

 B. Even if you're not, you should monitor yourself to remain safe in the knowledge that your pressure is in the normal—90/70 to 140/90—range.

 C. Get your blood pressure checked today, free of charge, at the Student Health Center and save a life—your own.

Action step: Listeners in a speech class can't do much to affect the national and community programs, but they certainly can implement the personal aspects of the solution. That's what the speaker stresses, telling what range to look for and where to get a blood pressure check free of charge.

Structuring Persuasive Speeches

Persuasive speeches stop short of a call for direct action, but nonetheless they're still easily structured with the motivated sequence. The primary difference is in the action step. Sometimes, no action is called for because there are no acceptable action plans formulated; so, everyone wants to reform the medical system of this country, but agreement on actions can't be reached. At other times, you simply want people to change how they think, not how they act. Asking parents to think about high school education as a primary method for gaining discipline in their children's lives won't change how schools operate, but it might get them to reconceive of their relationship to schools. Sure, in the long run you might want them to support tax increases for schools, but, at this point, those parents probably are not ready for such a request. Seek to change their attitudes and then later, perhaps, you can take them farther down to road to educational reform.

Notice how the action step in the outline that follows differs from the one built for an actuative speech.

Sample Outline for a Persuasive Speech

The Positive Negative Political Ad[15]

 Specific purpose: to persuade listeners to differentiate between destructive and constructive negative political ads.

INTRODUCTION

 I. Last summer, the editor of the *Des Moines Register,* Dennis Ryerson, asked readers to comment on the negative political advertising that was flowing through the state. Here's a sample of the comments he published in September 1996:

 A. Eugene and Norma Lister said that "Dirty campaigning is practiced because it is profitable."

 B. Stephen Litts said "I dislike political advertising that uses innuendo to smear an opponent."

Attention Step: *Cite recent citizen testimony to introduce the problem in a commonsensical way.*

C. Kay Luckett thought that negative advertising "demeans the other candidates, their ideas and their personal lives and make the voting public stay away from the polls on Election Day."

D. Jeff Mitchell was firm: "Iowans simply have to be aware of it and punish candidates who engage in it."

II. Editor Ryerson finished the article by saying that the *Register* would do more to report on campaign activities and urged readers to report negative advertising.

Use of an authority figure to specify the problem: "fair comment."

A. He said "Let me know when you see a campaign ad or other activity that reaches beyond fair comment."

B. That statement captures the problem I want to talk about today: what *is* "fair comment" during a campaign?

1. Are all attacks on your opponent destructive and unfair?

2. Can we distinguish between positive and negative attack ads?

III. Today I want to talk about the question of negative political advertisements and convince you if I can that some negative ads are very useful to voters—some negative ads are positive.

Forecast

A. First I'll describe and illustrate different sorts of negative ads.

B. Then I'll talk about criteria you should use in assessing attack ads.

C. Finally, I'll ask you to compare a world where all advertising is regulated with one where we use market forces to stop unfair ads.

BODY

Need Step: Begin by exploring definitions with the help of experts, finishing with one that will help to frame the need in a way you want to.

I. Before we can evaluate negative advertising, we first have to be clear what it is.

A. Too often, we think of all negative ads as dirty.

1. So, Professor Charles Stewart of Purdue University studies "mudslinging," and talks about political attackers as "untrustworthy, dishonest, incompetent, unqualified, unlikable, not self-confident, and immature."

2. Political commentator Edwin Diamond writes about "attack ads" as "[n]amecalling, direct personal attacks, man-on-the-street, and symbolic attacks" used to "discredit the opponent."

3. Of course these commentators think negative ads are political manure because that's how they define them.

B. But, I think we need to work with a broader definition.

1. I suggest we define "negative political ad" as any attempt to create an undesirable or unattractive image of one's opponent.

2. Such a definition is in tune with V. L. Tarrance's views that political voting always has been a matter of both voting *for* someone or something and voting *against* someone or something as well.

a. That is, citizens are always affirming one set of ideas and denying another set in their votes.

      b. Especially in a complex world, where few of us can under-
        stand most of the issues clearly, voting against ideas is at
        least as important as voting for others.

II. If you'll accept such a definition of negative political advertising, then
we can examine some of the different types. Let me work with a
simple classification system—three.

  A. The image definition ad is the kind you'll often see early in a campaign.

    1. In an image definition ad, candidates define themselves and
      their political agenda, often by contrasting themselves with
      their opponent.

    2. Here are some examples of image definition ads. (SHOW THEM)

  B. A second type of negative ad is the comparison ad.

    1. You see many of these, where candidates compare their stands
      on issues or their voting records with those of their opponents.

    2. Here are some comparative ads you saw last fall. (SHOW THEM)

  C. The third type is the direct attack ad.

    1. You can attack your opponent's character, actions, motives,
      and associates.

    2. Here are some examples of each kind of attack. (SHOW THEM)

III. Now, as you think about these three types of negative political
statements, I hope you can better understand the problem I'm trying to address:

  A. Image definition ads focus primarily on the candidate, and they gen-
    erally are quite useful to voters, who need to get to know some-
    thing about a candidate before being able to judge the person.

  B. Likewise, comparison ads help voters to see differences between
    candidates, to better understand their choices.

    1. Granted, the comparison ads aren't always perfectly fair.

    2. But, at the least, they're urging voters to make comparisons
      seriously before voting.

  C. Among all of the types of negative ads, it's the attack ad that
    should most concern us.

    1. It's in these ads that words like "ultra-liberal" and "reac-
      tionary," "personally profited," "the worst voting record,"
      "godless communism," and "immoral" get thrown around.

    2. Some (but not all) attack ads aimed at the candidate him- or
      herself make the electorate sick at heart, and in fact may con-
      tribute to people not voting at all.

IV. If the problem we face in thinking about negative political advertising
is that it's as often useful to voters as it is harmful to them, then
what kind of solutions to the tone of negativity that runs through
too many campaigns should we think about?

Construct a classification system that will permit you to argue that some negative ads are good. Show examples to involve the audience in the classification of appeals.

Appeal to the listeners' sense of need for good political information and to their sense of fairness.

Use a gentle fear appeal with references to the destructive vocabulary of some attack ads.

Satisfaction Step: *Start off by suggesting that listeners have the power to seize control of the system.*

A. The first thing we have to do is convince voters that they can make a difference in how campaigns are run.

1. If voters complain loudly, campaign managers get jumpy and adjust.
2. Citizens controlling electoral processes is an ideal.

B. Second, the press has got to remember that it often brags about being the citizens' voices and should start to act that way, which it has in some instances.

Use their sense of deference to the power of the press to create an ally for them.

1. Newspapers started running "truth boxes" examining campaign claims after the ugly presidential election of 1988.
2. NPR in 1990 had a program on every Thursday examining ads' claims.
3. C-Span call-in programs sometimes focus on ads.
4. Television networks and local stations periodically show opposing ads.
5. More examples of the press fulfilling its "watch-dog" function would help.

C. We've got to give the voters the tools to evaluate ads:

Appeal pridefully to the power of citizen education by showing how easy it is to ask good questions of candidates.

1. We must teach them to sort out the negative ads that give them important information and those that mislead them.
   a. We live in an era when, according to Montague Kern of Rutgers University, voters get over half of their political information from the candidates, not the press.
   b. In such a situation, voters must be educated to sort through the claims in ads with good questions:
      (1) Are claims backed up with factual evidence?
      (2) Are the claims focused on public, not private, matters?
      (3) Can and do others corroborate charges?
      (4) Is the charge actually relevant to political decision making?

Visualization Step:
Use a contrastive method, telling a "bad" story about overt attempts to regulate advertising and contrasting it to a system of voluntary constraint. Use authorities out of the media consulting business as experts.

V. If citizens and their press representatives focus on the job of sorting through positive and negative claims to find information relevant to voting, even the negative ads can contribute in positive ways to the political process.

A. If we try to legislate away negative political advertising, we'll be in a mess.

1. Setting up citizen boards, as some local groups have tried to do when confronting political claims, only confuses people more than it helps them.
2. All of the election time is taken up commenting on political process, not examining issues. (TELL THE STORY OF NASSAU COUNTY, NEW YORK)
3. We end up trampling on rights to free speech, trying to muzzle the very people we're asking to guard those rights.

B. But, if we end up using the voters' great strength—their active voting—together with a press focused on testing claims publicly, we'll end up with a system of voluntary control that runs on the philosophy for attack ads articulated by David Doak, a Washington, D.C., media consultant:

1. The statement of fact about your opponent must be accurate.
2. The allegation must be a fair representation of the factual occurences.
3. The allegation must be about the public record of your opponent.
4. "If you are thinking about deviating from these general principles," Doak says, "you should think long and hard. The more you deviate, the more you expose yourself and your client to counter attacks."

C. Doak's vision of political attack works, he says, thanks to the press.

1. "Negative campaigning is now cleaner and fairer because of the actions of journalists in reviewing ads."
2. In the best of all democracies, the people and the press cooperate to force the dirty campaigners off of the political stage.

VI. No one likes to see politics depend upon ads like this. (SHOW LYNDON JOHNSON'S "DAISY GIRL" AD FROM 1964).

A. Some might appreciate the artistry of Tony Schartz, the man who made that ad.
B. Yet, we don't want our politics to depend on such character assassination.

CONCLUSION

I. Yet, I hope you understand that we make our political decisions on the bases of both likes and dislikes, on positive judgments of people and their ideas as well as negative judgments.

A. In the words of media consultant Adam Goodman: "[Negative ads work] because they open up the process; they draw contrasts between competing candidates—or dueling interest on ballot issues; and they provide voters with the mother's milk of political decision making: information."
B. They worked with voters in California when Governor Pete Wilson attacked his opponent's stands on crime, taxes, and welfare reform before putting forward his own plans.
C. They worked in Washington when Senator Slade Gorton contrasted his work style with his opponent's lack of constructive voting record.
D. So long as negative political ads are the source of good information, they belong on the air and in the newspapers.

II. As a voter, use every piece of positive and negative data you can to make informed voting decisions—because if candidates know that you do, they'll wage positive campaigns even with their negative attacks. That's all you can ask for and all you should want.

Action Step: Because you're calling for a change of mind rather than a change of action, use the conclusion to bolster your position with another example, more testimony, and specific instances.

Issue a challenge to complete the speech.

Sample Speech

The following speech, delivered to a joint session of Congress on December 8, 1941, by President Franklin Delano Roosevelt, requested a declaration of war against Japan. Round-the-clock negotiations with Japan suddenly had been disrupted when, on Sunday morning, December 7, the Japanese launched a massive surprise attack on Pearl Harbor, Hawaii, sinking eight American battleships and other smaller craft and leveling planes and airfields.

The nation was numbed, Congress was indignant, and the president moved quickly. The joint session was held in the House chamber. The galleries were overflowing, and the speech was broadcast worldwide. Notice that this message contains only a short attention step because the surprise attack created all of the necessary attention, a longer need step (paragraphs 2 through 10) that details the situation in the Pacific, and a short satisfaction step (paragraph 11) that only hints at American military strategy. The visualization step (paragraphs 12 through 16) attempts to steel the nation for war, and it is followed by a concise, sharply drawn action step. The president's strategies seem clear. The fact that the need and visualization steps receive detailed development shows his concern for (a) providing an informational base for the action and (b) offering a psychological orientation to wartime thinking.

Attention step:
Attention is focused on the Pearl Harbor incident.

Need step: *National and international audiences are still shocked and confused. Therefore, President Roosevelt offers background information in paragraphs 2 and 3 as well as descriptions of the attacks in paragraphs 4 through 9, summarizing the need for American action in paragraph 10.*

For a Declaration of War Against Japan[16] Franklin Delano Roosevelt

TO THE CONGRESS OF THE UNITED STATES: Yesterday, December 7, 1941—a date which will live in infamy—the United States of America was suddenly and deliberately attacked by naval and air forces of the Empire of Japan./1

The United States was at peace with that nation and, at the solicitation of Japan, was still in conversation with its government and its Emperor, looking toward the maintenance of peace in the Pacific. Indeed, one hour after Japanese air squadrons had commenced bombing in Oahu, the Japanese Ambassador to the United States and his colleague delivered to the Secretary of State a formal reply to a recent American message. While this reply stated that it seemed useless to continue the existing diplomatic negotiations, it contained no threat or hint of war or armed attack./2

It will be recorded that the distance of Hawaii from Japan makes it obvious that the attack was deliberately planned many days or even weeks ago. During the intervening time the Japanese government had deliberately sought to deceive the United States by false statements and expressions of hope for continued peace./3

The attack yesterday on the Hawaiian Islands has caused severe damage to American naval and military forces. Very many American lives have been lost. In addition, American ships have been reported torpedoed on the high seas between San Francisco and Honolulu./4

Last night Japanese forces attacked Hong Kong./5

Last night Japanese forces attacked Guam./6

Last night Japanese forces attacked the Philippine Islands./7

Last night the Japanese attacked Wake Island./8

Japan has, therefore, undertaken a surprise offensive extending throughout the Pacific area. The facts of yesterday speak for themselves. The people of the United States have already formed their opinions and well understand the implications to the very life and safety of our nation./10

As Commander-in-Chief of the Army and Navy I have directed that all measures be taken for our defense./11

Always will we remember the character of the onslaught against us./12

No matter how long it may take us to overcome this premeditated invasion, the American people in their righteous might will win through to absolute victory./13

I believe I interpret the will of the Congress and of the people when I assert that we will not only defend ourselves to the uttermost but will make very certain that this form of treachery shall never endanger us again./14

Hostilities exist. There is no blinking at the fact that our people, our territory, and our interests are in grave danger./15

With confidence in our armed forces—with the unbounded determination of our people—we will gain the inevitable triumph—so help us God./16

I ask that the Congress declare that since the unprovoked and dastardly attack by Japan on Sunday, December 7, a state of war has existed between the United States and the Japanese Empire./17

Satisfaction step: The United States now is preparing for war and the secrecy that surrounds it; hence the president does not detail the actions taken. *Visualization step:* The president must gather in the American people and get them behind his war effort. Visualization is important for him to accomplish those goals, so he invokes history or memory (paragraph 12), the righteousness of the cause (paragraph 13), the treachery of the opponents (paragraph 14), the reality of warfare (paragraph 15), and optimism for a successful completion of hostile actions (paragraph 16). *Action step:* The action needed is obvious: President Roosevelt calls directly on Congress to pass the resolution declaring war.

Assessing Your Progress

Chapter Summary

1. Speeches to persuade and actuate have psychological or behavioral change as their primary goal.

2. Because need satisfaction is important to all human beings, the concept of motive need is central to an understanding of persuasion and actuation.

3. Keys to the achievement of persuasion are motivational appeals, which are verbally created visualizations that link an idea, entity, or course of action to a motive.

4. Occasionally motivational appeals are attached directly to other concepts in a verbal process known as attribution.

5. Commonly used motivational appeals can be grouped into three clusters: affiliation, achievement, and power.

6. Monroe's motivated sequence is an organizational pattern for actuative and persuasive speeches based on people's natural psychological tendencies.

7. The five steps in the motivated sequence are attention, need, satisfaction, visualization, and action. Each step can be developed by using appropriate rhetorical devices.

Key Terms

achievement motives (p. 236)

actuative speech (p. 233)

affiliation motives (p. 236)

attribution (p. 235)

desires (p. 234)

Monroe's motivated sequence (p. 243)

motivational appeal (p. 235)

motive cluster (p. 235)

motive need (p. 235)

needs (p. 234)

power motives (p. 236)

persuasive speech (p. 233)

Assessment Activities

1. Present a five- to eight-minute actuative speech in which your primary goal is to get class members to actually *do* something: sign a petition, write a letter to an official, attend a meeting, give blood, or take some other personal action. Use the motivated sequence to create attention, lay out needs, propose a solution, visualize the results, and call for action. On a future "Actuative Speech Check-up Day," find out how many took the actions you suggested. How successful were you? Why?

2. In a brief persuasive speech, attempt to alter your classmates' impression or understanding of a particular concept. Analyze their current attitudes toward it and then prepare a speech reversing those attitudes. Sample topics might include: pesticides, recycling, United Nations peacekeeping operations, in vitro fertilization, animal rights, or genetic counseling for prospective parents.

3. What relevant motivational appeals might you use in addressing each of the following audiences? Be ready to discuss your choices in class.

   a. A group of farmers protesting federal agricultural policy.

   b. A meeting of pre-business majors concerned about jobs.

   c. Women at a seminar on nontraditional employment opportunities.

   d. A meeting of local elementary and secondary classroom teachers seeking smaller classes.

   e. A group gathered for an old-fashioned Fourth of July picnic.

References

1.   For a fuller discussion of attribution, see Philip G. Zimbaro, *Psychology and Life,* 13th ed. (New York: Longman, 1994).

2.   For a fuller discussion of motivational appeals, see Bruce E. Gronbeck, Raymie E. McKerrow, Douglas Ehninger, and Alan H. Monroe, *Principles and Types of Speech Communication,* 13th ed. (New York: Longman, 1997), chap. 6.

3. The clusters we are using develop out of the work of David McClelland. See Katharine Blick Hoyenga and Hermit T. Hoyenga, *Motivational Explanations of Behavior: Physiological and Cognitive Ideas* (Monterey, Calif.: Brooks/Cole Publishing, 1984), chap. 1; Joseph Veroff, "Contextualism and Human Motives," in *Frontiers of Motivational Psychology: Essays in Honor of John W. Atkinson,* edited by Donald R. Brown and Joseph Veroff (New York: Springer-Verlag, 1986), 132–145; Abigail J. Stewart, ed., *Motivation and Society: A Volume in Honor of David C. McClelland* (San Francisco: Jossey-Bass, 1982); and Janet T. Spence, ed., *Achievement and Achievement Motives* (San Francisco: W. H. Freeman, 1983).

4. From an interview with Ron Mitscher, Vietnam veteran, for *Parallels: The Soldiers' Knowledge and the Oral History of Contemporary Warfare,* edited by J. T. Hansen, A. Susan Owen, and Michael Patrick Madden (New York: Aldine de Gruyter, 1992), 137.

5. From Douglas MacArthur, "Duty, Honor, and Country," in *The Dolphin Book of Speeches,* edited by George W. Hibbitt (New York: Doubleday, 1965).

6. Abraham Lincoln, "Gettysburg Address," speech delivered in 1863, reprinted in *Lincoln at Gettysburg: The Words That Remade America,* edited by Garry Wills (New York: Simon & Schuster, 1992), 261.

7. John Dickinson, "The Declaration on Taking Up Arms," speech delivered 6 July 1775, reprinted in *The World's Greatest Orations,* edited by David J. Brewer (St. Louis: Ferd. P. Kaiser, 1899), 5:1855.

8. Samantha L. Hubbard, "Irradiation of Food," speech reprinted in Bruce E. Gronbeck et al., *Principles of Speech Communication,* 11th brief ed. (New York: HarperCollins, 1992), 354.

9. William Pitt, Lord Chatham, "The Attempt to Subjugate America," speech delivered in 1777, reprinted in Brewer, 3:1070.

10. Ralph Waldo Emerson, "The American Scholar," speech delivered in 1837, reprinted in Brewer, 20:2005.

11. For more on the clusters and alternative treatment of appeals, see David C. McClelland, *Power: The Inner Experience* (New York: Irvington, 1975); and David C. McClelland, *Human Motivation* (Glenview, Ill.: Scott, Foresman and Co., 1985).

12. To see how Monroe originally conceived of the motivated sequence, see especially the Foreword to Alan H. Monroe, *Principles and Types of Speech* (Chicago: Scott, Foresman, 1935), vii–x.

13. We're not suggesting here that the other organizational patterns discussed in Chapter 8 be discarded; they're useful in particular situations. Here, we're noting that the motivated sequence is especially potent when offering motivationally oriented persuasive, especially actuative, speeches.

14. This outline is based on Todd Ambs, "The Silent Killer," *Winning Orations;* his materials were formed into an outline by special arrangement with Larry Schnoor, Director, Interstate Oratorical Association, Mankato State University, Mankato, MN.

15. Information for this outline is taken from Arhur H. Miller and Bruce E. Gronbeck, eds., *Presidential Campaigns and American Self Images* (Boulder, Colo.: Westview Press, 1994); Dennis Ryerson, "Readers' Advice to Candidates," *Des Moines Sunday Register,* 8 September 1996, C1; and three articles in *Campaigns & Elections,* July 1995: David Doak, "Attack Ads: Rethinking the Rules" (pp. 20–21); Adam Goodman, "Producing

TV: A Survival Guide" (pp. 22–24); and Richard Schlackman and Jamie "Buster" Douglas, "Attack Mail: The Silent Killer" (pp. 25–26, 62, 67). Fuller background on the issues can be found in essays in Frank Biocca, ed., *Television and Political Advertising*, 2 vols. (Hillsdale, N.J.: Lawrence Erlbaum Associates, 1991), and in Karen S. Johnson-Cartee and Gary A. Copeland, eds., *Negative Political Advertising* (Hillsdale, N.J.: Lawrence Erlbaum Associates, 1991).

16. Originally published in the *Congressional Record*, 77th Congress, 1st Sess., vol. 87, pt. 9 (8 Dec. 1941), 9504–9505.

15 Argumentation and Critical Thinking

The ability to think critically is central to your survival in the social world. You're constantly bombarded with requests, appeals, and pleas to change your beliefs or adopt new ways of doing things of the kind we discussed in the previous chapter. Sorting through all those appeals to determine which are justified and whether you should alter your thoughts or actions requires analysis and evaluation skills—and a cool head, not emotional responses. Before committing yourself, you've got to be able to analyze appeals, to determine if the reasons fit the claim being made. Skilled speakers, too, must be able not only to construct motivational appeals but also to work from data-based evidence to seemingly logical conclusions. You've got to use your head in reasonable ways, as Mario found out:

> *"Boy," said Mario, "I'm really bummed out. My girlfriend Ingrid and I had a big fight last night. She screamed at me for not taking politics seriously. I told her she was crazy for believing anything good could come out of politicians. She got so angry that she cried, and then I got scared and told her I'd take politics seriously if it would make her feel better, and then she got even more mad. It was a bad argument." "No it wasn't," his friend Romano replied. "You had a fight, not an argument." "So what's the difference?" queried Mario. "A lot," said Romano. "Arguments depend on your head. Fights depend on your volume."*

Mario needs to develop what's called a *critical spirit*—the ability to analyze others' ideas and requests.[1] Criticism is a process of careful assessment, evaluation, and judgment of ideas and motives. It's also a matter of supporting your assessment, evaluation, and judgment with reasons. As you engage in evaluation—assessing reasons or offering counter-reasons—you become a critical thinker. You also develop critical skills when you advance a claim and then offer reasons why others ought to accept it. And finally, a critical spirit requires fair-mindedness, an important dimension of a person's credibility.[2] Critical thinkers inspire confidence in others, thus, by demonstrating both reasonableness and ethical commitments. The critical spirit should be cultivated by both speakers and listeners.

Argumentation is a process of advancing claims supported by good reasons and allowing others to test those claims and reasons or to offer counterarguments. Through argumentation, people hope to come to reasonable conclusions about factual, valuative, and policy matters. The act of arguing does not consist merely of offering an opinion or stating information, and certainly not of screaming. An act of arguing is an act one step beyond the act of persuading by appealing to motives. It commits you to communicating by using good reasons.

You probably engage in argument in many ways. In public forums such as city council meetings, you might provide reasons your community should preserve a marshland rather than erect a dam or you might advocate better community regulation of local day-care facilities. You might write a letter to the editor of a newspaper proposing a pedestrian mall downtown. In conversations with friends, you probably argue over sports teams and players. In each of these cases, you'll be more effective if your arguments are sound, with clearly identifiable reasons given for each claim you make. In this chapter, we'll examine the structure of arguments, then offer ways for you to critically evaluate the arguments of others, and we'll finish with some tips to help you argue effectively.

Rational Thinking and Talking: Argumentation

To turn rational thought into powerful talk, you've got to learn how to construct an argument. An **argument** is built out of three essential elements that must work together to compel belief in another person: (a) the claim or proposition you are defending, (b) the

Different sorts of arguments appeal to different segments of your audience. Vegetarians argue that meat harms your body ("heart") for some people and that it is a sin against nature ("soul") for others.

FIGURE 15.1 The Elements of Argument

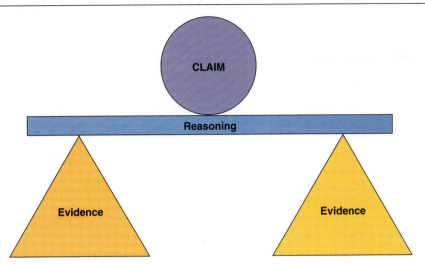

Why are all three elements necessary for an argument?

relevant evidence that you provide in support of that claim, and (c) the reasoning pattern that you use to connect the evidence with the claim. (See Figure 15.1.)

Types of Claims

Most argumentative speeches assert that: (a) something is or is not the case; (b) something is desirable or undesirable; or (c) something should or should not be done. Such judgments or assessments are the speaker's **claims** or propositions. Your first task as an arguer or listener is to determine the type of claim being argued.

Claims of Fact   A claim of fact asserts that something is or is not the case. If you're trying to convince listeners that "Using compact fluorescent lightbulbs will reduce your utilities cost significantly," you're presenting a factual claim—asserting that a given state of affairs exists. When confronted with this sort of claim, two questions can occur to the critically aware listener:

1. *By what criteria, or standards of judgment, should the truth or accuracy of the claim be measured?* If you're asked to determine someone's height, you immediately look for a yardstick or other measuring tool. Similarly, listeners look for a standard by which to measure the accuracy of a factual claim. Before agreeing with your claim, the critical thinker asks what you mean by "reduce your utilities costs significantly." What percentage reduction in your electrical bill is being considered significant? Against what standard, precisely, is the accuracy of the claim to be judged? As a speaker, you need to build those judgments into your speeches.

2. *Do the facts of the situation fit the criteria?* Now then, to the replacement of bulbs: how many have to be replaced to achieve the reduction you're after? First, get listeners to agree to certain standards of judgment, and then present evidence that a

given state of affairs meets those standards. In these ways, you work to gain the assent of listeners to your factual claims.

Claims of Value   When your claim asserts that something is good or bad, desirable or undesirable, justified or unjustified, you're advancing a **claim of value**—a claim about the intrinsic worth of the belief or action in question. Here, too, it is always appropriate to ask: (a) by what standards is something to be judged? and (b) how well does the item in question measure up to the standards specified?

For example, you can measure the quality of a college by the distinction of its faculty (intellectual value), the excellence of its building program (material value), the success of its graduates (practical value), the size of its endowment (monetary value), or the reputation that it enjoys according to surveys of educational excellence (educational value). You then can assess the worth of a particular college by each of these criteria to come up with the sorts of scores you find in books that rate colleges. In other words, value judgments are not mere assertions of personal preference—"I like Grand Valley State or Michigan State." Rather, they must be argued for, as if someone else is going to examine or challenge them.

Claims of Policy   A **claim of policy** recommends a course of action that you want the audience to approve. Typical examples are: "State standards for welfare eligibility *should be* tightened, "A test for English competency *should be* instituted as a graduation requirement." In both instances, you're asking your audience to endorse a proposed policy or course of action. When analyzing a policy claim, four questions are relevant to the judgments being made:

1. *Is there a need for such a policy or course of action?* If your listeners don't believe that a change is called for, they're not likely to approve your proposal.

2. *Is the proposal practical?* Can we afford the expense it would entail? Would it really solve the problem or remove the evil it is designed to correct? Does such a policy stand a reasonable chance of being adopted? If you can't show that your proposal meets these and similar tests, you can hardly expect it to be endorsed.

3. *Are the benefits your proposal will bring greater than its disadvantages?* People are reluctant to approve a proposal that promises to create conditions worse than the ones it is designed to correct. Burning a barn to the ground may be an effective way to get rid of rats, but it's hardly a desirable one. The benefits and disadvantages that will result from a plan of action must always be carefully weighed along with considerations of its basic workability. Would an English proficiency test, for example, be fair for international students?

4. *Is the proposal superior to any other plan or policy?* Listeners are hesitant to approve a policy if they have reason to believe that an alternative course of action is more practical or more beneficial. A program of job training may be a better way to remove people from the welfare rolls than new qualifications tests.

As you've seen, then, different types of claims make varying demands on you as an arguer. (See Table 15.1.) And, too, arguers must tell audiences how to assess their claims. Articulating criteria or standards for judgment is essential for the person who tries to win an argument. If you think tuition increases should be tied to the Consumer Price Index while your opponent believes tuition should be tied to rises and falls in state tax revenue,

TABLE 15.1 Types of Claims

Notice how each type of claim can be analyzed.

Claim	Description	Analysis
Claim of fact	Assertion of truth or that something exists	1. By what criteria is the truth or accuracy of the claim measured? 2. Do the facts of the situation fit the criteria?
Claim of value	Assertion that something is good or bad; desirable or undesirable; justified or unjustified	1. By what standards is something to be judged? 2. How well does the thing measure up?
Claim of policy	Recommendation of a course of action	1. Is there a need for this policy or course of action? 2. Is the proposal practicable? 3. Are the benefits of the proposal greater than its disadvantages? 4. Is the proposal better than other courses of action?

you have a serious disagreement over what standards to apply. Rather than haggling about increases and decreases in tuition, you and your opponent have to stop and see whose standard for judgment will be accepted by your listeners. When you agree on the criteria, you can conduct a meaningful debate.

Unless there are sound reasons for delay, you should announce your claim early in your speech. If listeners don't see where you're going in your argument, your strongest arguments may be lost on them. Take time to say something such as, "Today, I want to convince you that increases and decreases in student tuition should be coupled with the Consumer Price Index. If the Board of Regents takes this action, the cost of education will be more fairly distributed between the state and the students."[3]

Types of Evidence

As you discovered in Chapter 6, supporting materials clarify, amplify, and strengthen the ideas in your speech. They provide evidence for the acceptance of your central idea and its supporting points. Evidence is the base from which an argument builds. It can be presented in any of the forms of supporting materials with which you are already familiar: explanations, comparisons and contrasts, illustrations, specific instances, statistics, and testimony.

There's no single or easy rule for selecting relevant evidence. Supporting material that's relevant to one claim may be irrelevant to another, or it may provide logical proof but not compelling reasons for action. You should consider both the rational and the motivational characteristics of evidence as you select it: What does it prove? Whom does it affect?

Rationally Relevant Evidence The type of evidence you choose should reflect your claim. For example, if you're defending the claim that controls on the content of Internet chat rooms violate the First Amendment guarantee of freedom of speech, you'll

Both constructive and refutational arguments are usually necessary for argumentative victory, as we saw in the O. J. Simpson trial.

probably choose testimony by noted authorities or definitions of terms to advance your claim. On the other hand, examples, illustrations, and statistics work better for showing that a problem exists or a change is needed. For example, if you argue that the speed limit in your state should be raised by ten miles per hour on interstate highways and have surveys indicating that nine out of ten drivers in your state agree, you'll be showing that there is popular support for a change. The claim you present requires rationally relevant type of evidence. As you plan your arguments, you should ask yourself, "What type of evidence is logically relevant in support of my claim?"

Motivationally Relevant Evidence   If you hope to convince listeners to adopt your attitudes or actions, your claim must be supported by more than logically relevant evidence. You must get your listeners emotionally involved, as we saw in Chapter 14. That is, your evidence must be motivationally relevant to them. So, you should ask two questions:

What type of evidence will this audience demand? If you want to argue that your city needs to build a new sewage plant, many, many people will demand that you demonstrate the problems with the present system, a financial plan that won't bankrupt the city, incentives that the new plant will provide for new businesses, and even a plan for laying the lines that won't paralyze neighborhoods. On the other hand, if you're reviewing a

Speaking of . . . *apprehension*

The Personal Risk of Argumentation

As we've noted, debating someone face to face can be scary. You probably have some fears or at least anxieties when you argue because an opponent can force you into a contradiction, dispute your evidence, offer better evidence, talk faster than you do. There is a risk in argumentation that you'll be proved wrong in front of others. And that is humiliating, or so you think.

Much of this is true. A good opponent, better informed than you are, can take apart your claims, evidence, and sometimes even reasoning. But, so what? Yes, so what? You must remember that argumentation is an idea-testing process, an exercise in critical thinking. You must find ways to convince yourself that if you're proved wrong by someone, so much the better! If someone has found a flaw in your thinking, then they have improved your ability to work in the world. Be ready to say "I hadn't thought of that. Tell me more." "You're right: there is a problem in those data. I will go back and look again." "Well, then, maybe I can't prove definitively that that's the case, but . . . ."

The fear of being wrong should be greater than the fear of being proved wrong.

new video release for friends, an example from the plot, an analogy to other videos like this one, or an illustration of dialogue would be more forceful as proof than statistical word counts, box office receipts, or testimony from published movie critics. Careful audience analysis, as we suggested earlier, will help you determine what type of evidence is needed to move your particular group of listeners psychologically.

What specific evidence will generate the best response? You should pose this question once you've determined the type of evidence required by your argument. For example, if you've decided to use expert testimony to support your argument, whom should you quote? Or if you're using an illustration, should you use a factual example or develop one of your own? Will listeners be more moved by a personalized story or a general illustration?

To answer these and similar questions about your listeners, you need to analyze them. A homogeneous audience of townspeople may be suspicious of outsiders. They might react best to local experts or illustrations from the local community or common range of experience: the mayor, a reference to a particular neighborhood, or the town's experience in the flood of 1993. A heterogeneous audience of college students, on the other hand, will not know those local experts and probably will prefer geographically varied examples because it does not share experience and background. It will probably respond better to a nationally known expert and references to well-known communities across the country. You should consider your listeners' demographic or psychological characteristics in order to choose the most effective evidence for them.

Forms of Reasoning

Reasoning or *inference* is a process of connecting something that is known or believed (evidence) to a concept or idea (claim) that you wish others to accept. **Patterns of reasoning** are habitual ways in which a culture or society uses inferences to connect what is accepted to what it is being urged to accept. In our culture, there are five generally accepted reasoning patterns: from examples, from generalization or axiom, from sign, from parallel case, and from causal relation.

Often called *inductive reasoning,* **reasoning from examples** involves examining a series of examples of known occurrences (evidence) and drawing a general conclusion (claim). The inference of this reasoning pattern is, "What is true of particular cases is true of the whole class." This inference represents a kind of mental inductive leap from specifics to generalities. For example, the National Cancer Institute has studied hundreds of individual case histories and discovered that people with high-fiber diets are less prone to have cancers of the digestive tract develop. With an inductive leap, the Institute then moved to the factual claim, "High-fiber diets help control certain types of cancer." Commuters use a similar pattern of reasoning every time they drive during rush hour. After trial and error, they decide that a residential street is the best route to take home between 5:00 and 5:30 P.M. and the expressway between 5:30 and 6:00 P.M. In other words, after experiencing enough instances, they arrive at a generalization and act on it.

Reasoning from generalization (sometimes called *deduction*) means applying a general truth to a specific situation. It is essentially the reverse of reasoning from examples or induction. In high school consumer education class, you may have learned that buying goods in large quantities saves money (the generalization). Now, you may shop at discount stores because they purchase goods in quantity, thereby saving money and passing that savings on to you (the claim deduced from the evidence). Or, you may believe that getting a college education is the key to a better future (the generalization). Therefore, if you get a college degree, you will get a better job (claim). This inference gathers power because of experience (you learned it through observation) or by definition (one of the characteristics of education is self-improvement). You ultimately accept this inference because of the uniformities you believe exist in the world.

Reasoning from sign uses an observable mark, or *sign,* as proof of the existence of a state of affairs. You reason from sign when you notice the tickle in your throat (the evidence) and decide that you're getting a cold (the claim). The tickle in your throat doesn't cause the condition; rather, it's a sign of the virus that does cause it. Detectives, of course, are experts at reasoning from sign. When they discover that a particular suspect had motive, means, and opportunity (the signs), they make the claim that he or she might be the murderer. Your doctor works the same way every time he or she examines your respiration and heart rhythms for signs of ailments. Reasoning from sign works well with natural occurrences (ice on the pond is always a sign that the temperature has been below 32°F). However, reasoning from sign can be troublesome in the world of human beings (as when some people take body weight as a sign of laziness or skin color as a sign of dishonesty). Signs, of course, are circumstantial evidence—and could be wrong. Just ask detectives and doctors. Yet, we often must use signs as indicators; otherwise, we couldn't project our economy, predict our weather, or forecast the rise and fall of political candidates.

Another common reasoning pattern, **reasoning from parallel case,** involves thinking solely in terms of similar things and events. You probably designed your first Homecoming float by looking at others; they served as models of what people expect of Homecoming floats in your area. Those floats functioned as evidence; the claim was that you should make a similar mark of pride and identification. The inference that linked the evidence and the claim was probably something such as, "What was acceptable as a Homecoming float last year will be acceptable/expected this year." Your instructors might use parallel reasoning every time they tell you, "Study hard for this exam. The last exam was difficult; this one will be, too." Obviously this is not a generalization, since every exam will probably not be the same. However, your instructors are asserting that the upcoming examinations and past examinations are similar cases—they have enough features in common to increase the likelihood that careful study habits will benefit you.

Finally, **reasoning from cause** is an important vehicle for reaching conclusions. The underlying assumption of causal reasoning is that events occur in a predictable, routine manner, with causes that account for occurrences. Reasoning from cause involves associating events that come before with events that follow. (See Table 15.2.) When substance abuse appears to be increasing across the country, people scramble to identify causes: the existence of international drug cartels, corrupt foreign governments, organized crime inside our own borders, lower moral standards, the break-up of the nuclear family, and lax school discipline. The trick for the arguer is to assert causes that might reasonably be expected to produce the effects—to point to material connections between, for example, foreign governments' actual policies and the presence of drugs in Cleveland or other American cities. Overall, the inference in causal reasoning is simple and constant: every effect has a cause.

Evaluating Arguments

The reasoning process is the pulley around which the machine of argument runs. You must test reasoning in order to protect yourself, both as a speaker and as a critical listener, from embarrassment when you're arguing and from faulty decisions when you're

TABLE 15.2 Kinds of Reasoning
Try to think of additional examples of each kind of reasoning.

Reasoning	Description	Examples
Reasoning from examples (inductive reasoning)	Drawing a general conclusion from instances or examples	I enjoy the music of Bach, Beethoven, and Brahms. I like classical music.
Reasoning from generalization or axiom (deductive reasoning)	Applying a general conclusion to a specific example	Irish Setters are friendly dogs. I think I'll get an Irish Setter puppy for my niece.
Reasoning from sign	Using an observable mark or symptom as proof of a state of affairs	The petunias are all dead. Someone forgot to water them.
Reasoning from parallel case	Asserting that two things or events share similar characteristics or patterns	North Korea is developing nuclear technology; South Korea won't be far behind.
Reasoning from causal relation	Concluding that an event that occurs first is responsible for a later event	The engine won't start because the carburetor is flooded with gasoline.

Speaking of . . . *skills*

Evaluating Arguments

Undoubtedly you'll participate in disputes or arguments many times as an advocate or a bystander. Often, you'll have to determine if your arguments or those of others were effective. Here are four questions you can ask to help discover the effectiveness of an argument:

1. *What was its effect?* Did the argument convince people to vote? to boycott? to donate canned goods? Clearly, if your argument results in a desired response, it was effective. However, this is only one way of judging the effectiveness of arguments. You must also ask the next three questions.

2. *Was the argument valid?* Did the arguer follow a logical order of development? Did he or she use supporting materials to prove the points? Were those supporting materials relevant to the claim advanced? If the argument was sound, it can be judged valid.

3. *Was the argument truthful?* Did it meet the test of reality? If an argument doesn't correspond to the way things really are, then it fails the truthfulness test.

4. *Was the argument ethical?* Did it advocate what is morally good? Did the arguer use ethical means to achieve results? This is an especially important test in this age of ethical malaise.

For additional development of these ideas, see J. Michael Sproule, *Argument: Language and Its Influence* (New York: McGraw-Hill, 1980), 22–24.

listening to others. For each kind of reasoning, there are special tests or questions that help you determine the soundness of arguments. Consider the following questions as you construct arguments and evaluate those of others:

Reasoning from Examples

1. *Have you looked at enough instances to warrant generalizing?* If you live in Idaho, you don't assume spring has arrived after experiencing one warm day in February.

2. *Are the instances fairly chosen?* You certainly hope that a teacher doesn't judge your speech skills by listening only to your first speech, when you were confused and nervous. You want to be judged only after being observed in several speaking situations.

3. *Are there important exceptions to the generalization or claim that must be considered?* While presidential elections show that, generally, "As Maine goes, so goes the nation," there have been enough exceptions to this rule to keep presidential candidates who lose in Maine campaigning hard.

Reasoning from Generalization

1. *Is the generalization true?* Women are more emotional than men; woolly caterpillars come out when winter's about to arrive; private universities provide better

education than public universities. Each of these statements is a generalization. You need to determine if sufficient evidence exists to support the truth of the statement.

2. *Does the generalization apply to this particular case?* Usually, discount stores have lower prices, but if a small neighborhood store has a sale, it may offer better prices than a discount house. While the old saying "Birds of a feather flock together" certainly applies to birds, it may not apply to human beings.

Reasoning from Sign

1. *Is the sign fallible?* As we've noted, many are merely circumstantial. Be extremely careful not to confuse sign reasoning with causal reasoning. If sign reasoning were infallible, the weather forecaster would never be wrong.

2. *Is the observation accurate?* Some of us see what we want to see, not what's there; children see ghosts at night and jealous lovers can interpret each other's acts in erroneous ways. Be sure that the observation is reliable.

Reasoning from Parallel Case

1. *Are there more similarities than differences between the two cases?* College A and College B may have many features in common—size, location, programs, and so on—yet they probably also have many different features, perhaps in the subgroups that make up their populations, the backgrounds of their faculty, and their historical development. Too many differences between two cases rationally destroy the parallel.

2. *Are the similarities you have pointed out the relevant and important ones?* There are two children in your neighborhood who are the same age, go to the same school, and wear the same kinds of clothes; are you therefore able to assume that one is well-behaved simply because the other is? Probably not, because more relevant similarities than their clothing and age would include their home lives, their relationships with siblings, and so forth. Comparisons must be based on relevant and important similarities.

Reasoning from Cause

1. *Can you separate causes and effects?* We often have a difficult time doing this. Does stress lead to a propensity to drink too much, or does excessive alcohol consumption lead to stress? Does a strained home life make a child misbehave, or is it the other way around?

2. *Are the causes strong enough to have produced the effect?* Did Bill Clinton's appearance on MTV really win the 1992 election for him, or was that an insufficient cause? There probably were much stronger and more important causes

3. *Did intervening events or persons prevent a cause from having its normal effect?* If a gun is not loaded, you can't shoot anything, no matter how hard you pull the trigger. Even if Iraq cuts off the United States oil supply, prices may not go up if enough oil's been stockpiled, if other producers offer competitive rates, or if U.S. consumer gas consumption drops.

4. *Could any other cause have produced the effect?* Although crime often increases when neighborhoods deteriorate, increased crime rates can be caused by any number of other changes—alterations in definitions of crime, increased reporting of crimes that have been going on for years, or closings of major industries. We rationally must sort through all of the possible causes before championing one.

The heart of critical thinking is idea-testing. You must learn to use what you have available—the evidence others have presented, your own experience, your wits, and sometimes a trip to the library when the decision's particularly important—to test the rationality and force of others' arguments.

Detecting Fallacies in Reasoning

So, your primary job as a critical listener and arguer is to evaluate the claims, evidence, and reasoning of others. On one level, you're looking for ways that the ideas and reasoning of others are important to your own thinking; and, on another level, you're examining the logical soundness of others' thinking. A **fallacy** is a flaw in the rational properties of an argument or inference. There are many different fallacies. Let's look at eight common ones.

1. *Hasty generalization.* A **hasty generalization** is a claim made on the basis of too little evidence. You should ask, "Has the arguer really examined enough typical cases to make a claim?" If the answer is *no,* then a flaw in reasoning has occurred. Urging a ban on ibuprofen because some people have had liver problems with it and the closure of a pedestrian mall because of an armed robbery are examples of hasty generalization.

2. *Genetic fallacy.* A **genetic fallacy** occurs when someone assumes that the only "true" understanding of some idea, practice, or event is to be found in its origins—in its "genes," literally or metaphorically. People sometimes assume that if an idea has been around for a long time, it must be true. Many people who defended slavery in the nineteenth century referred to the biblical practices of slavery to support their claim. Studies of origins can help us understand a concept, but it's hardly proof of present correctness or justice.

3. *Appeal to ignorance.* People sometimes **appeal to ignorance** by arguing with double negatives: "You can't prove it won't work!" They may even attack an idea because information about it is incomplete. "We can't cure all varieties of AIDS so let's just stop therapies until we learn more." Both of these are illogical claims because they depend on what we don't know. Sometimes we must simply act on the basis of the knowledge we have, despite the gaps in it. In countering such claims, you can cite parallel cases and examples. So, you might say:

> *OK, so we don't have all of the answers to the AIDS puzzle. That doesn't mean we don't work with what we know. Consider the case of tuberculosis. The vaccines against it weren't developed until the 1950s, and yet thousands of lives were saved earlier in the century because TB sanitariums used the*

physical and pharmacological regimes they had available. Of course they couldn't save everyone, but they relieved suffering and even prevented the deaths of many with the partial knowledge they had. Give HIV-positive people the same chance—to use what we have now even while we're waiting for the miracle cure.

4. *Bandwagon Fallacy.* A frequent strategy is to appeal to popular opinion or to urge people to jump on the bandwagon. The **bandwagon fallacy** assumes that if everyone else is doing something, you should, too: "African Americans don't belong to the Republican Party!" or "But Dad, everyone else is going!" While these appeals may be useful in stating valuative claims, they're not the basis for factual claims. The world has witnessed hundreds of widely believed but false ideas, from the belief that night air causes tuberculosis to panic over an invasion by Martians.

5. *Sequential fallacy.* The **sequential fallacy** is often present in arguments based on evidence from causal relations. The fallacy arises from the assumption that if one event follows another, the first must be the cause. Thunder and lightning do not cause rain, although they often occur sequentially; and, even if you usually catch colds in the spring, the two are not causally related. That is, the season of the year does not cause your cold—a virus does.

6. *Begging the question.* **Begging the question** is rephrasing an idea and then offering it as its own reason. This kind of reasoning is circular thought. If someone asserts, "Abortion is murder because it is taking the life of the unborn," he or she has committed a fallacy by rephrasing the *claim* (it is murder) to constitute the *reason* (it is taking life). Sometimes questions can be fallacious, such as "Have you quit smoking on weekends?" The claim, phrased as a question, assumes that you smoke during the week. Whatever your answer to the question, therefore, you're guilty. Claims of value are especially prone to begging the question.

7. *Appeal to authority.* **Appeal to authority** occurs when someone who is popular but not an expert urges the acceptance of an idea or a product. Television advertisers frequently ask consumers to purchase products because movie stars or sports heroes endorse them. Michael Jordan promotes everything from underwear to telephone services. The familiar figure provides name recognition but not expertise. You can detect this fallacy by asking, "Is he or she an expert on this topic?"

8. *Name calling.* **Name calling** is the general label for attacks on people instead of on their arguments. Name calling may take the form of an attack on the special interests of a person: "Of course, you're voting for O'Casey—you're Irish." Or it may be an attack on a personal characteristic rather than on ideas: "You're just a dweeb (or nerd or retrograde male)." Even dweebs, nerds, and retrograde males sometimes offer solid claims. Claims ought to be judged on their own features, preferably their objective features, not on the characteristics of the person who makes them.

These are some of the fallacies that creep into argumentation. A good basic logic book can point out additional fallacies.[4] Armed with knowledge of such fallacies, you should be able to protect yourself against unscrupulous demagogues, sales personnel, and advertisers. The Roman phrase, *caveat emptor!*—"Buyer, beware!"—should be a part of thinking as an audience member. You share with speakers the responsibility of cultivating the sort of critical spirit we discussed in the opening of this chapter.

Tips for Developing Argumentative Speeches

As you get ready to pull all of your claims, kinds of evidence, and reasoning patterns together into coherent argumentative speeches, consider the following pieces of advice:

1. *Place your strongest arguments first or last.* This strategy takes advantage of the **primacy-recency effects.** Arguments presented first set the agenda for what is to follow, and a strong opening argument often impresses an audience with its power, thereby heightening the credibility of the arguer (the primacy effect). We also know that listeners tend to retain the most recently presented idea (the recency effect), so you might put your strongest argument at the end of your speech so that listeners will remember your best shot.[5] Decide which position will best help you with the particular audience you face, and then place your best shot there (but then, of course, summarize all of the arguments in your conclusion).

2. *Vary your evidence.* Different listeners are likely to prefer different kinds of evidence, and most listeners want supporting materials that are both logically relevant and psychologically motivating. For example, if you're arguing that more Americans must invest in solar power units for their home electrical needs, general statistics on energy savings and average reduction in costs of utilities are good, but a good, clear illustration with details on what it's like to live in a solar-assisted environment will more likely clinch the argument.

3. *Avoid personal attacks on opponents.* Maintain arguments on an appropriate intellectual level. This tactic enhances your credibility. If you can argue well without becoming vicious, you'll earn the respect—and perhaps the agreement—of your listeners; most know that the more someone screams, the weaker his or her arguments are. Hold your opponent accountable for arguments and reasoning, yes, but without name-calling and smear tactics (see "Speaking of . . . Ethics: Name-Calling").

4. *Know the potential arguments of your opponents.* The best advocates know their opponents' arguments as well as their opponents do; they have thought about those arguments and ways of responding to them ahead of time. Having thought through opposing positions early allows you to prepare a response and feel confident about your own position. Notice how presidential candidates are able to anticipate each other's positions in their debates.

5. *Practice constructing logical arguments and detecting fallacious ones.* Ultimately, successful argument demands skill in performing the techniques of public reasoning. You need to practice routinely constructing arguments with solid relationships between and among claims, evidence, and reasoning patterns; and you need to practice regularly detecting the fallacies in other people's proposals. Critically examine

Speaking of . . . *ethics*

Name Calling

Arguments often threaten to degenerate into fights, not always physical clawing and punching, but certainly into symbolic assaults: attacks on an opponent's intelligence, parentage (or lack thereof), associations, motives, appearance. Is that ethical? Where do you draw the line?

1. You're having a class argument about ways to control hate speech. You know that your opponent is gay—do you reveal that information in the debate?
2. Both Michael Dukakis in 1988 and Bill Clinton in 1992 were accused by the National Conservative Political Action Committee of being "card-carrying members of the American Civil Liberties Union." Is that a relevant issue in presidential politics?
3. "Well, you're over thirty, so how would you understand?" "You're a girl, so of course . . . ." "Now, you're Black and so I'd expect you to . . . ." "When you lived in the ghetto, didn't you . . . ?" Is it ethical to make statements like these when arguing with someone?

Name-calling—*argumentum ad hominem* (arguments to the person)—have been used since Homer wrote *The Iliad*. But are they ethical? Anytime? Sometimes? When?

product advertisements, political claims, and arguments that your neighbors make in order to improve your communication skills—as both a sender and a receiver of argumentative messages.

A Look at Debates

One final topic should be mentioned: debates. When groups or societies are trying to resolve major differences or select leaders, they often go to **debates**—face-to-face arguments usually executed within some sort of controlled environment and in front of an audience. In the United States, the Commission on Presidential Debates every four years now negotiates a series of debates with particular formats between the candidates. In 1996, two presidential debates and one vice-presidential debate were held; in 1992, there were three presidential debates and one vice-presidential encounter. In 1992, one was run by a moderator, one, by a panel of reporters, and another by a moderator who led an audience that was asking the questions. In 1996, Jim Lehrer of public television fame moderated both of the presidential debates, though in the second, questions were asked by audience members. The rules vary, but are almost always present.

A professional academic association often features debates over intellectual or social issues; a cable channel might set up a debate between advocates and opponents of land set aside for new parks; the U.N. Security Council regularly debates proposals for controlling particular countries.

In one sense, a debate is like any kind of argument; you're expected to advance claims, support them, and reasonably tie your evidence to those claims. But, in another sense, a debate is different because of the formal controls. Several aspects of your **argumentative** talk can be controlled:

✓ *Time.* In most debate situations, the overall time devoted to the issue is **controlled**, and you may find that the time you can talk is limited as well.

✓ *Turn-taking.* There likely are rules for who speaks when, who can follow whom, and who can "yield the floor" to whom.

✓ *Materials.* Some debate formats even control what can be said; so, in trials there are such things as "admissible" and "inadmissible" evidence.

✓ *Material relevance.* Often in trials, as well, some material is ruled irrelevant (e.g., a defendant's past record). The same can be true in intellectual debates, where some kinds of evidence for a theory are deemed irrelevant.

In preparing for a debate, therefore, (1) find out the rules ahead of time to make sure that you've adapted your materials to them; (2) probe to see if you're allowed to respond to charges or other arguments from your opponent(s); and (3) know enough about group traditions to understand what kind of arguments are important. For example, as you'll see in any presidential debate in the United States, making points about one's leadership skills is at least as important as setting out a policy on crime or foreign aid.

Being in a formal debate can feel risky, because you've got someone asking you questions face to face and because there's often an audience there, assessing how you're doing. Convince yourself that your opponent is facing the same situation, that the risk of debate is worth it because you're in a situation where you can knock out opposing ideas head-on, and because a careful probing of your arguments by an opponent will make them even stronger in the end.

Debates are seen by more voters than any other single political message in presidential campaigns.

Sample Arguments From the Second Presidential Debate, 1996

Incumbent President Bill Clinton and challenger Bob Dole met in the Shiley Theatre on the University of San Diego campus for the second of their televised debates on October 16, 1996. For ninety minutes they worked their ways through opening statements, argumentative statements, rebuttals, statements about credibility issues (trust, experience), value orientations, personal anecdotes, and closing statements. The exchange was much too long to reproduce here, though it can be found on the World Wide Web at publications-admin@whitehouse.gov. In what follows we print transcriptions of some specific exchanges between the candidates so that you can see some similar and some contrasting methods for arguing.

Opening statements on issues. Notice different argumentative strategies from the start. Dole tries to personalize, even with humor, his views on campaigning and public programs, and then lists issues as valuative priorities. Clinton as the incumbent instead goes to the record, with facts and figures and particular policies. Which approach works better for you?

Dole:

In 20 days you will help decide who leads this country into the next century. It's an awesome responsibility. And you must ask yourself, Do you know enough about the candidates? You should know as much as possible about each of us. Sometimes the views have been distorted. There has been millions and millions of dollars in negative advertising spent distorting my views. But I hope tonight you'll get a better feel of who Bob Dole is and what he's all about./1

I think first I should understand [that] the question on your mind is, do I understand your problems. What I understand is—it occurred to me, and I might just say that I'm from a large family, I've got lots of relatives, and they're good, average, middle-class, hard-working Americans. They live all across the country. They're not all Republicans. Maybe all but one. (*Laughter.*)/2

But in any event, I understand the problems—whether it's two parents working because one has to pay the taxes and one has to provide for the family; whether it's a single parent who just barely pays the pressing bills; or whether you're worried about an education for your children, going to the best schools; or whether you're worried about safe playgrounds, drug-free schools, crime-free schools. This is what this election is all about./3

And hopefully, tonight when we conclude this debate, you will have a better understanding, and the viewing and listening audience will have a better understanding./4

Thank you./5

Clinton:

I've had a simple philosophy that I've tried to follow for the last four years—do what creates opportunity for all, what reinforces responsibility from all of us, and what will help us build a community where everybody has got a role to play and a place at the table./6

Compared to four years ago, we're clearly better off. We've got 10.5 million more jobs. The deficit's been reduced by 60 percent. Incomes are rising for the first time in a decade. The crime rates and the welfare rolls are falling. We're putting 100,000 more police on the streets, 60,000 felons, fugitives and stalkers have been denied handguns./7

But that progress is only the beginning. What we really should focus on tonight is what we still have to do to help the American people make the most of this future that's out there. I think what really matters is what we can do to help build strong families. Strong families mean a strong economy. To me, that means we have to go on and balance this budget while we protect Medicare and Medicaid and education and the environment./8

We should give a tax cut, targeted to child-rearing and education, to buying a first home and paying for health care. We ought to help protect our kids from drugs and guns and gangs and tobacco. We ought to help move a million people from welfare to work. And we ought to create the finest education systems in the world, where every 18-year-old can go on to college and all of our younger children have great educational opportunities. If we do those things, we can build that bridge to the 21st century. That's what I hope to talk about tonight./9

Taking positions on valuative issues. The candidates were asked by a teacher to talk about the lack of political unity in this country. Dole first attacks Clinton's White House and then some members of his own party for promoting scandals and bigotry; in other words, Dole uses attack as a way of affirming his position. Clinton, on the other hand, tried to use a positive method for outlining his valuative position on unity in government. Which worked better?

Dole:

There's no doubt about it that many American people have lost their faith in government. They see scandals almost on a daily basis. They see ethical problems in the White House today. They see 900 FBI files of private persons being gathered up by somebody in the White House. Nobody knows who hired this man. So that there is a great deal of cynicism out there./10

What I've always tried in whatever I've done, is to bring people together. I said in my acceptance speech in San Diego about two months ago that the exits are clearly marked: if you think the Republican Party is someplace for you to come if you're narrow-minded or bigoted or don't like certain people in America, the exits are clearly marked for you to walk out of, as I stand here without compromise, because this is the party of Lincoln./11

Clinton:

One of the reasons that I ran for President is because not just children, a lot of grownups felt that way. If you remember, four years ago we had not only rising unemployment, but a lot of rising cynicism. I had never worked in

Washington as an elected official. It seemed to me that most of the arguments were partisan—Republican-Democrat, left-right, liberal-conservative./12

That's why I said tonight I'm for opportunity, responsibility, and community. And we've gotten some real progress in the last four years. I've also done everything I could at every moment of division in this country—after Oklahoma City, when these churches were burned—to bring people together and remind people that we are stronger because of our diversity. We have to respect one another./13

Using statistics. Especially when arguing politics and public policy, statistics are important for describing the general conditions of the country. When asked about health care programs, Clinton runs through what he sees as his accomplishments and then his plans by quantifying progress and future needs. Dole responds both with an attack on Clinton's statistics and 1994 health plan, and then looks to his own view: ways he believes the health care system would benefit from his tax-cut proposal. Thus, he tries to avoid Clinton's strengths by taking an economic rather than a medical policy approach to the question. In your opinion, do these counter-arguments work for Dole?

Clinton:

First of all, let me say what we have done. In the last four years, we've worked hard to promote more competition to bring down the rate of inflation in health care costs without eroding health care quality. The government pays for Medicare and Medicaid, as you know, and that's very important./14

Secondly, we've added a million more children to the ranks of the insured through the Medicaid program. We have protected 25 million people through the passage of the Kennedy-Kassebaum bill that says you can't lose your health insurance if you change jobs or if someone in your family has been sick. We just recently ended those drive-by deliveries, saying people couldn't be kicked out of the hospital by insurance companies when they just had babies./15

So that's a good start. In the next four years I want to focus on the following things. Number one, add another million children to the insured ranks through the Medicaid program. Number two, keep working with the states, as we are now, to add 2.2 million more people to the insured system. Number three, cover people who are between jobs for up to six months. That could protect 3 million families, 700,000 kids. And, number four, make sure we protect the integrity of the Medicare program and the Medicaid program, and not do anything in cutting costs which would cause hundreds of hospitals to close, which could have been the case if the $270 billion Medicare cut that I vetoed had been enacted into law./16

Dole:

Just let me say, there you go again, Mr. President, talking about a Medicare cut. Now, I've heard you say this time after time. And I've heard you say on one TV appearance, the media made me do it. You're trying to defend your cut—which was not a cut, either—but a reduction in the growth of spending.

And we always had at least a seven percent [growth written in our proposal]. You've said publicly that it's now three times the rate of inflation. We ought to cut the growth to twice the rate of inflation. It's about where we are now./17

Let's stop talking about cutting Medicare, and my economic plan will increase it 39 percent. Don't forget what he [Clinton] tried to do with health care. Seventeen new taxes, spend $1.5 trillion, 50 new bureaucracies. Can you believe that? You couldn't have ever been a cardiologist because they [the Democratic plan] had quotas. Your—cardiology wouldn't affect you, but if someone wanted to be a cardiologist 10 years from now you'd have to be certain you complied with some of the rules in this extreme medical plan the government was going to take over for all America./18

There are things we can do, like the Kassebaum bill, which contains many provisions I authored, covered preexisting conditions, portability. And there are other things we should do. We will need to cover about 20 million people and a lot of children./19

Humor and sharp rebuttal. Bob Dole was always well known for his humor, sometimes caustic humor, that could be used as a weapon to inflame an opponent (and audience). Bill Clinton, however, could also engage in the give-and-take of debate. Here's part of what they both said when the question of Dole's age and his ability to understand the "young voices of America today and tomorrow" came up.

Dole:

Well, I think age is very—you know, wisdom comes from age, experience and intelligence. And if you have some of each—and I have some age, some experience, some intelligence—(laughter)—that adds up to wisdom./20

I think it also is a strength, it's an advantage. And I have a lot of young people work in my office, work in my campaign. Now, this is about America. This is about—somebody said earlier, one of the first questions, we're together. It's one America, one nation./21

I'm looking at our economic plan because I'm concerned about the future for young people. I'm looking about drugs. The President's been AWOL [Absent Without Leave] for four years. I'm looking about crime. He'll claim credit now for crime going down, but it happens because mayors and governors and others have brought crime down. Rudy Giuliani, Mayor of New York, brought crime down 25 percent just in New York City. But, of course, the President will take credit for that./22

My view is, we want to find jobs and opportunities and education. This year, the Republican Congress—student loans went from $24 billion over the next six years—a 50-percent increase. It's the highest appropriation ever—$6 billion for Pell Grants—very, very important. We've also raised the amount of each Pell Grant./23

In our economic plan, the $500 child credit can be used for young people—rolled over and over and over [as a tax credit]. Of course, not this age, but if you have a child two years old, seven percent interest, it will be worth about $18,000 by the time that child is ready for college./24

Clinton:

I can only tell you that I don't think Senator Dole is too old to be president. It's the age of his ideas that I question. You're almost not old enough to remember this, but we've tried this before, promising people an election year tax cut that's not paid for./25

Dole:

We tried it last time you were in./26

Clinton:

Tell them they can have everything you've got. And let me just say this. Did you hear him say that Congress just voted to increase student loans and scholarships? They did after he left [after Dole resigned to run]. The last budget he led cut Pell Grants, cut student loans, I vetoed it when they shut the government down./27

My plan would give students a dollar-for-dollar reduction for the cost of a typical community college tuition, a $10,000 deduction a year for the most of college tuition, would let families save in an IRA and withdraw tax-free to pay for the cost of education. And it's all paid for./28

My whole administration is about your future. It's about what the 21st century is going to be like for you. And I hope you'll look at the ideas in it. Thank you./29

The 1996 presidential debates show you argumentation at work. Because these excerpts are transcriptions, you are seeing oral argument, with false starts, half-finished thoughts, interruptions, and the rest. Obtaining a videotape of the first and second presidential debates from the C-SPAN Educational Archive or other resource will show you even more dimensions of argumentation, and may even remind you why a critical spirit is absolutely essential for anyone trying to make good decisions about public policies and legislative proposals.

Assessing Your Progress

Chapter Summary

1. Argumentation is a process of advancing propositions or claims supported by good reasons and allowing others to examine those claims and reasons in order to test them or to offer counterarguments.

2. Criticism is a process of careful assessment, evaluation, and judgment of ideas and motives. Both listeners and speakers should engage in critical thinking.

3. Arguments are built from three elements—the claim, the evidence, and the reasoning pattern.

4. The types of claims common to arguments are claims of fact, claims of value, and claims of policy.

5. Evidence for arguments can be chosen to reflect the rational quality of the claim (rationally relevant evidence) or to stimulate audience involvement (motivationally relevant evidence).

6. Five forms of reasoning connect evidence and claims—reasoning from examples, reasoning from generalization, reasoning from sign, reasoning from parallel case, and reasoning from cause.

7. A fallacy is a flaw in the rational properties of an argument or inference. There are many kinds of fallacies; the most common fallacies are hasty generalization, genetic fallacy, appeal to ignorance, bandwagon fallacy, sequential fallacy, begging the question, appeal to authority, and name-calling.

8. In developing argumentative speeches: (a) organize your arguments by putting the strongest first or last, (b) vary the evidence, (c) avoid personal attacks on opponents, (d) know the potential arguments of your opponents, and (e) practice constructing logical arguments and detecting fallacious ones.

9. Debates are face–to–face arguments executed in a situation wherein the rules of conversation are controlled.

Key Terms

appeal to authority (p. 271)

appeal to ignorance (p. 270)

argument (p. 260)

argumentation (p. 260)

bandwagon fallacy (p. 271)

begging the question (p. 271)

claim (p. 261)

claim of fact (p. 261)

claim of policy (p. 262)

claim of value (p. 262)

fallacy (p. 270)

debates (p. 273)

genetic fallacy (p. 270)

hasty generalization (p. 270)

name calling (p. 271)

patterns of reasoning (p. 265)

primary-recency effects (p.272)

reasoning (p. 265)

reasoning from cause (p. 267)

reasoning from examples (p. 266)

reasoning from generalization (p. 266)

reasoning from parallel case (p. 266)

reasoning from sign (p. 266)

sequential fallacy (p. 271)

Assessment Activities

1. Choose a controversial topic and phrase it as a question of policy, such as, "Should the federal government privatize Social Security?" or "Should all 18-year-olds be required to complete two years of military or domestic service?" As a class, think of arguments for and against the policy. Then, determine what rationally and motivationally relevant evidence would be required to develop each argument.

2. Prepare a ten-minute argumentative exchange on a topic involving you and another member of your class. Dividing the time equally, one of you will advocate a claim and the other will oppose it. Adopt one of the following formats: (a) a Lincoln-Douglas format—the first person speaks for four minutes, the second speaks

for five, and then the first person returns for a one-minute rejoinder; (b) an issue format—both parties agree on two key issues and then each speaks for two-and-a-half minutes on each issue; (c) a debate format—each speaker presents a constructive speech for three minutes, and then each speaker gives a two-minute rebuttal; (d) a heckling format—each speaker has five minutes to speak; but, during the presentation of each speech, the audience or opponent may ask questions that the speaker must answer.

3. Turn the class into a deliberative assembly, decide on a motion or resolution to be argued, and then schedule a day or two for a full debate. Class members should assume argumentative roles: advocates, witnesses, direct examiners, cross-examiners, and summarizers. The deliberative assembly allows each speaker to be part of a team.

References

1. Harvey Siegel, *Educating Reason: Rationality, Critical Thinking, and Education* (New York: Routledge, 1988), 1–47. The importance of critical thinking has been underscored in two national reports on higher education: The National Institute of Education, *Involvement in Learning: Realizing the Potential of American Higher Education,* 1984; and the Association of American Colleges, *Integrity in the College Curriculum: A Report to the Academic Community,* 1985. For a summary of research on critical thinking in the college setting, see James H. McMillan, "Enhancing College Students' Critical Thinking: A Review of Studies," *Research in Higher Education, 26* (1987): 3–29.

2. Fairness or fair-mindedness is one dimension of a primary factor underlying positive source credibility, trustworthiness. See James B. Stiff, *Persuasive Communication* (New York: Guilford Press, 1994), esp. 90–92.

3. A full discussion of the logical grounding of claims in evidence and reasoning is presented in the classic book on argumentation: Douglas Ehninger and Wayne Brockriede, *Decision by Debate,* 2nd ed. (New York: Harper & Row, 1978).

4. See Irving M. Copi and Keith Burgess-Jackson, *Informal Logic,* 2nd ed. (New York: Macmillan, 1992); and Frans H. vanEemeren and Rob Grootendorst, *Argumentation, Communication, and Fallacies* (Hillsdale, N.J.: Lawrence Erlbaum Associates, 1992).

5. The debate over primacy-recency effects continues. For the position that primacy and recency are equally potent, see Stephen W. Littlejohn and David M. Jabusch, *Persuasive Transactions* (Glenview, Ill.: Scott, Foresman, and Co., 1987), 235–236; for the arguments championing the primacy position, see Robert E. Denton, Jr., *Persuasion and Influence in American Life* (Prospect Heights, Ill.: Waveland Press, 1988), 299–300.

Credits

Index

Accuracy of words, 151–152
Achievement motives, 236, 238–239
Acquisition, motivational appeal and, 238, 242
Action, as step of Monroe's motivated sequence, 243, 247, 249, 253, 255
Active listening, 37
Activity, as factor of attention, 130
Actual objects, 187–188
Actuative speech(es)
    defined, 233
    purpose of, 19
    sample, using motivated sequence, 254–255
    sample outline for, 247–249
    structuring, 243–247
Adventure, motivational appeal and, 238, 242
Affect displays, 179
Affiliation motives, 236–238
Aggression, motivational appeal and, 239
Alda, Alan, 155
Alliteration, 139
Analogical definition, 160
Appeal(s)
    to authority, 271
    development of, 78–79
    fear, 241
    to ignorance, 270–271
    motivational. See Motivational appeal(s)
Appreciative listening, 36
Apprehension
    breathing through fears and, 181
    first-time fears and, 10
    information overload and, 212
    personal risk of argumentation and, 265
    state, 25
    trait, 25
    xenophobia and, 45
Appropriateness of language, 156–158
Argument(s). See also Argumentation; Debate(s)
    elements of, 260–261. See also Claim(s)
    evaluating, 267–270

tips for developing argumentative speeches and, 272–273
Argumentation. See also Argument(s); Debate(s)
    critical thinking and, 259–281
    defined, 260
    personal risk of, 265
    tips for developing argumentative speeches and, 272–273
Articulatory control, 176
Assertion, 107
Atmosphere, creation of, 155–158
Attention
    capturing and holding, 129–132
    defined, 129
    factors of, 130
    as step of Monroe's motivated sequence, 243, 244, 247, 249, 254
Attitudes, 71–72, 73
Attribution, 235
Audience(s). See also Listener(s)
    age of, 66
    analysis of. See Audience analysis
    attention of. See Attention
    attitudes of, 71–72, 73
    beliefs of, 70–71, 73. See also Belief(s)
    changing minds and actions of, 233–243. See also Actuative speech(es); Persuasive speech(es)
    common ground and, 74
    cultural background of, 68
    distance between speaker and, 177
    diverse, persuasion of, 234. See also Actuative speech(es); Persuasive speech(es)
    education of, 67
    ethnic background of, 68
    eye contact with, 182
    gender of, 66
    group membership of, 67
    hostile, 78
    motivating, 212

orientation of, 22
patterns of organization centered on, 118–121
persuading, 233–243. *See also* Actuative speech(es); Persuasive speech(es)
segmentation of, 79
size of, adaptation of gestures and movement to, 182
support material required for, 84
understanding of, 65–82
values of, 72–74
visual aids use and, 195–196
Audience analysis
demographic, 66–69, 74–76
ethics and, 68
psychological, 69–76
responsible, 22
sample, 79–81
speech preparation and, 76–79
Audience-centered patterns of organization, 118–121
Audience orientation, 22
Audience segmentation, 79
Auditory imagery, 162
Authority
appeal to, 271
motivational appeal to use, 239
Autonomy, motivational appeal and, 241–242

Bandwagon fallacy, 271
Bar graphs, 191
Barrinson, Rod, 101
Begging the question, 271
Belief(s), 70–71, 73
defined, 70
fixed, 70, 71
supplying additional inducement to, 141
variable, 70, 71
Biographies, as sources, 89
Blondin, Charles, 99
Body, use of to communicate. *See* Nonverbal communication
Books, as sources, 23, 89
Bowers, John Waite, 156
Brainstorming, 18
Breathing
control of, 176
through fears, 181
Buckley, William F., Jr., 175
Burke, Kenneth, 164

Bush, Barbara, 134
Bush, George, 238, 240

Campbell, Ben Nighthorse, 4, 5
Cardozo, Benjamin, 137
Carter, Jimmy, 159, 243
Carter, Rosalynn, 243
Casals, Pablo, 10
Causal patterns, 117
Cause, reasoning from, 267, 269–270
Cause-effect pattern, 117
Cavett, Dick, 171
CD-ROM searches, 87
Central idea
defined, 18
determining, 18, 20–22
developing, 115
speaking purposes and, 21
Chalkboard drawings, as visual aids, 190
Challenge, issuing of, 140
Change, motivational appeal and, 238
Chapman, Joyce, 226–228
Charles, Ray, 237
Charts, as visual aids, 193–194
Chatham, Lord (William Pitt), 57, 239
Chronological patterns, 116
Chunking, 123
Claim(s)
as element of argument, 261, 262
of fact, 261–262
of policy, 262–263
types of, 261–263
of value, 262
Clarity, 208–210
Cleghorn, John E., 140
Clinton, Bill, 98, 153, 191, 197, 269, 273, 274, 275–279
Clinton, Hillary Rodham, 101, 102
Co-cultures, 48
Coherence, 153–155
Common ground, 74
Communication
community building and, 4
of feelings, 182
nonverbal. *See* Nonverbal communication
using body in. *See* Nonverbal communication
using voice in, 26–27, 169, 171–175, 176. *See also* Voice
visual aids and, 196. *See also* Visual aids

Community building, 4–5
Companionship, motivational appeal and, 236, 242
Comparisons, as supporting material, 99–100
Comprehension
  listening for, 36
  visual aids and, 187
Computer-generated visual materials, 198–200
Computerized database searches, 23, 85–88
Conclusion(s)
  for demonstrations, 216
  for informative speeches, checklist for, 219
  for instructions, 216
  for lectures, 220
  for oral report, 218
  sample outline for, 143–144
  for speeches of definition, 214
  types of, 135
Conflict, as factor of attention, 132
Conformity, motivational appeal and, 236–237
Context, 7
Contextual definition, 160
Contrasts, as supporting material, 99–100
Conventional gestures, 180
Cosby, Bill, 132
Creativity, motivational appeal and, 239
Credibility, 10
Critical listening
  public speaking and, 1–62
  for responsible speakers, 33–43
  techniques for, 36, 38–41
Critical thinking
  argumentation and, 259–281
  defined, 41
  use of supporting materials and, 106–108
Cultural diversity. *See also* Diversity
  accepting multiple paths to goals and, 53–55
  challenge of, 50
  communicating unity through, 50–59
  cultural processes and, 47–50
  ethics and, 57
  of "family values," 52–53
  maintaining self-identity when facing difference and, 56–59
  negotiating diverse values and, 52–53
  recognizing, 50–52
  working through the lifestyle choices of others and, 55–56

Culture(s)
  audience and, 68
  co-, 48
  defined, 44
  diversity and. *See* Cultural diversity
  dynamics of, 47–49
  as lived, 47–48
  multiculturalism and, 47
  oral, 56
  as performed, 49
  processes and, 47–50
  public speaking and, 44–62
  sub-, 47–48
  as thought, 48–49
Curiosity, motivational appeal and, 239, 242

Database searches, 23, 85–88
Debate(s)
  defined, 273
  Presidential, 273, 275
    Second, in 1996, sample arguments from, 275–279
DeBois, W. E. B., 234
Deduction, 266
Defense, motivational appeal and, 239–240
Deference, motivational appeal and, 237
Definitions, 158–160
Delany, Bessie, 99
Delany, Sadie, 99
Delivery of speech, 169–185. *See also* Presentation of speech
  confident, development of, 25–27
  using body in. *See* Nonverbal communication
  using voice in, 26–27, 169, 171–175, 176. *See also* Voice
Demographic analysis, 66–69
  discovering factors regarding, 74–76
  ethics and, 69
  responsible use of, 68–69
Demonstration(s)
  defined, 207
  sample outline for, 222–225
  structuring, 214–216
Dependence, motivational appeal and, 237
Descriptive gestures, 180–181
Desires
  analyzing, 233–234
  turning into motivational appeals, 233–234
Dialect, 173

Dickinson, John, 239
Dictionary definition, 159
Discriminative listening, 36
Display, motivational appeal and, 238
Distance
 interhuman, 178
 "public," 177
 between speaker and audience, 177
Diversity. *See also* Cultural diversity
 communicating unity through, 50–59
 of "family values," 52–53
 human, respect for, 11–12
 individual, 3–4
 recognizing, 50–52
 speechmaking and, 3–15
Documents, as sources, 23, 89
Dole, Bob, 191, 274, 275–279
Dominance, motivational appeal and, 239
Doublespeak, 157
Douglass, Frederick, 3
Drifting thoughts, 34–35
Dukakis, Michael, 197, 273
Dyer, Shannon, 136

Effect-cause pattern, 117
Ekman, Paul, 179
Electronic card catalog, 85–86
Elimination order, 120–121
Embodiment, 49
Emerson, Ralph Waldo, 242
Emphasis, vocal, 174–175
Enactment, 49
Encoding, 149
Encyclopedias, as sources, 23, 89
Enunciation, 173
Ethics, 9–11, 13
 audience analysis and, 69
 cultural practices and, 57
 deliberately misguiding listeners and, 40
 doublespeak and, 157
 name calling and, 273
 numerical data usage and, 104
 picture alteration and, 197
 revealing responsible intentions and, 133
 suppressing information and, 213
 using fear appeals and, 241
 using supporting material responsibly and, 93
Ethos, 10
Etymological definition, 160
Evidence. *See also* Supporting material(s)

as element of argument, 261–262
 motivationally relevant, 264–265
 rationally relevant, 263–264
Examples
 reasoning from, 266, 267, 268
 as supporting material, 23, 100–102
Exemplar definition, 160
Explanations, as supporting material, 98–99
Extemporaneous speech, 171
External perceptual field, 35
Eye contact with audience, 182

Facial expressions, 179–180
Fact(s), 71
 claims of, 261–262, 263
 defined, 70
 knowledge, information age and, 205–206
 as supporting materials, 23
Factors of attention, 130
Fallacy(ies)
 bandwagon, 271
 defined, 270
 detection of, in reasoning, 270–272
 genetic, 270
 sequential, 271
Familiarity, as factor of attention, 131
Familiarity-acceptance order, 119
"Family values," 52–53
Farrahkan, Louis, 234
Faulkner, William, 164–166
Fear(s)
 breathing through, 181
 first-time, 10
 motivational appeal and, 240–241, 242
Feedback, 7, 8, 34
Films, as visual aids, 188, 190, 198
First-time fears, 10
Fisher, Mary, 57–58, 101–102
Fixed beliefs, 70, 71
Flipcharts, 194
Flowcharts, 194
Flynn, Nicholas, 136
Forecasts, 153–154, 155
Friesen, Wallace V., 179

Gandhi, Mahatma, 106
Gender-linked words, 156
Gender-neutral language, 156–158
Generalization
 hasty, 270

reasoning from, 266, 267, 268–269
General purposes for speeches, 18, 19–20, 21, 22
Generosity, motivational appeal and, 237
Genetic fallacy, 270
Gestures, 169, 180–181, 182, 183
Goal development, 77–78
Gore, Al, 197
Government documents, as sources, 23, 89
Government reports, as sources, 23, 89
Graphs, as visual aids, 190–193
Greeting, use of, 134–136
Grune, George V., 137–138
Gustatory imagery, 162

Hall, Carl, 105
Hall, Edward T., 177–178
Hancock, John, 196
Hasty generalization, 270
Hearing, 33–34
Hegemony, 48–49
Helpful pauses, 175
Hubbard, Samantha, 239
Humor
    as factor of attention, 132
    use of, in story form, at beginning of
        speech, 137
Hunn, Hortense, 105
Huxley, Elspeth, 162–163

Idea(s)
    central. *See* Central idea
    clustering, 211
    coherence and, 153–155
    complex, using reiteration to clarify, 210
    familiar, association of, with new ones,
        210–211
    focusing on, 26
    framing of, 76
    major, summarizing, in conclusion, 140
    new, association of, with familiar ones,
        210–211
    phrasing, 76
    restatement of, 152–153
    supporting materials and, 98. *See also* Sup-
        porting materials
Ideology, 48
Illustration(s)
    as an example, 100
    at beginning of speech, 138
    as supporting material, 23

Imagery
    defined, 160
    types of, 161–164
Impromptu speech, 170, 171
Independence, motivational appeal and,
    241–242
Indicators, 181
Inductive reasoning, 266
Inference. *See* Reasoning
Informal language, 156
Information
    defined, 206
    overload of, 212
    recording of, 90–91, 92
    speech to provide. *See* Informative
        speech(es)
    suppressing, 213
Informational interview, 90
Informative speech(es), 205–230
    choosing topic for, 209
    conclusions to, checklist for, 219
    essential qualities of, 208–212
    introductions to, checklist for, 219
    outline for, 108–109
    purpose of, 19
    sample of, 226–228
    structuring, 212–217
    types of, 206–208
Inquiry order, 119
Instructions
    defined, 207
    structuring, 214–216
Intelligibility, 172–173
Intensity of word choices, 155–156
Interhuman distance, 178
Internet, 87–88
Interviews, 90–91
    conducting, 91
    informational, 90
Introduction(s), 133–139
    completion of, 138–139
    for demonstrations, 214–215
    for informative speeches, checklist for,
        219
    for instructions, 214–215
    for lectures, 218
    for oral report, 216
    sample outline for, 143–144
    for speeches of definition, 213
    types of, 135

Jackson, Jesse, 50–51, 54, 169
Jordan, Barbara, 73–74
Jordan, Michael, 271

Keller, Helen, 169
Kelly, Leontine, 141
Kennedy, John F., 131, 169
Kennedy, Ted, 197
Kinesthetic imagery, 163
King, Larry, 174
King, Martin Luther, Jr., 131, 164, 169
King, Rodney, 49, 53
Knowledge, 206

Language, 149–168. *See also* Words
    accuracy of, 151–152
    achieving clarity through, 209–210
    appropriateness of, 156–158
    coherence and, 153–155
    definitions and, 158–160
    dialect and, 173
    doublespeak and, 157
    encoding and, 149
    enunciation and, 173
    gender-neutral, 156–158
    imagery and, 160–164. *See also* Imagery
    informal, 156
    intensity of, 155–156
    metaphor and, 164
    oral, 150, 151
    pronunciation and, 173
    relevant visualization and, 211
    restatement and, 152–153
    simplicity of, 152
    strategic use of, 158–164
    style of. *See* Style
    trigger words and, 35
    written, 150, 151
Leathers, Dale G., 176
Lectures, 207, 218–220
Lehrer, Jim, 273
Limbaugh, Rush, 169
Lincoln, Abraham, 99, 131, 152, 153, 169, 237
Line graphs, 191, 192
Listener(s). *See also* Audience(s)
    attention of. *See* Attention
    defined, 6–7
    desires of, 233–235
    feedback and, 7, 8, 34
    looking at, 26

misguiding, 40
needs of, 233–235
note taking by, 37
observing, 75
questions of, raising and answering of,
        119–120
surveying, 74–75
Listening
    active, 37
    appreciative, 36
    for comprehension, 36
    critical. *See* Critical listening
    defined, 34
    discriminative, 36
    good, barriers to, 34–35
    hearing and, 33–34
    note taking and, 37
    practical techniques for, 35–41
    responsible, developing skills for, 41–42
    therapeutic, 36
Locke, John, 11
Lopez, Delores, 12–14
Loudness, 172
Love, Russell J., 134
Loyalty, motivational appeal and, 237
Lunden, Joan, 171
Lutz, Robert, 98

MacArthur, Douglas, 163, 237
MacKay, Harvey, 134–135
Madonna, 10
Magazines, as sources, 23, 88–89
Magic numbers, 123, 211
Magnitudes, 102–103
Mann, Jonathan, 160
Manuscript speech, 170
Mapping of movements, 123
Marx, Karl, 58
Mehrabian, Albert, 179
Mellor, David, 28–30
Memorized speech, 170
Memory
    organization and, 123
    visual aids and, 187
Message, 6
Metaphor, 164
Michaels, Al, 171
Miller, G. A., 123
Minow, Newton N., 161
Mitscher, Ron, 237

Mnemonics, 123, 139, 211
Models, as visual aids, 194
Molinari, Susan, 169
Monroe, Alan, 132
Monroe's motivated sequence, 243–255
  defined, 243
  organizing persuasive speeches using,
    243–247
  sample actuative speech using, 254–255
Morton, Henri Mann, 53–54
Motivated sequence. *See* Monroe's motivated
  sequence
Motivational appeal(s). *See also* Motive clus-
  ter(s)
  defined, 235
  turning needs and desires into, 235
  types of, 235–242
  using, 242–243
Motivationally relevant evidence, 264–265
Motive cluster(s)
  achievement, 236, 238–239
  affiliation, 236–238
  defined, 235–236
  power, 236, 239–242
Motive need, 235
Mount, Anson, 135
Movement(s)
  mapping of, 123
  by speaker, 178–179
Multiculturalism, 47

Name calling, 271, 273
Narrative, 100
Need(s)
  analyzing, 233–234
  motive, 235
  as step of Monroe's motivated sequence,
    243, 244, 245, 248, 250, 254
  turning into motivational appeals, 233–234
Negative definition, 159–160
Newspapers, as sources, 23, 88
Nonverbal communication, 26–27, 169,
  175–183
  adaptation of, to presentations, 181–183
  dimensions of, 176–181
Notecard(s)
  recording information on, 92
  speaking outline on, 125
Note taking, 37
Novello, Antonia, 102

Novelty, as factor of attention, 131

Occasion for speech
  analysis of, 22
  atmosphere and, 155
  formality of, 177
  referring to, at beginning of speech, 134
  visual aids use and, 195–196
Olfactory imagery, 162–163
Olivier, Sir Laurence, 10
Opinions, 70, 71
Oral culture, 56
Oral report(s)
  defined, 207
  sample outline for, 217–218
  structuring, 216–218
Oral style, 150, 151
Organic imagery, 163–164
Organization of speech. *See* Speech organization
Osborn, Michael, 164
Outline(s)
  for actuative speech, sample of, 247–249
  for conclusion, sample of, 143–144
  for demonstration speech, sample of, 222–225
  for informative speech, sample of, 108–109
  for introduction, sample of, 143–144
  making of, 23–24, 114, 121–128
    guidelines for, 125–127
  for oral report, sample of, 217–218
  for persuasive speech, sample of, 249–253
  for problem-solution speech, sample of,
    109–111
  rough, 121–124
  speaking, 124–125
    sample of, on notecards, 125
  for speech of definition, sample of, 220–222
  types of, 121–125
Overhead projections, as visual aids, 177, 190,
  198

Pace of presentation, 183
Paglia, Camille, 169
Parallel case, reasoning from, 266–267, 269
Passive listening, 34
Pattern(s) of organization, 116–121
  announcement of, in speech introduction,
    138
  audience-centered, 118–121
  causal, 117
  chronological, 116

Monroe's motivated sequence as. *See* Monroe's motivated sequence
spatial, 116–117
topical, 118
Patterns of reasoning, 265–266
Pauses, helpful, 175
Pavarotti, Luciano, 10
Payan, Janice, 106
Perot, H. Ross, 99, 191
Perseverance, motivational appeal and, 238
Personal enjoyment, motivational appeal and, 239, 242
Personal reference, use of, 134–136
Persuasive speech(es), 231–258
  defined, 233
  purpose of, 19–20
  sample outline for, 249–253
  structuring, 249
  visual aids and, 187
Philbin, Regis, 171
Photographs
  alteration of, 197
  as visual aids, 188, 197
Physical distractions, 35
Pictographs, as visual aids, 193
Pie graphs, 191–192
Pitch
  changing, 174
  control of, 176
  defined, 174
Pitch variation, 174
Pitt, William (Lord Chatham), 57, 239
Plagiarism, 91–94, 106
Planning of speech, 114–116
  steps in, 23
Policy, claims of, 262–263
Pontier, John, 138
Postman, Neil, 92–94
Posture, 169, 178
Powell, Colin, 142, 169
Power motives, 236, 239–242
Practicing speech, 24–25, 26, 175, 183
Preparation of speech
  appeal development in, 78–79
  audience analysis usage in, 76–79
  goal development in, 77–78
  purpose development in, 76–77
  steps in, 23
Presentation of speech. *See also* Delivery of speech
  adapting nonverbal behavior to, 181–183

atmosphere creation and, 155–158
integration of, with visual aids, 196–198. *See also* Visual aids
method of, selection of, 170–171
pace of, 183
responsible, 147–202
steps in, 23
wording and. *See* Language; Words
Prestige, motivational appeal and, 238, 242
Previews, 153–154, 155
Pride, motivational appeal and, 238, 242
Primacy effect, 129
Primary sources, 85
Print materials, 88–89
Problem-solution order, 120
Problem-solution speech, outline for, 109–111
Pronunciation, 173
Proxemics, 177–178, 182
Proximity, as factor of attention, 130
Psychological profiling, 69–74
  discovering factors regarding, 74–76
  using, 75–76
"Public distance," 177
Public speaking. *See also* Speechmaking
  critical listening and. *See* Critical listening
  cultural life and. *See* Culture
  ethics and. *See* Ethics
  as interactive process, 6
  training for, 5–6
Purpose for speech. *See* Speech(es), purpose(s) for
Pytte, Agnar, 137

Question(s)
  asking of, at beginning of speech, 136
  of listeners, raising and answering of, 119–120
Question-answer order, 119–120
Quotation, use of
  at beginning of speech, 137
  at end of speech, 140–141

Radio broadcasts, as sources, 23, 90
Rate, speaking, 173, 174
Rationally relevant evidence, 263–264
Rational thinking, talking and, 260–267
Reagan, Ronald, 101
Reality, as factor of attention, 130–131
Reasoning
  from cause, 267, 269–270
  defined, 265

detecting fallacies in, 270–272
as element of argument, 261
from examples, 266, 267, 268
from generalization, 266, 267, 268–269
inductive, 266
kinds of, summarized, 267
from parallel case, 266–267, 269
patterns of, 265–266
from sign, 266, 267, 269
Recency effect, 129
Recording information, 90–91, 92
Reeve, Christopher, 7–8, 9
Reference, personal, use of, 134–136
Relevant visualization, 211
Repetition, 139
Report(s)
oral. *See* Oral report(s)
as sources, 23, 89
Responsible speechmaking. *See* Speechmaking
Restatement of words, phrases, and ideas,
        152–153
Reverence, motivational appeal and, 237
Reward, motivational appeal and, 238
Rhetorical sensitivity, 11–12
Richards, Ann, 169
Rivera, Geraldo, 171
Roosevelt, Eleanor, 169
Roosevelt, Franklin Delano, 101, 134, 153,
        254–255
Rough outline, 121–124

Satisfaction, as step of Monroe's motivated se-
        quence, 243, 244, 245, 248, 251, 255
Saving, motivational appeal and, 238, 242
Schaillol, Charles, 164
Secondary sources, 85
Segmentation, audience, 79
Segments, statistical, 103–104
Self-fulfilling prophecies, 35
Sellnow, Deanna, 138
Sequential fallacy, 271
Sexual attraction, motivational appeal and,
        237–238
Shock treatment, 136
Sign, reasoning from, 266, 267, 269
Signposts, 154, 155
Simon, Carly, 10
Simplicity of words, 152
Slides, as visual aids, 188, 198
Spatial patterns, 116–117
Speaker(s)

advantages of speech training to, 5–6
communication by. *See* Communication
critical listening for, 33–43
defined, 6
distance between audience and, 177
facial expressions of, 179–180
gestures by, 169, 180–181, 182, 183
intentions of, 133, 142
movement by, 178–179
posture of, 169, 178
stance of, 178–179
voice of. *See* Voice
Speaking
public. *See* Public speaking; Speechmaking
style of, 149–151. *See also* Style
variety in, 173–174
Speaking outline, 124–125
sample of, 125
Speaking rate, 173, 174
Speaking volume, 172
Specialized databases, 86–87
Specific instances, 100
Specific purposes for speeches, 18, 20, 21, 22
Speech(es). *See also* Public speaking; Speech-
        making
actuative. *See* Actuative speech(es)
argumentative. *See* Argument(s); Argumen-
        tation
beginning of, 133–139. *See also* Introduc-
        tion(s)
central idea of. *See* Central idea
conclusion of, 139–143. *See also* Conclu-
        sion(s)
of definition. *See* Speech(es) of definition
delivery of. *See* Delivery of speech; Presen-
        tation of speech
demonstration. *See* Demonstration(s)
ending of, 139–143. *See also* Conclusion(s)
evaluation of, form for, 42
extemporaneous, 171
first, 12–14
impromptu, 170, 171
informative. *See* Informative speech(es)
introduction to, 133–139. *See also* Introduc-
        tion(s)
length of, 139
manuscript, 170
material for. *See* Supporting material(s)
memorized, 170
occasion for. *See* Occasion for speech
organization of. *See* Speech organization

outline for. *See* Outline(s)
to persuade. *See* Persuasive speech(es)
planning of, 114–116
 steps in, 23
practicing, 24–25, 26, 175, 183
preparation of. *See* Preparation of speech
presentation of. *See* Delivery of speech; Presentation of speech
problem-solution, outline for, 109–111. *See also* Outline(s)
purpose(s) for
 central idea and, 21
 determining, 18–22
 developing, 76–77
 general, 18, 19–20, 21, 22
 knowing, 35–36
 specific, 18, 20, 21, 22
sample, 28–30, 164–166, 226–228, 254–255
subject of, 16–18, 134
wording of. *See* Language; Words
Speechmaking. *See also* Public speaking
 apprehension and. *See* Apprehension
 community building and, 4–5
 diversity and, 3–15. *See also* Diversity
 ethics and. *See* Ethics
 first-time fears and, 10
 functions of, 3–4
 getting started in, 16–32
 process of, basic elements in, 6–8
 successful, responsibilities for, 8–12
 training and, 5–6
Speech material. *See* Supporting material(s)
Speech(es) of definition
 defined, 207
 sample outline for, 220–222
 structuring, 213–214
Speech organization, 114–121
 achieving clarity through, 208–209
 choosing plan for, 115–116
 defined, 116
 developing central idea and, 115
 memory and, 123
 patterns of, 116–121, 116–121. *See also* Pattern(s) of organization
 types of, 116–118
Speech training, 5–6
Stance of speaker, 178–179
Startling statement, 136
State apprehension, 25

Statement
 startling, 136
 thesis, 20. *See also* Central idea
Statistics
 defined, 102
 ethics and, 104
 magnitudes and, 102–103
 segments and, 103–104
 as supporting material, 102–106
 trends and, 104–105
 types of, 105
 using, 105–106
Stereotypes, vocal, 173
Stereotyping, 157–158
Stewart, James, 10
Stipulative definition, 159
Streisand, Barbra, 10
Stress, 174–175
Style
 oral, 150, 151
 selecting, 149–151
 written, 150, 151
Sub-cultures, 47–48
Subject
 referring to, at beginning of speech, 134
 selecting and narrowing of, 16–18
Success, motivational appeal and, 238
Summaries, 154, 155
Sunday, Billy, 152
Supporting material(s)
 assertion and, 107
 checklist for, 107
 choosing, 76, 100
 comparisons as, 99–100
 contrasts as, 99–100
 critical thinking and, 106–108
 determining kinds needed, 83–85
 examples as, 100–102
 explanations as, 98–99
 finding, 83–95
 forms of, 23, 97–106
 functions of, 96–97
 gathering, 22–23
 nature of, proxemics and, 177
 objectiveness of, 85
 quantity needed, 84
 recording information and, 90–91, 92
 relevant visualization and, 211
 sources of, 23, 85–90

responsible use of, 91–94
statistics as. *See* Statistics
testimony as, 106
using, 91–94, 96–113
visual aids as. *See* Visual aids
Suspense, as factor of attention, 131–132
Sympathy, motivational appeal and, 237

Tables, as visual aids, 193–194
Tactile imagery, 163
Talbot, Bruce, 159–160
Television broadcasts, as sources, 23, 90
Testimony, as supporting material, 106
Therapeutic listening, 36
Theriault, Brenda, 102–103
Thesis statement, 20. *See also* Central idea
The Vital, as factor of attention, 132
Thinking
   critical. *See* Critical thinking
   rational, talking and, 260–267
Topic
   narrowing of, 16–18
   selecting, 16–18, 209
   support materials for, 84, 85
Topical patterns, 118
Tradition, motivational appeal and, 237
Trait apprehension, 25
Transitions, 154, 155
Travis, Randy, 10
Trends, 104–105
Trigger words, 35
Twitchell, David, 141
Twitchell, Michael, 141

Value(s)
   of audience, 72–74
   claims of, 262, 263
   defined, 72
   diverse, negotiation of, 52–53
   "family," 52–53
Variable beliefs, 70, 71
Variety, 173–174
Veeck, Bill, 28–30
Victoria (queen of United Kingdom), 141
Videotapes, as visual aids, 188, 190, 198
Visual aids, 186–202
   business use of, 195
   communicative potential of, 196
   computer-generated, 198–200

distractions created by, 198
functions of, 186–187
integration of, with verbal presentation,
      196–198
relevant visualization and, 211
selecting and using, strategies for, 194–200
types of, 187–194
Visual imagery, 161
Visualization
   relevant, 211
   as step of Monroe's motivated sequence,
      243, 244, 246–247, 248, 252, 255
Vital, The, as factor of attention, 132
Vitale, Dick, 171
Vocabulary. *See* Language
Vocal control, 11, 175, 176
Vocal emphasis, 174–175
Vocal stereotypes, 173
Voice
   exercising, 176
   speaking, effective, 172–175
   speaking volume and, 172
   using to communicate, 26–27, 169,
      171–175, 176
   vocal control and, 11, 175, 176
   vocal emphasis and, 174–175
   vocal stereotypes and, 173
Volume, speaking, 172

Walters, Barbara, 175
Washington, Booker T., 53
Washington, George, 131
Wattleton, Faye, 140–141
White, E. B., 161
Winfrey, Oprah, 171
Wolfe, Tom, 162
Words. *See also* Language
   accuracy of, 151–152
   choices of, intensity of, 155–156
   gender-linked, 156
   restatement of, 152–153
   simplicity of, 152
   trigger, 35
Worship, motivational appeal and, 237
Written style, 150, 151

Xenophobia, 45

Yearbooks, as sources, 23, 89